Crisis and Choice
in European
Social Democracy

A Volume in the Series

Cornell Studies in Political Economy

EDITED BY PETER J. KATZENSTEIN

A full list of titles in the series appears at the end of the book

Crisis and Choice in European Social Democracy

Fritz W. Scharpf

Translated by Ruth Crowley *and* Fred Thompson

Cornell University Press

Ithaca and London

The publisher gratefully acknowledges the assistance of Inter
Nationes in defraying part of the cost of translation.

First published as Fritz W. Scharpf, *Sozialdemokratische Krisenpolitik in
Europa* (Frankfurt: Campus, 1987)

English translation first published 1991 by Cornell University Press.

International Standard Book Number 0-8014-2221-3 (alk. paper)
International Standard Book Number 0-8014-9942-9 (pbk.: alk. paper)
Library of Congress Catalog Card Number 90-55139

Printed in the United States of America

*Librarians: Library of Congress cataloging information
appears on the last page of the book.*

⊗The paper in this book meets the minimum requirements of the
American National Standard for Information Sciences—
Permanence of Paper for Printed Library Materials, ANSI Z39.48-1984.

Contents

Tables

Figures

Foreword

A book that analyzes how a social democratic government in a divided Germany dealt with one economic crisis in the 1970s can be instructive for Americans as they watch a conservative government in a united Germany address a different economic crisis in the 1990s.

Crisis and Choice in European Social Democracy analyzes the policy choices of social democratic governments in the Federal Republic, Britain, Austria, and Sweden during the economic crisis of the 1970s. The intrinsic merits of Scharpf's inquiry have made the German version of this book a classic in the field of comparative political economy. Scharpf's original, insightful, and imaginative examination is empirically firmly grounded and brilliantly illuminates the similarities and differences of four West European states that are continuing to deal with structural economic change.

Fritz Scharpf is one of Germany's leading social scientists. He is the rare scholar whose work always reflects the highest standards of excellence while he never loses sight of the social and political relevance of his research. For the past twenty years Scharpf has been a pioneer in institutionalizing policy research in Germany. Trained as a lawyer in both Germany and the United States, he taught briefly at the Yale Law School before he accepted a chair at the University of Constance in the late 1960s and helped to build there one of the leading public administration programs in Germany. Beginning in the 1970s, he was for more than a decade one of the foremost researchers into the dynamics of West German federalism and labor market policy at the Science Center in West Berlin. Scharpf's strong intellectual influence in the reform policy discussions of the SPD dates to the mid-1970s. And he continued to be an influential voice inside the SPD during the 1980s while he was also active in setting up a new social science research institute of the Max-Planck Society in Cologne, acting as its codirector.

For the student of contemporary Germany, before and after unification, Scharpf's comparative analysis conveys an important message: Germany's political economy is not unique. No secrets shroud a special Germanic essence that have made it such a successful trading state. Instead Scharpf's book highlights specific institutional features of Germany's political economy which have led to its amazing success—for example, in international export markets—and to some surprising failures, such as the structural unemployment of the 1970s and 1980s. The policies that West German elites found congenial as they coped with the problems of the 1970s are the results of institutional and political links among important political actors, including business and union leaders, party elites at the national and state level, the governing council of the Bundesbank, and bureaucrats regulating the labor market. In the 1970s these relations made possible the unexpected crisis policy of the Social Democrats, which combined a record trade surplus with a deflationary bias and only a modest labor market policy. The partisan composition of the West German government did not matter much. Heading a Social Democratic coalition government, Helmut Schmidt was frequently called the best CDU chancellor the Federal Republic had ever had.

The peaceful revolution in East Germany in the fall of 1989 and the modalities of unification in 1990 have apparently not altered the institutional structure of the united Germany's political economy. This outcome was not preordained in the rapid developments leading up to unification. Unification brought about by joining the two states under the provisions of Article 146 of West Germany's Basic Law would have permitted constitutional changes in Germany's governing institutions. But the accession of five East German states under the provisions of Article 23 of the Basic Law does not. Consonant with the imbalance in power, wealth, and prestige, East Germany has simply accepted all of the institutions of what in the 1970s was called the West German "model." From this perspective Scharpf's institutional analysis leads us to expect continuities in the ways successive governments of a united Germany will cope with the economic and social problems the country confronts in the 1990s.

But the relationships among the important political actors are not only institutional; they are also political. Here two sources of change are of possible relevance. As a result of unification the political spectrum in Germany may broaden. The centripetal drive of electoral competition and a perpetual system of coalition governments at the federal level may be modified by the increased social, political, and economic heterogeneity of the German population. It is too early to judge the extent and duration of this possible reversal of centripetal forces. But the rapidity of change and the magnitude of the task for reformist policies are so great that the political center in Germany is likely to lose some strength.

More important, within the West German institutions that have been transferred wholesale to East Germany, the new Germans will confront the troubling question of political identity and political purpose crucial to how consistent or experimental they will be in dealing with the challenges of the 1990s. If an economic miracle in East Germany in the 1990s were to repeat the economic miracle of West Germany in the 1950s, a consistent policy would remind us of the electoral slogan of the 1950s: "no experiments." But history rarely repeats itself. If it does not, what kinds of political experiments will emerge from the battles within Germany's dominant institutions over issues such as the enormous ecological crisis and the existence of a state-owned sector that may well resist even determined efforts at privatization?

Germany's period of political introspection resulting from these new challenges is likely to be brief. Its involvement in international markets, as Scharpf's analysis of the 1970s demonstrates, is irreversibly strong. So is its political entanglement with the United States through NATO and with the Soviet Union (or its successors) through a new system of bilateral relations as well as a common security framework in Europe, and with France, Britain, Italy, and the smaller states of Western and Central Europe through the European integration process. The institutional and political features of Germany's political economy will thus have a strong influence on its various partner countries; at the same time Germany's international ties are bound to affect the balance between institutional continuity and policy experimentation. This book will give readers an in-depth understanding of the important structural features of Germany's political economy, and those of some of its neighbors, which make European integration both politically feasible and at the same time extraordinarily difficult.

PETER J. KATZENSTEIN

Preface

My theme is the struggle waged by the social democratic governments of Western Europe to achieve full employment during the decade of global economic crisis that began about 1970. My subjects are the Federal Republic of Germany, Great Britain, Austria, and Sweden. I concentrate on these countries because all four started the decade in about the same position. All were developed industrial nations that were highly integrated into world markets. Consequently, they were affected by the crisis in approximately the same ways, at least until Great Britain became an oil-exporting nation. Moreover, at the beginning of the era, government in the four countries was in the hands of "reformist" social democratic or socialist parties, for whom full employment took priority over *all* other goals of economic policy. In this they had the support of well-organized, cooperative labor unions.

The second reason for concentrating on these countries is that their policies achieved remarkably dissimilar results. Although all four countries had achieved high levels of employment, comfortable rates of growth, and moderate prosperity at the beginning of the era, by 1979 (the year Great Britain turned to the right with the election of Margaret Thatcher) their economic performances had become widely divergent. From the standpoint of unemployment and inflation, the two major economic problems of the Western industrial nations in the 1970s, Austria performed best and Great Britain worst. The comparison between the two countries in the middle is perhaps even more interesting. The Federal Republic had the lowest rate of inflation of all of the Organization for Economic Cooperation and Development (OECD) countries during the 1970s; Sweden's inflation was higher than the OECD average. Conversely, Sweden's unemployment rate fell during the crisis,

xvii

whereas unemployment rates in the Federal Republic increased dramatically from a very low starting point. If we consider the number of jobs instead of registered unemployment, Sweden achieved large increases during the 1970s, while among the OECD nations only Switzerland lost proportionally more jobs than did the Federal Republic.

Many considered West Germany's social democratic policies and economic institutions to be models for the rest of the world. Yet West Germany failed to achieve the preeminent economic goal of the Social Democrats: full employment. The apparent contradiction between West Germany's reputation and its performance provided the initial impetus for this comparative study. I was further motivated to pursue the issues discussed here by a controversy between the Labor Market Policy Research Group of the Wissenschaftszentrum Berlin, where I then worked, and colleagues at the Institute for Employment Research of the German Federal Labor Institute, who claimed that our research approach overestimated the potential employment effects of an "active labor market policy" and neglected the central importance of macroeconomic policy.

As I was preparing a seminar on comparative employment policy in spring 1981, I became convinced that while the differences in the employment performance of the Western European nations could not be explained entirely by their labor market policies, neither could they be explained by differences in their macroeconomic policies. Perhaps these differences were caused by union wage policies or by government job creation, by the expansion of the public sector or part-time work, by incomes policies, or by international trade programs and practices. But if there are so many ways in which national policymakers could plausibly have influenced employment and unemployment, then all explanations focusing on the use of a single instrument must necessarily remain superficial. What seemed to matter was the conditions under which a variety of potentially available instruments could be combined into an internally coherent and effective strategy. Where that was feasible, defending full employment was also possible, at least under the economic conditions of the 1970s. Where achieving a coherent strategy was impossible, job losses were inevitable, and the only issue then was whether they would be fully reflected in official unemployment statistics.

Once I realized that any explanation of the unemployment puzzle would depend on identifying the political and institutional conditions under which it was possible to formulate and implement an effective national employment strategy, the question also became a challenge to my professional identity as a political scientist. As the director of a research institute on labor market policy at the Wissenschaftszentrum Berlin, I had spent ten years persuading reluctant labor market economists and sociologists of the importance of multidisciplinary work. A multidisciplinary project of my own, with a strong political science component, thus seemed an appropriate conclusion to this period of my intellectual biography.

Yet it is not clear that I would undertake such a project again, if I had it to do over. True, no single discipline can fully elucidate employment problems. But it is one thing to accommodate economic, sociological, and political science perspectives in the portfolio of projects of a multidisciplinary research institute and quite another to try to integrate these divergent approaches in a single book. Instead of generating clarity and understanding, the attempt could all too easily degenerate into a nightmare of interdisciplinary confusion for the author as well as for the reader.

If I have escaped that fate, it is thanks to the professionalism of my colleagues at the institute, who never tired of correcting my misperceptions. But I also profited from opportunities to expose my working hypotheses to much external criticism. Since I was not able to begin field work until the end of my directorship, the exploratory phase of my project was unusually long. When the interview phase finally began, I thus had a fairly good understanding of the various policy responses to the crisis and of their economic consequences.

Altogether, I interviewed fifteen to twenty persons in each country who had shaped or closely observed the policies of the government, the national bank, the labor market authority, and the social partners. Although these interviews seldom produced facts not available in the literature, they were essential for my project. One must meet the actors in their milieu before one can confidently interpret available "objective" data. My goal was to discover the economic constraints confronting the full employment policies of four social democratic governments. Within these constraints I then wanted to reconstruct the logic governing the actions of those multiactor systems that had actually determined the realization or failure of economic strategies. The analysis I offer is formulated within the rational-choice frame of reference that also underlies the economic theory of politics. But I have found myself unable to pursue this approach in a particularly rigorous fashion, since my study also demonstrates how the "rationality" of action is defined by historically contingent, institutionally shaped identities, goals, and perceptions of a situation that resist reduction to the universal assumptions used in economic analysis.

In any case, the explanation of real-world phenomena cannot be based on a single theoretical model. Like a judge who, in deciding a real case, cannot rely exclusively on the law of torts while ignoring the law of civil procedure, social scientists dealing with complex historical developments must take explanations where they find them. And just as the application of law develops new law when the existing body of rules does not seem to fit the case before the court, social science explanations of real-world developments are likely to cross the boundary between the interpretation of received theory and the inductive development of new theory. Even then, however, not all events can be interpreted as manifestations of a generalizable rule, and in many situations the best one can hope to achieve is narrative explanations. This book relies on them extensively.

For the same reason, my interviews also increased my respect for the actors whose practical intelligence must grasp and consider so much more real-world complexity than do our scientific theories. I am grateful for the patience and the didactic skill with which my informants imparted their worldviews to me. I am equally grateful to my colleagues, whose detailed work is at the basis of this summary even though many of my simplifications may make their hair stand on end. When the tables are turned I often have the same reaction—and in interdisciplinary communication we must all put up with that.

Above all, I owe special thanks to the the Labor Market Policy Research Group of the Wissenschaftszentrum Berlin and to its director, Egon Matzner, who for two years has cheerfully supported the work of his predecessor and who also took the time to read and, in a spirit of friendship, criticize new versions of the manuscript as I produced them. Earlier versions of the manuscript or parts thereof have also profited from suggestions and commentary by Marlene Brockmann, Michael Funke, Adalbert Hepp, Heinz Kluncker, Hans Maier, Gerhard Maier-Rigaud, Rudolf Meidner, Edda Müller, Bernd Reissert, Ronald Schettkat, Günther Schmid, Arndt Sorge, Heinz-Peter Spahn, Wolfgang Streeck, and Georg Voruba. In the course of our work, Sylke Nissen has progressed from a reliable research assistant to a rigorous critic of the content and style of the manuscript, while maintaining her spirit of unruffled cooperation. Finally, Ulli Goose impressed me with her ability to merge my flawed computer data with a completely incompatible text system. In addition, she organized and guided me and my project through all perils with cheerful competence.

Why, with all this help, the responsibility should still lie with the author is a mystery. Nonetheless, it is so.

FRITZ W. SCHARPF

Cologne, West Germany

PART I

CAPITALISM UNDER DEMOCRATIC CONTROLS

Chapter One

Crisis as Fate?

The Great Depression of the 1930s taught the Western industrial nations a crucial lesson: the crisis was not an irresistible natural catastrophe. It could have been avoided and, even after it began, its consequences could have been mitigated by appropriate countermeasures. Swedish Social Democrats, Hitler's minister of economics, and American New Dealers, independently and almost simultaneously, discovered that they could use government spending to stimulate aggregate demand and thereby achieve full employment and fully exploit the productive capacity of their countries. John Maynard Keynes subsequently created an economic theory to justify these successful experiments in deficit financing. His thought profoundly influenced postwar economic policy in all the Western industrial nations, ultimately even in the Federal Republic of Germany. Governments everywhere, guided by Keynesian theory, methodologically sophisticated empirical research, and complex macroeconomic models, assumed responsibility for the performance of the economy. And because the economies of the Western industrial nations performed better in the postwar era than in any previous period in history, their high growth, full employment, and stable prices were widely accepted as evidence of the soundness of Keynesian policies and the economic theories underlying them. The skeptical and critical voices of heterodox economists, both Marxists and conservatives, went unheeded.

The second great economic crisis of modern times has called into question the lessons taught by the first. It has shaken economists' confidence in their ability to manage the economy and shattered the theoretical consensus on which that confidence rested. Since the beginning of the 1970s, the Western industrial nations have experienced low growth, high unemployment and inflation, and unfavorable trade balances (see

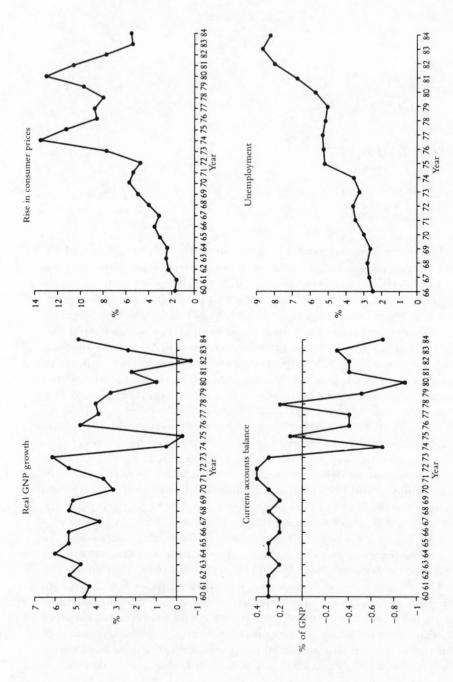

Figure 1.1. Economic development of the OECD nations, 1960–1984 and 1966–1984. Source: OECD *Economic Outlook.*

Figure 1.1). Although the crisis began more than a dozen years ago, economic policy makers have not yet succeeded in setting the world to rights. Keynesians failed almost everywhere in their fight against inflation and often against high unemployment as well. But the neoclassical conservatives who succeeded them in many countries have been equally unsuccessful. At best they were able to reestablish price stability, but growth rates remained low and unemployment levels often increased from one business cycle to the next.

DID THE CRISIS RESULT FROM GLOBAL AND LONG-TERM STRUCTURAL CHANGES?

As the OECD's McCracken Report (1977) testifies, the worldwide recession that began in the 1970s was initially attributed to the oil shock of 1973–74 and to a series of avoidable misjudgments of economic policy in the major industrial nations. As the crisis persisted, however, alternative explanations emphasized the normality of low growth and the significance of structural changes in the global economy. These explanations generally reject the notion that government management of the economy can replicate the high growth rates of the postwar decades. Knut Borchardt (1982; 1984), for instance, denies the existence of a causal link between Keynesian spending policies and the postwar boom. Instead, he attributes the exceptionally high growth rates after World War II to war, reconstruction, and catching up with the United States. Low growth is thus the norm on which future Western economic policies should be based. Burkart Lutz (1984) arrives at the same conclusion. According to his fascinating analysis, postwar prosperity resulted from the last great "land grab" of industrial capitalist development, which ended irrevocably with the complete mobilization of the undeveloped sectors of the economy. Michael Piore and Charles Sabel (1985) take a different approach to explaining the unique nature of postwar development. They argue that the rise of microchip technology and the increasing competition from developing nations have brought to an end the "Fordism" of mass production and, with it, the power of Keynesian demand management to influence the pace of economic development.

Manipulating aggregate demand is even less relevant in long-wave, or Kondratieff-cycle, explanations of the crisis (Eklund, 1980; Kleinknecht, 1984; Bieshar and Kleinknecht, 1984). In the 1920s Nicolai Kondratieff (1926), a Soviet economist, theorized that the capitalist development process was characterized by short periods of global growth and expansion, followed by longer periods of relative consolidation and contraction, comprising waves or cycles of fifty to sixty years. Joseph Schumpeter (1950:67ff.) and Gerd Mensch (1975), following Schumpeter, claimed that these cycles resulted from the introduction, industrial exploitation, and eventual stagnation of basic technological innovations. According to this theory, the impetus given to economic development by the innovations of the first industrial revolution was exhausted by 1820 and that given by the second or "railroad cycle" by 1875. The third Kondratieff cycle, driven by electrical engineering and chemistry, ran out around 1930, and the maturation of the automobile, synthetic fibers, and consumer electronics may be responsible for the current period of contraction and consolidation. Kondratieff-cycle theory holds that Keynesian policies could have done nothing to halt the inevitable decline. Thus Mensch predicted the failure of job creation programs even before the crisis had really set in (1975:34ff.).

At the most, government might have tried to stimulate a new growth cycle, however uncertain, by promoting technological innovation and the modernization of the economy (Hanff and Scharpf, 1975). Conservative theorists, however, would deny even this positive role to government. They attribute worldwide recession to a general overburdening of the productive forces of capitalism, either by a "profit squeeze" produced by the financial and regulatory demands of the welfare state and the redistributive successes of powerful unions (Lindbeck, 1980; Bacon and Eltis, 1978; Giersch, 1983) or by a more basic "institutional sclerosis" due primarily to the proliferation of organized interest groups and their influence on government policy (Olson, 1982). If these negative structural changes should be reversible (and Mancur Olson is less optimistic in this regard than the advocates of the profit squeeze theory), government's role would be to minimize welfare-state regulations that protect individuals from the rigors of competition, to reduce public expenditures and taxes, and to withdraw as much as possible from active involvement in the economy.

Each of these explanations for the worldwide recession refers to real changes in global economic conditions or in technological, social, political, and institutional conditions. Each also relies on plausible causal hypotheses linking these changes to slower growth. However, the very number of plausible hypotheses argues against the possibility that any one of them could explain the overall development. It appears that the worldwide recession is theoretically overdetermined—a situation that is hardly rare in the social sciences. Still, the plausibility of the numerous secular, cyclic, and structuralist explanations seems to render at least one conclusion inescapable, that the long-term climate of the capitalist economies has changed for the worse since the beginning of the 1970s.

Does this conclusion also imply the irrelevance of government control of the economy? Such an inference would be justified only if the economies of all the Western industrial countries had run the same course and their policies had produced the same results. But this is not the case. On the contrary: while the most important indicators of economic performance everywhere worsened at the beginning of the 1970s, the variation in growth, employment, and inflation among the highly developed industrial nations increased greatly (Table 1.1).

WHAT EXPLAINS VARIATIONS IN GROWTH, EMPLOYMENT, AND INFLATION RATES?

The developed industrial nations did not all experience the same decline after 1970. Instead, the less successful fell increasingly behind the rest. And as it became apparent that not all economic goals could be achieved simultaneously, individual countries seem to have pursued different priorities. Of course, these differences in economic performance cannot conclusively prove the effectiveness of national economic policy choices. But they are sufficient to challenge the explanatory power of the universal (secular, cyclic, or structuralist) crisis theories. And even if, despite their differences and contradictions, these global theories could explain the general decline from the early 1970s on, they do not explain the differences in the way countries coped with this decline. To explain these differences, we must supplement global theories with explanatory models that take account of national factors.

Under the general heading of "neocorporatism," a group of political scientists and students of comparative politics have elaborated just such explanatory models. Since the mid–1970s Harold Wilensky (1976; 1981), David Cameron (1978; 1984), Philippe Schmitter (1981), Manfred Schmidt (1982; 1983), Heikki Paloheimo (1984), and others have attempted to answer, on the basis of cross-national empirical comparisons, the question: Do politics matter?—a question that has long concerned political scientists. Worldwide economic decline both stimulated a reformulation of this question and provided almost ideal quasi-experimental conditions for answering it. This reformulation began with a disappointment. The simple left-right hypothesis, that countries with conservative governments would have higher unemployment and lower inflation than social democratic countries, had worked well during the 1960s (Hibbs, 1977) but was evidently invalidated by events after 1970. When political scientists realized that, they extended their search for possible explanatory factors to the interaction between government policy and organized

7

Table 1.1 Average annual growth rates and changes in employment and consumer price indexes in highly developed industrial nations (%)

	Growth in GDP		Employment		Consumer prices	
	1963–73	1973–83	1963–73	1973–83	1963–73	1973–83
Canada	5.70	2.80	3.60	2.30	3.70	9.30
USA	4.10	2.20	2.60	1.90	3.60	8.30
Japan	9.80	4.20	1.50	0.90	6.20	8.20
Australia	5.60	2.50	3.30	0.90	4.00	11.20
New Zealand	4.00	2.00	2.40	1.10	5.40	13.40
Austria	5.10	2.60	-0.10	0.00	4.20	6.10
Belgium	4.90	2.10	0.80	-0.70	4.10	8.00
Switzerland	4.10	0.60	0.80	-0.70	4.50	4.70
FRG	4.40	1.90	0.00	-0.70	3.60	5.00
Denmark	4.00	1.70	1.40	0.00	6.30	10.40
France	5.50	2.60	0.90	0.10	4.70	10.90
Finland	4.90	3.20	0.20	1.10	6.20	11.80
GB	3.30	1.60	0.20	-0.50	5.30	13.30
Italy	5.00	2.40	-0.50	0.70	4.90	16.20
Norway	4.30	3.90	1.70	1.80	5.30	9.40
Netherlands	5.10	1.90	0.70	0.60	5.50	6.70
Sweden	4.00	1.80	0.60	0.90	4.90	9.90
Mean	4.93	2.35	1.18	0.57	4.85	9.58
Standard deviation	1.42	0.86	1.20	0.94	0.91	3.10
Coefficient of variance (standard deviation/mean)	0.29	0.37	1.01	1.64	0.19	0.32

Sources: OECD Economic Outlook 28, 34, 38; author's own calculations.

societal interests, as it had been conceptualized by neocorporatist theory (Schmitter, 1974; Schmitter and Lehmbruch, 1979; Lehmbruch and Schmitter, 1982; Tarantelli and Willke, 1981; von Alleman, 1981).

Neocorporatism implies specific organizational structures of unions and employer associations, specific types of industrial relations, and specific relationships between the "social partners" and government policy makers. As an ideal type, which was approximated in Scandinavia and Austria during the 1960s and 1970s, the neocorporatist model is defined by the coexistence of the following characteristics: a monopolistic union movement without ideological cleavages or competing craft unions and with a high degree of organization; a similar degree of organizational concentration on the employer side; centralized collective bargaining; and participation by the peak organizations of labor and capital in the formulation of government economic and social policy. Comparative political studies that included quantitative indicators for the degree to which a country approached this neocorporatist ideal were relatively more successful in explaining economic performance during the 1970s than studies that used only indicators for the left-right dimension. In fact, countries with social democratic governments *and* with neocorporatist institutions were shown to be successful not only in their expansion of the welfare state but also in their fight against unemployment and inflation. Thus it seemed that, with the discovery of neocorporatist institutional arrangements, comparative political research had found a simple and powerful explanation for the economic policy success or failure of highly developed industrial countries.

In the meantime, enthusiasm for this discovery has waned. The variance in economic performance not explained by political and institutional factors was always large and now seems to be increasing. Some countries that ranked high on the corporatism scale—Denmark, Holland, Belgium, and the Federal Republic of Germany—have experienced increasing unemployment since the end of the 1970s. The countries that ranked highest on that scale, Austria and Sweden, have also had serious economic difficulties since the end of the 1970s. At the other extreme, the United States under the Reagan administration has been highly successful, not only in fighting inflation but also in promoting growth and employment. Its success raises doubts about the relative superiority of neocorporatist institutions and policies (Streeck, 1984a). The nexus between institutional arrangements and economic outcomes is thus either looser or more complicated than the neocorporatists had assumed.

Nevertheless, the political scientists' key working hypothesis retains its validity. Because the onset of the economic crisis increased differences among the economic success profiles of the industrial nations, explanations for this increase must take account of national differences. If we further assume that all countries were confronted with similar problems at the beginning of the 1970s and that all governments had the same interest in avoiding unemployment and maintaining price stability, there is much to be said for the presumption that the differences in economic performance may have been caused by political and social institutions, since these are the factors that most distinguish countries from one another.

Political and social institutions are like specialized tools; they can achieve much that would otherwise not be possible. They help to structure collective behavior by reducing the set of possible responses by all participants to a smaller set of rule-governed responses, which can be anticipated by others in their own plans. Hence, institutions permit us to design more complex strategies and to realize more ambitious goals. But the gain in power is achieved through selection. The action repertoire of institutions is constrained as its effectiveness increases, and it cannot be changed at will, or with any speed. This does not mean that we should see institutions as wholly rigid behavioral programs. Their repertoire usually consists of a variety of permissible solutions that can be matched to particular situations and refined and adapted to deal with new situations over time. Thus in the 1950s and 1960s, when conditions were both favorable and stable, most Western nations developed successful economic programs despite great institutional differences.

I believe that this dynamic explains both the convergence of economic and political trends during the 1960s—when the preferences of leftist or rightist governments still influenced tradeoffs at the margin between inflation and unemployment—and their divergence in the period that followed. Under crisis conditions, there is not enough time for incremental adaption of institutional repertoires. Policy responses then tend to follow a law of inertia according to which previous solutions are continued or even intensified until catastrophe compels a change of government that facilitates a radical break with past practices. Success or failure at the beginning of a crisis probably depends more than at any other time on the accidental coincidence between the existing policy repertoire and the requirements of the new situation (Scharpf, 1981; 1979).

We can thus interpret the findings of comparative studies as follows. Economic policy responses are institutionally constrained, but they can be changed. Before 1970 most of the industrial nations were relatively successful, and the remaining differences among them could be explained by their different political priorities. When the crisis began, it overwhelmed the institutional adaptability of all countries. In the early stages of the crisis, countries with neocorporatist institutions were particularly fortunate, because policy responses within their repertoires happened to be relatively successful under the new economic conditions. As the crisis continued, however, the coincidence diminished, either because economic problems persisted for so long that the resources of corporatist policies were exhausted; or because the problems changed so that originally "appropriate" policies ceased to be effective; or because the countries that had originally been unsuccessful were now able to adapt their own policy repertoire to the demands of the new economic situation.

If we follow this interpretation to its logical conclusion, it becomes clear why quantitative analyses could only partially explain economic performance during the crisis. The relationship between economic outcomes and institutional arrangements was mediated by the economic strategies that were actually pursued. These strategies are excluded from the analytical design of quantitative comparative studies, and their exclusion is not an accidental or easily corrigible defect but a fundamental methodological limitation. This becomes clear when one looks at the causal relations underlying the regression coefficients.

Neocorporatist literature offers two complementary hypotheses that could explain the positive correlation between economic success and corporatist structures. The first interprets corporatism in class theoretical terms, as a power resource of the labor movement that assures its influence on government policy even when social democrats are out of office or when economic conditions weaken the bargaining power of the unions (Korpi, 1983; Esping-Andersen and Korpi, 1984). This hypothesis is quite plausible in explaining the achievement of redistributive goals. The goals that become important in the course of the crisis, however—economic growth, full employment, and price stability—could not be obtained through victories in the distributive battle between labor and capital. For their explanation, therefore, the power structure hypothesis by itself seems inadequate.

Instead, a second hypothesis gains in plausibility. It maintains that neocorporatist institutions will increase the "governability" of the political system as a whole. By drawing large, monopolistic interest organizations into the government process itself (Schmitter, 1981), they are able to oblige these organizations to contribute to the achievement of public policy goals and to create favorable conditions for macroeconomic policy coordination. That seems reasonable enough, but whether the postulated connection did in fact exist during the crisis is a question that cannot be further discussed at the present level of theoretical abstraction. It depends on a closer examination of the potential relationships between institutional arrangements, economic policy strategies, and economic success.

Policy Strategy as an Explanatory Concept

Economic problems are, of course, influenced by the policy measures that are taken and not by the institutions that make economic policy. But even policy measures do not affect economic problems directly. Whether they take the form of direct commands or indirect incentives, their results are achieved only by influencing the behavior of "economic subjects": individual investors and savers, producers and consumers, employers and workers. In a pluralist state open to the world economy, however, such signals do not emanate from a single source but from many sources at once: from the national bank, from the ministers of economic affairs, or of finance, from the budget committee of the legislature, from the labor authority, from the states and municipalities, from the unions—or even from the European Commission, the Federal Reserve Board of the United States, or a meeting of the Organization of Petroleum-Exporting Countries (OPEC).

To be effective, the parties whose behavior is to be influenced by government policy must be able to recognize it over the "white noise" generated by the multiplicity of other signals—intentional and unintentional—broadcast by a chaotic world. This effect can be produced either by a particularly powerful individual signal, such as that sent by OPEC in 1973–74, or by bundling an array of policy measures whose signals would cancel each other out if they were uncoordinated. Thus it may be generally sufficient to define "strategy" as a recognizable "pattern in the stream of decisions" by individual actors or organizations (Mintzberg and McHugh, 1985; Mintzberg and Waters, 1985), but in the area of economic policy such a pattern can be created only if the decisions of several or many participants are effectively coordinated. However, the various economic policy makers are likely to pursue their own different economic and institutional interests, and they are likely to be guided by their own interpretations of the situation. Thus, their participation in concerted strategies is problematic in principle. The difficulties will vary with the degree to which their interests conflict (Axelrod, 1970), but they are also affected by the prevailing power relations and institutional arrangements that either permit certain interests to be suppressed or facilitate the development of common worldviews and agreement on compromise solutions. It is in this context that the second corporatism hypothesis is of obvious relevance. Under the institutional arrangements postulated, union and management elites are continuously and jointly involved in economic policy making; they are likely to be fully aware of each other's interests and interpretations; and if opportunities for improving overall economic performance through joint action exist, they are more likely to make use of them.

Nevertheless, joint participation in policy making can only be half of the explanation. A successful economic policy strategy depends not only on coordination but also on the strategy's suitability for achieving the desired effect in a given situation. Corporatism can be made to account for superior economic performance in the post–1970 era only if it can be established that the strategies adopted by corporatist institutions were particularly well suited to prevailing economic conditions. It is theoretically possible to show that this was in fact the case, but it is not nearly so easy as the neocorporatists had claimed.

Western industrialized nations did not all face the same economic conditions, and these conditions did not even remain stable over the entire crisis period. Empirical tests would thus depend on detailed structural and time-series analyses of individual countries. Moreover, the theoretical distinction between situational "conditions" and "strategy" is difficult to maintain empirically, in view of the interactive relationship between "cause" and "effect." Favorable initial conditions can be made worse by the wrong economic strategy and unfavorable conditions can be improved by the right strategy. More important, however, economic strategies are not clearly circumscribed states of affairs that can easily be isolated or measured. To use Georgescu-Roegen's (1986) distinction, they are not precisely defined "arithmomorphic" constructs but diffuse "dialectic constructs" in need of interpretation.

THE NORMATIVE-COGNITIVE AMBIVALENCE OF STRATEGIES

Before 1970 most politicians probably agreed on the desirability of economic growth, full employment, stable prices, and balanced external accounts (while today some would question the benefits of growth and some, perhaps, also those of full employment). But even then no political consensus existed with respect to the second-best combination of goals when not all of them could be achieved simultaneously. Once the necessity for choice became apparent, the various political parties assigned different priorities to fighting inflation and fighting unemployment, since those problems by no means posed equal threats to the economic interests they represented. At the same time, cognitive conflicts over the interpretation of changing economic conditions and the efficacy of specific policy instruments became more serious. A conservative government's monetarism differed from a social democratic government's Keynesianism not only in terms of the goals it pursued and the instruments it employed but also in its interpretation of economic developments and conditions and its understanding of the relationships between policy instruments and targets, measures and results. Governments that gave up on job creation programs, for example, were not necessarily signaling disinterest in full employment. They may have been convinced that the most effective full employment policy was to fight inflation and improve business profits. Consequently, different governments contended with different problems, recognized different facts, and experienced different victories and defeats. Each can be evaluated fairly only on its own terms.

In short, by themselves, objective indicators and certainly the results achieved cannot tell us what strategy a country was actually pursuing. Like all human action, economic policy is possible only within a cognitive framework that pairs goals with available means and the critical conditions of the decision environment. And neither the goals pursued nor the causal efficacy of economic policy instruments, nor the conditions of the economic environment, are sufficiently beyond dispute to be simply taken as facts that could be plugged into cross-national multivariate regression equations. That does not rule out the possibility of scientific explanations, but in the turbulent world of economic policy making under conditions of international crisis, all strategies must also be seen as exploratory natural experiments. If we try to assess the findings they yield, we must first understand the questions that were posed.

STRATEGIES AS HISTORICAL EXPERIMENTS

The key question of this book, whether government economic policy could have avoided or mitigated the consequences of the worldwide recession after 1970, cannot be answered without reference to the specific priorities guiding the policy makers' choices and to the way they interpreted prevailing economic conditions. Both changed during the period under study. At the beginning of the 1970s, the Keynesian-neoclassical synthesis dominated economics, both theoretical and applied, in the Western industrial nations. Ten years later, economic policies nearly everywhere were guided by the tenets of monetarism or supply-side economics. Equally dramatic shifts took place in the policy priorities of the governments in power. In the early 1970s, most would have agreed with Helmut Schmidt's maxim that 5 percent inflation is better than 5 percent unemployment. By the early 1980s, nearly all the governments of the Western nations gave priority to price stability. This shift entailed not only a change in political evaluation but also a change in the object of scientific explanation. It makes no sense to try to explain the failure of *A* if *B* was the policy target.

Researchers may investigate and even explain these changing orientations. But when the goal is a systematic examination of the potential scope for and effects of economic policy options during the crisis period, the researcher must also adopt one of the competing working hypotheses that have in fact guided political actors in their real-world experiments. For the same reason, the demise of Keynesian action perspectives that occurred in many countries during the crisis also limits the opportunities for new insight. From a purely scientific point of view, it is poor practice to change the experimental design in mid-course. Recognizing this difficulty, this book concentrates on the economic policy of four European countries, the Federal Republic of Germany, Great Britain, Austria, and Sweden, whose policies at the onset of the crisis were shaped by social democratic governments, and it pursues their experiences only to the end of the Social Democrats' participation in government: to 1979 in Great Britain and to 1982 in the Federal Republic. Sweden had a centrist coalition government between fall 1976 and fall 1982 but maintained its social democratic commitment to full employment. Events in Sweden, as in Austria, will therefore be explored up to the mid–1980s. Two reasons bearing on research strategy speak in favor of this choice.

Social democratic parties (including the British Labour party and the Austrian Socialist party) have historically evolved from workers' movements and they continue to represent workers' interests, although these have become more differentiated and the parties have broadened their class base to the point where they could even be described as "catch-all parties" (Kirchheimer, 1957; von Beyme, 1982:86–116). Nonetheless, despite all the differences of interest among their constituents, they all remain committed to one priority above all other goals of economic and social policy: for them, the achievement and maintenance of full employment ranks first, above increasing real incomes or other distributional goals (and, of course, above the maintenance of price stability or of reducing the public sector deficit).

Social Democrats have many reasons for assigning priority to full employment. According to the platform of the Social Democratic Party of Germany (SPD), paid work is a "basic precondition of human existence."

It not only ensures "material survival" but also "changes, develops, and educates" human beings (SPD, 1986:50). Tight labor markets enhance the individual's life chances, opportunities for personal choice, and the possibility of "walking tall." Only full employment, according to British Labour party economist Thomas Balogh, "removes the need for servility, and thus alters the way of life, the relationship between classes. It changes the balance of forces in the economy" (1982:47). But hard-headed power considerations are at least as important as spiritual concerns in giving weight to full employment. Tight labor markets enhance the economic power of workers relative to employers and increase the probability that union demands will be met. From this strategic perspective, full employment is a public good and not merely a private good, since it benefits even those workers whose jobs are not in jeopardy.

Thus, when economic conditions left them any choice at all, social democratic governments must have had a preference for full-employment strategies in keeping with their own self-understanding and with the unambiguous interests of their political constituents and of the unions representing those interests. And given their presumed clarity and seriousness of purpose, it may also be presumed that social democratic governments exploited all economic policy options available to national governments under the specific conditions of their respective countries in order to avoid, or to eliminate, mass unemployment. From a research point of view, these are more promising experimental conditions than would be provided by the analysis of perhaps halfhearted efforts undertaken by less committed governments.

Moreover, the "reformist" Social Democrats and unions of the four countries we will compare had a stronger—and hence, despite all disappointments, a longer—commitment to Keynesian economic policies than did other political parties. Their strategies and their results can be interpreted within a fundamentally common political and economic frame of reference. We will present its outlines before we proceed to discuss the real historical experiences of the four countries.

CHAPTER TWO

Prerequisites for Control of the Economy

Not all economists believe that the performance of capitalist economies can be, or even should be, controlled by government intervention. Since market economies are by definition highly decentralized, the goals of government economic policy cannot be directly realized by government action. They are produced by the innumerable microeconomic decisions of producers and consumers, employers and workers, capital owners and investors. All of them are generally assumed to pursue their own microeconomic goals, and they are not directly concerned with the impact of their choices on the overall performance of the economy. Instead, their decisions are supposed to be coordinated through the "invisible hand" of the price mechanism working in anonymous markets.

Disagreement on the relative efficacy of market coordination is the principal issue dividing the three leading schools of economics in the Western world today: the neoclassical, the neo-Keynesian, and the neo-Marxist. However, neither Keynesians nor Western Marxist economists deny the superior microeconomic efficiency of market coordination, even though they are generally more impressed with the practical importance of monopoly, externalities, and other market failures than their neoclassical counterparts. Rather, the crux of their disagreement is in their evaluation of the macroeconomic consequences of "capitalism" in the technical sense—the existence of free markets for the investment of accumulated capital. While neoclassical economists tend to assume that all markets are alike in principle, both Keynesians and Marxists begin with the assumption of a hierarchy of markets (Ostleitner, 1979; Spahn, 1986:170–92). In their view, the markets for yield-seeking capital determine the level of productive investment, which, in turn, determines production and employment. These then circumscribe the income and consumption opportunities of households and the revenue obtainable by government. At first blush, of course, that argument seems insufficient to establish the unilateral dependence of all other markets on the capital market, since capital accumulation itself results from the savings of firms, households, and governments. The relationship among markets would be one of circular dependencies rather than of unidirectional hierarchy. The postulated asymmetry becomes more plausible, however, when one compares the relationships among the two sides in each market. In goods markets, for example, businesses can make a profit only when they offer goods for sale, while households can increase their material welfare only by acquiring goods offered in the market. Similarly, in labor markets, households must sell their labor to earn the income they use to buy goods, and firms must buy labor to produce goods for sale. The dependency relationships between the supply side and the demand side in goods markets and labor markets are thus of a mutual and exclusive nature, with the implication that neither side would be able to withhold its own supply for any length of time without incurring serious disadvantages.[1] It follows that market clearing prices will reflect the relative scarcity of supply and demand in each of these markets.

Financial markets, however, are not constituted by the bilateral relationship between two homogeneous sides. On the one hand, there is the market for production investments, which is of particular importance for government economic policy. In this market, the savings of firms, households, and government confront investment opportunities or projects in need of financing. Each of these investment projects promises to yield a specific combination of risks and returns. If the market is efficient, only investment projects with expected profits equal to or greater than the average rate of interest will be exploited. This guarantees that capital will first flow to the most productive opportunities available. But even if capital markets are efficient at the microeconomic level, they can give rise to macroeconomic problems because their market-clearing rates of return are not determined solely by the availability of real investment opportunities. Business can invest in plant and other structures, equipment, and inventories only if it finds the funds to do so, but savers do not have to put their funds at the disposal of business. They have two other options.

First and foremost, savers do not have to invest. They can hoard cash

1. Of course, both sides of the goods and labor markets could restrict their performance for a time. But because human labor cannot be stored, any restriction of supply has a permanent opportunity cost, as is also the case with the failure to sell perishable wares. For the rest, functioning markets rarely create conditions under which hoarding would be worthwhile for the individual seller.

if available investment opportunities appear too risky. Consequently, savings may at least temporarily disappear into Keynes's liquidity trap. This implies a macroeconomic investment gap in which funds for investment become scarce and expensive, constraining output, employment, and consumption. Generally, however, holding liquid assets implies a zero rate of return, so that low-cost sources of finance should still be available for reasonably secure and profitable investment opportunities. But that is strictly true only when investment opportunities compete exclusively against money-hoarding pure and simple. It is not true when alternative opportunities are available in the market for nonproductive but potentially high-yield investments in national and international money or currency markets, in government securities, or in speculative investments in gold and other valuable assets.

The supply side of the capital market thus has a choice among a number of options, with the crucial consequence that the market-clearing price for capital is not exclusively defined by the relationship of relative scarcity between the supply of capital and the supply of profitable opportunities for productive investment. As a consequence, capital owners depend less on the investment opportunities provided by enterprises than enterprises depend on the supply of capital. This fundamental asymmetry accounts for the fact that "subordinate" goods and labor markets depend on developments in the hierarchically "superior" capital markets. If interest rates climb while business profits are unchanged, savers will redirect their assets to unproductive monetary investments, thereby constraining the economy's capacity to produce and reducing output and employment first in capital-goods industries and then more generally. Even if all monetary investments were to flow immediately back into domestic economic circulation as income (but not as investment), the consequence would be involuntary unemployment. This conclusion holds a fortiori for capital outflows from the country.

Hence "capitalism," defined by the existence of free financial markets, has a Janus face. On one side, it guarantees that society's resources, including its capital, will be invested productively and efficiently. This is a claim that no other economic system can make, because no other system provides equally effective incentives to allocate real assets to their most profitable uses. On the other side, capitalism also implies private choice between productive and nonproductive monetary investments, and hence the risk of macroeconomic imbalances that may escalate into world-wide crises. The debate between Keynesian, Marxist, and neoclassical economists results primarily from the varying significance each assigns to this dilemma and the conclusions each draws from it for the formulation and execution of government policy.

Marxist and left-Keynesian economists (represented in West Germany by the Memorandum Group and in Great Britain by the Cambridge School) stress capitalism's inherent instability, as well as the highly inequitable distribution of property and income it produces. They also stress the ubiquity of monopolies and external effects, the existence of which raises doubts about the relative efficiency of capitalism. Given these concerns, it should come as no surprise that Marxist economists frequently recommend the suppression of financial markets, even where they favor markets in other respects. Demands for nationalization on the part of the orthodox Left do not therefore necessarily imply a desire to create a full-fledged "command economy" with centrally planned production, consumption, and employment—the specter that so horrified Hayek (1944), von Mises (1944), and Eucken (1959). Instead, those demands and—with greater precision—the debates of the 1970s about guided investment in West Germany (Meißner, 1974; Besters et al., 1975) and the workers' fund in Sweden (Meidner, 1978) focused on the desirability of socializing the investment function—a prospect that Keynes himself had also contemplated. But even these moderate proposals were rejected out of hand by many Keynesians, as well as by the great majority of neoclassical economists.

The neoclassical position, which once again predominates in Western industrial nations, is characterized by the following principles: (1) all markets tend to equilibrium; (2) in equilibrium all production opportunities are exploited, all job seekers are employed, and all realizable consumer demands are met; and (3) actual markets will approximate equilibrium conditions when a workable degree of competition and flexible prices are assured. From this point of view, there are no fundamental differences between financial markets and other markets except perhaps that financial markets, with their greater transparency and mobility, should reach equilibrium even more rapidly. In a neoclassical world, therefore, long-term imbalances (e.g., long-term involuntary unemployment) should be impossible. If they nevertheless occur, they must result from monopolistic wage or price setting or government interventions that have reduced the flexibility of market adjustments.

Governments are expected to pursue a vigorous antitrust policy. Apart from that, neoclassical economists would minimize government intervention in economic processes, and they would prefer to see inevitable interventions take the form of market-like incentives and disincentives rather than of command and control regulation. Yet if neoclassicists are critical of state intervention, their attitude toward unions can only be characterized as hostile. In their view, the only function that unions could possibly have is the exercise of monopoly power to fix wages above the market equilibrium—which must, of course, produce unemployment. Accordingly, neoclassical recommendations for combating unemployment always imply a reduction of real wages, to be achieved through moralistic appeals to the unions' macroeconomic conscience or through proposals for "union-busting."

Finally, neo-Keynesian economists emphasize the crisis-prone character of capitalist economies as much as the Marxists do. In their view, crises have their origin in the capital market and the ever-present danger of "liquidity traps" that may entail labor market equilibria below the full-employment level (Rothschild, 1981). In their description of all markets, moreover, Keynesians emphasize the significance of market imperfections. They expect to find price rigidities everywhere, not just in the labor market. Hence Keynesians do not share the neoclassical belief that a reduction of real wages is a sure-fire cure for persistent mass unemployment (Kromphardt, 1985), nor do they regard nonintervention as a generally optimal strategy of government economic policy.

In contrast to the Marxists, however, Keynesians tend to appreciate the microeconomic efficiency of profit-oriented private choices. They thus reject not only outright nationalization but also direct government controls on the quantity, quality, timing, and location of private investments. But of course that does not preclude the prohibition of certain kinds of investments, or of investments at certain locations, for reasons of health, safety, environmental protection, or land-use planning. Nor does the Keynesian credo preclude the use of positive and negative incentives to stimulate regional or sectoral development or technological innovation. Above all, Keynesians do believe in the possibility of a global management of the macroeconomic business cycle (Thoss, 1975).

Thus Keynesians believe that governments need to manage economic processes. But since they have set out to stabilize and correct capitalism rather than to replace it, they must depend on indirect and global instruments of control that are supposed to influence private economic calculations without undermining the efficiency of capitalist choices. Compared to the simpler concepts and more straightforward recommendations of Marxist and neoclassical economics, Keynesianism thus occupies a more difficult intellectual and practical position. Its theoretical constructs are more dependent on empirical data and its interpretations of given economic situations are more contingent than is true of its more apodictic competitors. From the point of view of government practice, Keynesian economics is also more demanding in its requirements for the precise specification and variation of fine-tuned policy measures.

All that must have seemed highly attractive to academic economists. Once John Hicks and Paul Samuelson had created the neoclassical-Keynesian synthesis that conferred academic respectability on Keynes's heretical doctrine, macroeconomists experienced a gratifying increase in political influence and professional opportunities. This was the time when big economic research institutes competed in constructing ever more complex and larger macroeconomic simulation models on the basis of which Keynesian policy makers, supported by high-powered economic advisers, attempted to smooth out the last flurries of the business cycle. Clearly, such a degree of arcane professional competence could not have been obtained with the simpler and more accessible doctrines of the Marxists or the neoclassicists (Lindberg, 1983). However, when it became apparent at the end of the 1960s that the neo-Keynesian fine-tuning of the economy was working less and less well in practice, the neoclassical-Keynesian synthesis began to crumble in theory as well. While a leftist strand of Keynesianism returned to the more radical positions of the original Keynes, the monetarist and supply-side revival of older neoclassical doctrines gained first in academic respectability and then very rapidly in practical influence as well.

I suspect that the difficulty of popularizing Keynesian diagnoses and recommendations at least accelerated the change of the political tide. The nostrums neoclassical (and Marxist) economists prescribe always tend to point in the same direction. They are easily simplified in editorials, and even their vulgarized versions are essentially correct. Keynesian prescriptions, however, cannot be reduced to a simple rule of thumb (e.g., more "market" or more "state"). Their validity is entirely contingent on the specific economic circumstances of the moment. For that reason, Keynes's theories are not only invalidated by oversimplification, but they are also much more easily falsified by practical applications that do not precisely fit a given situation. In short, despite all the hopes that Keynesianism engendered in the postwar period, the contingent nature of its analyses and the conditional nature of its prescriptions were always a potential ideological or political weakness. On the level of principles and of practical political maxims, Keynesianism never offered the relief of a clear yes-or-no answer to policy questions but only the ambivalent "on the one hand . . . and on the other," or the hesitant "it depends."

THE SOCIAL DEMOCRATIC–KEYNESIAN SYMBIOSIS

Yet precisely this fundamental ambivalence of Keynesianism corresponded almost ideally to the ideological needs of "reformist" social democrats in the postwar period. As the political arm of the labor movement, and historically shaped by Marxism, these social democrats could not accept capitalism as it was. Under the given power relations, however, they could not abolish it either, even if they still seriously wanted to. Their own economic insights as well as the practical economic experiences of the Soviet Union and its satellites had persuaded the social democratic parties in the four countries in our study to back away from old-line Marxist concepts. They were searching instead for a middle way between the "real existing" socialism of scarcity and the prewar capitalism of exploitation and depression. Their goal was, to put it bluntly, no longer to overcome capitalism but only to "humanize" the capitalist mode of production, and then only to the extent that this would not impair the capitalist potential for creating material welfare. For the rest, social democratic programs focused on the progressive social utilization and the just distribution of the wealth that was so created. Social democrats gave priority to developing social security, creating equal access to educational opportunities and health services, and improving the public infrastructure. Unions fought for higher real incomes, shorter working hours, and better working conditions—to which list one should add the equalization of primary incomes for Sweden and the extension of worker participation and codetermination for West Germany.

Before the advent of Keynesianism, however, the reformist position was intellectually vulnerable in the ideological disputes with the Marxism of the Old Left. As long as capitalist crises could happen at any moment, whatever gains unions and social democratic parties might have achieved in the redistribution of incomes or the expansion of public services must have seemed extremely insecure. Indeed, the unions had been helpless during the Great Depression of the early 1930s, as the welfare state collapsed under the burden of mass unemployment. Social democrats could thus make their reluctant peace with capitalism only if they could also hope to avoid its recurrent crises or at least to dampen them sufficiently to assure the continuous economic growth that was necessary to maintain full employment and expand public services. That hope was provided by Keynesian economics. It was only in alliance with Keynesianism that social democratic concepts could achieve the intellectual hegemony that shaped the postwar era and made it meaningful to speak of a social democratic consensus even in countries where social democratic parties rarely had the opportunity to participate in government (Dahrendorf, 1979:147ff.).

On the other hand, however, Keynesian economics also posed to reformist social democracy a subtle danger to which both the Old Left and the centrist parties were immune. While Marxists condemned capitalism on moral grounds and wanted to abolish it, centrist parties were committed to its moral acceptance and practical maintenance. Social democrats, however, supported capitalism on grounds of economic and political expediency even though they continued to reject its moral implications: the pursuit of egoistic self-interest, competition at the expense of social solidarity, and the allocation of life chances according to the criteria of market success. Under the constant pressure to legitimate their "middle way" against the criticism of the Old Left and the New Left within their own parties, in the trade unions, and (in some countries) in competing Marxist parties, social democrats were often provoked to promise the fulfillment of socialist ideals even under capitalist conditions—and Keynesian economics made the temptation to translate this rhetoric into political action almost irresistible.

Keynesians, after all, could not oppose the moral and political rigor of the Left on moral grounds; all they could draw upon were technocratic arguments. But as the optimistic belief in fine-tuning the economy began to spread under the influence of the neoclassical-Keynesian synthesis, social democrats tended to forget what both Marx and Keynes had known: that capitalism was a dangerous and untamable beast that needed to be handled with utmost caution. The technocratic warnings of Keynesian economists thus lost their political persuasiveness, at least in countries large enough that their external vulnerability itself was not sufficient to structure debates about economic policy. Unlike the centrist parties, which were always concerned about the health of the economy (and unlike the orthodox Left, which never tired of predicting the next depression), social democrats tended to concentrate on idealistic re-forms, and some were quite happy to "test the robustness of the capitalist economy" with ever more financial, regulatory, and procedural burdens. In some countries, this surely contributed to the depth and duration of the crisis in the early 1970s.

For the same reason, the social democrats were long unable to re-nounce their optimism about macroeconomic fine-tuning even after the crisis began. They depended on it to justify and defend their political and moral identity, whereas the centrist parties had merely followed the rules of political competition. As long as the credibility of the Keynesian program went unchallenged, and as long as the interests of their constit-uents were met by an economy in which the government took care of growth, stability, and full employment, it was politically advantageous for them to endorse that program. But when Keynesian control proved ineffectual and the consequences of its failure became more significant in the 1970s, neither the interests of their constituents nor their own convictions kept the centrist parties from returning to neoclassical analy-sis and policies.

It was different with the social democrats, whose political fate was inextricably bound to the promise of successful management of the capitalist economy. They had no choice but to adhere to Keynesianism as long as possible and try everything to realize its promise, even under unfavorable conditions. Because their efforts were desperately serious, an examination of their successes or failures ought thus to give us more information about the possibilities and limits of the political management of crisis-prone capitalism than can the policies of the centrist governments, which were never really committed to Keynesianism. But before I present and analyze the experiences of the four countries in our study, I need at least a short overview to clarify the problems at which the Keynesian controls were directed and the instruments they had at their disposal.

ECONOMIC PROBLEMS AND THE INSTRUMENTS OF ECONOMIC POLICY

There are basically four kinds of macroeconomic problems: unemployment, inflation, weak economic growth, and chronic foreign trade deficits (which result in balance-of-payments crises under a regime of fixed exchange rates and in currency devaluation under flexible exchange rates). Keynesian policy instruments can thus be directed at any one of these problems. Chronic foreign trade surpluses, on the other hand, which are equally disturbing from the standpoint of international equilibrium, are generally seen as beneficial from the perspective of the nation experiencing them.

In Europe inflation and unemployment were perceived to be the most serious macroeconomic problems during the 1970s. Each can appear in two forms and, depending on whether its cause is to be found on the demand side or the supply side of the goods market, can make different demands on economic managers. However, because changes in price indices or employment statistics do not include information about their origins on either side of the market, macroeconomic managers must depend on theoretical interpretations to explain these changes—which, of course, are the subject of vigorous dispute among the various schools of economics (Malinvaud, 1977). Figure 2.1 shows the general pattern of potential interpretations.

The interpretation reflected in field (1)—demand-gap unemployment—is distinctly Keynesian. The most important economic concern is unemployment and its cause is insufficient aggregate demand (which manifests itself in capacity underutilization). Firms could be induced to produce more and hire more workers if demand were higher. For Keynesians, this diagnosis calls for government intervention aimed at expand-

25

| | Causes | |
	Demand side	Supply side
Problems *Unemployment*	(1) Due to lack of demand (Keynesian)	(2) Due to lack of jobs (classical)
Inflation	(3) Demand-pull inflation	(4) Cost-push inflation

Figure 2.1. Typology of macroeconomic problems

ing aggregate demand. Neoclassical economists, however, contend that if prices and wages were flexible (downward), unemployment due to lack of demand could not occur. Their diagnosis calls for reducing real wages and prices so that sales, production, and employment can grow, even if wage reductions should entail further declines in consumer demand on the part of workers.

On the other hand, the interpretation of investment-gap unemployment reflected in field (2) is distinctly neoclassical. Even if unemployment is presumed to be the most serious economic problem, its causes are found not on the demand side of the goods market but on the supply side. Firms fail to hire all job-seekers despite sufficient demand (indicated by stable or rising prices), because increased production would be unprofitable given existing factor costs and goods prices. "Classical" unemployment has two basic etiologies, however, each of which has a distinct prognosis. Where unemployment coexists with unfilled (technologically and economically "modern") jobs, lower real wages would in the neoclassical view be sufficient to reduce unemployment. Keynesians, on the other hand, are aware of the difficulty of lowering wages and would instead try to increase profits by increasing aggregate demand and prices and thereby the demand for labor. If, on the other hand, existing production capacity is fully employed, only an increase in the profitability of productive investment can achieve increases in employment. Under these conditions, even Keynesians would not recommend stimulating aggregate demand. Nevertheless, they would not limit supply-side measures to wage restraint and tax cuts but would emphasize the importance of lower interest rates for reducing the opportunity cost of productive investment.

Monetarists favor the interpretation reflected in field (3), demand-pull inflation. When existing productive capacity is fully utilized or firm profits are too low, an increase in aggregate demand will lead to an increase in the inflation rate, not to increased production and employment. Under such conditions, even from a Keynesian perspective, the proper remedy is tight government fiscal and monetary policies to reduce aggregate demand.

Finally, field (4), cost-push inflation, like demand-gap unemployment, is inconceivable in a neoclassical world. Given flexible prices and wages, an exogenous price increase (e.g., the petroleum price shock) could affect only relative prices but could not raise the general level of inflation. Inflation, therefore, necessarily demonstrates that the money supply has been expanded too rapidly and should be constricted to stabilize prices. In contrast, Keynesians believe that prices and wages are often relatively inflexible and that the wage-price spiral, in which cost increases induce price increases, which in turn induce increased wage demands, and so on, is an important inflationary mechanism in economies characterized by imperfect competition and administered prices. Hence, most Keynesians believe that fighting a wage-price spiral by restricting the money supply would merely generate unemployment. In their view, the best way to fight cost-push inflation is directly, by reducing factor costs, and indirectly, by promoting price competition among firms.

The two remaining problems—low growth and balance-of-payments deficits—did not occur in isolation during the 1970s but were usually accompanied by inflation or unemployment. Keynesians tended to attribute anemic growth to overly aggressive efforts to combat inflation, while neoclassical economists tended to attribute balance-of-payments deficits to overly aggressive expansionary policies intended to increase employment. We have to look all the way back to the 1960s to find an economy—Great Britain's—that had weak economic growth and recurring balance-of-payments crises, despite near-full employment and price stability. At the time, there was nearly universal agreement that Britain's problems were structural in nature—that its sluggish economic growth and balance-of-payments crises were due to the chronically low productivity of British industry relative to its most important competitors. The treatments prescribed for the "British disease" were therefore primarily institutional rather than economic in the narrow sense, and were explicitly aimed at the development of corporatist "productivity coalitions" among employers, unions, and the state (Shonfield, 1965; Middlemas, 1979). Elsewhere, however, structural measures were assigned a minor role in the policy repertoire proposed by both neoclassical economists and Keynesians. In practice they were employed primarily as a means of minimizing regional disparities by promoting industrial investment in agricultural and other backward regions.

But what were the policy instruments on which social democratic–Keynesian hopes rested? At the outset, we should recall that in theory both neoclassical (monetarist and supply-side) and Keynesian economists were opposed to interventions that would directly control micro-economic decisions. Both Britain and the United States experienced episodes in the 1960s and 1970s, however, when the governments tried to combat inflation with wage and price controls. Even West Germany, oriented as it was toward a free market, imposed exchange controls in its campaign against imported inflation in the early 1970s. But such interventions were criticized even at the time as being either ineffective or counterproductive on theoretical grounds, and practical experiences were disappointing except in cases where direct controls were imposed for very short periods to dramatize the situation and to support other measures taken by government (Frye and Gordon, 1981; Penceval, 1981).

On the whole, therefore, the Keynesian response to the variety of conceivable macroeconomic problems concentrated on measures that would affect microeconomic decisions only indirectly through positive and negative incentives and, most important, through changes in the macroeconomic environment. The instruments available for these purposes include expansionary and restrictive fiscal policy, expansionary and restrictive monetary policy, exchange rate policy, and—under specific institutional preconditions—the possibility of influencing union wage policy. I summarize the probable effects of these policy instruments on demand and supply-side economic problems below.

Expansionary monetary policy permits banks to create more money and provide more credit, at lower interest rates, which makes possible an increase in aggregate demand. The actual increase in demand will depend, however, on other factors affecting the liquidity preferences of households and firms and on their inclinations to save and invest. On the supply side, lower interest rates will reduce capital costs. But whether the opportunity cost of productive investment will also be reduced depends not only on domestic interest rates but also on the yield on other, especially foreign, investment options.

A restrictive monetary policy will move the economy in the opposite direction. If it is in fact possible to reduce the domestic money supply and raise interest rates, which was difficult during the regime of fixed exchange rates, the impact on effective aggregate demand will be achieved with greater certainty than is true in the expansionary case. Equally certain is a supply-side cost increase, and if domestic interest rates are pushed up sufficiently, it is also certain that the higher opportunity costs of capital will inhibit productive investment. Thus, while stimulation of the economy through monetary expansion is associated with a good deal of uncertainty, a tight-money policy must be seen as a very effective instrument of economic policy.

The effects of an expansionary fiscal policy, where government outlays exceed revenues, largely parallel those of an expansionary monetary policy, but they differ in several important respects. In the first place, the effect of fiscal stimulus on aggregate demand is more certain, but only if the deficit is produced by increased public investment or public consumption. But if the deficit is achieved by cutting taxes or increasing transfer payments to households, firms, or local jurisdictions, the desired fiscal stimulus may be blunted by an increase in savings or by substitution effects. On the supply side, an expansionary fiscal policy will have positive effects only if tax reductions or increases in government outlays are targeted at increasing business profits. Whether that will stimulate productive investment depends, again, on the opportunity cost of capital and hence on the impact of the deficit on domestic interest rates.

Today governments usually finance deficits by borrowing in the financial markets rather than by "printing money." Consequently, the public fisc must compete with private borrowers for credit, which means that deficit spending may have the effect of increasing interest rates. Whether this effect has indeed occurred was and is the object of the still-undecided crowding-out controversy (Placone, Ulbrich, and Wallace, 1985). A fully financed deficit has a second effect, however, that is both more important and more certain, although it is frequently overlooked. Any increase in government borrowing necessarily increases the supply of risk-free financial securities. During recessions (precisely when an expansionary fiscal policy is used), investment projects in the private sector are often unable to compete with this option. The supply-side effects of an expansionary fiscal policy are thus not entirely predictable.

A tight fiscal policy is the mirror image of an expansionary policy. Fiscal restraint is produced by reducing the public sector deficit or by realizing a surplus (where government revenues exceed outlays). As a consequence, aggregate demand is reduced; supply-side effects again depend on how the surplus and the cutbacks in expenditure are allocated. The opportunity cost of capital could also decrease unless it is held up by other measures (a policy of monetary restraint, say, or increased interest rates in international financial markets).

The effects of currency devaluation are similar to those of an expansionary monetary or fiscal policy, again with certain important distinctions. Devaluation increases import prices and reduces export prices, so that if it is price sensitive, demand for domestic goods will increase at home as well as abroad. On the supply side, devaluation increases the costs of imported raw materials and intermediate goods and services (and possibly wages, if unions try to compensate for the increase in prices). Persistent devaluation also increases the cost of capital, because investments abroad promise to increase in value as devaluation continues. As might be expected, revaluation reduces aggregate demand, lowers the prices of imports, and reduces the cost of capital.

Wages, finally, to the extent that they can be influenced by government for the purposes of economic control, can have a particularly strong effect on domestic demand and on supply-side cost-push, while they will not directly influence financial markets.

It should be clear by now that each school of economics has its favorite instruments of macroeconomic policy. For neoclassical economists of both the monetarist and the supply-side persuasion, the world is simple. They presuppose a workable competition, and it follows that inflation can occur only when the money supply grows faster than the economy's productive capacity. To fight inflation and stabilize prices, therefore, one must first reduce the money supply and then firmly tie its expansion to the growth of capacity. The complement of this belief is that wage flexibility will preclude the possibility of involuntary unemployment. But since by definition collective bargaining forestalls "workable competition" in the labor market, unemployment merely indicates that wages are higher than the market-clearing equilibrium. The solution to unemployment then is to ask the unions to accept lower real wages. Of course, it would be even better if collective wage bargaining could be eliminated entirely, and if competition were established in labor markets as well.

For reasons discussed above, Keynesians believe that labor markets are dependent on the conditions prevailing on financial and goods markets. When investment and output are constrained, the willingness to work for lower wages cannot produce a full employment equilibrium. The preeminent danger against which Keynesians are on guard is a liquidity trap in which households, uncertain about the future, increase their savings at the expense of consumption while savers, out of fear of loss, avoid productive investment even when interest rates are low. The downward spiral of mutually reinforcing fears can be reversed only if the state is willing to increase effective demand substantially by an expansive, deficit-financed fiscal policy. Then, as expectations stabilize, incomes of households and firms and their willingness to consume and to invest will also increase. Thus fiscal policy is the Keynesians' favorite weapon against unemployment, while low interest rates—even though necessary—could not by themselves reverse deflationary expectations.

In the case of inflationary overheating, on the other hand, Keynesians agree that government must not further increase aggregate demand. But since they are less sanguine about "workable competition" and hence about the flexibility of prices in the goods markets, they are wary of the monetarist recommendation to fight inflation with a tight-money policy, which in their view would be associated with an unacceptable increase in unemployment. Instead, they suggest that price competition ought to be increased by a further liberalization of foreign trade, by a revaluation of the currency, and by a moderation of union wage policy that would reduce the cost pressures on industry.

Both mainstream schools of macroeconomic thought thus tend to emphasize particular constellations of economic problems and to orient their economic-policy recommendations to the problem so defined. But to an interested outsider who has no stake in their battle, the historical evidence points to the conclusion that each of the demand-side and supply-side problem constellations discussed above may in fact really occur. Therefore it now seems more sensible to change our perspective and to discuss the consequences and undesirable side effects of available instruments of macroeconomic management with reference to the full range of macroeconomic pathologies that may in fact obtain. Let us begin with problems on the demand side.

When unemployment is caused by lack of demand, the Keynesian formula is plausible. In this situation an expansionary fiscal policy, supported by permissive monetary policies, should bring quick relief. Among the likely side effects are increases in imports and a deteriorating balance of payments. But if an expansionary policy continues after the available production capacity is fully utilized (say, because unemployment is not yet fully eliminated), the result will be demand-pull. If it is allowed to persist and is anticipated in collective bargaining, a further consequence may be cost-push inflation. On the other hand, if unemployment is of the demand-gap variety, the neoclassical remedy of lower real wages appears to be counterproductive. There is no reason to believe, at any rate, that the resultant decrease in consumer demand would be offset by increased business investment.

When demand-pull inflation is the problem, however, only monetary restraint will decisively reduce both consumer and investment demand. By contrast, private demand might offset the effects of fiscal restraint, and wage drift (a tendency for earnings to grow more rapidly than contractual rates permit) or increases in demands of other kinds in the economy could neutralize union wage restraint. If prices are inelastic, however, as the Keynesians predict they will be, restricting the money supply will also reduce output and employment. Furthermore, as a consequence of lower profits and higher interest rates, firms are likely to reduce their investment in new plant and equipment. Hence the long-term effect of monetary restraint is likely to be investment-gap unemployment, which, unlike demand-gap unemployment, can no longer be reversed at short notice by a return to demand inflation.

In the case of investment-gap unemployment, the expansionary policies that the Keynesians recommend can increase employment only if they increase profits, that is, if prices rise faster than production costs and especially faster than wages. This implies demand-pull inflation. At the same time, the Keynesian remedy presupposes either that workers are suffering from a "money illusion," taking nominal wage increases for rising real incomes, or that unions are willing and able to hold the increase of unit labor costs below the rate of inflation so that profits will in fact be able to rise. Monetarists and supply-side theorists, on the other hand, recommend increasing profits by reducing real wages. However, that implies the risk that negative repercussions on consumer spending might also dampen the willingness of firms to invest in new jobs. Finally, while a reduction of the opportunity costs of capital is essential for both strategies, neither side emphasizes it, presumably because both monetarists and Keynesians assume that with high unemployment, interest rates will be low as a matter of course.

In the case of cost-push inflation, the restrictive monetary and fiscal policies recommended by the monetarists should reduce the scope for price increases but would not directly reduce exogenous factor-cost pressures. The immediate consequence would be a profit squeeze and a reduction of output and investments, which would first lead to demand-gap unemployment and later to investment-gap unemployment. Only when rising unemployment forces wage costs down could one expect an alleviation of cost-push inflation, at the end of a long chain of causation. On the other hand, Keynesians—starting from the presumption that prices and wages will be relatively inflexible under most circumstances— would have to rely mainly on hopes for union wage restraint (in addition to revaluation and the liberalization of foreign trade). But as we shall see, this is a solution fraught with institutional difficulties.

Finally, in the case of a balance-of-trade deficit, a tight monetary policy would decrease domestic consumption and hence imports. At the same time, higher interest rates would attract foreign capital imports, which should improve the balance of payments. But since this will increase production costs, reduce domestic investment, and raise the exchange rate, the country that adopts a policy of monetary restraint is likely to further damage its international competitiveness. If the country were to use monetary expansion instead, it would achieve the opposite effects, but the overall balance of outcomes would be equally unsatisfactory. Fiscal policy would be somewhat less effective and somewhat less harmful, when employed in either direction.

The conclusion is clear. If economic policy is limited to the instruments of government fiscal and monetary policy, it is likely to succeed only when it confronts problems originating on the demand side of the economy. And even in those cases, protracted reliance on expansionary or restrictive policies is likely to entail serious secondary problems in the long run. But when causes are located on the supply side, economic problems are likely to be resistant to monetary and fiscal strategies. Their undesirable side effects on the demand side will occur earlier and with greater certainty than the intended positive effects on the supply-side problem. In short, government economic policy is relatively helpless when confronted with investment-gap unemployment, cost-push inflation, or a negative balance of current accounts if its set of policy instruments is limited to the expansionary or restrictive use of fiscal and monetary policy.

This is even more true when supply-side and demand-side problems appear in combination, as they did during the stagflation period of the 1970s. Regardless of whether the dominant manifestation was a combination of (oil) cost-push inflation and demand-gap unemployment or a combination of demand-pull inflation and investment-gap unemployment, any attempt to fight one problem by increasing or decreasing aggregate demand would entail an immediate worsening of the other problem. If, as Jan Tinbergen (1967, chap. 3) explained, economic policy needs as many independent policy instruments as there are policy targets, it seems that the degrees of freedom provided by monetary and fiscal demand management were insufficient to cope with the constellation of economic stagflation in the 1970s.

From the foregoing analysis we can also derive a better understanding of the peculiar double role of wage policy in economic-policy discussions. On the one hand, wages are an essential determinant of macroeconomic problems, because they constitute by far the largest single element of both aggregate domestic demand and aggregate production costs. On the other hand, they also constitute one of the potentially most powerful instruments of economic policy. While wages are the price for labor as a commodity, they are not exclusively determined by anonymous forces in atomistic markets. Instead, in all Western industrial nations, nominal wages are to a large extent determined by collective bargaining between unions and employers' associations. In that regard, they are political prices which, under certain circumstances, may be fixed above or below the level corresponding to a hypothetical market equilibrium. Potentially, therefore, an incomes policy influencing wage settle-

33

ments could be an important instrument of macroeconomic policy, even if we realize that wage drift will always modify collectively determined nominal wages to some extent and that their translation into real wages is affected by unforeseen changes in the rate of inflation.

The unique value of an incomes policy in the context of macroeconomic control derives from the fact that wages influence the demand side and the supply side of the goods market in opposite directions. Both monetary and fiscal policy have simultaneous expansionary or restrictive impacts on demand and supply, and have a stronger effect on demand than they have on supply. An expansionary incomes policy, on the other hand, will stimulate aggregate demand and reduce the profitability of production and investment, and a restrictive incomes policy has opposite effects. Moreover, in both cases, the change in wages will be fully reflected in production costs, while savings and imports reduce the impact on domestic demand. Thus the availability of an incomes policy creates important additional degrees of freedom for macroeconomic policy makers.

Ever since the beginning of the crisis, however, incomes policy has been associated with wage restraint, meaning that unions were asked to accept wage settlements below the level that they could have obtained by fully exploiting their bargaining power. Moreover, the meaning of wage restraint changed over time. During the 1970s the unions were merely asked to hold the increase of unit labor costs below the current rate of inflation in order to achieve greater price stability. In the 1980s, however, wage restraint came to mean the voluntary acceptance of real-wage losses in order to increase the profitability of productive investments. In either case, however, a restrictive incomes policy gave policy makers an otherwise unattainable means of using a single strategy to achieve a reduction of aggregate demand and a simultaneous reduction of the factor costs that firms had to bear. From this analysis it is easy to derive its attractiveness in precisely those situations in which monetary and fiscal policy instruments would be either ineffective or associated with unacceptable side effects.

Used alone, a restrictive incomes policy is the ideal weapon to combat cost-push inflation as well as balance-of-payments deficits produced by excessive domestic demand and high production costs. It should also be effective against demand-pull inflation, without the adverse supply-side consequences associated with monetary and fiscal contraction. It is less clear how reducing wages would affect investment-gap unemployment. Production costs would be reduced, but so would consumer demand. Thus the overall effect on firm profits is unpredictable, as is the effect on employment and investment. A restrictive wage policy would be unambiguously detrimental only in the case of demand-constrained unemployment, which does not mean, however, that large wage increases would solve that problem.

Even more important are the effects of incomes policy when used in combination with other policy instruments. The asymmetry of its effects makes incomes policy an ideal complement to monetary and fiscal demand management. With investment-gap unemployment, a restrictive incomes policy can fully restore firm profits—and employment—if government fiscal policy compensates for the demand shortfall and government monetary policy provides low interest rates to encourage investment. Even when unemployment is due to a lack of demand, the government can employ an expansionary policy with less trepidation if it knows it will not also have to contend with cost-push inflation. According to this economic logic, incomes policies are the key to solving problems of stagflation.

If demand-constrained unemployment and cost-push inflation occurred together, an alliance between government and unions would permit the government to fight unemployment by means of a decisively expansionary monetary and fiscal policy, while the unions would fight inflation by restraining in their wage demands. At any rate, the negative side effects resulting from such a division of labor may be less than those resulting from an attempt to fight stagflation using only one set of instruments. If stagflation's etiology lies in a combination of investment-constrained unemployment and demand-pull inflation, voluntary wage restraint would reduce cost push and increase firm profits, even if government reduced demand less drastically than the monetarist formula recommends.

This discussion is summarized in Figure 2.2, which shows that monetary and fiscal policy can react appropriately either to problems of inflation or to problems of unemployment, but not to both simultaneously. It can do less to solve supply-side problems than problems on the demand side. The figure also demonstrates that the possible effects of a restrictive incomes policy are particularly strong with respect to those problems which present special difficulties for monetary and fiscal policy. And the figure illustrates the conclusion of our analysis: that for supply-side problems, and especially for the combination of problems called stagflation, economic policy would be well served by close cooperation between government and unions. If these parties made their decisions jointly and coordinated their actions, they could achieve a better total result than either side could achieve alone.

To summarize: this introduction should have shown that social democratic hopes for steady economic growth and continuous full employ-

| | Monetary and financial policy | | Wage policy | |
	Expansionary	Restrictive	Expansionary	Restrictive
Unemployment due to lack of demand	Helps	Harms	(Helps)	Harms
Demand-pull inflation	Harms	Helps	Harms	Helps
Unemployment due to lack of jobs	(Helps)	Harms	Harms	(Helps)
Cost-push inflation	Harms	(Helps)	Harms	Helps
Current accounts deficit	Harms	(Helps)	Harms	Helps

Figure 2.2. Effects of monetary and fiscal policy and of wage policy on macroeconomic problems

ment were precarious, because the policy instruments directly available to government would not offer protection against all theoretically possible constellations of economic deviation from the optimal path. Keynesian theory was best prepared to deal with the one constellation that had inspired it: demand-gap unemployment coupled with a deflationary fall in prices, as experienced in the Great Depression of the 1930s. It is true that Keynes himself, and Kalecki (1943) even more so, had foreseen that once the depression was over, full employment might generate permanent inflationary pressures. Neither, however, had formulated a viable solution to that problem. Within a social democratic–Keynesian frame of reference, neoclassical-monetarist remedies that would fight inflation with higher unemployment were, of course, unacceptable. At the same time, no one regarded permanently imposed wage and price controls as a practicable solution to the inflation problem.

All things considered, it should have been clear that governments did not have direct access to fully half of the arsenal of necessary policy instruments. Even when confronted only with the usual swings of the business cycle, successful economic policy depended on the voluntary cooperation of the unions. This was even more true of problems rooted in the supply side of the goods market, "classical" unemployment and cost-push inflation. Here, fiscal demand management, the Keynesians' favorite policy instrument, was completely ineffective without full union support. But even when union wage restraint was assured, the effect of a Keynesian therapy for supply-side problems was less certain than it was with demand-side problems. Finally, when demand-side and supply-side problems appeared in combination, the only certain thing was the ineffectiveness of simple solutions. Nothing in Keynesian theory helped to define the economic and institutional conditions under which a successful combination of strategies could conceivably be achieved.

In a certain sense, then, the social democratic–Keynesian vision of the postwar decades was overly optimistic, because economic theory had neglected a whole series of possible constellations of economic problems. Keynesian social democrats could not alert their followers as to how demanding and precarious their attempt was to eliminate capitalist crises through state action. Fascinated by fiscal fine-tuning, Keynesian economic theory was particularly deficient in its attention to the central role of incomes policy (Weintraub, 1978). As a result, the institutional conditions that might have permitted concerted strategies were not specified with the necessary theoretical clarity and were not politically supported with the necessary sense of urgency. Where they were in place, as in Austria, they did not owe their origins to Keynesian theory; and where they were created to support a Keynesian policy, as in the Federal Republic, their importance was not understood clearly enough and political support was not strong enough to prevent their disintegration at the very beginning of the crisis.

This argument, however, anticipates the historical descriptions of subsequent chapters. Here, my purpose has been to demonstrate that the vision of efficient and crisis-free capitalism, controlled with a light hand by democratic policy makers managing macroeconomic aggregates, was extraordinarily demanding but not theoretically impossible. In the following chapters I first describe and interpret the historical experience of four social democratic countries during the worldwide economic crisis. Then, in Part 3, I provide a comparative analysis of the economic and institutional conditions that explain the relative success or failure of social democratic–Keynesian economic strategies during the crisis period.

Part II

FOUR EUROPEAN EXPERIENCES

Chapter Three

A Comparison of Performance Indicators

The Yom Kippur War in the fall of 1973 gave OPEC the opportunity
to impose an oil embargo against several Western industrial nations and
then, in the following months, to limit crude oil production and to raise
prices by a factor of twelve. At first, the problem of scarcity dominated
public attention in the West. Already sensitized by the ecological movement and its argument about the "limits of growth," people saw carless
Sundays and the waiting lines at gas stations as eloquent symbols of the
finiteness of material resources and of the necessity of conserving energy and raw materials. The price increase seemed of secondary importance by comparison.

Today, we would place the emphasis differently. Petroleum scarcity
was soon followed by surplus. But the OPEC cartel successfully defended
the price increases for a whole decade. The increases in the price of this
essential energy source and industrial raw material, which was in the
short run irreplaceable, were at least the catalyst if not the cause for the
longest and deepest world economic crisis since the Great Depression.
Although it was not readily recognized at the time, the crisis-inducing
effect of the oil price shock resulted from the stagflationary combination
of two apparently contradictory mechanisms.

1. The rise in crude oil prices meant a marked increase in the price
level for the whole economy (Gerstenberger and Hölterhoff, 1983). The
prices of other forms of energy were drawn along, and these cost increases were passed through into the prices of all energy-intensive and
raw-material-intensive goods and services (for instance, transportation).
Hence the oil shock provided an additional cost push to the inflation
already raging in the Western industrial nations. Given increasing prices,
the unions had every reason to demand higher wages to protect real

incomes. In the absence of effective remedial action, the result of the oil price shock would have been an accelerating cost-price-wage spiral.

2. At the same time, the increase in oil prices meant a substantial decrease in the industrialized nations' buying power. Even if the OPEC nations had been able immediately to convert their increased wealth to effective demand for goods and services, the structural adjustment required by the differences in the demand streams before and after the oil shock would have probably brought on a substantial crisis. In fact, the "absorptive capacity" of the OPEC nations was initially overloaded by the new wealth. The current account surplus of the OPEC nations climbed from $8 billion in 1973 to $60 billion in 1974 (OECD Economic Outlook 28, 1980:125), decreased again, and then, after the second oil price shock, climbed to $65 billion in 1979 and $111 billion in 1980 (ibid. 37, 1985:135). These OPEC surpluses corresponded with equivalent reductions in aggregate demand in the industrial nations. Again, in the absence of effective remedial action, the consequence of this aspect of the oil shock had to be decreased production and rising unemployment in the industrialized nations.

Hence, in the winter of 1973–74, the OPEC cartel shocked the Western industrial nations with the dual threat of increased inflation and rising unemployment. As was shown above, this was a constellation to which conventional Keynesian demand management had no satisfactory response. Government could either respond to rising unemployment by increasing aggregate demand and letting inflation take its course, or it could fight inflation and accept the consequent increase in unemployment. Given this choice, the priorities of the social democratic governments in the Federal Republic, Austria, and Sweden—as well as the British Labour party, which returned to power in February 1974—were clear. They wanted both full employment and stable prices, but since they had to choose, they chose full employment. Helmut Schmidt had clearly articulated the priorities of the Social Democrats in 1972 when he categorically stated that 5 percent unemployment was worse than 5 percent inflation.

When the crisis began in 1973, all four countries shared a similar macroeconomic situation (Table 3.1). By the standards of the recent past, Britain's economic growth was a bit above average and that of the other three countries was average. All four (also by comparison with the recent past) faced substantial inflation; the Federal Republic was somewhat better off than the other three and Austria somewhat worse off. The Federal Republic and Austria had excess demand for labor, while in Sweden and especially in Great Britain unemployment was already somewhat disquieting according to the standards of the time.

Table 3.1 Growth, inflation, and unemployment, 1973 (%)

	Austria	FRG	GB	Sweden
GDP growth	4.9	4.6	7.9	4.0
GDP inflation	8.0	6.0	7.1	7.2
Unemployment	1.1	0.8	3.3	2.5

Sources: OECD *Historical Statistics,* 1960–1984; OECD *Economic Outlook* 39.

It is worth noting that at the beginning of the period, the symptoms of the "British disease" were not particularly prominent. The British position was, considering all three indicators of economic performance, quite average compared with the positions of the other three countries. If one had wanted to choose one of the four countries as a problem case on the eve of the crisis, the most likely candidate would have been Sweden rather than Great Britain.

GROWTH, INFLATION, UNEMPLOYMENT

Drawing an intermediate balance for the period ending six years later, at the beginning of the second oil price shock, we find that the performance indicators for the four countries are much further apart (see Table 3.2). Great Britain now stands out as a clear problem case. During the period from 1974 to 1979, Great Britain had the lowest economic growth, the highest inflation rate, and the highest rate of unemployment. Austria took the lead with the highest rate of growth, the second-lowest rate of inflation, and, together with Sweden, the lowest rate of unemployment, in keeping with the definition of full employment in force at that time. The Federal Republic had the lowest rate of inflation and higher unemployment; Sweden had the second-lowest rate of unemployment and a higher rate of inflation.

Table 3.2 Average growth rates, inflation rates, and unemployment rates, 1974–1979 (%)

	Austria	FRG	GB	Sweden
GDP growth	3.0	2.4	1.5	1.8
GDP inflation	6.0	4.8	16.1	10.6
Unemployment	1.8	3.2	5.0	1.9

Sources: OECD *Historical Statistics,* 1960–1984; OECD *Economic Outlook* 39.

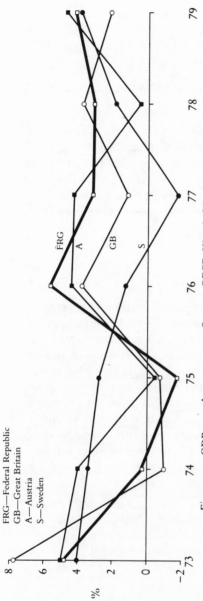

FRG—Federal Republic
GB—Great Britain
A—Austria
S—Sweden

Figure 3.1. GDP growth, 1973–1979. Source: OECD *Historical Statistics*, 1960–1984.

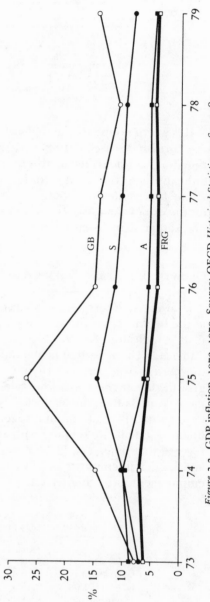

Figure 3.2. GDP inflation, 1973–1979. Source: OECD *Historical Statistics*, 1960–1984.

44

Figures 3.1–3.4 depict the six years between the first and the second oil price crises. The rates of growth run largely parallel in Austria, Great Britain, and the Federal Republic, with a steep decline in 1974–75 and an equally steep climb in 1976, a minirecession in 1977 (1978 in Austria), and a new climb in 1979, in which Great Britain did not participate (Figure 3.1). The development of the Swedish economy is particularly noteworthy. Sweden avoided the decreased growth at the beginning of the crisis but experienced it three years later, in 1977. Sweden therefore did not participate in the "intervening high" in 1976 but did participate in the later upward cycle in 1978–79.

Inflation rates were even more varied (Figure 3.2). Germany and Austria peaked in 1974; after 1976 their inflation rates remained low. Inflation in Sweden and especially in Great Britain continued to climb steeply until 1975. After 1976 Sweden slowly decreased its inflation rate, while the inflation rate in Great Britain first fell steeply, then dropped to 10 percent in 1978, but climbed back to 15 percent in 1979.

The fluctuations in official unemployment rates were again completely different (Figure 3.3). Austria and Sweden for the whole period enjoyed full employment in the ambitious sense of the term then current. In the Federal Republic unemployment climbed in 1974 and 1975, and in Great Britain it climbed in 1975 and 1976. It then remained far above the previous levels in both countries.

What Does "Full Employment" Mean?

Registered unemployment is a problematic indicator of the success of the social democratic goal of full employment. Unlike the rate of growth or the rate of inflation, official unemployment figures do not measure a single-dimensioned variable but reflect changes on the supply side as well as on the demand side of the labor market. The unemployment rate increases when more people are looking for work or when there are fewer jobs available in the labor market, and it sinks when the number of those seeking work goes down or when more jobs are filled. But while changes in the number of jobs can plausibly be ascribed to government policies, changes on the supply side are partly determined by demographic and cultural factors and therefore cannot simply be interpreted as policy successes or failures. Even when government action decreases the labor supply in the interests of fighting unemployment, the reduction is not always a policy success. Prolonging education and training may be desirable in many ways, but when young people are kept in schools and universities that have nothing more to offer them, the reduced pressure on the labor market becomes a plague for educational policy. In the same way, it may be desirable to offer older people a choice between working and retiring, and especially between forms of part-time work and part-time retirement (Bruche and Casey, 1982). But when early retirement leads to a forced exclusion of older people from gainful employment, the improvement in unemployment statistics comes at high human and social cost. The same is true of administrative measures repatriating foreign workers, who had been actively solicited before the crisis began. In short, the social democratic goal of full employment can be taken seriously in a moral sense only when it is interpreted as a right to gainful employment for all who are looking for paid work, as it is defined in the Swedish model (Meidner and Hedborg, 1984:46ff.).

This ambitious interpretation of full employment makes the choice of a performance measure very difficult. The statistics on unemployment are less informative than data on the number of employees and on changes in the number of gainfully employed members of the labor force, because both dependent employment and self-employment contribute to the goal of full employment (Figure 3.4). Here we see extreme differences between the Federal Republic and Sweden. Gainful employment in the Federal Republic decreased by more than 5 percent between 1973 and 1977; only part of the loss was later recouped. In Sweden, by contrast, gainful employment increased from year to year, and in 1979 was almost 8 percent higher than it was in 1973. Developments in Austria and Great Britain lay between these two extremes; both countries were able on balance to achieve small gains in employment between 1973 and 1979.

But the number of employees alone is still a highly imperfect measure of the degree to which the goal of full employment has actually been met. This goal also includes persons who would accept work if they had the opportunity. It includes not only those who are registered for unemployment assistance but also the "silent reserve" of those who are not counted by the various national processes for registering the unemployed (Freiburghaus, 1979) but who would seek and find work in a more favorable labor market. Estimating their number for even a single nation is a difficult undertaking (Mertens and Klauder, 1980; Klauder, 1982). Making these estimates comparable on an international level is probably impossible. Consider, for example, the question of gainfully employed women (Schmid and Weitzel, 1984). Differences in the availability of part-time work slots, day-care facilities, and all-day schools, in the regulation of maternal and parental leave, in the way the income of marriage partners is treated by the tax system, and finally in the evaluation of the work of "mere housewives" are simply too great to be recon-

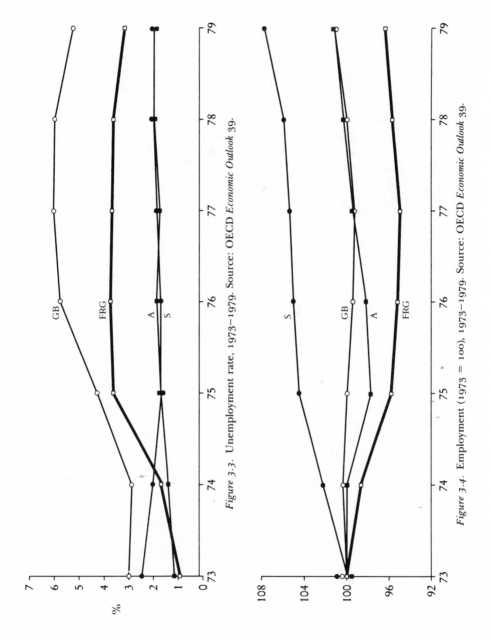

Figure 3.3. Unemployment rate, 1973–1979. Source: OECD *Economic Outlook* 39.

Figure 3.4. Employment (1973 = 100), 1973–1979. Source: OECD *Economic Outlook* 39.

ciled. Similar problems arise in drawing comparisons about the employment of young people, older people, or the handicapped.

Since there is no prospect of an internationally standardized definition of the "silent reserve," only one reference point remains for comparison: the total number of persons of working age (conventionally defined as the years between 15 and 64). The best measures of the success of full employment programs across countries are thus the labor force participation rates, that is, the proportion of 15-to-64-year-olds that is gainfully employed and the changes in that figure over time (corrected, of course, for immigration and emigration by foreigners). The use of these measures as proxies for full employment does not mean that all persons of 15-to-64 years of age should ideally be employed. But it does mean that we can compare the relative success of full employment programs by establishing a relationship between actual gainful employment and the maximum possible work force.

The comparison in Table 3.3 shows that the employable population grew slightly in all four countries between 1973 and 1979; it grew most in Austria and least in Sweden. In the Federal Republic the number of gainfully employed people declined, in Great Britain and Austria it increased slightly, and in Sweden it increased greatly. Correspondingly, the participation rate of 15-to-64-year-olds grew only in Sweden; it fell markedly in the Federal Republic and slightly in the other two countries.

During the crisis of the 1970s, only Sweden continued to approach the goal of full employment as we have defined it here. Although Austria and Great Britain achieved respectable results, their increases in employment were insufficient to maintain their participation rates in the face of a growing population. West Germany had the least favorable results in terms of participation since its paid work force actually declined.

The full extent of Sweden's accomplishment becomes clear, however, only when it is compared to Sweden's initially high level of participation in the paid work force. Figure 3.5 shows that Sweden started off at a high level in 1973 and substantially improved on its performance after

Table 3.3 Changes in the employable population, number of gainfully employed, and participation rate, 1973–1979 (%)

	Austria	FGR	GB	Sweden
Employable population, age 15–64	2.57	1.60	1.77	0.86
Gainfully employed	1.36	−2.04	0.91	5.50
Participation rate, age 15–64	−1.17	−3.58	−0.85	4.61

Source: OECD *Labour Force Statistics*, 1970–1981.

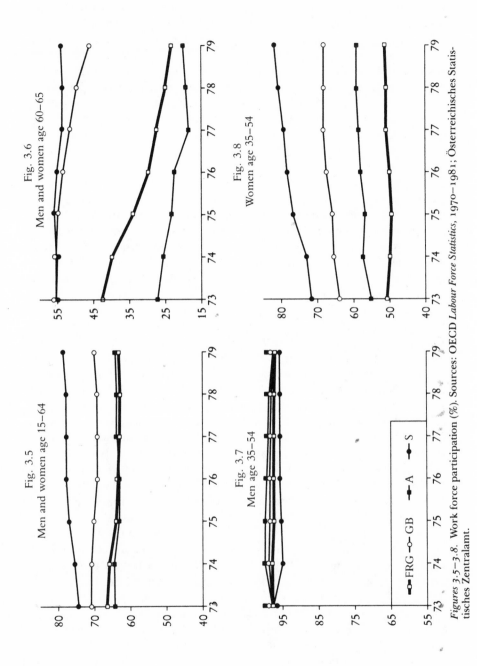

Fig. 3.5
Men and women age 15–64

Fig. 3.6
Men and women age 60–65

Fig. 3.7
Men age 35–54

Fig. 3.8
Women age 35–54

●—● FRG   ○—○ GB   ■—■ A   ●—● S

Figures 3.5–3.8. Work force participation (%). Sources: OECD *Labour Force Statistics*, 1970–1981; Österreichisches Statistisches Zentralamt.

that time. During the years of its last Labour government, Great Britain was also able to maintain a relatively high level of participation in the labor force, while Austria and to a greater extent the Federal Republic started with lower participation rates that declined still further. These results can be further refined by examination of the supply side, that is, by asking which groups of persons were primarily affected by changes in employment, and of the demand side, by asking which economic sectors declined or expanded. Both aspects reveal further differences among the countries.

Advantaged and Disadvantaged Groups

Beginning with the supply side, the first substantive difference among the four countries is their treatment of foreign laborers. In Great Britain the question is moot. Immigration is restricted to persons from Commonwealth countries, and those persons are not distinguished from British workers in the employment statistics. In the three other countries, the percentage of foreigners who were gainfully employed in 1978 was 5.2 percent of the work force in Sweden, 5.9 percent in Austria, and 7.4 percent in the Federal Republic. In Sweden, however, even during the years of crisis the employment of foreign workers (primarily from Finland) was not restricted by administrative measures, and it increased slowly. In Austria and the Federal Republic, recruitment of foreign workers was stopped after 1973, and it became more difficult to extend their work and residence permits. The number of foreign workers employed thus declined between 1973 and 1978 by 19.9 percent in Austria and by 22.7 percent in the Federal Republic (*Internationale Chronik* 4, April 1981:4). As the economy began to recover, the number of foreign workers again increased, so that the labor market was unburdened for only a limited period. The following comparisons therefore do not break out the fluctuations in foreign worker participation in the labor force. Instead they are based on the total number of persons registered in the country in the employable age group or in the age classes.

For the rest, the question who lost and who gained in the 1970s can be answered in terms of age and gender. Both answers are elucidated by Figures 3.5–3.8 and Table 3.4. In 1973 the participation rate for the group aged 60 to 64 was much higher in Sweden and Great Britain than in the Federal Republic and in Austria. While Sweden was able to keep the participation rate of older workers at its initial high level, by 1979 rates had declined moderately in Great Britain and in Austria and sharply in the Federal Republic. In contrast, middle-age groups were not affected by the employment crisis in the Federal Republic and in Austria

Table 3.4 Work force participation of 60-to-64-year-olds and of men and women in the middle-age groups, 1973 and 1979 (%)

	Austria	FRG	GB	Sweden
Work force participation, Ages 60–64				
1973	26.8	41.9	55.5	55.1
1979	19.2	22.6	46.8	53.9
Difference, 79–73	−7.6	−19.3	−8.7	−1.2
Participation of 35-to-54-year-old men (Austria: 30–49)				
1973	98.0	97.3	97.9	97.4
1979	96.5	96.8	97.3	95.8
Difference, 79–73	−1.5	−0.5	−0.6	−1.6
Participation of 25-to-54-year-old women (Austria: 30–49)				
1973	55.7	50.5	63.8	71.3
1979	59.1	51.6	68.0	82.5
Difference, 79–73	+3.4	+1.1	+4.2	+11.2

Sources: OECD *Labour Force Statistics*, 1970–1981; Österreichisches Statistisches Zentralamt; author's own calculations.

(Figures 3.7 and 3.8; Table 3.4). There are, however, clear distinctions between the countries in the change in work force participation for men and women between 1973 and 1979.

In all four countries the employment of middle-aged men changed very little. For women, there were much greater differences both in the initial level and in the rate of change. In the Federal Republic the employment of women stagnated at the relatively low 1973 level. In Austria and Great Britain, the somewhat higher initial level increased, and Swedish women, who started with the highest employment participation in the Western world, increased their rate by an almost unbelievable 11 percent between 1973 and 1979.

We can thus summarize developments on the supply side of the labor market between 1973 and 1979 as follows. The work force participation of the population of employable age climbed overall in Sweden, remained constant in Great Britain, declined somewhat in Austria, and declined more sharply in the Federal Republic. The work force participation of men in their middle years was completely unaffected by these various developments. In all four countries that figure remained at its initial high level. If overall employment declined, older workers were the group affected by loss of jobs. Their participation in the work force declined moderately in Great Britain and in Austria and steeply in the Federal Republic. If overall employment increased, women were the beneficiaries, most in Sweden and least in the Federal Republic.

Growing and Shrinking Sectors

Let us now turn to the demand side of the labor market to see which sectors gained or lost jobs. We can begin by ascertaining that the percentage of the work force employed in the industrial sector between 1973 and 1979 declined in all four countries, most in the Federal Republic and least in Austria (Figure 3.9). The service sector grew everywhere, most in Sweden and least in the Federal Republic (Figure 3.10). The orders of magnitude are important here. In the industrial sector, the Federal Republic and Great Britain began with a relatively high initial level and suffered large losses, whereas Sweden and Austria had a low initial level and suffered light losses. On the other hand, Sweden started out with a very high level in the service sector and experienced a disproportionately large growth, while employment in the service sector in Austria and the Federal Republic started out at a low level and also climbed less.

Of particular interest in the service sector are developments in the public sector (Figure 3.11). Here, too, Sweden is clearly in the lead, in terms of both initial level and rate of growth. In the three other nations public employment increased less, in the Federal Republic least of all. Finally, employment in the agrarian sector deserves special consideration (Figure 3.12). This figure reveals that whereas the restructuring of agriculture was largely complete in the other countries, in the 1970s Austria was still in the midst of the process. The loss in agrarian employment in Austria was consequently much more serious than in the other countries.

Table 3.5 summarizes and compares the differing basic patterns for sectoral employment in the four nations. Total job growth in Sweden was on about the same order of magnitude as the expansion of its public sector. Without this expansion the Swedish employment figures would even have declined somewhat. This fact explains much of the spectacular success of Sweden's full employment policy in the 1970s, although even Sweden's losses in industrial and agricultural employment were slightly below the average of the four nations.

Despite the negative assessment of Great Britain's economy in the 1970s, that country had the second-best participation rate of the four nations. It suffered minimal losses in its (very small) agricultural sector and showed a moderate increase in its service sector. Industrial employment losses in Britain, on the other hand, were greater than average.

The development in Austria was the exact reverse. During the 1970s employment in the (still very large) agricultural sector declined much more sharply than in the other three countries. Austria was, however,

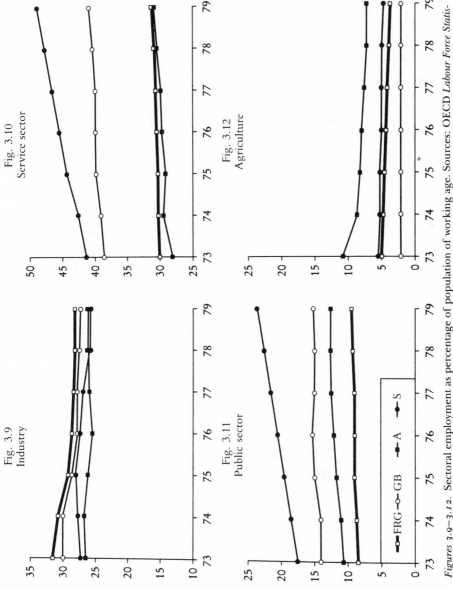

Fig. 3.9
Industry

Fig. 3.10
Service sector

Fig. 3.11
Public sector

Fig. 3.12
Agriculture

FRG—○—GB ■ A ● S

Figures 3.9–3.12. Sectoral employment as percentage of population of working age. Sources: OECD *Labour Force Statistics,* 1970–1981; OECD 1982.

Table 3.5 Changes in employment in industry, in the service sector, and in agriculture for the population of working age, 1973–1979 (%)

	Austria	FRG	GB	Sweden
(1) Participation rate in general	−1.17	−3.58	−0.85	+4.61
(2) Industry	−0.50	−3.69	−2.78	−1.47
(3) Service sector	+3.27	+1.35	+2.62	+7.26
(4) (Service sector, public)	(+1.59)	(+0.64)	(+1.01)	(+4.70)
(5) Agriculture	−3.72	−1.20	−0.23	−0.67
(6) Sum of (2) and (3)	+2.77	−2.34	−0.16	+5.79
(7) Difference between (6) and (4)	+1.18	−2.98	−1.17	+1.09

Sources: ILO *Yearbook of Labour Statistics*, 1983; OECD 1982; OECD *Labour Force Statistics*, 1970–1981.

the only country that kept its (relatively small) industrial employment stable throughout the crisis period. In Austria, too, the growth of the service sector was topped only by Sweden (and in Austria only half of that growth was in the public sector, as compared to two-thirds in Sweden). If we disregard the losses in the agricultural sector as unavoidable, then Austria shows a markedly positive development in the two "modern" sectors of industry and services (line 6 of the table). If we consider only the private sector (line 7), Austria is the most successful of the four nations, while Great Britain and especially West Germany suffered losses even from this adjusted perspective. Austrian employment gains were thus primarily achieved in the nonagricultural private sector.

West Germany shows the worst employment picture overall, corresponding in magnitude to the high job losses in the industrial sector. If industrial employment had been more stable, as in Austria, then West Germany would largely have avoided its decline in overall employment. However, its growth in service sector employment, especially public sector employment, was also below average. If the nation had achieved employment growth rates in its service sector like those of Austria or Sweden, its overall employment performance would have been average or better. To explain the particularly poor course of employment participation in the Federal Republic, we must thus analyze developments in both the industrial sector and the service sector.

The Bottom Line

Despite similar political priorities and initial situations, the four nations weathered the global period of crisis between the first and second oil price shocks in very different ways. Conventional performance indicators—economic growth, inflation, and unemployment (Table

3.2)—show Austria performing best and Great Britain worst. Sweden and the Federal Republic take a middle position, if we consider all indicators, but their profiles vary greatly. Sweden paid for its defense of full employment with high inflation, and the Federal Republic bought its lead in price stability with a marked rise in unemployment.

If instead of looking at unemployment rates, however, we consider the number of those employed, the picture changes dramatically. Now Austria and Great Britain constitute a middle group with somewhat stable employment figures, whereas Sweden's employment numbers have risen and those in West Germany have dropped sharply. We can make further distinctions and determine that the gains in Swedish employment were due solely to public sector employment and primarily benefited women in the paid work force. West Germany, on the other hand, took its losses in the industrial sector, and the burden fell especially hard on older workers. The rather stable figures in Great Britain resulted from an even development in the three sectors. In Austria stable industrial employment and growth in the service sector did not compensate for losses in the agricultural sector. In the following chapters I sketch the historical events that led to the different developments and distributional outcomes in the four nations.

CHAPTER FOUR

Austria: Collective Mistakes Jointly Corrected

At the beginning of the 1970s, Austria was still in the midst of the process of restructuring and modernizing its economy, a process that the Federal Republic had gone through in the 1950s and early 1960s. The agricultural sector employed more of the work force and accounted for a higher proportion of GNP than in the other three countries; per capita income was also lower (see Table 4.1).

The real "Austrian economic miracle" began in the mid–1960s and lasted until 1974 (Butschek, 1981:9–18). It was initiated by a restrictive wage policy and the government's promotion of industrial investment in order to improve Austria's international competitive position. It continued when Austria chose not to participate in the revaluation of the German mark between 1969 and 1973, which in effect devalued the schilling by more than 12 percent with respect to the Federal Republic, its most important trading partner, with a 31 percent share of exports and a 45 percent share of imports in 1980 (Abele et al., 1982:468).

Austrian economic policy makers had no desire to interrupt this long boom, which had given the nation a chance to join the more advanced industrial nations. Thus Austria failed to take decisive measures to control the boom even as real wages and prices began to increase in the early 1970s, when the labor supply was fully employed. At that point the unions felt entitled to compensation for the wage restraint they had exercised during the 1960s, and it was expected that prices would level off as the boom wore itself out. Unlike the Federal Republic, Austria was not trying to put on the brakes when the crisis hit. Instead, it was attempting to extend its boom and to treat the problems of overheating with Band-Aids, for instance by introducing a short-term investment

Table 4.1 Agricultural sector's percentage of total
employment and gross per capita domestic product,
1970–1980

	Austria	FRG	GB	Sweden
Agricultural sector's percentage of total employment				
1970	18.8	8.6	3.2	8.1
1975	12.5	7.0	2.7	6.4
1980	10.5	5.6	2.6	5.6
Gross per capita domestic product (U.S. $; exchange rates and prices of 1980)				
1970	7,176	10,276	7,948	12,718
1975	8,573	11,165	8,747	14,187
1980	10,184	13,216	9,470	14,938

Sources: OECD *Labour Force Statistics,* 1964–1984; OECD *National Accounts,* 1960–1984.

tax. A number of factors peculiar to Austria also made its economy and labor market less susceptible to crisis, at least initially.

Since the oil shock was initially misunderstood as a problem of scarcity, the fear of other raw materials cartels led to worldwide purchases of raw materials and increases in buffer stocks and work-in-progress inventories. The Austrian (and Swedish) raw materials industry thus profited from the inventory boom in 1974, while the West German investment and consumer-goods industries already suffered from the worldwide decline in demand. Moreover, the firms in the Austrian raw materials industry, which had been nationalized after 1945 (less for ideological reasons than to save them from the Soviet occupation army's confiscation of German property), were always employers of a special kind. Their consolidation into one single holding company increased the visibility of governmental responsibility for the decisions of the firms. In the second half of 1974, when demand receded precipitously after the end of the raw materials boom, political considerations thus precluded widespread layoffs. The high proportion of nationalized firms made a marked contribution toward stabilizing industrial employment in the first years of the crisis (Nowotny, 1979).

During the economic recovery between 1976 and 1977, the nationalized firms, with the labor they had hoarded, also had every interest in fully exploiting market opportunities, whereas comparable West German firms were understandably reluctant to hire new workers after painful and costly layoffs. The number of workers in Austrian industry thus rose in 1974, declined slightly in 1975–76, and climbed again in

1977. In West Germany, the number fell sharply in 1974–75 and continued to decline until 1977.

Another development peculiar to Austria took place in the service sector (Butschek, 1981:46–59). In this sector there was a severe shortage of personnel during the boom because tourism, the retail trade, and the lower ranks of the public sector had been unable to compete with the rising wages in industry. Many jobs in the private service sector went unfilled, as did public sector positions in municipalities, police departments, and the post office. As the crisis began, the service sector was therefore able to soak up workers and fill many long-empty jobs without the need for approval of new positions. In the Federal Republic, on the other hand, where a scarcity of labor had existed not merely since the early 1970s but since the early 1960s, the unoccupied jobs in the private service sector had disappeared. Incomes in public service had also been adjusted to the conditions of scarcity by "structural improvements," so that there was no manifest shortage of workers either in the service sector generally or in public service. In Austria, the service sector contributed substantially to the overall positive employment picture (see Figure 3.10 above).

Finally, changes in the laws governing working hours and retirement age that had been passed long before the crisis began also contributed to the overall positive employment picture. The gradual shortening of the legal workweek from 45 to 40 hours between 1970 and 1975 had a demonstrably favorable impact on employment. Two hours a week were dropped in 1970, one in 1973, and the remaining two in 1975. Studies estimate that this measure increased total employment by about 1.5 percent (WIFO, 1982:53). The number of foreign workers was also reduced by 19.9 percent between 1973 and 1978, which amounted to 2 percent of the work force (*Internationale Chronik* 4, April 1981:4). Still, the working-age population grew more in Austria than in the other countries between 1973 and 1979: by 2.57 percent, as opposed to 1.77 percent in Great Britain, 1.6 percent in the Federal Republic, and a mere 0.86 percent in Sweden (see Table 3.3 above).

THE SHARED MISPERCEPTION

The crisis thus hit Austria later than other countries. In summer 1974 the WIFO Institute for Economic Research was still predicting a "national boom all on our own" and a real economic growth rate of 4 percent for 1975, which could, however, be restricted by labor shortages (WIFO Monatsberichte 6/1974:269, 271). Based on this consensus evaluation of the situation, which was shared by the government, the National Bank, and the social partners, wage settlements in the fall of 1974 amounted to an average increase in nominal weekly wages of 13.4 percent for 1975 (as opposed to 8.4 percent in the Federal Republic) despite the two-hour reduction in the workweek. Hence, when the recession hit Austria in the winter of 1974–75, its incomes policy was pointing in the wrong direction. This put it at a distinct competitive disadvantage with respect to its most important trading partner, West Germany, and it impaired business profits. Nevertheless, domestic demand benefited from the high wage increases of 1975 (Marin, Maurer, and Wagner, 1984).

Expansionary Fiscal and Monetary Policy

In comparison to that of the Federal Republic of Germany, the Austrian economic success during the 1970s is generally ascribed to an expansionary fiscal policy that was accommodated by a permissive monetary policy. Nevertheless, it is not entirely correct to attribute its successs in maintaining nearly full employment entirely to Keynesian deficit spending in 1975 and 1976 (Seidel, 1979; Lehner, 1982). The Austrian government's 1975 spending plans were based on the consensus economic forecast of the summer of 1974. When circumstances invalidated those forecasts, the Austrian government did not try to reduce the unanticipated deficit produced by the recession, as did the Federal Republic with its 1975 deficit reduction legislation. On the contrary, in the words of one of the participants, Austria "plunged joyously into deficit" in order to demonstrate the capabilities of an expansionary fiscal policy. Spending programs were carried out as planned or in a few cases were actually increased. Moreover, Austrians put aside their commitment to balancing the budget over the economic cycle and for the first time authorized an operating deficit, which was financed primarily through foreign credit to avoid crowding out private productive investment (Hankel, 1979). These measures were clearly intended to encourage private investment and probably did.

However, the differences between Austria's budget policies and West Germany's should not be overestimated. In comparisons of budget policies, the focus of attention is usually on the central government, and from this perspective Austria did indeed adopt a more expansionary policy than did West Germany. The Austrian federal budget deficit was 4.5 percent of the gross national product in 1975 and climbed to 4.7 percent in 1976. The German deficit was only 3.3 percent in 1975 and fell to 2.5 percent in 1976. It makes more economic sense, however, to

59

focus on the total public sector deficit. When we do so, it turns out that Austria's budget deficit was not in fact larger than the Federal Republic's. In West Germany the states and the municipalities contributed substantial deficits to the total, whereas in Austria subnational jurisdictions contributed a surplus. Thus the Federal Republic's total deficit in 1975 was 6.4 percent of the GNP, while Austria's was only 4.3 percent. In 1976 the two nations' total public sector deficits were approximately equal as a percentage of GNP (see Table 10.3 below).

Nevertheless, it does seem that Austria's budget deficit probably provided proportionally greater fiscal stimulus than West Germany's, since Austria had had public sector surpluses in 1973 and 1974, whereas West Germany had already been in deficit. Since the shift in fiscal thrust was greater in Austria, presumably so too was the effect. In any case, this is the finding of a comparative study conducted by the German Institute for Economic Research, which ascribes an especially strong expansionary effect to the Austrian budget deficit (Teschner and Vesper, 1983).

A discrepancy between attribution and reality exists with respect to Austrian monetary policy as well. In the mid–1970s, according to the memory of everyone I interviewed, monetary policy was guided exclusively by the principle of constant nominal interest rates, and no serious effort was made to control the money supply. The Austrian National Bank, unlike the German Federal Bank, was never the "ruler of everything" but always "financed whatever the social partners decided." Hence it is claimed that in Austria fiscal stimulus was automatically accommodated by an equally expansionary monetary policy.

A closer look, however, shows that until mid–1974 the money supply was as tight as in the Federal Republic and that between 1973 and 1974,

Table 4.2 Long-term nominal interest rates (government loans of at least five years) and long-term real interest rates (deflated with the GDP deflator), 1972–1980

	1972	1973	1974	1975	1976	1977	1978	1979	1980
Long-term nominal interest rates									
Austria	7.4	8.2	9.7	9.6	8.8	8.7	8.2	8.0	9.3
FRG	7.9	9.3	10.4	8.5	7.8	6.2	5.7	7.4	8.5
GB	9.2	10.9	15.2	14.6	14.2	12.2	12.0	11.3	11.9
Sweden	7.3	7.4	7.8	8.8	9.3	9.7	10.1	10.5	11.7
Long-term real interest rates									
Austria	−0.2	0.2	0.2	3.0	3.0	3.3	2.8	3.7	4.0
FRG	2.4	2.8	3.7	2.4	4.0	2.3	1.4	3.3	3.5
GB	0.9	3.5	0.2	−9.9	−0.6	−1.5	0.7	−2.7	−6.6
Sweden	0.3	0.3	−1.5	−5.0	−2.3	−0.7	0.5	2.3	0.0

Source: OECD Historical Statistics, 1960–1983.

because of higher rates of inflation, nominal interest rates increased faster in Austria than in the Federal Republic. Although real interest rates were substantially below those of the Federal Republic in 1973 and 1974 because of higher inflation rates, they were allegedly ignored in formulating Austrian monetary policy. By 1975 real interest rates were actually higher in Austria than in West Germany (see Table 4.2). If monetary accommodation is part of the explanation for Austria's superior economic performance compared to the Federal Republic's, then its contribution must have been produced by the earlier increase in the money supply in the summer of 1974 and lower real interest rates throughout 1974.

HARD CURRENCY AND WAGE RESTRAINT

According to conventional explanations of Austria's success, its comparatively good showing in controlling inflation rates was due primarily to its traditional hard currency policy (Seidel and Szopo, 1983). But this too developed very gradually into the dogma that it now seems in hindsight. After 1969 Austria effectively devalued the schilling with respect to the West German mark. Thereafter, the exchange value of the schilling was set with reference to a "currency basket" that included all major Western European currencies. Only after significant devaluations of the Italian lira, the British pound, and the French franc, and the appreciation of the Swiss franc, none of which Austria wanted to reflect in its exchange rate, did the Austrians tie the schilling to the mark (and to the Dutch guilder, to assuage Soviet worries about a rapprochement with the Federal Republic in violation of its commitment to neutrality). Even then the schilling fluctuated to a certain extent (Table 4.3).

Tying the schilling to the German mark did not, of course, mean that the two hard currency nations experienced the same economic conditions. The schilling followed the revaluation of the mark with respect to the currencies of other nations. But because the German market is much more important for Austria than vice versa, more than a third of Austria's exports and almost half of its imports were traded at constant rates of exchange, whereas the revaluation of the mark significantly affected German exports. This difference is clearly reflected in the trade-weighted exchange rates of the two countries. At the same time, the primary goal of Austria's hard currency policy—forcing its economy to adjust to the greater price stability of the Federal Republic—was unimpaired.

In a press statement in 1973, the National Bank first expressed the

Table 4.3 Comparative rate of exchange and effective rate of exchange of the schilling and German mark (weighted according to trade streams), 1970–1981

	1970	1971	1972	1973	1974	1975	1976	1977	1978	1979	1980	1981
Change in the schilling exchange rate relative to the mark (%)	−7.5	−1.2	−1.0	−1.1	+1.5	+2.0	−0.6	+0.1	−1.6	−0.9	+2.4	+1.0
Effective rate of exchange (first quarter of 1970 = 100)												
Schilling	99	100	100	104	108	111	114	119	120	121	125	125
Mark	101	104	106	116	123	123	131	141	149	155	157	152

Sources: Abele et al., 1982; OECD Economic Outlook 38.

notion that where there is a current account deficit, a hard currency policy can contribute to domestic price stability and hence also to improved international competitiveness. Since then the notion has been elevated to part of the fundamental dogma of the "Austrian model." It is also an essential condition for the third basic element of the "Austro-Keynesian strategy": a conservative incomes policy, which Austria has adhered to since 1976 (Blaas and Guger, 1985; Tichy, 1984; Seidel, 1982). It is claimed that pressure from stable import prices and threatened losses in export markets were needed to justify to union members the low wage increases that union leaders considered economically necessary. Interview subjects in the National Bank frankly characterized the hard currency policy as a whip for employers, to keep them tough in wage negotiations, but it was the unions that most strongly defended the hard money policy, as for instance when Chancellor Bruno Kreisky considered devaluing the schilling during the minirecession of 1978. Cynics even claim that union support of its hard money policy is the National Bank's strategic masterpiece, permitting it to practice an imported monetarism free of all political controversy by merely defending the sacrosanct rate of exchange.

Initially, however, tying the schilling to the mark led to predictable difficulties. The wage settlement of 1975 and the Austrian inflation rate, which was higher than the German, reduced Austrian exports and increased imports. Austrians thus paid for their expansionary policy with a sudden increase in the current account deficit from 5.6 billion schillings in 1975 to 26 billion in 1976 and 49 billion in 1977 (Abele et al., 1982:467). In the industrial sector, cost increases due to the shorter work week and higher wages could not be completely passed through into prices because of the hard currency policy. Therefore, profits and productive investment suffered. From the point of view of the unions and the Social Democrats, these were threatening developments that demanded immediate correction.

Austrians, however, were unwilling to rely on a tight fiscal and monetary policy to achieve this correction, because that would have entailed reduced employment. Nominal interest rates were gradually reduced between 1975 and 1978, although real interest rates remained at the high 1975 level because of reduced inflation (see Table 4.2). And as has been noted, Austria did not immediately try to control its deficit, as the Federal Republic did. In 1976 it even intentionally *increased* its deficit. When it seemed possible and necessary to reduce the deficit in 1977–78, Austria did so by increasing revenues rather than by cutting expenditures, for instance by a 30 percent increase in the value-added tax on "luxury goods" (falling mostly, and not coincidentally, on imports). But by mutual agreement of all parties, the incomes policy had to bear the primary burden of making the needed corrections.

Just as collective memory insists that the monetary policy sought constant nominal interest rates while statistics show otherwise, there is also a discrepancy between memory and statistics with respect to wage policy. According to a rule ascribed to the chairman of the Austrian Federation of Unions (ÖGB), real wages should have increased about 3 percent a year from the late 1960s on, without regard to the economic cycle. In fact, however, between 1970 and 1975 the average increase in real wages was between 8.5 percent and 4.5 percent per year, well above the "Benya formula" of 3 percent. Nonetheless, no one in Austria thought that wages were out of control, although after the fact it was agreed that the 1975 increase had been a dangerous error. Then, after 1976, the increase in real wages dropped so sharply that it was well below the ÖGB formula each subsequent year. Correspondingly, the increase in unit labor costs in industry (15 percent in 1975) was only 0.5 percent in 1976, well below the inflation rate. Without an increase in unemployment, wage settlements had become a factor in controlling inflation instead of one driving it. Accordingly, Austrians ascribe the decline in the inflation rate from 8.4 percent in 1975 to 3.6 percent in 1978 to the combination of hard currency policy and restrictive wage policy (Table 4.4).

ECONOMIC PROMOTION UNDER DIFFICULT CONDITIONS

After the immediate results of the oil price shock were mastered without noticeable increases in unemployment and without increased inflation, Austrian fiscal and monetary policy makers undertook a hesitant, gradual readjustment to the new world-market conditions. They reduced domestic consumption to lessen Austria's high current account deficit, and firms were encouraged to produce for export markets. Consumer credit was tightened and made more expensive, depreciation allowances were eliminated, and taxes and social security contributions were increased. At the same time budget deficits were reduced to a level that was acceptable in the long term (to about 2.5 percent of the GNP, according to the "Seidel formula," named for the minister of finance).

The desired results were promptly achieved. The budget deficit was reduced and the balance-of-payments deficit fell from 49 billion schillings in 1977 to 20 billion in 1978. But undesired side effects were just as quick to arrive. The growth rate fell from 4.4 percent in 1977 to 0.5 percent in 1978; investment fell by 4.0 percent in real terms between 1977 and 1978; and unemployment rose to 2.1 percent (Abele et al.,

Table 4.4 Earnings, real wages, and unit labor costs in the manufacturing industry, with consumer prices: Austria, 1970–1980 (changes from the previous year in %)

	1970	1971	1972	1973	1974	1975	1976	1977	1978	1979	1980
Wages	9.4	13.6	11.7	12.7	15.9	13.4	9.9	8.4	5.8	5.5	6.1
Real wages	4.7	8.5	5.1	4.8	5.8	4.5	2.4	2.7	2.2	1.7	0.2
Unit labor costs	4.4	13.1	5.6	10.8	9.7	15.1	0.5	5.6	1.2	1.8	5.9
Prices	4.4	4.7	6.3	7.6	9.5	8.4	7.3	5.5	3.6	3.7	6.4

Sources: OECD Historical Statistics, 1960–1983; IFO, 1982.

1982:464, 467, 470). In short, the Austrians had gone counter to the rhythm of the international economic cycle to create a homemade recession. This ended political tolerance for consolidation policies, although the unemployment rate was still very low. A reflationary correction was considered necessary, and even more so after the second oil price crisis began in the fall of 1978.

Monetary policy rather than fiscal policy was supposed to carry the main burden of the expansion. In early 1979 monetary policy makers lifted restrictions on credit and lowered the discount rate to stimulate consumption and investment by providing more and cheaper money. But this program was defeated by international constraints, which for the first time set real limits on national action. As soon as the interest rates fell below those in West Germany, liquid capital drained out of Austria. The National Bank lost one-third of its reserves within a few weeks and was barely able to maintain parity with the German mark.

Austrians were unprepared for this development. At various times Austrian interest rates had been lower than the German rates without creating difficulties. But by 1979 Austrian banks had increased their operations abroad to an even greater extent than the banks of other OECD nations (Table 4.5). The banks and other large enterprises had also built up their capacity for managing foreign investments so that they could rapidly transfer very large sums to locations all over the world. Their investment policy had thus become much more sensitive to fluctuations in domestic interest rates, so that the unilateral attempt to make money cheaper in Austria resulted in capital flows that threatened the international stability of the schilling exchange rate. Controls on capital flows, which nominally still existed, proved ineffective, and since devaluation had also become a political impossibility, the National Bank lost its autonomy with respect to interest rates (Koren, 1982). As usual, the Austrians responded to this turn of events by embracing a new rule of

Table 4.5 Business with nonresidents as share of assets and liabilities of commercial banks, 1970 and 1981 (%)

	Assets		Liabilities	
	1970	1981	1970	1981
Austria	10.7	24.5	9.8	27.8
FRG	8.8	10.2	5.6	8.1
GB	46.1	67.9	50.2	69.9
Sweden	7.0	9.7	5.4	18.2

Source: Pecchioli, 1983.

thumb. From now on the money market interest rate in Vienna must always be about one-fourth of one percent above that offered in Frankfurt.

Austrian policy makers have not tried to use expansion of the money supply as an economic policy instrument since 1980. Instead, they have adhered to their rule, even when West German or international interest rates were higher than desirable for Austria, and this was the case from the end of the 1970s on (Socher, 1982). Consequently, to maintain full employment—and even the Austrian opposition never suggested abandoning that goal—Austria had to rely entirely on fiscal policy. Moreover, it had to offset the influence of an excessively tight monetary policy on domestic demand and the effects of overly high interest rates on business investment, and hence on the supply side of the economy.

As a matter of fact, Austria was better prepared to deal with the second problem than most other nations. Austro-Keynesianism had always been oriented more toward the supply side than had British or German economic policy. After 1975, Austrian policy makers expanded and improved their instruments for indirect (tax-based) and direct economic and investment promotion (Lehner, 1979; Leibfritz and Meurer, 1985; Kitzmantel, 1986), which were already unusually well developed and well tended. In particular, they structured depreciation allowances so that profitable firms were practically compelled to increase their capital stock. When recession made taxable profits rare, Austria shifted to measures independent of profit levels to promote investment (Reitzner, 1983). Quantitatively the most important of these were programs to subsidize interest rates. According to an internal survey by the National Bank, about 40 percent of the volume of domestic credit was subsidized as early as 1977.

Thus it was predictable that Austria would react to the minirecession of 1978 primarily with another program to subsidize interest rates. This program was huge, encompassing 16 billion schillings. As a result, Austrian investment was not only protected from the increase in capital costs but businesses, which represented a greater share of national income than in most other nations, were able to maintain and even increase this share during the crisis period (Paloheimo, 1984:27). Consequently Austria had higher investment rates well into the 1980s than did the other three nations; they were also higher than in any other OECD nation except Japan (Table 4.6).

Austrian investment promotion has been criticized for a lack of clear priorities. It is composed of more than four hundred individual programs, and because their criteria are insufficiently rigorous, it is said that they contribute more to maintaining overcapacity in stagnating indus-

Table 4.6 Investment rates (gross capital investment as % of GDP), 1973–1982

	1973	1974	1975	1976	1977	1978	1979	1980	1981	1982
Austria	28.5	28.4	26.7	26.0	26.7	25.6	25.1	25.5	25.2	23.0
FRG	23.9	21.6	20.4	20.1	20.2	20.7	21.8	22.7	21.8	20.5
GB	20.0	20.9	19.9	29.4	18.6	18.6	18.8	18.1	16.4	16.4
Sweden	21.9	21.5	20.9	21.2	21.1	19.4	19.8	20.2	19.2	18.8

Source: OECD *Economic Outlook* 39.

tries and sectors than to modernizing the economy (Tichy, 1980). This criticism may be accurate, but still the cost of capital is reduced even when subsidies are unselective. Moreover, if one doggedly pursues an investment policy aimed at maintaining jobs despite the worldwide growth recession, one can hardly apply selective allocational criteria (E. Schmidt, 1985). The risk the Austrians were prepared to run is most clearly illustrated by the export financing practices developed by one of the national monetary institutions, the Control Bank. At the end of the 1970s that bank, with government guarantees, began to buy cheap hard-currency credits in Switzerland for use in financing Austrian exports, especially those to developing and Eastern bloc nations. The Austrian government was thus directly liable to foreign creditors, a serious problem if the international debt crisis intensified.

Regardless of all reservations and warnings, the foreign observer must conclude that the calculations underlying the Austrians' economic choice were for the most part correct, not only up to 1979 but to the present. The combination of hard currency and a moderately restrictive voluntary incomes policy has assured Austria of a preeminent place in the ranks of nations with price stability. Austria's investment promotion program may be unselective, but it is comprehensive and is obviously responsible not only for the highest investment rates of the four countries but also for the most positive development of industrial employment and for one of the lowest unemployment rates in general.

Austria has paid a price for these victories, a price the Austrians I interviewed mentioned over and over, with different emphases. The modernization of the economy has been retarded rather than accelerated by subsidies that maintain existing jobs. The nationalized firms in particular have suffered from government interventions sheltering them from market pressures that would otherwise force them to adapt and innovate (Matzner, 1986; Bauer, 1986). The structural balance-of-trade deficit has not gone away, although the current account is temporarily in surplus. The consolidating of public finances has yet to be undertaken. And the distribution of income and wealth has shifted to the disadvan-

Table 4.7 Indicators of economic development in Austria, 1980–1984 (changes from previous year in %)

	1980	1981	1982	1983	1984
GDP growth	3.0	0.1	1.2	2.1	2.0
Balance of trade as % of GDP	−2.7	−2.0	−1.1	0.6	0.8
Consumer prices	6.4	6.8	5.4	3.3	5.6
Industrial wages	6.3	7.2	3.9	4.9	3.9
Real wages	−0.1	0.4	−1.5	1.6	−1.7
Unemployment (%)	1.9	2.5	3.5	4.1	3.8

Sources: OECD *Economic Surveys: Austria,* 1985; OECD *Economic Outlook* 38.

tage of workers, whose position with respect to real wages since 1979 has worsened more dramatically than in any other comparable country (SVR, 1984–85:25, Table 2). Business profits meanwhile have been given favorable tax treatment, and investments have been highly subsidized.

Remarkably, however, Austrians do not seem to be upset about this last point. The government, the Socialist party, and the unions have succeeded in convincing the public and themselves that Austria has managed to achieve the best possible outcome for workers in a worldwide situation that was extremely difficult for workers (SWS, 1986), a claim that has some objective truth (Table 4.7). One spokesman in my interviews offered a more cynical interpretation. Pointing out the close identification of the "socialist camp" with the interests and problems of the nationalized firms, he assured me that distributive issues were of no political concern for economic policy makers, since "the Socialist party of Austria goes along with anything that will help the nationalized industries."

Nevertheless we must remember that between 1973 and 1979 Austria was the most successful among the social democratic European nations at managing a capitalist economy. At least during that period, it shielded Austrian workers from the consequences of the global crisis, which is more than the German Social Democrats were able to do. Developments in the following years have not clearly discredited the "Austrian model" even in the judgment of observers with extremely diverse points of view (Rothschild, 1985; OECD *Economic Surveys: Austria,* 1985; Kahn et al., 1983; 1984). It can well serve as a standard against which we can weigh and evaluate the economic policy efforts of the other three countries. I shall address the institutional reasons for Austria's success after a discussion of developments in the three other nations.

CHAPTER FIVE

Great Britain: The Drama of Incomes Policy

In the introductory section I pointed out that, contrary to the general assessment of the British economy, the macroeconomic indicators for the year before the first oil price crisis were relatively positive. Nevertheless the growth of Britain's economy lagged behind that of the other three nations during most of the postwar era. Moreover, in the decade immediately preceding the oil shock, its inflation rates were higher than in the three other countries, and, while the postwar years were unusually prosperous for Great Britain by historical standards, per capita incomes fell behind the average of Western industrialized nations. Only in terms of unemployment did Great Britain do as well as other nations (Table 5.1).

There was general agreement about the reasons for Britain's slower growth as early as the 1960s, and the Labour government under Harold Wilson tried nearly the same solutions between 1964 and 1969 as the Conservatives did under Edward Heath between 1970 and 1974. Unless we wish to delve into alleged tensions between the aristocratic values of English culture and the demands of industrialism (Wiener, 1981), Britain's economic problems resulted from a particular configuration of governmental fiscal policy and union wage policy.

In the postwar era Great Britain decided earlier and more consistently than other nations to pursue full employment through Keynesian demand control, and the constitutional tradition according to which all tax laws must be passed anew by Parliament every year provided Britain with a fiscal instrument of unique flexibility. The anticipation with which both taxpayers and the financial press await the annual budget address of the chancellor of the exchequer demonstrates how much room there is for short-term variations in public revenue. None of the other nations enjoys a comparable degree of fiscal flexibility, certainly not West Ger-

Table 5.1 Average GDP growth, average increase in consumer prices, and average unemployment rate, 1963–1973 (%); GDP per capita 1963 and 1973 (U.S. dollars, at 1975 prices and exchange rates)

	Austria	FRG	GB	Sweden
GDP growth	5.1	4.4	3.3	4.0
Inflation	4.2	3.5	5.3	4.9
Unemployment	2.5	1.0	2.0	2.0
GDP per capita (in constant U.S. $)				
1963	3,065	4,720	3,187	6,140
1973	4,838	6,872	4,200	8,232

Sources: OECD *Economic Outlook* 28; OECD *National Accounts*, 1951–1980.

many, whose fiscal constitution allows a change in tax rates only after exhaustive negotiations between the federal government and the states.

On the other hand the British pound sterling was an important reserve currency all during the postwar era, and London was one of the most important financial capitals of the world. From the beginning the British balance of payments was thus susceptible to speculative financial transactions, while in the Federal Republic (and even more so Sweden and Austria) the balance of payments in the 1950s and 1960s was determined almost exclusively by real transactions.

Both factors, the ease of fiscal control and the volatility of the balance of payments, produced the "stop-and-go" pattern that characterized British economic policy in the postwar decades (Surrey, 1982). Whenever economic growth slowed and unemployment figures began to rise, the government responded with fiscal stimulus aimed at expanding demand—always supported by the monetary policy of the Bank of England, which is dependent on the government. But with the upswing, wages and prices would rise and imports increase, causing balance-of-payments problems and threatening a capital drain. To keep the pound steady and to protect the always scarce British currency reserves, fiscal policy makers would then switch to restraint, often before that was justified in domestic economic terms. The upswing would come to a premature end, especially for businesses that were able to realize only part of the profits from additional investments. Thus Great Britain always had the lowest investment rate of the four nations, and hence the lowest rate of increase in labor productivity (Table 5.2).

The negative consequences of the stop-and-go policy were matters of public discussion in Britain from the early 1960s on. But since no one was willing to question the international position of the pound or Lon-

Table 5.2 Investment rates and increases in productivity

	Austria	FRG	GB	Sweden
Gross capital investment as % of GDP				
1965	27.3	26.1	18.5	24.7
1969	25.1	23.3	18.9	23.2
1973	28.5	23.9	20.1	21.9
Increase in hourly productivity in industry (%)				
1954–63	54	77	28	54
1964–73	80	61	45	86

Sources: OECD *Economic Outlook* 38; Guger, 1983; WIFO Economic Data Bank; author's own calculations.

don as a financial capital, the British had to accept the vulnerability of their economy to the balance of payments. A steadier economic policy could be achieved only by avoiding rapid wage and price increases, and thus a worsening of the balance of trade, during the upswing. Since the late 1940s both socialist and conservative governments had employed statutory wage and price controls for this purpose, with only short-term success and over the increasing opposition of the unions (Bornstein and Gourevitch, 1984; Barnes and Reid, 1980).

In the 1960s, political discussions began to center on increased productivity as an independent means of improving the growth rate and the international competitive position of the British economy (Middlemas, 1979). The Conservative government had established the National Economic Development Council and its branch committees, "Little Neddys," in which employers, unions, and government representatives were supposed to develop a shared understanding of the requirements and opportunities of industrial policy (Middlemas, 1983; Coombes, 1982). After 1964, the new Labour government under Harold Wilson also relied most heavily on strategies involving industrial policy to accelerate economic growth by promoting investment and modern technologies. Its policy of "indicative" economic planning and modernization was to be supported by an agreement with the Trades Union Congress (TUC) about "voluntary" wage restraint and complementary price controls.

But when a balance-of-trade deficit nevertheless arose, the policy of investment promotion immediately gave way to fiscal restraint, which was considered necessary to protect the pound. The wage agreements, which had been based on considerably higher expected growth rates, were thus well above the level that the economy as a whole could support. Consequently the government turned to compulsory wage controls, contrary to its original intent. In summer 1966 it even instituted a wage freeze. The union leadership provided halfhearted support for the freeze, but union membership rebelled. As a result, wildcat strikes and "wage drift" increased to such an extent that in 1968 the government gave up its attempt at direct wage control. Meanwhile, it had also failed to protect the pound and had gone through a massive devaluation.

The government now saw the main cause of all these negative developments in the greater-than-average frequency of strikes and the generally confrontational nature of labor relations in Britain, blaming them for both poor productivity and inflationary wage increases. The Donovan Report (1968), prepared by a royal commission established in 1965, laid the intellectual groundwork for this political conclusion. The report identified as problems the fragmented organization of the more than 600 individual unions, of which only 183 (including, however, most of the larger ones) belonged to the TUC in 1960; the extreme decentralization of wage negotiations; and the complete lack of any legal regulation and limitation of labor-management conflicts. The shop stewards in the plants were responsible for negotiations and strikes without being bound by central collective bargaining agreements (Degen, 1976). Their position favored the exploitation of all local abilities to pay higher wages, and competition among the many small unions then favored whipsawing, whereby one union would use another union's new wage agreement to bolster its own case for a raise. Thus local wage increases quickly spread throughout the economy (Bain, 1983; Brown, 1981). These structural problems were intensified by the fact that British governments had not regulated labor relations since the turn of the century but had created a space where management and labor could stage and resolve conflicts outside the jurisdiction of the court system. Thus there were no laws to structure and limit labor-management conflict, and of course there was no statutory "duty of peace" as in West Germany during negotiations.

Although it considered the idea desirable in theory, the Labour government did not think that it could reorganize the unions on an industry-wide rather than a craft basis or centralize wage negotiations. Therefore, in its white paper "In Place of Strife" (1969), it concentrated on the attempt to reform labor law. The draft, supported by leftist Barbara Castle, called for the use of mediation and arbitration to resolve conflicts about jurisdiction and responsibility among the individual unions. It also advocated giving the government the right to issue temporary injunctions against strikes and lockouts, and to compel a vote of the membership prior to a strike. The TUC, although impressed by the analysis of the Donovan Report, saw the government draft as so intolerable an incursion on union autonomy that it decided to mobilize union influence within the Labour party to force the government to give up its

73

plans. The election victory of the Conservatives in spring 1970 was ascribed primarily to this conflict between the unions and the Labour government.

At first, the newly elected Heath government did not try to regulate wages either on a voluntary basis or through the legal system. Instead, it focused on reforming organization and labor-management relations, which had brought the Wilson government down. Thus, in its intentions, the Industrial Relations Act of 1971 was not particularly hostile to the unions. Seeing that the weakness of the union headquarters made it much more difficult to achieve an economically responsible wage policy, the government attempted to strengthen the authority of union leaders at the expense of the shop stewards (Streek, 1978; Crouch, 1982:70–84). In the TUC at least, there was substantial interest in such an undertaking. However, the law combined this goal with new (for Britain) conditions on the internal operations of the union and on members' free entry into and exit from the union, which were unequivocally aimed at weakening the unions' organizational strength. The closed shop was to be abolished. Only unions that met these conditions could register, and only registered unions and their authorized representatives (and not the shop stewards acting on their own) should be free of civil liability for breaches of contract during labor conflicts. In other words, all strikes that were not officially led by a recognized union would now be subject to the general law of contracts and torts, as they had been before the turn of the century.

After some hesitation, the TUC decided to oppose the new law. Unions that were already registered because they met the legal conditions of the act were moved to rescind their registration under threats of exclusion from the TUC; otherwise, other TUC unions could have competed for members. After several union leaders were arrested under the new Industrial Relations Act for disregarding regulations, the opposition became universal. The law remained without practical effect but nonetheless destroyed the possibility for pragmatic cooperation between the unions and the conservative reformism of the Heath government. The consequences became apparent in 1973.

The government, which had initially wanted to forego the instruments of an incomes policy, used a tight fiscal and monetary policy to reduce the inflationary burden it had inherited from Wilson. But while inflation rates fell only slightly (from 9.4 percent in 1971 to 7.1 percent in 1972), the unemployment rate rose to the record high of 4.2 percent in 1972. Expansion became politically mandatory, and in order to avoid inflationary overheating, the government had to try to hold down wage increases once again. In view of the smoldering political conflict, Heath's proposals for a contractual incomes policy were unacceptable to the TUC. Still, preliminary discussions came close enough to substantive agreement that the government could expect most unions to give tacit support to a policy of statutory wage controls and hoped for the tacit approval of most unions in the case of government wage controls. In the first phase, in which all wages, prices, rents, and dividend payments were to be frozen from November 1972 to March 1973, unions in fact gave their support without exception. That was largely true in the second phase as well, which allowed wage increases especially for the lower-income groups.

In terms of economic policy, the expansion was a brilliant success. The growth rate rose in 1973 to a record 7.6 percent, and the unemployment rate dropped from 4.2 percent to 3 percent. For most unions, therefore, the third phase of Heath's incomes policy, which began in November 1973, with somewhat more flexible wage standards and threshold rules to compensate for inflation, was still acceptable. But the militant miners' union rejected it. The miners went on strike in support of their demand for a wage increase of 25 percent (with average annual inflation then running at 9.2 percent).

Since the TUC had not formally assumed responsibility for the government's incomes policy, the rest of the union movement had to support the miners. Nevertheless, the TUC did signal to the government that settling the strike with a wage agreement above legal norms would not be treated as a precedent by the other unions. The Heath government, however, was no longer interested in (uncertain) compromises. Instead, it sought open conflict. Since the miners' strike coincided with the oil crisis, three-day weeks were introduced to dramatize the national emergency. At the same time, Heath scheduled parliamentary elections for February 1974. The voters were asked to determine "who governs Britain," the elected government or the unions. The result was a narrow plurality for Harold Wilson, who had conducted his campaign with the slogan "Back to Work with Labour" and who now had to deal with the consequences of the miners' strike and the oil crisis.

First Responses to the Crisis

While they were out of power, the Labour party leaders came to believe that conflict with the unions had caused the party's election defeat in 1970 and must in future be avoided at any price. The unions had also rediscovered their sympathy for the Labour party during the controversy about the Heath government's Industrial Relations Act. As the price

75

for their active political support of the Labour party, they proposed an agreement about economic policy. The TUC–Labour Party Liaison Committee was established in 1972 to work on such an agreement. In early 1973, after approval by the highest decision-making bodies of both sides, that committee published a joint position paper that was declared to be a new Social Contract. The obligations of the Labour party were much more precisely drawn in the paper than were those of the unions. The unions, after all, would have already met their part of the bargain, supplying political support; only after an election victory would Labour's obligations begin (Crouch, 1982a).

If Labour returned to power it was to repeal the Industrial Relations Act and to introduce improved mediation mechanisms and better job protection during strikes (the "shop stewards' charter"). Labour was to improve work safety regulations and health service programs, to increase pensions substantially, and to raise family allowances. To hold price increases down, rents in council housing were to be frozen and price controls tightened. The agreement explicitly excluded statutory wage controls. Instead, the unions declared themselves prepared to adjust their wage demands to economic circumstances.

Despite its political weakness, in 1974 the new Wilson government began immediately to meet its quasi-contractual obligations to the unions. An implicit term of this contract was complete satisfaction of all demands of the striking miners. However, in contrast to the TUC's earlier offer to Heath, wage agreements in other unions were now guided by the miners' agreements. Even more problematic was another legacy of the Heath government. The threshold rule, introduced in the public sector and copied in other sectors, provided that any rise in consumer prices of one percentage point or more would trigger the same increase in wages and salaries. The inflationary push of the oil price crisis was thus almost immediately translated into general wage increases, which in turn drove prices up. The TUC's halfhearted admonitions about moderation in negotiated wage increases remained ineffectual. As a consequence, consumer prices rose inexorably, by 16 percent in 1974 and 24.2 percent in 1975.

The government, whose hands were tied with respect to the incomes policy, did not want to respond to the oil crisis by instituting a deflationary policy that would increase unemployment. Thus its initial measures against galloping inflation were purely cosmetic. A newly created ministry highlighted the symbolic significance of price controls and tightened them in practice. Food subsidies were also greatly expanded and raised in order to retard a cost-of-living increase (and to postpone the threshold of wage increases). The effect of such programs on inflation was

76

limited. But since the increase in consumer prices in 1975 was 2.7 percent below the general price increase of 29.6 percent, workers clearly felt the effect on their real incomes, which increased by 4.8 percent between 1974 and 1975. As the unemployment rate also receded further in 1974, the unions had every reason to be pleased with their government, despite the global crisis (Table 5.3).

The combination of overly high wage increases and effective price controls was catastrophic for firm profits, however, which receded greatly after 1973. As a consequence, industrial employment also declined significantly in 1975. At the same time, the balance-of-trade deficit increased in 1974, and it appeared that a new crisis was developing for the pound (Table 5.4). Nonetheless, the Wilson government remained passive in terms of economic policy. In the autumn 1974 elections it had won a very slim parliamentary majority (which soon evaporated again in subsequent by-elections) and had also survived the referendum on whether Great Britain should remain in the European Community. Still, there was no sign of a firm and credible strategy against the "South American" inflation rates, the rising unemployment figures, and the threatening balance-of-payments problems.

INCOMES POLICY WITH THE UNIONS

Almost unnoticed politically, the Treasury under Dennis Healey had returned to its traditional line in 1975 (Haines, 1977; Barnett, 1982). Together with the Bank of England, it had introduced a cautious policy of restraint to stabilize the pound, which was, however, ineffective—in part because of its low profile. At the same time, in the early summer of 1975, Treasury officials were working on a top-secret proposal to Cabinet to reintroduce statutory wage controls. Regardless of how Cabinet handled it, this proposal would have broadcast political signals, but the prime minister's planning staff, a new entity created under the second Wilson government, was alert enough to block the attempt. Still, the existence of the proposal sufficed to make clear to the unions how serious the situation was.

Jack Jones, president of the Transport and General Workers' Union (TGWU), picked up the signal. The TGWU, with approximately two million members, was the largest single union of the TUC. Jones, a former stevedore and a veteran of the Spanish Civil War, had impeccable leftist credentials. He was convinced that the government had fulfilled its obligations under the new social contract to the letter and that the unions must now come to the government's aid with a wage policy to

Table 5.3 Earnings, real incomes, and unit labor costs in manufacturing; consumer prices (changes from previous year in %); unemployment (% of the paid work force): Great Britain, 1970–1980

	1970	1971	1972	1973	1974	1975	1976	1977	1978	1979	1980
Wages	10.0	12.5	13.6	13.0	17.1	30.1	19.8	4.8	18.2	14.8	17.2
Real wages	3.5	2.8	6.0	3.6	1.9	4.8	3.5	-9.7	8.4	1.4	-1.0
Unit labor costs	13.1	10.3	5.0	4.8	24.0	32.6	12.7	11.7	14.9	17.2	21.0
Prices	6.4	9.4	7.1	9.2	16.0	24.2	16.5	15.8	8.3	13.4	18.0
Unemployment	3.0	3.7	4.0	3.0	2.9	4.3	5.7	6.1	6.0	5.1	6.6

Sources: OECD Historical Statistics, 1960–1983; IFO, 1982; OECD Economic Outlook 38.

Table 5.4 Profits in industry, industrial employment, and balance of trade: Great Britain, 1973–1980

	1973	1974	1975	1976	1977	1978	1979	1980
Profit as % of value added	19.7	12.8	8.9	10.1	16.3	16.7	11.5	8.8
Change in industrial employment in %	+1.6	−0.3	−4.2	−2.8	−0.3	−0.2	−0.0	−3.8
Balance of trade (billions of U.S. $)	−2.6	−7.9	−3.5	−1.6	−0.2	+1.9	−1.6	+7.2

Sources: OECD *Historical Statistics,* 1960–1983; ILO *Yearbook of Labour Statistics,* 1981; OECD *Economic Outlook* 39.

combat galloping inflation and avert the threat to the pound. At the same time he rejected any kind of statutory wage control. He also opposed the Treasury's suggested percentage limitation on wage increases because he believed an acceptable incomes policy should produce a decrease in wage differentials. His proposal of a strictly egalitarian wage increase of six pounds a week across the board met with approval in his own union's governing committee (a strong majority of its constituents belonged to lower-income groups) and in the governing committee of the TUC before it was submitted to the government in summer 1975. Even though the Treasury expressed concern about leveling the wage structure, the government accepted the proposal with relief. It amounted to a wage raise of about 10 percent for skilled laborers, which was far below the inflation rate. For the lower-income groups, the raise amounted to more than 20 percent. Women did especially well under this plan; in the first year of this incomes program they came closer to wage parity than ever before or since.

However, to make the proposal binding on unions of skilled workers and white-collar employees, whose interests it did not serve, required a majority vote at the annual TUC congress in September, where more than a hundred individual unions were represented in proportion to their membership numbers. To accomplish this, the government and the TUC launched a joint publicity campaign with the motto "Give a Year to Britain," which was designed to demonstrate how important the proposal was for stabilizing the British economy during a global crisis. Moral pressure was intense enough to deliver a solid majority at the congress. Aided by the media and internal sanctions, it also guaranteed observance of the six-pound upper limit for wage increases during the first year almost without exception. The extreme simplicity of the policy guidelines was a crucial factor in the success of the program.

In 1976 price increases were noticeably less than in the prior year, but they were still at 16 percent, far above the level in comparable countries. Confronting a new crisis for the pound, the Treasury considered it necessary to tighten the incomes policy in 1977. This time, however, it did not want to surrender the initiative to the unions. Therefore, it persuaded the chancellor of the exchequer to take a public stand for a 3 percent wage increase before any kind of preliminary talks. That was the end of mutual trust and cooperation for Jack Jones, who would have considered a fixed sum increase necessary and acceptable for another year. Instead, the following discussions between the government and the TUC resembled collective bargaining negotiations and resulted in a compromise. Wages and salaries were to increase by 5 percent in 1977, with an upper limit of £6 and a lower limit of £4.5 per week. In a formal sense the principle of linear wage increases favored by the Treasury won out, but since there was such a narrow spread between upper and lower limits on increases, the proposal was also close to the fixed-sum approach Jones had advocated. However, the union central committees provided less moral support than in the previous year, and firms and shop stewards began to look for ways around the agreement by promotions, change of function, extraordinary raises, or payments in kind. There was trouble when it became known that the government itself had not applied the six-pound rule to seniority raises. Nevertheless, wage increases in the second year were lower than in the first, and with prices still rising because of the pound crisis, real wages fell by nearly 10 percent in 1977, after having risen by 3.5 percent the year before. The unemployment rate in 1977 also rose to a new record high of 6.1 percent. The results of two years of voluntary incomes programs were thus very negative for the unions (see Table 5.3).

The Pound Crisis and IMF Negotiations

The pound crisis of 1976 played a large role in bringing about this unfavorable result (Barnett, 1982:97–111). Considering the exorbitant inflation rates of 1975, the crisis was late in arriving. Apparently, the exchange rate for the pound was initially stabilized by the currency reserves of the OPEC countries, which were traditionally oriented toward London as a financial capital. But in early 1976, several Labour deputies wondered aloud about a "competitive pound" and some interventions by the Bank of England could be similarly interpreted. Thus the impression arose that the government was working toward a devaluation in order to stimulate the economy, and the Arabs began to withdraw their funds. The result was a self-reinforcing speculation against the pound, which pushed the exchange rate vis-à-vis the U.S. dollar to 1.7:1,

Table 5.5 Exchange rate of British pound and U.S. dollar, 1973–1980

	1973	1974	1975	1976	1977	1978	1979	1980
U.S. \$/Pound	2.32	2.34	2.02	1.70	1.90	2.03	2.22	2.38

Source: IMF *International Financial Statistics*, 1977; 1980; 1985.

far below the 2:1 ratio the government may have been working toward (Table 5.5).

The consequences of such a drastic increase in import prices spelled disaster for the stabilization policy that had begun with the help of the unions. But the international currency market could not be persuaded, despite denials of any intent to devalue and despite repeated interventions by the Bank of England defending the pound. Instead, these interventions drained Great Britain's currency reserves and exhausted its regular line of credit from the International Monetary Fund (IMF), as well as a three-months' credit in the amount of \$5.3 billion that had been extended by an international bank consortium in July 1976. Even though this line of credit was extended by a further three months, it was clear as early as September that Britain would not be able to repay it in December. Thus the government had to secure a longer-term special loan from the IMF, which was available only after an IMF examination of Britain's finances and under conditions specified by the examiners.

The London financial press, extraordinarily influential on what happens in the market, had long felt that such an examination was necessary. It was deeply concerned about the seeming dependence of government policy on the unions; it was also skeptical about any kind of incomes policy (Brittan and Lilley, 1977). Fiscal conservatives to begin with, the influential columnists had turned more and more toward a monetarist worldview since the early 1970s. The Keynesian premises of the Wilson government (advised by Nicholas Kaldor) must have appeared very dubious to them. The Treasury's moderately restrictive course of action, in effect since 1975, was judged unsatisfactory, because the government held fast to its Keynesian rhetoric to pacify the unions and the left wing of the party and could thus desert the Treasury's course at any time. Only a public, credible commitment on the part of government policy could regain the trust of these columnists—and nothing was better suited for that purpose than the explicit conditions of an IMF loan.

In essence, the economic policy makers in the government shared this view after Harold Wilson left office in Summer 1976 and Foreign Minister Jim Callaghan became prime minister. In the earlier Wilson government he had been the chancellor of the exchequer responsible for the devaluation of the pound, and he was determined to wipe out this disgrace. The planning staff he inherited from Wilson, the top officials in the Treasury, and the chancellor of the exchequer, Healey, were convinced of the need for consolidation. A regular discussion group called "The Seminar," which included the governors of the Bank of England and several Oxford economists, confirmed the government circle in its "reluctant conversion to monetarism," as one of the participants put it. The public sector's demands on the GNP had to be contained, the public sector borrowing requirement had to be reduced in order to lower interest rates, business profits had to be raised, and the influence of the unions on government policy had to be lessened in order to revitalize the British economy. In his first speech as prime minister at the Labour Party Congress in 1976, Callaghan thus uttered a clear rejection of Keynesian hopes, which shocked many in his audience: "You cannot spend your way out of a recession and increase employment by cutting taxes and boosting government spending."

The inner circle of Labour economic policy makers thus saw a need for structural consolidation, although according to a Keynesian analysis the British economy showed no symptoms of economic overheating in summer 1976. But since their philosophy would not have gained the support of the Labour party (Coates, 1980; Berrington, 1982), the conditions imposed by the IMF were in fact welcome. To be sure, the IMF examiners' initial demands that net borrowing be reduced by five billion pounds sterling were considered absurd, but after the examiners became more realistic, the Treasury was negotiating only over austerity measures that it too considered necessary. In December the Treasury agreed to a reduction of net borrowing by £2.5 billion (which was covered to a large extent by the sale of British Petroleum stock). What mattered was its symbolic value. With the IMF seal of approval, the British government regained its credibility in the world of international finance. The pound ceased to be an object of speculation, foreign investors returned, and the pound's exchange rate rose again. In any case, the whole uproar was almost anachronistic from the Treasury's point of view. Just one year later, North Sea oil began to flow, and the chronic balance-of-payments deficit and recurring pound crises were a thing of the past, at least for the next decade.

INCOMES POLICY WITHOUT THE UNIONS

The policy of restraint agreed upon with the IMF had its domestic price, however: unemployment rose in 1977, and the end of the food

subsidy programs, together with loosening price controls, kept the inflation rate from declining further. In spite of its "reluctant conversion to
monetarism," the government thus had a strong interest in continuing
an incomes policy that would be supported by the unions. Otherwise, as
Callaghan and Healey tried to browbeat their own party and the unions,
the only recourse was monetary stabilization achieved by means of an
extremely tight monetary and fiscal policy. Since the inflation rate was
still over 15 percent, the government proposed that the unions accept a
10 percent wage increase as the upper limit for 1978. In return, the
government introduced the Youth Opportunity Program to combat unemployment among the young, raised family allowances, and offered
"conditional" tax cuts (conditioned on the unions' willingness to cooperate).

But relations between the government and the TUC leaders had
cooled. Moreover, the TUC leadership had to take into account the
increasing tensions between the wage interests of the various member
unions as well as a spreading unease about government policy, which
seemed completely oriented toward the interests of capital (Barnes and
Reid, 1980:209–20; Crouch, 1982:90–110). In short, the TUC leadership did not refuse the wage guideline proposed by the government, but
it was no longer prepared to take responsibility for pushing it through.
On the contrary. The TUC congress in autumn 1977 passed a resolution
that demanded a return to free collective bargaining for the coming
wage negotiations. The TUC's explicit support for the government was
thus limited to strict observance of the twelve-month rule, which functioned to bar premature termination of wage rates currently in effect.
For the rest, the TUC tacitly assumed that the government would now
get Parliament to authorize statutory wage controls, contrary to the
agreements of 1973.

But this path, although it would have corresponded to earlier patterns,
was no longer open to the Labour minority government tolerated by the
Liberals. Neither the left wing of the Labour party nor the Conservatives
under the new and explicitly monetarist leadership of Margaret
Thatcher would have agreed to a statutory incomes policy. Without the
support of the unions, the government thus could rely only on administrative measures as sanctions against nonobservance of its wage guidelines. Firms that approved higher wage increases ran the risk of losing
public contracts and public subsidies; and price officials would not count
the higher wages as increased costs. The effect was minimal. Nominal
wages in industry rose by 18.2 percent in 1978, much more than the
government guidelines. Thanks to the low wage agreements of the prior
year, which still had some effect, and the rising exchange rate of the
pound, the inflation rate nevertheless fell below 10 percent. In keeping

with this development, real wages climbed steeply by 8.4 percent, after an equally steep fall in the previous year. Because unemployment receded somewhat in 1978 and the number of workers in the paid work force increased markedly, the government found itself on a successful economic course in summer 1978, which seemed to suggest early elections and smooth relations with the unions. But Callaghan was out to break inflationary expectations completely, and thus tried to extend the incomes policy for a fourth year.

THE WINTER OF DISCONTENT: INCOMES POLICY AGAINST THE UNIONS

In summer 1978, the Callaghan government, as one of its members pointed out critically, was "obsessed with the problem of inflation." They considered the current improvement to be unstable and thought it was possible at any moment for galloping inflation to return. On the other hand, the government reasoned that because the unions were now benefiting from the positive effects of falling inflation rates on real income, they should be ready to cooperate out of economic self-interest. Reasons of election strategy played a role as well. The next House of Commons elections had to take place no later than autumn 1979, but in view of the government's weakness in Parliament, people speculated that the elections would be held in autumn 1978. Callaghan, however, thought his chances in early elections were poor, and he believed that a further decline in the inflation rate to about 5 percent in 1979 would bring substantial political advantages. Such a decline was held to be economically feasible. On the other hand he counted on the political loyalty of the union leaders as long as the elections were in the future, whereas union willingness to impose voluntary wage discipline would probably decrease after an election victory. From Callaghan's point of view, the battle against inflation was a now-or-never matter. He decided to present the unions with a tough guideline for a maximum 5 percent wage increase and to postpone the elections to the latest possible moment.

Some members of Cabinet pleaded instead for a soft guideline at about the current inflation rate and for elections in autumn 1978, which they hoped to win with the solid support of the unions, despite unfavorable opinion surveys. Afterward, they argued, one could be more uncompromising in pursuing a policy of stability with a new political mandate. This point of view was not pushed, however, and in July Callaghan and Healey found a large majority of Cabinet in favor of the 5 percent guideline. The prime minister reserved the decision about the election date.

84

Both sides in Cabinet, however, had unrealistic and overly optimistic ideas about the situation of the unions. Several developments coincided in the unions, any one of which made TUC support for the government's guidelines nearly impossible. First, there was the long pent-up dissatisfaction of the skilled laborers' unions. From their perspective the wage structure had become distorted in the first two years of the incomes program, and now that the economy was in an upswing they wanted to exploit their bargaining strength fully at long last. After the inflation rate sank below 10 percent, they felt they had sacrificed enough and were no longer prepared to have either the government or the TUC impose a moral duty on them.

Second, the shop stewards in all unions were increasingly restless, because their primary function had been practically eliminated by the incomes policy. Instead of hammering out the best result for their own constituents in negotiations with management, they had been asked to implement centralized wage regulations for three years. At shop floor meetings they were no longer able to present their voters with the triumphs they themselves had achieved; at best they could report on successful negotiations between the TUC central committee and the chancellor of the exchequer about changes in the tax law. By the same token, they could hardly present the general improvement of the economic situation as a result of their own efforts. In short, the institutional structure of British wage bargaining provided few opportunities for key actors to take political advantage of the favorable overall balance between incomes policy and workers' interest that characterized the macroeconomic situation of 1978. Thus, after the extreme moral pressure of the first two years was relaxed, it became necessary to restore to shop stewards the responsibility for wage negotiations—unless one were willing to destroy their organizational bases of power altogether. But that was an option that the government had foregone with its repeal of Heath's Industrial Relations Act in 1974.

Finally, to the same degree that the official economic policy moved to the Right, the left wing of the Labour party and of the unions became ideologically more radical, making cooperation with government policy difficult (Berrington, 1982). Behind the move to the Left was not only the growing militancy of Trotskyite groups in party and union locals, but also the academically respectable economic position of the post-Keynesian Cambridge Economic Policy Group. Instead of the moderate consolidation practiced by Healey, this group advocated a determined expansion of public and private demand, protected by limitations on imports and controls on capital exchange (Cripps and Godley, 1978). After the political leader of the Left and minister of industry, Tony

Benn, failed in his ambitious plans for public controls on private investment and was placed in a second-rank Cabinet post, the interest of the Left focused on the unions, particularly on the leftist public sector unions.

The budget restraint of the past years had imposed sacrifices on those unions, and they had been the strictest practitioners of the incomes policy. Among the members there was a feeling that they had gotten the short end of the deal, and it was easy to mobilize them politically. The most prominent sacrificial victim of this spirit was Jack Jones, the father of the incomes policy. At the congress of his Transport and General Workers' Union in May 1978, he suffered a decisive defeat in the vote on the future attitude toward incomes policy. As a consequence, and partly because of his age, he did not run for the presidency of his union again. The political lesson for other union leaders was clear. In addition, a change of generations took place in other large unions as well, so that the government could no longer count on the cooperative and effective TUC partners of summer 1975.

TUC leadership was outraged at the 5 percent guideline, but even a 10 percent guideline could not have produced a consensus at that moment. The unions simply needed another period of free collective bargaining and could not allow themselves to serve any longer as instruments of government economic policy, however reasonable. From the TUC leadership's perspective, agreement to the guidelines was out of the question. The best that one could do politically was to try to keep the most militant unions quiet until an election that would be set as early as possible, and delaying the inevitable confrontation until afterward. Thus came as a complete shock when, immediately after the TUC congress in September, Callaghan announced that there was no question of elections in autumn 1978 and reaffirmed his determination to push the 5 percent guideline through.

The mobilization of the public sector unions had been targeted for late fall and could no longer be stopped, even if the central committees had wanted to. But the first open confrontation occurred in the private sector, when British Ford reacted to a strike in October and November with an offer that amounted to income increases of 17 percent including productivity bonuses. Ford wanted to be able to take advantage of the automobile boom. The government tried to exclude Ford from all public contracts, as it had threatened. But it had to retract its sanctions after it failed to win a majority in the House of Commons in a vote that technically did not count as a vote of confidence. It lost because the Liberals, expecting fall elections, had canceled the "Lib-Lab" treaty of tolerance. Thus the wage guideline in the private sector was reduced to a nonbinding recommendation. In November the government again negotiated with the unions about the possibility of an incomes policy. In a tie vote the TUC leadership rejected the suggested compromise, wage increases of 8.5 percent for the lower-income groups. The government's only hope to save anything of its wage guidelines was to remain tough in its negotiations with the public sector.

The confrontations began in November, when the tank truck drivers went out on wildcat strikes. Other truckers struck in sympathy and the new leadership of the TGWU soon declared these strikes official. Stevedores, locomotive engineers, health service workers, teachers, and municipal employees all followed suit. During the "winter of discontent," which lasted from November 1978 to March 1979, the unions were able to halt the administration and delivery systems of the modern welfare state. Wares were not transported, public transportation collapsed, children were not taught, sick people were turned away, and the dead remained unburied.

From January on the government fought only to settle the extremely unpopular strike rather than for its stabilization policy. The TUC helped in the attempt to give the inevitable capitulation the color of a politically defensible solution. The discussions resulted in a document called a "concordat" under which the wage structure in the public sector was to be examined for its comparability with private sector wages according to the principle of equal pay for equal work. As soon as this bill was signed (and adopted by Margaret Thatcher in her election platform as well), all strikes were ended with wage agreements that on average were actually somewhat below the level of the prior year. In any case, the financial consequences of the comparability negotiations would make themselves felt only after the next government took office, just as was the case in 1974 with Heath's cost-of-living thresholds.

After Callaghan lost a vote of confidence in March over the issue of the devolution of responsibilities to the regional parliament in Scotland, new elections were held in May 1979, before the voters had been able to forget the traumatic winter. The Conservative government under Margaret Thatcher never even tried to reach an arrangement with the unions about incomes policy. In its view, free collective bargaining was acceptable as long as a monetarist money and fiscal policy set the right conditions to constrain wage settlements. From this perspective, therefore, the subsequent steep rise in the unemployment rate to more than 12 percent was no longer the government's fault but solely the consequence of misguided union wage demands. But this period is not part of our study of full employment policies in a social democracy.

The Labour government fell because, under the prevailing institutional conditions, it was unable to achieve the necessary degree of coordination between government monetary and fiscal policies and union wage policy. Without this coordination, it was impossible to guide a troubled economy like Britain's successfully through the crisis of the 1970s.

CHAPTER SIX

Sweden: The Erosion of Hegemonic Institutions

Unlike Austria and Great Britain, at the onset of the crisis Sweden was neither one of the industrial West's latecomers nor one of its problem cases. On the contrary, the Swedish economy, with special strengths in wood products, high-grade ores, steel production, shipbuilding, tool and die making, and the automotive industry, had consistently led in international economic comparisons since the 1940s. Unimpaired by World War II, Sweden had profited from both European armament in the 1930s and rearmament after the war and was able to reinforce its lead position by thorough modernization during the 1950s and 1960s. Under a social democratic government since 1932, Sweden had also become the most progressive and most expansive welfare state in the Western world, apparently without sacrificing the vitality of its capitalist economy (Lundberg, 1985; Martin, 1984; Anton, 1980). The Swedish unions, under the uncontested leadership of the federation of blue-collar unions (the Swedish Labor Organization, or LO), also performed exceptionally well. On the basis of the "peace agreement of Saltsjöbaden," concluded in 1938 with the central employers' organization (the Swedish Employers' Association, or SAF), the unions had achieved not only top ranks in international comparisons of wage levels almost without strikes but also an increasing equalization of primary incomes. Government tax policy did what remained necessary to bring Sweden closer than any other capitalist nation to the social democratic ideal of full employment, social security, and income parity (Sawyer, 1982). In short, at the beginning of the 1970s Sweden was the most admired or feared (Huntford, 1971) model of what could be achieved by an intelligent and consistent social democratic policy under the conditions of developed industrial capitalism.

The elements of the "Swedish model" developed in the 1950s and 1960s that concern us here are economic policy and employment policy. What is remarkable at the outset is the somewhat conventional character of Swedish economic policy. In comparison to the course of development in Austria and Great Britain, the nationalized sector in Sweden remained small after the war. After a failed attempt to combat the inflation of the late 1940s by voluntary wage restraint, the government also dropped incomes policy from its economic policy repertoire. Until recently it was considered a truism of Swedish economic policy that in a capitalist economy neither the government nor the union was able to hold effective wages below the level defined by scarcity in the labor market. Rather, it was the task of the government monetary and fiscal policy to adjust macroeconomic demand so that excess demand could not arise in the labor market.

If these principles did not lead to a British-style stop-and-go policy, it was partly because the Swedish krona was much less susceptible to currency speculation and balance-of-payments crises. More important, however, was the fact that until well into the 1970s, Sweden was able to avoid two inflationary factors that were somewhat independent of macroeconomic demand: a wage-price spiral driven by wage competition among individual unions and inflationary bottlenecks in local labor markets. The complex strategy that made it possible to avoid both dangers had its theoretical basis in the 1951 work of Gösta Rehn and Rudolf Meidner (Meidner and Hedborg, 1984). The LO had commissioned this work and adopted the "Rehn-Meidner model" as soon as it appeared, but it took nearly a decade for government and management to accept it and fully incorporate it into the institutional practice of labor relations and government policy (Korpi, 1978; Martin, 1984). With the adoption of this model, economic policy and employment policy became conceptually coherent and politically acceptable to an extent not even approached by the other three nations in this study.

The normative starting point for the Rehn-Meidner model was a "solidaristic" wage policy aiming to reduce wage differentials not only between women and men but also between different firms, branches, or regions, according to the principle of equal pay for equal work. The LO was also committed to reducing the traditional income distinctions between the various classes of skilled and unskilled workers and the professions. This goal was inconsistent both with union wage competition and with the development of substantial discrepancies between wages actually paid and the standard wages determined by collective agreement. Establishing a solidaristic wage policy thus depended on centralizing wage negotiations and effectively containing "wage drift."

The first condition was satisfied in the mid–1950s with the help of the SAF, which had its own reasons for wanting centralized wage negotiations. Unlike the blue-collar unions of the LO, which were organized by craft or industry, the white-collar employees' unions, in the umbrella organizations TCO and SACO, were organized according to educational levels or professions (Elvander, 1983). This structure favored wage competition almost to the same extent as in Great Britain, since the demands of the white-collar employees were guided by blue-collar settlements in the most prosperous industries. These in turn became the basis for the demands put forward by blue-collar unions in the less favored branches. To put this escalation machine out of commission, the SAF found it desirable to engage in centralized wage negotiations with the LO in order to arrive at uniform wage increases across all industries. Both the SAF and the LO expected that white-collar unions would continue to orient their own demands by the blue-collar settlements. The employers' association centralization was in fact achieved in the mid–1950s, and the second condition also continued to hold until the late 1960s.

But this solved only one of the problems connected with a solidaristic wage policy. In the three-stage system of wage negotiations established in the mid–1950s, the results of central negotiations between the LO and the SAF effectively guided the branch unions in their wage agreements, but they could not prevent wage drift at the third level of negotiations, that is, within individual firms, when employers were willing (owing to high labor demand or under threat of strikes) and able (perhaps owing to above-average profits) to grant wage increases that were higher than the standard. Clearly, this kind of wage drift violated the principles of wage solidarity, thereby subverting the legitimacy of the strategy pursued by union leadership and ultimately the legitimacy of the union leadership itself in the eyes of the employees. The self-interest of the central union organizations would thus have required them to minimize wage drift by anticipating in the collective bargaining process all opportunities the firms had to raise wages. Because wage scales were to be made uniform, this would have required wage agreements to be set according to the ability to pay of the most lucrative firms, branches, and regions.

Such a policy would, however, have caused bankruptcies, layoffs, and foregone investments in firms with average earnings, resulting in an unacceptable level of unemployment. Nor could the unions count on an expansionary government monetary and fiscal policy to maintain employment under those conditions, because even apart from the inflationary consequences of such a policy, it would only have reconstituted the conditions facilitating wage drift. The leaders who were committed to

the principles of wage solidarity thus had to choose between two conflict-
ing goals in setting wage levels. If they effectively pursued income equalization, they risked increased unemployment; if they chose to work toward full employment, they had to accept wage drift and substantial
wage differences. The Rehn-Meidner model offered a way out of this
dilemma. Its concerted deployment of various instruments could not
even have been seriously discussed in the other three countries, but in
Sweden it was successfully practiced for almost two decades—a triumph
probably unique for the applied social sciences.

   According to the model, wage settlements were to be based on the pay
scales of firms with above-average earnings, but not the top firms, to
control wage drift. Because this standard would impinge on business
profits, business savings would be insufficient to finance the desired
levels of productive investment. Hence other sectors had to contribute to
capital formation to compensate for reduced business savings. Rehn and
Meidner unambiguously elected to make the public sector responsible
for this contribution. Part of the wage increases, which were too high
from a macroeconomic perspective, had to be diverted to establish a
permanent budget surplus that could flow back into the private sector in
the form of investment capital (Rehn, 1952). A technically practical way
to achieve this recycling of public surpluses was provided by the introduction, in the late 1950s, of a supplemental old-age pension scheme
financed through payroll deductions. The reserves of this new pension
plan were invested in loans and later in the stocks of Swedish firms
(Martin, 1984:213–18). Because Sweden never had a problem with capital drain and there were no competing investment options available,
businesses were willing to invest domestically as long as new projects
promised positive cash flows, even if, to a greater extent than previously,
their investments had to be financed externally rather than from internal savings.

   However, this scheme could, of course, guarantee desired levels of
macroeconomic activity only on average. If it was effective in equalizing
salaries and wages, then the wage levels would necessarily be too low for
some firms, industries, or regions and too high for others. Firms in the
first group would thrive, invest, and expand; those in the second group
would suffer losses, contract, or fail. The intellectual integrity of the
Rehn-Meidner idea consisted in its refusal to deny these implications;
rather, it embraced them. High profits were supposed to encourage the
quick growth of the most competent firms and the most productive
sectors of the economy; as for the rest, the solidaristic wage would either
goad them to increase productivity or drive them to the wall. Any other

92

outcome would be excessively costly for an economic system that was so dependent on its international competitive position.

The unions, though they had commissioned the Rehn-Meidner model, could not be entirely satisfied with its effect on the labor market under conditions of normal mobility: structural unemployment in the shrinking sectors and surplus demand and rising wage drift in the expanding sectors. These two problems could be addressed only by the government, which had to develop new programs to minimize the costs of transition for the workers who were adversely affected by the structural adjustments brought about by economic development and to maximize labor mobility so as to eliminate the labor bottlenecks that threatened the solidaristic wage. After long consideration the social democratic government was ready to implement the necessary programs by the end of the 1950s.

Given the economic conditions of the 1950s and 1960s, however, problems of excess demand were more pressing than problems of structural unemployment. As a consequence, the intruments of structural adjustment remained underdeveloped. As long as a sufficient number of jobs was available in the economy as a whole, theoretical and practical interest concentrated instead on the mobility-increasing instruments of an "active labor market policy" (which was also propagated by the OECD, under Gösta Rehn's leadership, and eventually imitated by almost all industrial countries).

Active labor market policy called for shifting workers whose jobs were threatened by structural unemployment as quickly as possible into new (and often better) jobs in competitive and growing sectors of the economy. If this could be done, businesses in expanding industries and growing areas would not be forced to offer overscale pay to attract labor from other firms or regions. Instead, labor market authorities were expected to train workers for high-demand jobs and make them available where they were most needed, at the standard wage. In the 1960s the Swedish government developed a network of training centers to educate and retrain unemployed and underqualified workers. The Swedish labor administration also sought to increase the mobility of job seekers by paying their moving expenses and a moving allowance. Only if workers took advantage of these programs and still failed to find new jobs would the Swedish government use subsidies to maintain jobs, take measures to create work, or provide employment in "protected shops" in order to avoid actual unemployment. In contrast to the Federal Republic, Sweden financed these measures out of general revenues and not by unemployment insurance contributions (Schmid, 1984).

93

Promotion of an active labor market policy completed the structure of the Rehn-Meidner model. The solidaristic wage would equalize actual wages and had to limit firm profits, both to avoid wage drift and to increase labor's share of the social product. But it should not be allowed to jeopardize the profitability of new investments. Some of the investment capital that the economy needed in order to grow and develop would be generated by government through permanent budget surpluses. High profits in the efficient economic sectors and losses in the weaker areas were acceptable, because they would accelerate structural change. An active labor market policy would prevent both structural unemployment and threats to the solidaristic wage by retraining workers to meet the needs of the labor market and by encouraging worker mobility. This was the model accepted by LO unions, the Social Democratic party, the government, and in principle also by management at the end of the 1950s. It shaped Swedish practice in the 1960s and early 1970s, although its individual elements were not all equally well thought through and were employed with varying success.

During the 1960s, the active labor market proposal was adopted by many OECD nations, including the Federal Republic in its Labor Promotion Act of 1969, but no other nation relied so heavily on this program to avoid overt unemployment (Rothstein, 1985; 1985a). Sweden used the new programs for the first time to cope with the economic downswing of 1957–60, and from then on the number and scope of the measures it took to implement the active labor market increased from economic low to economic low. During upswings they decreased only a little. During the year before the oil supply shock, Sweden devoted 1.54 percent of its gross national product to these measures—as compared to 0.41 percent in the Federal Republic. The policy involved 2.82 percent of the paid work force at that point as against 1.6 percent in the Federal Republic (Schmid, 1982:56). The active labor market program eventually came to be the most completely developed of all the elements of the Rehn-Meidner model, as it was refined and improved over the years. Its effectiveness was uncontested when the 1970s began; and for that very reason it was taxed to the limits during the crisis years that followed.

The other elements of the Rehn-Meidner model never achieved the same reputation of unchallenged success, although the solidaristic wage was consistently pursued, and it successfully reduced wage differences over the years (OECD, 1978:28; Meidner and Hedborg, 1984:66 ff.). But during the 1960s, the government and LO disagreed often about the timing and intensity of fiscal policy measures, arguing from positions that reversed the pattern in other countries. The unions charged that the government's fiscal policy was generally too expansionary or at least that its restrictive impulses were too little too late and therefore failed to avert inflationary price increases and overscale wage increases. In fact wage drift increased so much during the 1960s that it accounted for most of the yearly growth in incomes (Flanagan et al., 1983:312ff.). That incomes nevertheless continued to become more equal was even then due to compensation rules adjusting the wages of the disadvantaged groups.

For LO unions, which tried to accommodate central wage agreements to macroeconomic aggregates, this development was unsatisfactory. Because they did not want to relinquish the goal of income equalization, they had to take steps in subsequent stages of the bargaining process to generalize the effects of any wage drift that occurred, which entailed average wage increases higher than what they wanted. This constant disavowal of their own wage policy and the resulting inflationary push could have been avoided, they believed, if the government's economic policy had been less stimulative and had not made high wage drift possible in the first place. The government for its part pointed out that wages had risen so much that the restrictive monetary and fiscal policy demanded by the LO would have resulted in unacceptable job losses. The surprising lesson of this dispute seems to be that the loss of jobs had lost its terrors for the unions although not for the government, perhaps because the government-financed active labor market program had evidently eliminated overt unemployment. But if this had been the only issue dividing them, the government and the labor organization might have been able to work things out. The difficulties, however, lay deeper.

They resulted from the fact that the system of centralized wage negotiations that SAF and LO had established in the 1950s had already begun to erode in the late 1960s. The member unions of the LO remained loyal to the principle, but the white-collar and the public sector unions grew tired of adjusting their wages based on the decisions of others. Because their own organizational strength had grown steadily since the 1950s, they sought to put aside that subservient role. Moreover, the unions outside the LO were not oriented toward social democracy in a traditional sense, and even those in the umbrella organization TCO were only loosely linked to one another. Thus whenever circumstances were favorable, they proceeded on their own and pushed wage agreements for white-collar employees as high as they could, until at the end of the 1960s the TCO unions renounced LO leadership in matters of wages entirely, by refusing to synchronize their wage periods with those adopted by LO and SAF. The higher wage agreements for private-sector white-collar employees then set standards for wage agreements in the public sector and induced blue-collar unions at the plant level to aim for similar settlements in the local wage rounds. The government thus had a point when it asserted that an expansionary fiscal policy was needed to accommodate wage increases, and the LO was correct in refusing responsibility for the wage level and blaming instead the high wage drift.

The initiative to control wage competition came, once again, from the employers' association SAF, which had proposed that wages be based on objective or even scientific criteria. Subsequently, the chief economists of the three central organizations, TCO, SAF, and LO, had worked out what came to be called the EFO model, after its authors, Edgren, Faxén, and Odhner (1973). The model, which was derived from an earlier Norwegian study (Aukrust, 1977), aimed at an explicit understanding about the parameters that should be considered for wage determination. Its starting point was the distinction between a sector of the Swedish economy that was exposed to international competition and a protected sector. The model assumed that prices in the exposed sector would be dictated by the world market; in the protected sector it assumed markup pricing tied to the increase in wage costs. It further assumed that wages in both sectors would rise at exactly the same rate. Given these assumptions, the international competitive position of the Swedish economy could be maintained only if the exposed sector assumed wage leadership and if the increase in nominal wages in that sector did not exceed the sum of world market inflation (at fixed exchange rates) and domestic productivity growth. Because productivity growth was lower in the protected sector, the same wage increases would produce a slight inflationary push, which was tolerable as long as the exposed sector remained competitive.

The advantage of the EFO model was that, instead of tying white-collar pay to the labor organization agreements, which was increasingly difficult for reasons of organizational policy, it offered an "objective" formula that would serve as a guideline for everyone. In principle, every union could now figure out the economically responsible upper limit for its wage demands. For the rest, the model (contrary to the original intentions of the SAF) left enough play for discussions and compromises across a distributive range with broad outer limits. Thus the model served to reduce conflicts between the unions and made possible a relatively harmonious wage policy well into the second half of the 1970s. This organizational policy advantage of the EFO model proved, however, to be a security risk for economic policy as economic conditions, which the model, with its simplifying assumptions, had presumed constant, changed both at home and abroad.

I should note in passing two other factors that influenced Sweden's development in the 1970s. Between 1969 and 1971 Sweden switched

from taxing the income of married couples jointly to taxing each partner's income separately. This change contributed to the steep increase in
the number of married women in the paid work force during the 1970s.
Second, there were the political controversies about codetermination
and the workers' fund, which, employers felt, challenged the foundations of the postwar Swedish model. Both issues will be discussed in their
specific context below. Finally, I note that the Social Democrats suffered
significant losses in the parliamentary elections of 1973; even with the
support of the Communists they had only half the votes in the "lottery
parliament." In 1970 the Social Democrats, in the course of a constitutional reform aimed at making political life more democratic or at least
more dynamic, did away with the indirectly elected Second House, in
which they had always had a sure majority. Thus they were now dependent on support from the centrist opposition parties.

FIRST RESPONSES: BRIDGING THE CRISIS

In an attempt to suppress inflation, the government pursued a very
restrictive fiscal policy up to 1973. As a consequence it had to accept
unemployment of 2.5 percent, an unusually high rate for Sweden. At
the onset of the crisis, the government then relaxed its fiscal and monetary policies and raised consumer demand by temporarily reducing the
value-added tax. The unions also were satisfied with minimal increases
in real wages in 1973 and accepted very moderate wage agreements for
1974 as well. While this pattern of responses was unplanned, hindsight
tells us that it was precisely the optimum response. Wage restraint reduced cost-push inflation, and fiscal expansion filled the demand gap.

Unfortunately, however, the demand gap was not immediately manifest. As in Austria, Swedish exports benefited from the short-lived
boom in 1974 that resulted from the worldwide expansion of raw material stockpiles. Consequently, despite its expansionary policies, Sweden's
current account deficit stayed within bounds and its inflation rate increased only a little. Real economic growth also dropped only from 4
percent in 1974 to 2.2 percent in 1975, rather than becoming negative,
as was the case in the other three countries. Indeed, at the end of 1974 it
appeared that the world economic crisis had bypassed Sweden (Table
6.1).

Two years of low wage increases and the favorable export situation
caused firm profits to climb steeply in both 1973 and 1974. At the same
time unemployment dropped and the propensity to wage drift resumed.
According to the EFO model, the unions were thus fully justified in

Table 6.1 GDP growth (%), trade balance (% of GDP), rise in consumer prices, rise in nominal wages in industry, rise in real wages in industry, and rise in unit labor costs in industry; unemployment (%): Sweden, 1973–1980

	1973	1974	1975	1976	1977	1978	1979	1980
GDP growth	3.9	4.3	2.2	1.2	−2.0	1.3	4.3	1.9
Trade balance	2.8	−1.0	−0.5	−2.1	−2.6	0.0	−2.2	−3.5
Consumer prices	6.7	9.9	9.8	10.3	11.4	10.0	7.2	13.7
Nominal wages	8.4	11.1	17.2	13.5	8.2	10.3	7.8	8.8
Real wages	1.7	1.2	7.4	2.2	−3.2	−0.3	0.6	−4.9
Unit labor costs	4.6	12.9	19.3	16.7	11.1	8.3	−0.1	9.3
Unemployment	2.5	2.0	1.6	1.6	1.8	2.2	2.1	2.0

Sources: OECD Economic Outlook 32; OECD Historical Statistics, 1960–1983; IFO, 1982.

demanding significant wage increases for 1975, both to suppress wage drift and to adjust the distributive relation between capital and labor. Following the trend toward longer contract periods, these settlements applied to 1976 as well. Nominal wages in industry thus increased 17.2 percent in 1975 and 13.5 percent in 1976; real wages increased a record 7.4 percent in 1975. In addition, 1975 saw a marked rise in employer contributions to pension insurance. The initial consequence of these increases was an increase in inflation. The GNP price index rose 14.8 percent in 1975, compared with 8.4 percent in 1974, and consumer prices rose 9.8 percent. But this was just the beginning of Sweden's problems.

Like Austria, Sweden joined the "West German–mark bloc" of European hard-currency countries after the system of fixed rates of exchange was dissolved in spring 1973. But since past discussions of economic policy models had always assumed stable currency exchange relations, Sweden at first hardly noted the upward movement of the mark, which began in 1975. Moreover, projections under the EFO model had ignored the possibility that inflation rates would again decline in the world market in 1975 and 1976. As a result, the competitive position of Sweden's exposed sector worsened drastically in 1975 and 1976, both because of above-average domestic wage and price increases and because of the revaluation of the mark, which Sweden followed. The balance-of-trade deficit increased steeply in 1976 and 1977, and the exposed sector experienced a dramatic decline in profits. Business's return on investment, which had averaged 11 percent in 1974, fell to 4 percent in 1977 (OECD Economic Surveys, Sweden, 1984:39).

There were also structural problems. The international inventory boom was followed by a deep recession that severely affected Swedish raw material and steel exports. And the Swedish shipbuilding industry,

which had been the third largest in the world before the crisis, had
specialized exclusively in supertankers. The supertanker market collapsed completely just after the first oil crisis; afterward, it was dominated by South Korea and other newly industrialized nations. Unlike
Austria, Sweden was also affected by stagnation in the automotive industry. Although unemployment did not increase, employment in the industrial sector fell by 8.2 percent between 1976 and 1978, after running
counter to the general trend by climbing until 1976.

CENTRIST CRISIS MANAGEMENT

The Social Democrats lost the legislative elections of 1976 more because of the controversy about nuclear energy, forced on them by the
ecologically engaged Farmers' party, than because of political criticism of
their economic policy. The centrist coalition that came into office consisted of conservatives, liberals, and the Farmers' party. Of these, only
the Farmers' party had any experience in government, as an erstwhile
coalition partner of the Social Democrats. The coalition was divided over
many issues, and the battle about nuclear energy soon produced serious
internal tensions. But the coalition members were in accord that the first
centrist government after forty-four years should not have to shoulder
the responsibility for widespread unemployment. Thus one of the few
issues on which the coalition agreed was the continuation of the Social
Democrats' full employment policy. In executing this policy, however, the
coalition stood several social democratic principles on their heads.

The first to be overturned were social democratic principles in currency and fiscal policy. The centrist coalition began its government with a
minor devaluation of the krona in October 1976, followed by two much
larger devaluations in April and August 1977 (by 15 percent in total),
and with Sweden's removal from the European hard-currency bloc. The
goal of these actions was to restore Sweden's international competitive
position by lowering the price of Swedish exports. Sweden usually judges
the effect of a devaluation strategy in terms of its bilateral relationship
with the Federal Republic. According to this measure, the success of the
devaluations was short-lived and was soon consumed by higher prices. A
more accurate evaluation would consider a nation's exchange relations
with all its trading partners, and this measure shows that Sweden was
indeed able to improve its very unfavorable competitive position
through the strategy of devaluation it pursued from 1976 on (Table 6.2).

The price of devaluation was a lasting 10 percent inflation rate (see
Table 6.1), while nearly all other industrial nations again approached

Table 6.2 Effective rates of exchange and relative export prices (both trade weighted), 1974–1983

	1974	1975	1976	1977	1978	1979	1980	1981	1982	1983
Effective rates of exchange (first quarter of 1970 = 100)										
Austria	108	111	114	119	120	121	125	125	128	131
FRG	123	123	131	141	149	155	157	152	161	169
GB	83	76	66	63	64	68	75	77	74	70
Sweden	98	101	103	99	89	89	89	89	80	72
Relative export prices (1970 = 100)										
Austria	101	103	104	105	102	101	98	95	96	96
FRG	111	109	101	104	108	107	104	97	98	98
GB	88	90	88	91	96	103	114	113	107	105
Sweden	102	107	111	106	99	100	100	98	92	89

Source: OECD *Economic Outlook* 38.

price stability in the late 1970s. The Swedish government could not bring itself to fight inflation with a tight fiscal policy. On the contrary, while the Social Democrats had been prevented from following their traditional tight fiscal policy by the "lottery parliament," they had nevertheless held the deficit to 2 percent of GNP in 1976. Under the centrist coalition, however, it was allowed to rise from 5.2 percent in 1977 to 12.2 percent in 1982. Because the coalition was in no position either to cut expenditures or to raise taxes, it came to practice, in its own present judgment, a combination of "socialist spending policy and conservative taxing policy" (Table 6.3).

The coalition used deficit spending mainly to subsidize jobs, especially in the industrial sector, and to expand active labor market programs. In 1974, the Social Democrats had established a program of inventory maintenance subsidies to help out communities in the depressed north. Under the coalition this program became the most important means of maintaining industrial jobs. The Swedish shipyards were thus subsidized to produce their unmarketable supertankers "for inventory," only to have them scrapped later at government expense. When even this program was unable to save the firms, the government shifted its focus to nationalizing the steel industry, shipbuilding, and the raw materials industries in order to save endangered jobs or at least to slow down their elimination.

Critics allege that the inventory maintenance subsidies and the policy of nationalization were the main reasons that Swedish industry was so slow to adjust to global economic conditions after 1976. For instance, in 1979 the Volvo factory in Göteborg was unable to take full advantage of the export boom because it lacked workers, whereas in the nationalized shipyards next door, thousands of skilled workers were drawing higher

Table 6.3 Expenditures, revenues, and deficits of the national government (% of GNP): Sweden, 1973–1982

	1973	1974	1975	1976	1977	1978	1979	1980	1981	1982
Expenditures by the national government	26.3	29.0	29.5	30.0	32.1	32.9	35.9	35.0	34.8	41.9
Revenues of the national government	23.5	24.9	25.5	28.1	26.8	24.6	26.3	24.8	24.1	29.8
Deficit	2.8	4.1	4.0	2.0	5.2	8.4	9.6	10.2	10.6	12.2

Source: BMF Finanzberichte.

wages than in the automobile industry for doing nothing or for producing scrap. But the steel industry has now shrunk to a healthy size and is again competitive; in 1984 the mining industry made a profit again for the first time; and the shipyards were largely shut down after 1980 (the remaining yards were converted to building drilling islands for the high seas). On its own terms, therefore, the unplanned expedient of nationalization must be considered successful.

The Labor Market Administration (AMS) also tended to focus its efforts on inventory maintenance subsidies during this period. It substantially increased spending to maintain jobs in the private sector and to create jobs in the public sector, while expenditures for retraining to encourage regional mobility were stagnating (Schmid, 1982:48). This shift in focus was due not only to the worsening situation in the labor market (whose uneven development would have called for more funds to encourage mobility) but also to the changed composition of the government.

The Farmers' party, to which the new prime minister belonged, had increasingly come to criticize the Rehn-Meidner model as practiced by the AMS. It charged that forced mobility led to the depopulation of the northern regions (AMS was said to stand for "All Must [Go] South") and that it—like social democratic policy in general—overtaxed the human capacity to adjust to changes in the natural, social, and work environment. Even though in the cabinet the AMS was attached to the Liberal party, which was closely associated with industry, it had to respond to this change in political priorities. Moreover, worker willingness to move to new jobs had in fact declined noticeably. The Farmers' party claimed the decline was due to a stronger emotional attachment to home and locality, but it was more likely because the participation of married women in the labor force had grown rapidly since the beginning of the 1970s. Two attractive new jobs were simply harder to find than one.[1]

In any case, total expenditures for active labor market policy rose from 1.8 percent of GNP in the fiscal year 1975–76 to 3.1 percent in 1977–78, and the number of persons absorbed through labor market policy measures rose from 2.2 percent of the paid work force in 1975 to 3.6 percent in 1978. The net employment effect (including multiplier effects) was estimated to be 3.9 percent of the work force in 1978 and 4

1 Within the AMS a third argument, also supported by the OECD, is now emphasized. It challenges the Rehn-Meidner concept from yet another angle. Solidaristic wage policy and the government's egalitarian tax policy are believed to have reduced financial incentives for changing jobs or vocations so much that the instruments of the labor market policy alone can no longer guarantee a vocational and geographical mobility sufficient to meet the demands of the changing economic structure.

percent in 1979 (Schmid, 1982:57). In other words, in the absence of these measures, registered unemployment in Sweden would not have been a mere 2.2 percent in 1978 but would have been 6.1 percent, much higher than the West German rate of 3.8 percent.

Today, even the AMS believes that this development, rather than representing an unqualified success, overtaxed its active labor market policy and made it deviate from its original goals. In particular, according to AMS specialists, threatened unemployment made it impossible to maintain the Rehn-Meidner model's focus on the personnel needs of expanding firms and industries. Instead, the administration had to focus on protecting existing jobs and expanding substitute employment in the worker's place of residence. An additional factor was the political interest of the Liberal party, which was responsible for the labor market policy. This party did not want to see the volume of labor market policy measures reduced during the economic upswing of 1978–79. The inexperienced centrist coalition had grasped the active labor market policy as a lifesaver. Because it was unanimously held to be a successful tool, the coalition saw it as a chance to eliminate unemployment and to prove that the government had a social conscience. The clarity of this proof was not to be obscured by fiscal stinginess or technocratic doubts about the efficiency of individual measures of the policy. Thus it was the Social Democrats who instituted a commission to examine the organization of the Labor Market Administration and the efficiency of the labor market policy after their victory in 1982.

There was thus little political maneuvering room in the new coalition for the neoliberal or monetarist opinions held by some of its members. Their only practical influence was on the monetary policy of the Swedish Imperial Bank. In the directorate of that bank, a kind of secondary government appointed anew at the beginning of each parliamentary term by proportional vote, the government in power always has a majority of the votes, but the formal independence of the bank shields its decisions from political influence unless the finance minister intervenes in his oversight function. The finance minister after 1976 was a member of the Conservative party, which was closely allied with business interests; he would have preferred a restrictive policy from the outset. Since he could not prevail in this position in the cabinet, he at least supported the tight credit policy of the Imperial Bank, which was hardly discussed in the cabinet. However, the influence of monetary policy was much more limited than in other countries because housing finance is completely subject to government plans setting the number of new units to be built each year and the appropriate interest rates for financing. The government then pays the mortgage bank the difference between those rates and market rates. Another factor was the large role the pension fund played in capital formation and the commercial banks' obligation to keep a certain proportion of their active portfolio in low-interest government paper, which was in force until 1982. The restrictive monetary policy was thus significant only for investment loans in the private sector. Even conservatives believe that the only reason this policy did not do more damage there was that firms were generally unwilling to invest after 1976 in any case.

The Expansion of the Public Sector

In contrast to the relatively negative industrial employment picture, employment in the public sector virtually exploded during the crisis. Between 1973 and 1979 the public sector share of the paid work force rose from 24.1 to 29.9 percent, while the share in the Federal Republic rose only from 12.6 to 14.7 percent. However, this development contributed very little to relieving the pressure on the branches of industry affected by the crisis. Instead, it reflected the expansion of a largely independent "second labor market," which was generated by two complementary processes: the inclination of married women to work outside the home and the expansion of municipal services. All my interviews made clear that both factors were operating before the crisis, and even a generous interpretation cannot read their effect as part of an employment strategy used to fight industrial unemployment (Sterner and Mellström, 1985).

The work-force participation of Swedish women, which had been close to the European average in the early 1960s, has far surpassed all comparable nations (Table 6.4) and has almost reached parity with male participation, even for middle-aged women (Schmid, 1984:18). Apparently this was not due to a "feminist" policy of equal opportunity on the American model (Braun, 1984). Women are not more heavily repre-

Table 6.4 Participation of 15-to-64-year-old women in the paid work force (%), 1963–1983

	1963	1968	1973	1978	1983
Austria	n.v.	50.1	48.5	48.7	49.7
FRG	49.3	47.7	49.6	49.4	49.5
GB	47.4	49.8	53.1	56.7	57.8
Sweden	54.6	56.6	62.6	71.3	76.6

Source: OECD Labour Force Statistics, 1963–1983.

sented in the upper ranks of business, public administration, politics, or science in Sweden than elsewhere in Europe (and seemingly less than in Great Britain or even in "male chauvinist" Austria). What seems to have brought about the strong work-force presence of women was rather that Sweden places such a high social value on paid work that working becomes almost a compulsion. As a consequence, husbands, unions, employers, municipalities, and the national government were also compelled to take seriously the problems of wives and mothers in the paid work force. The result was impressive union advances in realizing the principle of equal pay for equal work (Meidner and Helborg, 1984:68), the expansion of communal day care, kindergartens in plants, all-day schools, generous parental leave provisions, and a supply of part-time jobs that was unique on the international scene. Tax law also provided a strong incentive. In 1969–70 the law had changed from joint assessment to individual assessment for married couples. That meant that with the same family income, the tax burden on two-earner households was much lower than in households with only one member of the couple employed (Gustafsson, 1984:139). The more the overall tax obligation increased, the more such considerations came to determine behavior.

Many factors thus contributed to making a career as a housewife unattractive to Swedish women and to making it easier to take paid work—which still did not mean that they reached effective parity with men. Wage differentials for the same work were almost eliminated, it is true, but professional segregation of women within the work force apparently increased at the same time (Jonung, 1984; Rein, 1985). With a certain irony one might thus conclude that the successful social democratic policy helped Swedish women out of the housewife's ghetto and into the closed society of women's professions and jobs. Kindergarten teachers, nurses, social workers, and geriatric care givers perform precisely the same kind of stereotypically female functions as housewives and mothers. The only difference is that women in these professions have the double burden of household and paid work, because the Swedish world record of 25 percent part-time employment in practice means part-time jobs for women (50 percent) rather than for men (5 percent).

But irony or cynicism are poor interpreters of the difficult struggle to discover new and practicable means of making social progress. The more interesting question is how public sector employment could have increased by 26 percent in Sweden between 1973 and 1979, as opposed to a mere 9 percent in the Federal Republic and in Austria. The answer seems almost too simple when one considers the ideological and fiscal resistance to increasing public sector employment elsewhere. In Sweden there was a coincidence of public needs and fiscal arrangements that could be used to satisfy them. The expansion was driven by a perfect example of social democratic circular reasoning. Married women wanted to work outside the home and should be helped to enter the paid work force. As a consequence, they had to be relieved of household duties, which implied the need to expand community services to care for children, old people, the sick, and the otherwise needy. Meeting this need required more jobs for women in the public sector. So far, so good—but how was one to pay for this expansion of community services?

In Sweden, as in the Federal Republic, municipalities have primary responsibility for the provision of community and social services for children, the aged, and other needy persons, while the county governments are responsible for medical and psychiatric care. Both levels of government have independent tax bases in Sweden, a proportional income tax whose rates they are free to set as they please. But subsidies from the national government were critical to the expansion of community services. These covered a fixed percentage of the operating costs of the community service facilities: about half for day-care centers (Gustafsson, 1984:141) and up to 80 or 90 percent for psychiatric clinics (which had been passed from the national government to the counties in the 1960s). In addition, the federal health insurance program paid for ambulatory care and subsidized parents' contributions to day-care centers. Thus the subnational governments financed only part of the overall cost of expanding community services, and this part could be increased by increasing local income taxes. Unlike the situation in the Federal Republic, therefore, municipal revenue constraints were not an argument against increasing public sector employment. The Swedish situation thus presented social democratic municipal politicians with the ideal conditions for meeting service sector needs. It also inspired a certain amount of competition among municipalities and counties to offer better services. The resulting inequalities of local tax burdens gave rise to tax oases, but these seem to have generated few controversies or further problems.

Women were chief beneficiaries of the expansion of community services. Most of the new jobs paid low wages and required few qualifications. They were filled by younger women, many with small children, who were interested in part-time work, a preference the public sector employers were happy to accommodate. Although unions generally opposed the expansion of part-time work as an instrument of employment policy in Sweden as elsewhere, they raised no objections in this instance; as long as jobs met the minimum of eighteen hours per week, the level at which workers are required to contribute to social security. More recently public sector employment in Sweden has stopped expanding. The young mothers of the 1970s are now interested in increasing their number of working hours. Given that the total volume of work in the public sector is stagnant, this means that overall community service employment is decreasing again.

THE NEED FOR CONSOLIDATION

Conflict over economic and fiscal policy and nuclear energy resulted in the fall of the first centrist coalition in early 1979. Afterward the Liberals formed a minority government, tolerated by the Social Democrats, and pursued an expansionary course on their own. The large gains by the Conservatives, who emerged as the strongest force on the center-right in the autumn elections that followed, marked a shift to monetary and fiscal consolidation, which, however, coincided with the second oil price crisis, as in Great Britain.

But as the new coalition cautiously curbed expenditures for industrial subsidies and the labor market program and attempted to check wage increases in the public sector, it ran into a confrontation with the unions that had been unimaginable since the peace agreement of Saltsjöbaden more than forty years earlier. Strikes in the public sector extended into the private sector and the government and private employers responded with lockouts. As a result, in spring 1980 strikes brought economic and public life in Sweden to the same kind of impasse as had occurred in the British "winter of discontent" (1978–79). As in Great Britain, the government gave in and largely met the demands of the strikers in the public sector. It also persuaded private employers to come around, although they had wanted to remain firm. As a consequence the inflation rate, which had been falling until 1979, accelerated again; Sweden's international competitive position declined once more; and in spring 1981 the Swedish krona was devalued by 10 percent against the West German mark, which in turn contributed to inflation. The current account deficit, which had dropped for a short time after reaching an all-time high in 1980, increased sharply again in 1982.

Under such conditions, consolidation was generally beyond reach. On the contrary, the deficit of the national budget, which during the first centrist coalition had climbed from 2 percent of GNP in 1976 to 9.6 percent in 1979, now continued to increase until it reached a record high of 12.3 percent of GNP in 1982 (Table 6.5). Even more remarkable, perhaps, was the budget's composition. By 1982, central government borrowing mounted to almost half of its regular revenues, and at 16.2

Table 6.5 National budget deficit (% of GNP)

	1973	1974	1975	1976	1977	1978	1979	1980	1981	1982
Austria	+0.3	+0.1	4.5	4.7	3.8	4.2	3.5	3.0	2.6	4.1
FRG	0.2	1.0	3.3	2.5	1.8	2.1	1.8	1.9	2.5	2.4
GB	2.9	4.3	6.1	6.6	5.2	5.1	4.2	6.1	3.5	4.0
Sweden	2.8	4.1	4.0	2.0	5.2	8.4	9.6	10.2	10.6	12.3

Source: BMF *Finanzberichte.*

percent of expenditures, debt service was already then the largest single component of public spending, larger than social security expenditures and twice as much as expenditures for defense. All this happened, it should be noted, in the country that raised more revenue than any other in the Western world, with taxes and social security contributions amounting to more than 50 percent of GNP in 1982. But, at 67 percent of GNP, public expenditures were still higher.

The one area in which the policy of consolidation proved to be more than rhetoric was local government employment. Here, the center-right government was not only able to replace the open-ended commitment to match county and local government outlays for community services with cash-limited appropriations, but it was also able to reach a general understanding with the subnational governments to hold the line on public employment. Consequently, county and local governments did not raise local income taxes to compensate for the lower increases in national support, something the national government could not have prohibited. Growth in public employment thus slowed considerably in the early 1980s and did not accelerate again under the new social democratic government.

The center-right coalition lacked the political power to bring about a major shift in economic and fiscal policy. Still, it managed to halt the further expansion of the public service sector. It also dramatized the need for consolidation. Thus when the Social Democrats returned to the government in autumn 1982 they were able to use center-right claims to justify a strategy to promote private-sector economic growth, to an extent that would not have been politically acceptable in Sweden previously.

SOCIAL DEMOCRATIC GROWTH POLICY

The most important element of the growth policy of the Social Democrats was a further 16 percent devaluation of the Swedish krona, carried out immediately after the election in October 1982. The rate of devaluation was surprisingly high; compared to purchasing power parity, it was objectively too high. Its purpose was to stimulate Swedish exports, to eliminate the current account deficit, and to stop all speculation about further devaluation, which had begun to matter for the krona as well. The strategy was successful in both respects. Exports increased and the balance of trade improved markedly. Profits for export firms grew disproportionately, since they had passed on only part of the devaluation in lower prices. Then, after a considerable lag, investment started to increase as well in 1984.

At the same time, the Social Democrats undertook to close the gap between public sector income and expenditure, an attempt that the centrist coalition had talked about but not begun (Table 6.6). In principle the LO unions supported this attempt, even if they did not support all details of the policy. From their point of view, the escalating national debt was less an expression of progressive economic policy than a dangerous increase in the power of private capital, and they longed for the time when private investment had had to be financed from public savings instead of the other way around. Since there was near unanimity that the tax rate could not be raised again for a time, it was necessary to exhaust all socially responsible avenues for trimming expenditures (for instance, by eliminating subsidies for industries that were once more profitable) and to check further increases in national expenditures. Therefore, the Social Democrats retained the cash limits placed by the coalition on subsidies to the localities and initiated a review of the active labor market policy with the goal of limiting it to the functions foreseen by the Rehn-Meidner model. Nevertheless, debt service, which was largely owed abroad and in foreign currencies, increased as a result of the devaluation.

Table 6.6 Expenditures, revenue, and deficits of the public sector and the national government (% of GNP); debt service of the national government (% of expenditures): Sweden, 1982–1985

	1982	1983	1984	1985
Public sector				
Expenditures in % of GNP	63.4	58.1	57.9	55.8
Taxes + social security contributions	51.4	48.0	48.0	49.3
Deficit	12.0	10.1	9.9	6.5
National government				
Deficit	12.2	10.1	9.7	6.3
Interest as % of expenditures	15.6	17.9	19.0	23.0

Sources: BMF *Finanzberichte,* 1985; 1986; 1987; author's own calculations.

Table 6.7 Exchange rates (trade weighted) and relative export prices (1982 = 100), balance of trade and current accounts: Sweden, 1982–1986

	1982	1983	1984	1985	1986
Effective rate of exchange (index)	100	89.7	93.1	93.9	93.7
Relative export prices (index)	100	97	99	99	100
Trade balance (billions of U.S. $)	1.0	3.1	4.7	3.3	5.8
Current accounts (% of GDP)	−3.3	−1.1	0.1	−1.5	−0.5

Source: OECD Economic Outlook 38. Values for 1985 and 1986 are OECD prognoses.

Since the budget could no longer be used in the offensive against unemployment, increased economic growth became the most important factor in stabilizing employment. The government counted on achieving this growth almost exclusively by revitalizing Sweden's export industry. The overly high devaluation, the effect of which was intensified by the rise in the dollar's exchange rate and the American boom, provided a much more substantial boost than any subsidy programs by the previous government. But the government's plans could be realized only if the competitive advantages produced by the devaluation led to an increase in export quantity and hence in production and employment at home. These expectations were fulfilled only in part (Table 6.7).

It seems that the huge devaluation did not significantly reduce the prices of Swedish exports, so that the subsequent improvement in the balance of trade must have owed more to the improvement in worldwide economic conditions than to the price competitiveness of Swedish exports. Still, the devaluation was not without effect, but its success derived more from the lessons of neoclassical supply-side economics, about which the Social Democrats and the unions were skeptical, than from the Keynesian logic on which the government had counted (Faxén and Normann, 1984). When, as the EFO model had assumed, firms set their prices by the world market, without taking the effects of devaluation into account, and when unions are ready and able to tolerate the consequent rise in import prices without demanding offsetting wage compensation, then profits should rise, as they did in the Swedish case. And as soon as profits exceeded the yield on investment in Swedish or foreign government loans, businesses began to reinvest them within Sweden. This is the simple logic of supply-side economics, which was confirmed rather than contradicted by the Swedish data (Table 6.8). After 1982 wages were somewhat below the inflation rate, real unit labor costs fell, profits increased, and when they surpassed the interest rate on loans, investment, production, and employment all increased. The only question is how this turn to the supply side came about.

Table 6.8 Indicators of Swedish economic performance, 1981–1984
(changes from the previous year in % unless otherwise indicated)

	1981	1982	1983	1984
Consumer prices	12.1	8.6	8.9	8.0
Industrial wages	10.5	7.5	8.0	9.6
Unit labor costs	9.6	4.9	5.4	—
Profits (% of capital stock)	7.0	8.7	11.5	12.9
Interest on government loans (%)	13.5	13.0	12.3	12.0
Gross capital investment	−5.3	−1.1	1.1	3.6
Industrial production	−2.0	−1.0	6.2	6.5
Employment	−0.2	−0.1	0.1	0.7

Sources: OECD *Economic Outlook* 38; OECD *Economic Surveys: Sweden*, 1985.

The Social Democrats had linked devaluation to the promise that wage increases would be sufficiently restrained to quash inflation and to provide a competitive advantage for Sweden's exports. They took it for granted that the unions would support them, believing that the failure of incomes policy under previous governments had resulted from political tensions and conflicts that no longer existed. Objectively speaking, higher economic growth coupled with reduced inflation was in the interest of the workers, and it was now the joint task of the government and the unions to realize that interest. But as the following years showed, Prime Minister Olof Palme and his finance minister, Feldt, had great difficulties in translating their economically plausible strategy into practice. The Swedish unions of the 1980s no longer resembled those of the 1950s and 1960s, as government politicians had known them. Then it had been possible for Prime Minister Erlander to agree on wages in informal conversations with the LO leader, but now the LO leadership was no longer able to enter into such arrangements on its own.

The structural changes in the union movement that emerged in the late 1960s were suppressed by agreement on the EFO model but became almost irresistible in the 1970s. The organizational strength of the white-collar unions had continued to increase. After both of the umbrella organizations, the TCO and the SACO, failed to prevail in their competition to represent all of them, the white-collar unions organized a bargaining cartel, the PTK, in 1973. This organization represented all white-collar unions in peak (centralized) negotiations with the association of private employers (SAF) and with nationalized industry (SFO). Similar cartels represented the individual public sector unions in their negotiations with national and local governments. In both sectors there were thus organizations that could legitimately claim to define the workers' interest and to develop appropriate bargaining strategies of their own that directly challenged LO's traditional claim of leadership. From the outset there had been conflicts of interest over wage differentials. While the LO had made it a high priority to abolish them, the PTK unions found this increasingly problematic as they succeeded in organizing more qualified and highly placed employees. In addition, there were political tensions between the social democratic unions in the LO and the politically neutral white-collar and government workers' unions, whose members tended to sympathize with the Conservatives, the Liberals, or the Communists (who in Sweden correspond in many respects to the West German Green party [Micheletti, 1985]).

Union rivalry also reflected the intense controversy about the workers' fund, whose issues can only be touched on here (Meidner, 1978; Öhman, 1982). The controversy had its roots in the leftist or radical democratic criticism of the compromises accepted by the Social Democrats during the postwar era. These criticisms increased in scope and intensity after the mid–1960s (Martin, 1984; Esping-Andersen, 1985). Within the LO unions they were initially manifested in demands for codetermination at the firm or plant level, which were shared by the white-collar unions and were enacted into law by a wide majority in the "lottery parliament" between 1973 and 1976. When codetermination proved to be something of a disappointment, the unions pinned their hopes on a plan developed by Rudolf Meidner to give workers a greater share in the ownership of capital assets. This plan, which was developed under the auspices of the LO, was influenced by similar proposals in the Federal Republic in the 1960s, but it opted clearly for a "collective solution" that would transfer capital shares to workers' funds organized by regions. Although the white-collar unions and the Liberal party were initially sympathetic to the plan, the proposal led to ideological polarization in the second half of the 1970s such as Swedish politics had not seen since the 1940s.

Radicals within the LO unions and left-wing Social Democrats saw the workers' fund as a means of promoting socialism through the "socialization of the investment function." On the other hand, conservatives, soon followed by most of the self-employed, skilled workers, and professionals, interpreted it as a unilateral abrogation of the postwar "Swedish model," which had been based on a pragmatic combination of capitalist production and social democratic distribution. The Social Democrats won the election in 1982 and, with the help of the Communists, enacted a watered-down version of the fund proposal, despite the lack of consensus that Swedish governments usually seek in matters of structural reform (Elder and Thomas, 1982; Anton, 1980). This act confirmed the worst fears of the centrist camp and was taken as proof that the Left was playing power politics plain and simple.

It did not matter that the finance minister explained over and over again that the regional funds (financed by a tax on windfall profits and limited in their acquisition of shares) were not the first step toward socialism but the first and last step toward the workers' funds and nothing else. In October 1983, to their own surprise, private employers succeeded in organizing their first mass demonstration in Stockholm: 75,000 entrepreneurs and white-collar employees marched to protest against the funds. For the Social Democrats and the unions, this demonstration also symbolized the end of the Left's ideological hegemony in Sweden. From now on, neoliberal and neoconservative notions enjoyed a degree of attention and respectability that was incompatible with the monopoly position that the Social Democrats and LO had achieved in the late 1950s and 1960s. In the 1980s, at any rate, their definitions of political and moral goals and their interpretation of the economic situation would no longer be accepted without challenge by the centrist parties and the other unions. This was also true for wage policy. The desirability of greater income equality was no longer accepted as a moral given, and a new generation of neoclassical or monetarist economists hardly even understood the economic policy functions attributed to a solidaristic wage policy in the Rehn-Meidner model.

Moreover, the structural conditions that permitted wage settlements oriented toward the condition of the economy as a whole have deteriorated considerably. Within the LO unions themselves the movement toward democratization in the early 1970s has strengthened the rank and file in the plants and made them more independent of the central leadership. Union leaders can no longer prevent wage drift and local strikes by ordering the rank and file to support government policy. The "compensation clauses" that had governed the structure of wage negotiations since the 1970s have become even more critical. They were particularly important in the public sector, where there were no negotiations at the individual plant level and no inherent tendency to wage drift. Thus public sector wage agreements generally include compensation for wage drift in the private sector. Similar clauses are included in PTK contracts linking white-collar wages to blue-collar wage increases, and they are even used by blue-collar unions in branches that would otherwise be immune to wage drift. Compensation is now nearly universal, so that everyone is compensated whenever anyone else receives an increase in wages or benefits. Thus, when piece rates increase in the export industry, pastors' salaries must also increase. Such circumstances are surely not conducive to the implementation of a program to generate high profits in export industries while keeping general wage increases down.

Finally, the employers' association (SAF) had temporarily abandoned centralized wage negotiations under the pressure of employers in the metal industry, and in 1984 wages were negotiated by branch in all industries. One reason for this change was the growing irritation of large firms at the increasing detail of central bargaining agreements. These firms hoped that in negotiations with branch unions they would be able to achieve greater wage differentiation and more flexible wage structures. Moreover, employers were still under the impression of the general strike of 1980 and its consequences, feeling that centralization could no longer guarantee industrial peace and moderate wage increases. But if the employers had hoped that decentralization would lead to wage settlements that were distinguished between various industrial branches on the basis of their ability to pay, they were disappointed. On the contrary, in 1984 the wage push generated by the ubiquitous compensation clauses was accelerated by wage competition among blue-collar unions, which were no longer guided by the average increase specified by the LO but by the highest settlements obtained in individual branches. Even though the LO was not strong enough to prevent the decentralization that many of its member unions supported, solidarity among LO unions was still sufficiently high to reinforce the bargaining power of unions in the weaker branches through officially approved sympathy strikes. In the light of these experiences, the SAF once again returned to centralized negotiations in the bargaining rounds of 1985–86.

The institutional conditions were thus anything but favorable when the government announced explicit guidelines for an incomes policy in late 1983, for the first time in several decades. The inflation rate (which was 8.9 percent in 1983 and had eaten into the competitive advantage gained by the devaluation) was projected to be 5 percent in 1984 and 3 percent in 1985. The government wanted wage increases to be limited to 6 percent in 1984 and 5 percent in 1985. The bargaining rounds for 1984 were already concluded, however, with an average wage increase of over 9 percent. The 1985 round of wage talks began in March 1984 with a public sector wage agreement that was nominally within the upper limit of the guidelines. But since the agreement also contained a clause guaranteeing full compensation for wage drift in the private sector, real wages in the public sector were well above the guidelines. For unions in the industrial sector, whose members had suffered real wage losses nearly every year since 1977, this was a provocation. They set out to obtain even higher wages for their members than public sector unions had obtained for theirs. Had they abided by government guidelines, they would have had to accept no wage increase, owing to the effect of previous compensation clauses and wage drift. In fact the wage increase in the metal industry was over 9 percent, and the PTK won an additional increase for its members of over 6 percent during supplemental negotiations in June 1984.

The government was alarmed and reacted in spring 1984 by imposing a short-term wage and price freeze to dramatize the seriousness of the situation. At the same time it invited the unions and employers in the private sector to summit discussions on an incomes policy. The public sector employers and unions were not invited, since they had complied, at least nominally, with the guidelines. The result was predictable, despite sympathy with government goals on the part of the LO, PTK, and SAF. Neither employers nor the unions felt able to hold wage increases down effectively. The unions had old scores to settle, and the export boom gave employers every incentive to avoid strikes. Both sides criticized the government for its economically irresponsible accommodation of the public sector unions (where the government had merely anticipated high agreements in industry). In short, the guidelines were obeyed neither in 1984 nor in 1985. Instead of the desired inflation rates of 5 and 3 percent, price increases were 8 percent in 1984 and 7.4 percent in 1985 (OECD *Economic Outlook* 39, May 1986).

The government thus did not reach its ambitious goals of stabilization, but neither was its economic policy a complete failure. Swedish inflation rates did fall, helped by the decreasing oil prices, and the strong revaluation of the West German mark against the dollar gave a further boost to Sweden's export industry. Moreover, after the shock of Olof Palme's assassination, the wage rounds of 1986 were closer to the government guidelines than in previous years. Unlike events under the centrist governments, the competitive advantage gained by devaluation was thus not immediately undercut by wage and price increases. Unemployment, which had reached a high of 3.5 percent in 1983, again fell well below 3 percent.

Nevertheless, basic problems remain. The solidaristic wage policy of the LO is unpopular with white-collar and public employee unions. Appropriate coordination could perhaps overcome the structural problems this creates for organized labor. But the more important underlying conflict of interest cannot be so easily papered over. On the one hand, rapid technological development has increased the demand for highly qualified skilled workers: technicians, engineers, information science specialists, marketing specialists, and managers. On the other, the success of the solidaristic wage policy has apparently diminished the willingness of workers to obtain the qualifications needed to fill these positions.

In any case, the export boom has created skill shortages that strengthen the bargaining power of precisely those groups whose interests are most inimical to the LO goal of leveling incomes (Micheletti, 1985; De Geer et al., 1986).

The Swedish Social Democrats and the LO unions face different dilemmas. The Social Democrats can maintain their majority only if they win the support of the highly qualified specialists and technicians (Esping-Andersen, 1985). Moreover, structural modernization, which is increasingly at the forefront of economic policy discussions, depends on the qualifications and productivity of this group of workers. Thus the Social Democrats have good political and economic reasons for meeting their demands, but the Social Democrats dare not jeopardize their alliance with the blue-collar labor unions. The unions in the LO for their part cannot prevent the white-collar employees from gaining salary increases, but they are strong enough to push through compensation clauses for their memberships. The end result of this conflict could be a wage spiral that threatens full employment. Under current conditions, an economically efficient incomes policy is not consistent with increased distributive equality. So far, the LO has been unwilling to accept this fact.

Therefore, although the "Swedish model" has met the challenges of the 1980s, its partial successes now owe more to favorable special circumstances than to the pursuit of a coherent social democratic strategy as in the 1970s. The Swedish Social Democrats and unions see clearly that they must find a new path, but they are less agreed than ever about the direction to travel: "forward" to egalitarian democratic socialism or "backward" to the Western European norm of crisis management—mitigated by a commitment to the welfare state and an active employment policy, but nevertheless compelled to respect the requirements of international capitalism with no ifs, ands, or buts.

CHAPTER SEVEN

The Federal Republic of Germany:
The Limits of Antagonistic Cooperation

Keynesian theory and practice came later and under more dramatic conditions to the Federal Republic than to other comparable nations. The "economic miracle" of the postwar years was generally interpreted, when it was attributed to government policy at all, as a success of supply-side economics rather than of demand management. As a consequence of the wartime destruction, domestic demand for consumer and investment goods was almost unlimited, as long as consumers and investors had enough faith in the future to borrow. Based on the spectacular successes of currency reform and decontrol of the economy, Ludwig Erhard's economic policy generated precisely this faith in the future. Moreover, the worldwide boom caused by the Korean War brought German exports back onto the world market and rapidly eliminated a current account deficit that had once seemed immutable. Given these conditions, the economic miracle depended on only two further factors: German prices had to remain internationally competitive under fixed rates of exchange, and domestic production had to remain profitable for investors. The economic policy of the 1950s and early 1960s saw to it that both conditions were met (Hennings, 1982).

The Bank Deutscher Länder, which later became the Deutsche Bundesbank (German Federal Bank), pursued a consistent policy of limiting the scope for price increases in the domestic market after the inflationary phase immediately following the currency reform, which had forced a massive devaluation of the mark. Government fiscal policy offered large tax incentives for private investment but held domestic consumer demand in check by collecting substantial surpluses to finance future rearmament. Then, at the end of the actual reconstruction period in the late 1950s, the legislature liquidated the fund, thereby stimulating aggregate demand. Thus the fiscal policy of the federal government had a countercyclical, stabilizing effect on aggregate demand, although neither Economics Minister Erhard nor Finance Minister Fritz Schäffer planned things that way—nor would they have approved of such a design.

The unions in the early 1950s were still haunted by the impression of wartime destruction and postwar dismantling of plant and equipment, widespread unemployment, and the undiminished stream of refugees from the east. For them, jobs were all-important—much more important than wage increases. While they prevented wages from falling (Lutz, 1984), their reluctance to ask for wage increases permitted investments to be financed from profits during the early reconstruction period that was characterized by extreme capital shortages.

When the German unions reorganized on an industry basis after the war, they pinned their hopes on the development of codetermination within firms and industries and throughout the whole economy. They hoped to participate fully and equally with management and government in the formulation and execution of decisions in enterprises and of public economic policy. Their goal was to transform their members from economic subjects to economic citizens. These hopes were disappointed. The Adenauer government, despite a national protest strike, refused to extend the coal and steel model of equal codetermination to all firms covered by the business constitution act of 1951. The coal and steel model dated from the early postwar years and owed its existence to Allied distrust of German heavy industry, but now times had changed. At the same time, the neoliberal hostility to planning that characterized Erhard's economic policy also gave little purchase for union demands for macroeconomic codetermination.

It was only after the consolidation of capitalism had buried the hopes for codetermination of the early postwar years that the German unions became more interested in distributional issues. Victor Agartz, the leftist theorist of the union movement, developed the concept of an active wage policy to redistribute income between capital and labor (Agartz, 1953; Markovits and Allen, 1984). Nonetheless, actual wage increases remained moderate, and wages did not become a concern of government economic policy makers until the early 1960s, with the onset of the labor shortage that followed the erection of the Berlin Wall. Even then government reaction was limited to moral suasion directed at the negotiating parties to moderate their demands. Erhard rejected any kind of interventionism as a matter of principle; he even opposed establishing a council of economic advisers. The German central bank finally lost patience with Erhard's continued passivity despite an overheated economy and used its monetary authority to bring the postwar economic boom to a screeching halt in 1965. The end was so abrupt that it caused the Federal Republic's first recession, with more than half a million unemployed. This brought the Social Democrats into the federal government for the first time in autumn 1966, as part of the Grand Coalition (with the moderate Keynesian Karl Schiller as minister of economics).

Erhard's fall discredited neoliberal economics in the Federal Republic for the time being and opened the gates to the active management of aggregate demand as practiced in the United States and nearly all other Western nations. The German approach to macroeconomic control was enacted by the Stability and Growth Act of 1967, which largely reflected the Keynesian ideas of the Social Democratic party (SPD). The act committed the federal and state governments to countercyclical fiscal policy, but contrary to Keynesian logic it left the autonomy of the central bank entirely unimpaired. The only way the federal government could influence the bank was through the "Concerted Action" program, whereby the bank would be morally but not legally bound by a broad consensus (Adam, 1972; Hardes, 1974). Schiller made good use of the possibilities of informal understandings in the first years of the act but did not take advantage of the chance for institutional consolidation.

As a result, the recession was quickly overcome by an almost ideal coordination of macroeconomic control instruments. The central bank, surprised by the effectiveness of its tight money policy, returned to a less restrictive monetary policy; the federal government enacted a series of supplementary budgets authorizing increased outlays for public investment at all levels of government; and the unions accepted agreements that were even below the targets in Schiller's annual economic report. From today's perspective it seems evident that the rapid success of these measures (Table 7.1) was primarily due to the looser monetary policy and secondarily to the unions' restraint in their wage demands. Given fixed exchange rates and the Vietnam War boom, these factors made possible robust growth in German exports. The public works program, on the other hand, received a great deal of attention at the time, but circumstances prevented it from getting under way until after the recovery had started. Direct fiscal stimulus in the form of outlays for public investment, therefore, had procyclical rather than countercyclical effects (Kock, 1975; Reissert, 1984).

Despite this success, Concerted Action did not lead to stable and viable corporatist institutions in the Federal Republic (Bonß, 1980). From the beginning it was not conceived as a decision-making body but as a forum for discussion, where the Ministry of Economics, the central bank, the top employer organizations, and the unions could meet and exchange

Table 7.1 Unemployment (as % of dependent work force members), GDP growth, consumer prices, standard hourly wages, gross wages per worker, and unit labor costs in industry (changes from previous year in %): Federal Republic, 1965–1970

	1965	1966	1967	1968	1969	1970
Unemployment	0.7	0.7	2.1	1.5	0.8	0.7
GDP growth	5.5	2.9	−0.1	5.6	7.5	5.1
Consumer prices	3.4	3.5	1.4	2.9	1.9	3.4
Standard wages	7.2	10.7	4.6	4.3	6.6	11.2
Effective wages	8.8	6.9	3.0	6.4	8.9	15.0
Unit labor costs	2.8	4.9	−0.6	−0.8	3.9	10.4

Sources: OECD Historical Statistics, 1960–1983; SVR, 1971–72; 1977–78.

their views of the macroeconomic situation. The attitude of employers and the central bank toward Concerted Action was one of benign skepticism from the outset: it could not hurt, and it might be useful to keep the unions in line. The unions' reaction to the federal government's invitation to join the forum was more ambivalent. They could not turn it down after having tried for so long to convince Erhard that economic policy making should be more public. Moreover, the invitation reawakened the hope that they might yet achieve macroeconomic codetermination and play an active role in economic and social planning. On the other hand, they saw serious risks for the autonomy of collective bargaining agreements and hence for their own function.

Even before Concerted Action, the unions had favored a formula according to which wage increases should be approximately governed by the growth in productivity plus the expected rate of inflation (Markovits and Allen, 1984:126ff.). But that was not the same as respecting government guidelines or bargaining over future wages within the constraints of Concerted Action. The reasons for this reservation about any form of explicit incomes policy are the same in principle as in the other three nations, but in the Federal Republic they were more compelling than elsewhere.

In international comparison, the German labor unions are relatively weak (Table 7.2). Germany's constitution and its labor law outlaw the closed shop and the union shop, which are taken for granted in other countries. Unions cannot seek special consideration for their members in wage negotiations. Their officers are not even permitted to represent their members to management within individual plants, except where they win elections for works council seats—and are willing to stick to the union line thereafter (Streeck, 1981; 1984). Thus the German unions are much closer to voluntary organizations than are unions in Austria,

Table 7.2 Degree of organization in national umbrella associations of unions, early 1970s

	Austria	FRG	GB	Sweden
Degree of organization in %	58	35–40	45–50	85

Source: von Beyme, 1977.

Sweden, or Great Britain. Their authority over their members and their ability to regulate wage levels through collective bargaining thus depend entirely on the ability of union leadership to gauge the mood of its members, management's bargaining strength, and the current economic situation and to react tactically to all of these factors in setting realistic goals. Any commitment in advance would impair the unions' capacity to react and would thus undermine their ability to control wages and working conditions altogether.

The unions had an additional internal problem. Wage policy was and is the responsibility of the individual unions. As early as the 1950s the central committee of the German Labor Union Federation (DGB) had been unable to fulfill its statutory function of coordination because of the dominance of the large individual unions, especially the metalworkers, and it even avoided the internal consultations about a wage policy line that might still have been possible. The DGB thus would not have been in a position to speak for the unions as a whole in Concerted Action meetings. On the other hand, the presidents of the large individual unions represented there could have determined the union line for any bargaining round through their sheer "weight," but the niceties of interunion diplomacy precluded recognition of this influence in negotiations with the employers and with the government. On the employers' side the situation was similar. Negotiations about wage policy or binding agreements with the government on the pattern of the British Social Contract were simply not possible for the German unions within the framework of the Concerted Action program.

Nevertheless, informal and open discussions between the presidents of the major unions and the employer organizations on the one side and the responsible federal ministers and the president of the central bank on the other served a purpose in the early years. They increased each side's understanding of the other's perspective on the economic situation, as well as of the constraints that it faced and its goals. Each participant knew where the others stood and what could be expected of them. This benefit, which Schiller probably underestimated, was reduced as the number of participants was increased. Not wishing to be excluded, the farmers, the private banks, the retail trades, their individual unions, and so on wanted to take part. At the same time powerful political figures like the minister of finance and the minister of labor tired of their role as extras in Schiller's show and sent officials to represent them. Discussions in the original small group setting had been serious and controversial but were still aimed at mutual understanding. This was no longer the case after meetings of Concerted Action became media events where leaders read prepared statements and negotiations about the closing statement were conducted two weeks in advance at the staff level.

The unions had hoped to participate in social planning. But that had never been the purpose of Concerted Action. Instead, from 1969 on, the meetings turned more and more into a concerted criticism by other participants of "excessive wage demands." In short, participation in Concerted Action had become increasingly unpleasant for the union leaders, and after Schiller's resignation in summer 1972 and his replacement by Hanns Friedrichs of the Liberal Democratic party (FDP) that fall, even the government no longer seemed to know what to do with the institution. Nonetheless, it dragged along for several more years before employers launched a constitutional challenge to the codetermination compromise of 1977, which finally gave the unions the pretext to end their participation. But I anticipate later events.

In the first years of Concerted Action the elements needed to ensure success were present to a certain degree. Moreover, the unions, which had expected pressure to reduce wages, were relieved that Schiller's macroeconomic picture included real wage increases and envisioned the future reestablishment of "social symmetry." Wage agreements in 1967 and 1968 were close to or even below Schiller's projections on average (Adam, 1972:54). The central bank was thus able to retain its expansionary monetary policy without jeopardizing price stability, and after 1968 government investment programs began to take effect. At the same time moderate domestic price increases and the worldwide Vietnam War boom caused German exports to grow so fast that the revaluation of the German mark demanded by Schiller and refused by the Christian Democratic Union (CDU) and the Christian Social Union (CSU) became the dominant issue during the parliamentary campaign of 1969. In sum, 1969 was a dream year for economic policy. Inflation was 1.9 percent, real economic growth rose to a high of 7.5 percent, and unemployment was down to 0.8 percent.

For the unions, however, 1969 became a year of crisis. They had accepted wage settlements that were in keeping with the overly cautious forecasts of the Ministry of Economics. Now the legal obligation to abide by agreements and keep the peace prohibited them from demanding supplemental negotiations, while firm profits exploded and effective wages, with labor in short supply, left standard wages far behind. Then in the "hot autumn" of that year wildcat strikes broke out all over West Germany, forcing employers to grant wage concessions they had previously denied the unions. At this point the unions had only one priority. They needed to wipe out the distributive setback they had suffered and to reinstate their seriously damaged authority in the plants. Wage increases in industry for 1970 and 1971 were thus far above the rates of increase of the past years, and even the increase in unit labor costs was clearly above the inflation rate. After this show of strength, however, the unions were willing to return to a policy of moderate wage increases guided by productivity growth and expected inflation (Table 7.3).

But in the meantime prospects for macroeconomic control had worsened considerably in the Federal Republic. Because the American government financed the Vietnam War with bank notes instead of through higher taxes, the dollar supply available worldwide increased and with it the average inflation rate in the Western industrial nations. Countries with above-average price stability were expected to revalue their currencies and thus attracted speculative capital streams, especially when, like the Federal Republic, they were enjoying high trade surpluses. When the Bundesbank tried to neutralize the influx of capital through a tight money policy, it only made the German mark more attractive to international speculators. Only massive revaluation would have helped the situation, but during the Grand Coalition such a move was blocked by the CDU and CSU. In the following years revaluations, pushed through over the loud protests of trade associations, were always too little and too late to staunch the inflow of speculative capital.

Since demand pull from abroad could not be stopped, the government and the central bank were all the more interested in restricting the domestic cost push. The unions were thus placed under considerable pressure in the Concerted Action meetings. From their point of view,

Table 7.3 Consumer prices, standard hourly wages, real hourly wages, and unit labor costs in industry (changes from previous year in %): Federal Republic, 1970–1975

	1970	1971	1972	1973	1974	1975
Consumer prices	3.4	5.3	5.5	6.9	7.0	6.0
Industrial wages	12.4	13.3	8.5	9.8	12.0	9.1
Real wages	8.7	7.7	2.8	2.6	4.7	2.9
Unit labor costs	10.4	8.9	5.7	7.9	9.4	6.9

Sources: OECD *Historical Statistics*, 1960–1983; SVR, 1977–78.

however, such criticism showed not only a complete lack of understanding of the internal problems with which they had been contending since 1969 but also a denial of the "social symmetry" in Keynesian economic policy that Schiller had promised earlier. If wage restraint was the key to overcoming the recession and to fighting inflation, when would the distributive claims of the workers finally be met? The only economically plausible answer might have been some form of wealth sharing. But this answer could not be proposed as long as the German unions remained deeply divided about the way in which wealth was to be shared. The metalworkers' union in particular was adamant in its refusal to accept the one model that could have won political consensus: individual stock ownership, which in their view would have turned the workers into "little capitalists."

At any rate, the unions had to make up foregone wages in 1970 and 1971 and were, for internal reasons, unable to respond to appeals for wage moderation issued by the federal government and the central bank. But apparently they still accepted their joint responsibility for the climbing rate of inflation. Wage agreements in 1972 were lower again and unit labor costs were stabilized. Nevertheless, inflation continued to increase. The social-liberal coalition's majority in the legislature was waning, and it lacked the strength to push through Schiller's recommended revaluation. The central bank's attempts to stabilize the money supply were defeated by the influx of foreign funds. Thus from the union point of view, the sacrifices they had made on behalf of stabilization were worthless. They had merely increased firm profits and accelerated wage drift. Because the government seemed unable to protect the Federal Republic from the worldwide tendency to inflation, the unions now had to adjust to inflationary expectations as well. The wage negotiations of 1973 reflected this change of mind, with demands aiming at a substantial redistribution of incomes and anticipating further increases in the rate of inflation.

From the central bank's perspective, committed as it was to stable prices over any other economic policy goal, the unions' wage demands were a catastrophe, especially since the bank no longer considered the federal government a reliable ally. Alex Möller stepped down as finance minister in 1971 because he could no longer hold his own in the cabinet against the spending plans of the departments. Willy Brandt gave workers in the Ruhr region an unconditional guarantee of full employment without mentioning wage restraint as a necessary precondition. Karl Schiller's resignation in summer 1972 gave the public a further signal. Finally, during the 1972 elections even Helmut Schmidt declared that 5 percent inflation was preferable to 5 percent unemployment. Thus after

Willy Brandt's election landslide in autumn 1972, the Bundesbank feared that social democratic reform and expenditure programs would no longer be constrained by voluntary moderation.

It was no wonder that the central bank deployed all possible administrative means to contain at least the foreign risks to economic stability and accepted direct exchange controls as part of the bargain. But its ultimate goal remained a changeover to flexible exchange rates. This goal was finally achieved in spring 1973, after a series of crises over the dollar and revaluations of the mark and a number of failed attempts to save the Bretton Woods regime of fixed exchange rates (Black, 1977).

Most economists, especially those of a neoclassical or monetarist bent, had for some time recommended floating exchange rates, which would continuously adjust the external value of a currency to its internal purchasing power. With the demise of fixed exchange rates, every country was free to decouple itself from the international "inflation alliance" and to pursue its own goal of stability undisturbed by speculative influxes of foreign currency. Because rates of exchange were continuously adjusted by the market, theorists also expected no extreme fluctuations in exchange rates that could attract currency speculation. These theoretical expectations were thoroughly disappointed, however. Speculators seemed to consider many factors more important than the differences in national inflation rates, and when exchange rates were no longer set by governmental policy, there was no fixed point of orientation for the currency trade, and hence no plausible upper and lower limits for future rates. As a consequence, it was only now that currency speculation could really take off.

Nevertheless, the transition to floating exchange rates markedly improved conditions for the Bundesbank's policy of stability. According to the Federal Bank Act, monetary policy was the bank's responsibility, but setting the rates of exchange had been a government matter. And it was precisely the politically motivated delay in adjusting the exchange rate that had not only attracted inflationary money inflows from abroad but also caused import prices to rise. But with flexible rates of exchange, the government's responsibility for currency rates lost its practical significance. It was replaced by currency markets and the factors influencing them. Among these factors were direct interventions in the currency markets, which continued to be dependent on government approval. Much more important in practice, however, are the regular operations of interest and money supply policy.

If a currency is attractive to international investors, as the German mark was in the 1970s, then tight money and high interest rates will attract international capital, improve the balance of payments, and thus raise the rate of exchange. Import prices will fall, and the pressure on export prices will restrain domestic price levels. However, the influx of foreign currency must be "sterilized," for instance by increasing the minimum reserves in the banks and also by additional tightening of credit for households and firms, which have no access to the international capital market. Revaluation can thus substantially increase the effectiveness of a national stabilization policy, but only if it is conducted as part of a consistently tight monetary policy. To be sure, it also intensifies the undesirable effects of a restrictive policy on domestic production and employment by making imports more competitive and by depressing profits in the exposed sector. But the politically decisive factor is that with flexible exchange rates this effective weapon of revaluation passed from the hand of government into that of the independent central bank.

The economic policy consequences of transferring responsibility for the exchange rate to the central bank, whose priority is price stability, were not noticed at the time, or at least they were not addressed in political and technical discussions. From today's perspective the importance of the move becomes clear as soon as one raises the hypothetical question whether any national government would have been able to shoulder political responsibility for the extreme revaluation of the German mark against the U.S. dollar and to a lesser extent against the currencies of its other trade partners in 1973. Still, one can guess that Helmut Schmidt, who negotiated the transition from the Bretton Woods system to flexible exchange rates during his time as finance minister, saw these implications sooner than other political figures. As chancellor, at any rate, he worked hard to build the European Monetary System, which limited the fluctuations of exchange rates between participating countries. The central bank was highly skeptical about these efforts, in part because they removed exchange rates between West Germany and its important European trading partners from the direct control of monetary policy and placed then again within the government's sphere of responsibility. But I am again anticipating historical developments.

Speculation against the dollar reached a new high in 1973. It did not diminish despite a renewed devaluation of the dollar in February and extreme discrimination against foreign investment under the Bundesbank's minimum reserve policy. In early March currency exchanges were closed for two weeks. When they reopened, the transition to floating rates was complete. Central banks were no longer obliged to intervene in support of the U.S. dollar, and at the same time six Common Market countries (the Federal Republic, France, the Benelux countries, and Denmark) as well as Norway and Sweden (and Austria too, in a practical sense) agreed to float their currencies jointly. By limiting fluctuations within this "snake" of floating currencies, it was possible to calculate the rates of exchange at least between the Federal Republic and its close trading partners with some certainty. However, in the following years, not all of these countries were ready or willing to imitate the German stabilization policy. Sweden and France left the European Monetary System permanently or temporarily in order to protect their competitive position, while new countries joined the "snake" under conditions that allowed their currency to fluctuate within greater margins.

Initially, dollar outflows pushed the German mark to the bottom of the European "snake," which finally gave the Bundesbank the chance to pursue price stabilization undisturbed by foreign economic events. By April 1973 consumer prices were up 7 percent, and the bank saw every reason to take drastic measures. It more than doubled the discount rate, from 3 percent in autumn 1972 to 7 percent in July 1973, where it remained until October 1974. It also retained the restrictions on the money supply that had been introduced to neutralize foreign money and reduced the rediscount quota of banks still further. The federal government also contributed to the bank's tight money policy by raising a forced loan whose proceeds were neutralized by the central bank. As a consequence, the free liquidity reserves of the banks sank to zero in May (Bundesbank, 6/73:7ff.). But because the inflation rate kept rising, the government decided to introduce a second stabilization program in May, which taxed private investment and added a surcharge to income and corporate taxes. At the same time public expenditures were reduced or stretched out over longer periods of time.

Thus, following the shift to floating exchange rates, the central bank and the federal government acted in concert to slam on the brakes. The money supply (M1) actually fell and at year's end was still 2.9 percent below what it had been in March. At the same time the discount rate for bank loans increased rapidly, from 5.38 percent in August 1972 to 12.37 percent in August 1973 (Bundesbank, 2/74). These measures were highly effective in transforming the boom into a homemade recession. Even the inflation rate for consumer prices, which had reached its high in June with 7.6 percent, receded to 6.2 percent by September. But afterward, it rose again until the end of the year. The goals of the deflationary policy were thus not yet achieved; they were not even in sight when the oil crisis began in autumn 1973.

FIRST RESPONSES TO THE CRISIS

In the Federal Republic as elsewhere, the oil crisis was first understood as a problem of oil scarcity, which was symbolically dramatized by "carless Sundays." The limits to growth, which had previously been ignored by most, now seemed to manifest themselves as the real limits of the energy supply and were seen as direct threats to full employment and affluence in the industrialized nations. The planning bureau of the Finance Ministry, however, staffed with economists whom Helmut Schmidt had brought along from the Ministry of Economics, had a different view. From the beginning it emphasized not supply shortages but the consequences of increased energy prices for macroeconomic demand. According to its interpretation, withdrawal effects would be felt at least until the OPEC nations were able to channel their surplus income back into the world market as additional buying power. In the meantime the gap could and should be filled by increased domestic demand. These considerations were taken into account at the last minute during the federal budget discussions for 1974; the budget was thus much more expansionary than originally planned. At the same time in December the measures that had been taken to discourage investment were repealed, and in February 1974 measures were taken to promote private and public investment. The first response of government policy makers to the crisis was thus perfectly congruent with a Keynesian analysis, the perspective that had also determined policy in Austria, Great Britain, and Sweden. Because subnational jurisdictions also initially maintained their spending programs despite reduced tax revenue, the overall fiscal effect was clearly expansionary in 1974.

But the reaction of the central bank was different. Its first interpretation of the oil crisis also emphasized the problem of supply. When shortages proved not to be a problem, however, the bank saw no reason to fill any demand gaps. In its view, the real economy could absorb the income transfer effected by the OPEC cartel only by reducing real incomes in the industrial nations. Artificially induced domestic demand could not substitute for the reduction (Bundesbank, 2/74:8). For the bank the main problem caused by the oil crisis was an increase in the pressure on prices, and it was unwilling to give up its battle for stability, which had just begun in earnest, before it saw any real victories. Thus its restrictive monetary policy continued for the time being, because otherwise the increase in oil prices was likely to be followed by accelerated wage-cost inflation. As the Bundesbank saw it, all signs pointed in that direction.

MONETARY POLICY VS. WAGE POLICY

The stabilization policy mounted by the government and the central bank was unable to influence wage levels for 1973 or to halt inflation. The unions' direct contacts with the central bank and the Ministry of

Economics, which had passed to the FDP after the election in autumn 1972, had worsened considerably; it was therefore not obvious to them that appeals to stabilization were now more serious. For the rest, conditions at the beginning of the wage rounds of 1974 were highly uneven. The construction industry was in the midst of a deep depression, and sales in the automobile industry were so impaired by the oil crisis that shorter work weeks and finally widespread layoffs became necessary. Otherwise, however, the feared consequences of the oil shock remained in abeyance. Domestic demand receded perceptibly, but exports rose, against all expectations. Keynesian responses to the crisis in the other industrial nations had their effect, and domestic monetary constraint improved German competitiveness at least vis-à-vis the other members of the currency "snake." In this unclear situation negotiations in the public sector, which opened the wage round this time, sent a special signal to the other unions—and to the central bank as well.

The major union representing public sector employees (all except the railroad and postal workers) in the Federal Republic is the Public Service, Transportation, and Traffic Union (ÖTV). This union set high goals for the wage round of 1974 and prepared its campaign long beforehand. In the previous decade its main concerns had been questions of social security, structural improvements, and vacation time; now it was concerned with catching up with wages in the private sector (where the high wage drift of recent years had widened the gap). The ÖTV initially sought identical raises favoring low wage groups in the public sector. Because that was unacceptable to the federal government, where Liberal Minister of the Interior Genscher was charged with conducting negotiations, the union shifted its emphasis to high percentage increases.

The government for its part wanted a demonstration of wage moderation in the public sector. Chancellor Brandt therefore declared early on that wage agreements with double-digit percentage increases were out of the question. This provoked ÖTV leader Heinz Kluncker to do battle. Brandt's statement was interpreted as an attack on the principle of autonomous collective bargaining, obliging other unions, which had been somewhat critical of ÖTV claims and negotiating tactics, to rally to its cause. The basic situation was as follows.

The ÖTV negotiates with the federal government and the collective bargaining associations of the states and communities in a single collective bargaining round (in which the postal and railroad workers' unions participate as observers). Although several legally separate collective bargaining agreements are concluded, all the participants are committed to the results reached in the single collective bargaining round. Different terms are unusual and would be contrary to ÖTV interests, since its capacity to secure benefits for all its members derives primarily from its ability to threaten municipal governments with strikes. That strike threat is used on behalf of white-collar employees in the federal government and the states as well (and it also determines the salaries of civil servants, ministers, and deputies). Brandt's preliminary commitment—if interpreted as an exercise of the chancellor's responsibility to set guidelines—would have limited Genscher's ability to negotiate for the federal government. Such a limitation would have either split the negotiations or prejudiced the result for the states and communities. Either outcome was unacceptable to Kluncker. In the wage battle that followed, which was carried on primarily by the municipal garbage workers, in local utilities, and in public passenger service, both sides were fighting for a principle. The federal government was fighting for the credibility of its stabilization policy and for the authority of the chancellor; the ÖTV was fighting for the public sector's claim to equal pay with the private sector and for the autonomy of collective bargaining. Ultimately, the communities and states caved in under the pressure of the extremely effective and unpopular strikes, and the federal government, which had never sought a separate agreement, agreed to wage and salary increases of more than 12 percent.

For the other unions, unless they had reasons to be moderate because of the branches they represented, the ÖTV agreement guided the 1974 bargaining round. They also had initially feared the worst from an oil shortage. When the worst did not occur, they did not expect any additional impairment of the world economy, and they "certainly saw no reason to expect unfavorable developments on the labor market front" (Wirtschafts- und Sozialwissenschaftliches Institut der Gewerkschaften [WSI], 1974:79ff.). On the other hand, they thought they had learned in 1973 that the brakes applied by the central bank and the federal government hardly affected the inflation rate. From this, union economists concluded that because of the increasing concentration of markets, macroeconomic control had lost its effectiveness. When aggregate demand was limited, quantity effects appeared earlier and more markedly than the price effects. Thus, in their view, "macroeconomics has only these alternatives left: either to throttle a boom so hard that a price effect appears (while accepting the grave risks for growth and employment), or to tolerate inflation" (WSI, 1974:78). Since the first alternative seemed politically impossible, union economists anticipated even higher inflation rates and greater real economic growth in 1974 than the federal government's optimistic annual economic report had projected in February.

The wage policy of most unions followed these assumptions. Wage scales in industry rose by 12 percent in the crisis year of 1974, even more than in the previous boom year (9.8 percent). In fact, however, the 7 percent rise in consumer prices and 0.5 percent rise were both well below the government's forecasts. Unemployment averaged 600,000 in 1974, well above the projected 450,000 (which WSI had criticized as too high an estimate). By year's end the number of unemployed exceeded a million, and the number has not been significantly below that ever since. How could this have happened?

The government's capitulation in the face of the ÖTV strike damaged Willy Brandt's authority, although one cannot prove the often-asserted connection between the wage battle and his resignation in May. In any case, for the Schmidt/Genscher government that came to power in May, the goal of stabilization had a very high political priority from the outset. Helmut Schmidt was a Keynesian when it came to filling temporary demand gaps. But like Dennis Healey in Great Britain, as finance minister he had become increasingly skeptical about the pressure from social democratic legislators to increase public expenditures without also taking political responsibility for higher taxes. From his perspective, which was shared by his secretary of state and other officials who had moved from the Finance Ministry to the chancellor's office, the federal budget had been in structural deficit even before the oil price crisis began, and that deficit had to be corrected as soon as possible. This situation explains the subdued tenor of Schmidt's official address on May 17, 1974. He did not rule out the possibility of new programs, but they were accepted with resistance and as unavoidable impediments in the way of the necessary consolidation.

The necessity for additional spending programs was not apparent at first. The demand gap in the world market projected by the economists in the Finance Ministry in late autumn did not occur, and firms were able for a time to compensate for the central bank's restrictive policy by increasing their export efforts—although with much lower profit margins. The Ministry of Economics thus was more optimistic about economic developments in June than it had been in its February annual report. It warned about the danger of a new inflationary overheating in view of tax cuts and increases in family allowances already planned for 1975. In terms of fiscal policy, therefore, budgetary restraint seemed more urgent than new, countercyclical spending programs. The major part of the federal deficit of 10.3 billion marks in 1974 and 33.1 billion in 1975 was thus due not to programs inspired by economic or employment policy but to the "automatic stabilizers" of lower revenues and increased expenditures caused by the downswing in the economic cycle. Still, the federal government and the states accepted these deficits, and

according to calculations by the Deutsches Institut für Wirtschaftsforschung (DIW), they generated additional demand of about 2.5 percent
of the GNP in 1974 and more than 4 percent in 1975 (Teschner and
Vesper, 1983).

Government financial policy may not have plunged joyously into deficit, as in Austria, but it did toe the Keynesian line. The Bundesbank,
however, became all the more determined in its own conversion to monetarism. The wage agreements in the public sector and then in all economic branches had confirmed the bank's doubts about the macroeconomic good sense of the unions as well as the government's
reliability. The OPEC nations' higher income had to be absorbed by
decreases in domestic income, but now it seemed out of the question that
this could be achieved with the agreement of the unions. An intensification of the domestic distributive battle was unavoidable, but the bank
wanted at least to avoid fighting it out in an inflationary race between
wages and prices.

It is thus not fair to suggest that the Bundesbank was trying, against all
economic reason, to neutralize the inflationary effect of oil price increases by its restrictive policy. It had displayed that inflationary effect
separately in its monthly reports and it measured the distance from the
goal of stabilization against the inflation rate corrected for the effect of
oil prices. But in contrast to the national banks in Austria, Great Britain,
and Sweden (and in nearly all other Western industrial nations, except
Switzerland), the Bundesbank central committee was not prepared to
resign itself to the wage-price inflation that was a secondary effect of the
oil crisis, letting it take its course in the short run and creating price
stability as a medium-term goal. It was not enough that German inflation
rates were at the very low end of the international rates; they had to be
lowered markedly and for good, even if that impaired other goals of
economic policy.

This, I believe, is the heart of the Bundesbank's conversion to monetarism. It had made this turn as early as spring 1973, when the transition to floating exchange rates freed it from the obligation to exchange
foreign currency supplies in the banks into German marks at any time.
The central bank took advantage of this chance to reduce the increase of
the money supply to zero in summer 1973, and it maintained this policy
of extremely tight money (and extremely high interest rates) until the
Federal Republic's economy slid into the deepest recession of the postwar years in the winter of 1974–75.

The monthly and annual reports of the central bank from those years
and the reports of the Council of Economic Advisers (SVR) supporting
and explaining its policy show that government policy makers and the

social partners were clearly warned about the disastrous consequences of the threatening collision between tight money and expansionary wage and fiscal policy. Two questions are thus of interest. Why did the unions not take these warnings seriously? And why did the government not intervene to stop a deflationary monetary policy after it was clear that the wage increases of 1974 were well above the level tolerated by the central bank? As with all questions about unrealized historical options, the answers must be speculative, but they seem to me plausible in view of the perspectives of that time.

In direct contrast to the completely different responses of monetary policy in the three other nations, there is an almost conventional "institutional" answer to the second question. Its greater legal and organizational autonomy allowed the Bundesbank to pursue the goal of stabilization in opposition to the government's full employment policy. This would have been institutionally impossible in Austria, Sweden, or Great Britain. That argument is not incorrect, and I will investigate it in greater detail later. In conversations with active participants, however, this argument gets less and less support the closer the actors were to the center of government policy in those years. Even if we take into account the human inclination to harmonize cognitive dissonance, the recurring emphasis on excellent relations and close contacts between government and central bank is remarkable. Even more remarkable, it is said that Helmut Schmidt had described the monetary restraint as his own idea.

In any case, after what he considered to be disastrous public sector wage agreements, Schmidt announced that he and the president of the Bundesbank had decided to combat inflation jointly (Bundesbank, press release 17/74:1). And as in Great Britain, there was a group of politicians and top officials not only in the Ministry of Economics (led by the FDP) but also in the Finance Ministry and the chancellor's office whose view coincided with that of the central bank in many respects. They thought the expenditure policy of the SPD faction was as dangerous as the inflationary redistribution policy of the unions, and they favored a dramatic change of course. Since the legislature and the government were not politically able to bring that about, they welcomed an increase in the Bundesbank's capability for autonomous action, at least as long as personal relations with the leading members of the directorate were as good as they were at that time.

Of course, that does not mean that the Social Democrats in the federal government intentionally brought about persistent mass unemployment or even that they anticipated it as part of the bargain. The worst that they expected was a short recession, which could easily be corrected according to the pattern of 1967–68. At the same time, there are indications that economic policy makers underestimated the importance of the monetary supply for economic and employment policy. Even the Bundesbank often spoke of a division of roles according to which monetary policy was charged with "keeping the money supply tight," while fiscal policy was to "compensate for the reduced domestic demand due to the higher oil prices by moving to a cautiously expansionary course" (Schlesinger, 1975:1; Bundesbank, 1974:18). Such a (theoretically nonsensical) description probably satisfied the "fiscal" Keynesians in the federal government. Furthermore, while the government would probably have been able to win an open political battle with the central bank, the loss of confidence in the financial press and in national and international capital markets could have had results like those in Great Britain in 1976. In short, the leading people in the federal government probably agreed more or less with the Bundesbank's policy in 1974, and they would have incurred a high political cost had they tried to change it.

Thus the search for an explanation for the Federal Republic's path into its employment crisis reduces to the question why the unions did not, at the last moment, avoid a collision with the central bank's deflationary policy. I consider it crucial that the unions in 1974 did not yet believe in the economic effectiveness of monetary constraint. Their doubts derived not only from the bitter experiences of 1969 and 1972, when their goodwill in reaching low wage agreements was punished by climbing profits, rising inflation rates, and a rising wage drift, but also, and to an even greater extent, from the insidious coincidence of theoretical models of interpretation with atypical real events.

In the "bastard Keynesianism" (the phrase is Joan Robinson's) of American provenance, which was adopted in the Federal Republic and implemented by the Stabilization and Growth Act of 1967, fiscal policy was considered by far the most important instrument of countercyclical macroeconomic control. But that theory still assumed that monetary policy would follow fiscal policy and assigned it a subordinate and supporting role. German Keynesians, in their enthusiasm about the "Keynesian" solution to the recession, initially ignored the fact that under the institutional conditions of the Federal Republic, the leading role of fiscal policy was not a foregone conclusion, just as they lost sight of the fact that the restrictive policy of the central bank had caused the recession of 1966. Moreover, German monetary policy had actually lost its domestic effectiveness during the decline of the Bretton Woods system. At this point, therefore, it was still possible to conduct the theoretical battle against monetarism and the concept of a "control of money supply oriented toward potential growth" as it was recommended by the Council of Economic Advisers (SVR, 1970–71:359) with plausible empirical and pragmatic arguments (Köhler, 1973). The transition to a floating exchange rate and the more effective control of the central bank money supply had changed the underlying conditions and endangered the goals of the unions, as a few experts in the Keynesian camp realized (Simmert, 1974; Pohl, 1974), but such insights came too late to influence the 1974 wage negotiations.

Moreover, union economists had become convinced that control of macroeconomic aggregates had become largely ineffective. In order to reduce the inflation rate perceptibly in concentrated markets, one would have had to curtail macroeconomic demand so rigorously that high unemployment became inevitable (WSI, 1974). According to the unions' theoretical evaluation of the instruments of economic policy, however, that was possible only if both monetary policy and government fiscal policy had continued to follow a very restrictive course. But government fiscal policy had been expansionary since autumn 1973, so the unions saw no reason to count on a major recession in 1974. Unhappily, the facts seemed to support this interpretation. When both monetary and fiscal policy were restrictive, the boom seemed to collapse and even the inflation rate began to fall in summer 1973. But when fiscal policy became expansionary in late autumn, despite monetary restraint, prices and new orders increased again.

The worldview of the unions in spring 1974 was thus not shaped by an acute consciousness of crisis. The unions counted instead on continued inflation and on relatively stable employment. Given that point of view, it was understandable that the wage round of 1974 was still determined by the distributive offensive that had begun in 1970. Since that time, the adjusted wage share had risen clearly above the long-term average of about 62 percent of national income, and in 1974 there was another leap, to a high of 66 percent (SVR, 1978–79:129). Because unemployment did not increase dramatically at first, the unions considered 1974 a successful year even in hindsight (WSI, 1975). Monetary policy and wage policy were thus on a collision course in 1974. From the unions' point of view the central bank's warnings were not credible and its exhortations were apparently motivated not by macroeconomic concerns but by distributive preferences. The bank, however, was no longer prepared to permit cost increases to be passed through into prices after what it considered the disastrous wage round of 1974. The unions had been warned; now let them take the consequences. The crash thus had become inevitable.

Predictably, the first victims were profits and investments. Gross incomes from employment rose 10 percent in 1974, but incomes from entrepreneurial activities and capital fell by 0.5 percent. In keeping with

Table 7.4 GDP growth, consumer prices, incomes from dependent employment, rents, profits, interest, and proprietors' income (changes from previous years in %); adjusted wage share, investment rate, and unemployment rate (%): Federal Republic, 1972–1979

	1972	1973	1974	1975	1976	1977	1978	1979
GDP growth	4.2	4.7	0.3	−1.6	5.4	3.0	2.9	4.2
Consumer prices	5.5	6.9	7.0	6.0	4.5	3.7	2.7	4.1
Income from employment	10.1	13.5	10.2	4.2	7.5	7.0	6.7	7.7
Rents, profits, interest, and proprietors' income	8.9	8.1	−0.5	3.0	14.8	5.0	10.8	7.6
Adjusted wage share	63.6	64.2	66.0	66.1	64.6	64.6	63.6	63.4
Investment rate	25.4	23.9	21.6	20.4	20.1	20.2	20.7	21.8
Unemployment rate	1.1	1.2	2.5	4.7	4.6	4.5	4.3	3.7

Sources: OECD *Economic Outlook* 38; SVR, 1982–83.

those figures, gross investment fell from 23.9 percent of GNP in 1972 to 21.6 percent in 1974 (Table 7.4), and real investment by firms in plant and new equipment decreased by 10.9 percent from 1973 (the year of the investment tax) to 1974. At the same time private consumption stagnated as a consequence of tighter credit and nervous saving. Real domestic demand decreased by 2 percent in 1974 (SVR, 1978–79: Appendix, Tables 16, 20, 22).

Because of the remarkably long export boom, the symptoms of the developing crisis were not felt immediately in the labor market (which might have awakened the unions from their false sense of security in time to correct the situation). While new orders in industry from domestic sources were stagnating or decreasing from summer 1973 on, orders from abroad increased at extremely high rates up to late summer 1974 (Bundesbank, 2/75:66). The export surplus grew from 29 billion marks in 1973 to a high of 43 billion marks in 1974, which was almost obscene in the context of the balance-of-trade problems of other industrial nations. Employment remained relatively stable until the second half of the year, largely because of the successful flight of German firms to foreign markets. But in autumn 1974 the long-predicted decline of world market demand finally occurred, because expansionary policy in other industrial nations was becoming constrained by increasing trade deficits (due in great part to the overwhelming success of the German export offensive). In the Federal Republic there now was no stable domestic demand to act as a safety net to mitigate the steep plunge of exports. The restrictive policy of the central bank finally took effect, but the consequences for employment were more severe than in other comparable nations. The number of employed persons fell from 26.9 million in 1973 to 25.8 million, while the number of unemployed jumped from a yearly average of 273,000 in 1973 to 1.1 million in 1975. The inflation rate, however, contrary to the unions' expectation, did not climb in 1974, and it began to fall markedly in 1975.

The central bank had thus won the showdown of 1974. Now, regardless of all theoretical controversies (Neumann, 1973; Pohl, 1973), there could be no doubt that a restrictive monetary policy could neutralize expansionary fiscal stimuli (Trapp, 1976; Neumann, 1978; 1981) and produce unemployment on its own. But the very visibility of its success (which was a necessary condition for the future credibility of monetary policy) also meant a political risk for the Bundesbank. The unions used it to support their demand that monetary policy be explicitly obligated to pursue all four goals of the Stabilization and Growth Act of 1967 (Simmert, 1974:56), and SPD members in the federal legislature began to draft the appropriate changes in the federal bank act. In this situation, the Bundesbank's concept of how the money supply was to be controlled gained a strategic importance quite independent of its economic plausibility and practical effectiveness. This concept, which had originally been proposed by the SVR, suggested that the growth of the money supply should be strictly tied to the expected growth of real productive potential, including unavoidable inflation (Bundesbank, 12/1974; SVR, 1974–75:316). The importance of this idea becomes clear when it is interpreted in coordination and game-theoretical terms.

In the Keynesian spirit of the Stabilization and Growth Act of 1967 and of Concerted Action, the Bundesbank had allowed itself to be made part of the attempt to pursue all four macroeconomic goals simultaneously by coordinating fiscal policy, monetary policy, and wage policy. But when its first legal priority, price stabilization, was impaired by the behavior of other actors, the bank faced a dilemma. Either it had to accept inflation rates higher than it found acceptable or it had to reject the demand for coordination in order to pursue price stability without consideration of its consequences for employment. Such a course of action would probably have brought it into conflict with its own statute (Köhler, 1985); in any case it would have taken a highly vulnerable position that would have challenged the legislature to revise the federal bank act. The concept of potential-oriented control of the money supply offered a brilliant escape from this dilemma, permitting the bank to act unilaterally while rhetorically honoring the demand for coordination, and to burden the government, and especially the unions, with making the adjustments necessary for a successful coordination.

The solution was for the Bundesbank to commit itself publicly by announcing its money supply goal a year in advance, before the beginning of the new wage round. In game-theoretical terms, the bank had won the advantage of the first move. From now on it was able to advocate better coordination in economic policy from a position of authority, because the social partners and the government had been put on notice about the available monetary supply for the coming year. It was now their responsibility to take account of this parameter in their own decisions. If the sum of all demands on GNP did not exceed the monetary supply made available by the bank, the nation could fully exploit its economic growth potential and could realize the maximum employment possible under the given circumstances. If not, then output and employment would be constrained by the money supply—but that would no longer be the bank's responsibility. If this situation arose, one would have to extend the argument, even deficit-financed government employment programs would not help. On the contrary, such measures could only continue to overtax the already short money supply, resulting in higher job losses in the private sector.

Thus union economists were right when they criticized the Bundesbank's new concept as reprivatizing the risk of unemployment (Pohl, 1974:467). That was its whole point. And they were also right when they noted that if the concept were applied systematically, every kind of price increase (and not only those occasioned by wage increases) would always be punished by rising unemployment (Simmert, 1974). The same result would arise if market prices did not yield flexibly enough when the money supply was reduced in order to lower the inflation rate. One need not even assume concentrated markets to reach this conclusion, an assumption that was somewhat overworked by the union economists at that time. Even under effective competition, price reductions are a rational microeconomic reaction only when quantity is already constrained (Spahn, 1986:212–13).

Moreover, we know today that too tight a money supply also constrains the possible growth of real productive potential, so that any mistake in potential-oriented monetary policy must entail cumulative losses in future growth (Flassbeck, 1982; Maier-Rigaud, 1982; 1983). In short, even if the unions had been prepared to subject their wage policy to the money supply dictates of the Bundesbank, that would not have been enough to neutralize the negative employment consequences of a monetary policy oriented exclusively toward the goal of price stability. Even the SVR has since conceded this point (SVR, 1984–85:326).

But in the political situation of 1975, even strong theoretical arguments would no longer have made a difference. Public opinion blamed the economic misdevelopment on the unions (along with the "oil sheiks"), while there was widespread public approval for the Bundesbank as the defender of stability. Thus the rather hesitantly espoused demand for a "new organizational form for monetary policy" (WSI, 1975a:447) was not even considered in parliament; it failed at the level of the federal government. The government was now dependent on the bank's support to overcome the acute economic crisis. And once its point was made, the bank began to loosen its monetary restrictions in autumn 1974 so that even the unions had no more cause for further demands by summer 1975 (Pohl, 1975:460). The acute conflict was defused, and the government had more urgent concerns than staging a highly risky political battle of principle about the Bundesbank's mandate.

Thus the political conditions for pushing through the concept of potential-oriented money supply could hardly have been more favorable (Kloten et al., 1985:390–95). Unlike the shift in responsibility for the exchange rate that had accompanied the transition to a floating rate, the strategic positional gain of the central bank did not remain unnoticed. Nevertheless, the bank was able to consolidate its strategic gains because neither the unions nor the federal government were prepared to expend their limited potential for battle on an institutional issue that no longer seemed critical. It was this fact, rather than the formal provisions of the Federal Bank Act, that allowed the Bundesbank to win a dominant role in German economic policy. The full price for this development, in economic policy terms, was to be paid only after 1980, when monetary policy for the first time conflicted directly with the priorities of government policy.

1975–1977: Vote for Recovery but Consolidate the Budget

Late 1974 introduced the most severe economic crisis in the history of the Federal Republic. Real GNP fell by 1.6 percent, the volume of work by 4.8 percent, and the number of registered unemployed workers rose to 1.074 million on average for 1975. Under the shock of the crisis, the Federal Republic now also found a way to coordinate its economic policy.

In the fourth quarter of 1974 the central bank began to reduce its discount and lending rates very gradually, until in autumn 1975 they were almost at the low level of 1972. Its monetary supply goal for 1975 was also rather generous. Interest rates for discountable loans fell from their high point of 13 percent in early 1974 to just 5 percent by the end of 1975. But this drop in interest rates did not produce a wave of consumption or investment; instead, it was a sign that the economy was not prepared to take on more debt despite the much more plentiful money supply. As Karl Schiller had often said, you can lead a horse to water, but you can't make it drink. The experience also demonstrated the fundamental asymmetry of monetary policy. While it is extremely effective when used restrictively, when used for expansionary purposes it is almost powerless to overcome the reluctance of firms to invest and the fears of private households about higher debts. To quote another macroeconomic homily, you can't push with a string.

For their part the unions, for good or ill, had learned the lesson of the Bundesbank. Under the pressure of widespread unemployment, standard hourly wages, which had increased by 13 percent in 1974, rose by only 9.3 percent in 1975, and in 1976 by only 6 percent. Because productivity increased at the same time, the rise in unit labor costs, which at 9.4 percent had been well above the inflation rate of 7 percent in 1974, decreased to 1.2 percent in 1976, well below the 1976 inflation rate of 4.3 percent (SVR, 1978–79: Table 4). The unions thus made a substantial cost-side contribution to reestablishing price stability, while the tax and family allowance reform of 1975 averted the drop in workers' incomes to be expected with low wage agreements and rising unemployment (Bundesbank, 2/1981: Tables VII, 7, and 8).

Monetary policy no longer prevented a rise in effective domestic demand but was powerless to effect such a rise. Unlike the situation in Austria, Sweden, and Great Britain, however, wages did not function as a support for demand in 1975. Thus it was up to fiscal policy alone to overcome the employment crisis. At first, the impulses emanating from the public budgets were clearly expansionary. Net borrowing for all levels of government reached an all-time high of 53.6 billion marks in 1975, which was, at 5.2 percent of the GNP, even higher than in Austria. And unlike Austrian subnational governments, in West Germany the states were involved in the attempt as well, although the federal government bore the main brunt with 30 billion marks (Simmert and Wagner, 1981:483).

The tax and family allowance reform of 1975 played a large role in the high deficit. It had been decided on before the crisis and burdened federal and state budgets with increased expenditures and foregone income to the tune of 18 billion marks. In light of uncertain economic prospects, however, the increase in disposable private income was only partly converted into effective demand. Instead, the already high savings rate rose again and reached an all-time high of 16 percent in 1975. Like an expansionary monetary policy, an expansionary fiscal policy aimed at increasing private income cannot make the horse drink. A large part of the fiscal impulses of 1975 were thus lost to fear-induced savings.

The remaining fiscal impulses of 1975 were due to automatic stabilizers. Outlays from the additional spending programs authorized by
the federal government in December 1974 and August 1975 were hardly
noticeable in fiscal 1975; most of the outlays (4.5 billion marks) actually
did not occur until fiscal 1976, when the government was once more
trying to put the brakes on the economy (SVR, 1976–77:221, Table 31).

But more was probably not intended. In conversations with policy
makers one gets the impression that the federal government had not
expected the crisis to last. As with the recession of 1966–67, people were
waiting for a quick, self-propelled recovery—where the most one could
do was hurry it along a bit. Since mid–1975 marked the bottom of the
cycle (SVR, 1976–76:255), federal financial planners approved the August program only reluctantly and under political pressure from the
forthcoming state elections in Nordrhein-Westfalen. They assigned
much more urgency to reducing what they considered to be a horren-
dous budget deficit.

Even during the election campaign, which the government conducted
and won with the slogan "Vote for Recovery!", meetings were held to
discuss expenditure cuts and tax increases designed to reduce the
federal deficit by 23 billion marks in 1976–78. Following the motto that
one must plug financial holes where they occur, the measures were
chiefly directed at the unemployment insurance fund. That fund, which
is financed by insurance contributions of employers and workers, had
run a deficit of 8.6 billion marks in 1975 because of the steep rise in
unemployment and short-time compensation. By law, this deficit had to
be covered by the federal government, a huge budget outlay that fiscal
planners had not counted on. In response, the Budget Structure Act of
January 1, 1976, introduced higher unemployment contributions and
lower unemployment benefits that succeeded in reducing the deficit so
rapidly that the fund was again in surplus by 1977—even though the
number of registered unemployed workers had barely decreased at all.
Further targets of the austerity campaign were student support and
doctoral stipends, savings promotion and public sector employment and
pay. In addition, the value-added tax and several consumer taxes were
raised in 1977.

The success of the consolidation campaign was impressive in terms of
fiscal economies realized. The rise in expenditures was slowed markedly;
revenue, which had stagnated in 1975, rose again; and the deficit of all
levels of government went from 63.8 billion marks in 1975 to 31.2 billion
in 1977 (Table 7.5). Economically, however, the success of the budget
consolidation was problematic. According to calculations of the DIW,
based on comparisons with the prior year, public budgets generated

Table 7.5 Net national expenditures and income (changes from previous year in %); public sector deficit (billions of marks); deficit as proportion of GNP (%): Federal Republic, 1975–1982

	1975	1976	1977	1978	1979	1980	1981	1982
Growth in expenditures	13.3	4.5	4.9	9.7	8.4	8.4	6.4	3.7
Growth in income	2.0	10.8	10.7	8.2	7.6	6.8	3.1	5.5
Deficit in billions of marks	63.8	48.0	31.2	39.6	46.6	57.1	75.7	69.9
Proportion of GNP	−6.2	−4.3	−2.6	−3.1	−3.3	−3.8	−4.9	−4.4

Source: BMF Finanzbericht, 1986.

strongly negative demand impulses in 1976 (Teschner and Vesper, 1983:74). But even according to the SVR concept of a cyclically neutral budget, the expansionary impulses were weak in 1976 and had disappeared altogether in 1977. Since foreign demand was stagnating at a level well below its high of 1974, the economic recovery that began in late 1975 was fed exclusively by the massive fiscal stimulus of 1975 and by increasing household demand. These were sufficient to allow the GNP, which had fallen by 1.8 percent in 1975, to rise the next year by a spectacular 5.4 percent, but in 1977 the growth slowed again to 3 percent.

At the same time it became clear that the recovery was insufficient to overcome unemployment quickly, as it had done in 1967–68. Between 1973 and 1975 the Federal Republic lost 1.1 million of its 26.9 million jobs, and despite increased production it lost an additional 0.3 million in 1977, reducing the total to 25.5 million. Despite a substantial reduction in the work force due to early retirement and the forced repatriation of foreign workers, 1.03 million workers were still unemployed in 1977, only fifty thousand less than in 1975. Obviously the government had throttled the recovery prematurely. Even the Council of Economic Advisers, looking at the fiscal policy of 1976 and 1977, agreed: "After the fact it was evident that restraint was excessive" (SVR, 1978–79:173). By that time, however, the government had once again switched to fiscal expansion.

1977–1980: "MODEL GERMANY" AS THE LOCOMOTIVE OF RECOVERY

In the federal elections of 1976, the social-liberal coalition had campaigned on its success in overcoming the global economic crisis with proud reference to "Model Germany." While the coalition was returned to power, however, the Social Democrats lost to the CDU/CSU the position Willy Brandt had gained for them in 1972 as the strongest party in the country. The union wing of the party, with which Helmut Schmidt had very good relations, blamed this loss on the coalition's willingness to consolidate the budget at the expense of full employment. Since even according to the calculations of the SVR, the structural budget deficit had been almost eliminated by early 1977, such ideas found attentive ears again in the chancellor's office. The planning department under Albrecht Müller, which otherwise was responsible for "progressive" public relations, took the opportunity to propose a "Program of Investment in the Future" (*Zukunftsinvestitionenprogramm* [ZIP]) that deviated in several respects from earlier economic and employment programs. To be sure, public investment was focused on tangible construction projects, as it always had been. It concentrated especially on improving transportation infrastructure, developing environmentally acceptable sources of energy, building sewage treatment plants, renovating inner cities, and constructing professional training centers. But the planned duration of the program, four years, was much longer than usual, and its cost, 13.8 billion marks—roughly equal to the total savings produced by the Budget Restraint Act—was greater than that of earlier economic and employment programs. The program, which was approved in March 1977 and begun in 1978, gave everyone enough time to identify and implement cost-effective projects. Thus, in terms of both employment policy and environmental policy, the program was indeed highly successful (Vesper and Zwiener, 1982).

In addition, 1977 saw the enactment of additional tax benefits for housing construction and for commercial investment, increased family allowances, and reduction of wage, income, and business taxes. Moreover, a 2 percent increase of turnover tax originally planned for 1977 was postponed. Even the central bank was willing to lend a hand. In view of the rising exchange rate, moderate wage agreements, and falling inflation, the bank lowered the discount rate from 3.5 percent to its earlier low of 3 percent and revised its goal for the 1978 money supply upward. With that, however, financial planners, the central bank, and the Council of Economic Advisers believed that the economy had received all the stimulus that was reasonable.

But when, in spring 1978, the recovery had not yet materialized, political pressure increased again. In June the ZIP was supplemented by a new long-term program to subsidize energy-saving investments in buildings. Nor was that enough. In the meantime foreign criticism of West Germany had come to a head. The Federal Republic's current account surplus remained very high despite a substantial revaluation of the mark against the dollar and other currencies. In the United States and elsewhere these surpluses were attributed to a selfish deflationary policy that excluded imports from the German market and exported unemployment to countries with more expansionary policies. Because the United States (the object of Helmut Schmidt's criticism because of its high inflation rate and trade deficit) had exhausted its capacity to promote worldwide prosperity, the Federal Republic (together with Japan) was now expected to become the locomotive of growth that would pull the Western world to recovery (Putnam and Bayne, 1984).

At the Bonn economic summit meeting on July 16 and 17, 1978, the Federal Republic finally ended its tenacious resistance to this role and committed itself to an immediate increase in aggregate demand of at least 1 percent of GNP. It was agreed that the measures necessary to fulfill this commitment would be introduced in the legislature by August. This startling announcement caused furious activity in the ministries. The new minister of finance, Hans Matthöfer, had hoped at first that he could develop a program to modernize the economy along the lines of the ZIP, but before work could begin on designing such a program, the locomotive was stoked by various projects that happened to be available for immediate implementation.

The details of the resolutions passed in cabinet on July 28 included uncontroversial measures like raising the family allowance once more and increasing the personal income tax exemption, as well as controversial ones like eliminating the payroll tax accruing to local governments (a measure that worked to the disadvantage of social democratic cities in the Ruhr region: Fürst, Hesse, and Richter, 1984:265–90). In the long run the most costly of these measures was the increase in maternity leave from two to six months, combined with a new federal maternity allowance of 750 marks per month. Minister of Labor Ehrenberg pushed this project through in the heat of the moment. The unanimous opinion at that time was that he would not have had a chance of succeeding in the regular budget process. The net effect of these measures was to increase the budget deficit by about 27 billion marks in 1979 and 1980. The deficit of all levels of government thus climbed from 31.2 billion marks in 1977 to 46.6 billion in 1979, providing as much economic stimulus as in 1975 (SVR, 1982–83: Table 28).

The initial resistance to foreign pressure, the haphazard way in which the package was put together, and the flaws of some of the specific measures tarnished the reputation of the locomotive strategy among policy professionals in the Federal Republic and prevented them from taking the offensive in presenting the new strategy to the public. Thus it became common, after 1979, to attribute the negative effects of the second oil shock on West Germany's current account balance to the "fall from grace" at the Bonn summit. This perspective has largely obscured the real successes of ZIP and the locomotive strategy.

For the first time since the onset of the crisis, the Germans succeeded in coordinating their macroeconomic control instruments according to the Austrian model. An expansionary fiscal policy was supported by a moderately expansionary monetary policy, which in turn was facilitated by constant revaluation of the German mark and moderate wage settlements, which limited the increase of unit labor costs to the inflation rate, less than 3 percent in 1978. Profits increased faster than income from employment, and the adjusted wage share receded from a high of 66.1

percent of national income in 1975 to 63.4 percent in 1979. At the same time new orders in manufacturing firms, which had stagnated in 1976, rose by 16 percent between 1977 and 1979. Under these favorable conditions, business investment in plant and new equipment rose by 25 percent (by 18.7 percent in real terms) between 1977 and 1979, markedly more than the increase in output (SVR, 1982–83: Table 14, and Appendix, Tables 19, 21, 27, 39).

Real economic growth accelerated from 3 percent in 1977 to 4.2 percent in 1979. And finally there were improvements in the labor market. Total employment actually increased by 729,000 between 1977 and 1980. However, because 588,000 people joined (or rejoined) the labor force, official unemployment fell by only 141,000—from 1.03 million in 1977 to 889,000 in 1980 (SVR, 1982–83: Appendix, Table 16). Thus even respectable economic growth failed to eliminate unemployment quickly. From an economic perspective, however, the locomotive strategy was a brilliant success that has not been repeated since. Unfortunately, this fact was soon obscured by the second oil crisis and has now evidently been forgotten in economic-policy debates.

1979–1982: FROM THE SECOND OIL CRISIS TO OPERATION 83

After the revolution in Iran the dollar price of oil began to rise, from $13 to $33 per barrel between late 1978 and autumn 1980. As in the period from 1973 to 1975, the result was an inflationary cost push in the industrial nations and a growth-inhibiting transfer of buying power to the OPEC nations. Their trade surplus had shrunk after the first oil crisis, but it was back to $60 billion by 1979 and $110 billion by 1980. However, despite these parallels to the crisis of 1974–75, the basic factors influencing economic policy were considerably changed from the first crisis.

First, the Federal Republic started the second crisis with a currency that was clearly overvalued in comparison to its buying power. Moreover, Japan, Germany's supposed partner in the locomotive policy, responded to the second oil crisis by immediately devaluing the yen, lowering its dollar exchange rate by a fourth between October 1978 and March 1980. Japanese exports became much cheaper and it became even more difficult to export to Japan. During the same period the foreign value of the mark increased further by 8 percent (Bundesbank, 2/1981: Tables 10, 11). Thus West Germany was unable to export its unemployment as it had during the first crisis (Table 7.6).

Table 7.6 Trade-weighted effective rates of exchange and relative export prices
(1970 = 100) and trade balance (% of GDP): Federal Republic and Japan, 1975–1982 ·

	1975	1976	1977	1978	1979	1980	1981	1982
Effective exchange rate (first quarter of 1970 = 100)								
Federal Republic	123	131	141	149	155	157	152	161
Japan	109	114	128	157	146	141	157	147
Relative export prices (1970 = 100)								
Federal Republic	109	101	104	108	107	104	97	98
Japan	104	100	103	114	104	99	104	95
Trade surplus (deficit) (% of GDP)								
Federal Republic	1.1	0.9	0.8	1.4	−0.8	−1.8	−0.8	0.5
Japan	−0.1	0.7	1.6	1.7	−0.9	−1.1	0.5	−0.7

Source: OECD *Economic Outlook* 38.

Second, West Germany was unable to free ride on expansionary policies in the other industrial nations and the Third World. On the contrary. In autumn 1978 the new chairman of the American Federal Reserve Bank, Paul Volcker, responded to the steadily climbing inflation rate under the Carter administration with a sharply restrictive monetary policy, and the Fed held to this deflationary course until autumn 1982. The consequence was a deep recession in the United States, beginning in 1979 and lasting until 1982. After 1980 there was also a steep increase in real interest rates in the United States and a steady climb of the dollar exchange rate. For similar reasons and with the same effect, Great Britain also pursued a highly restrictive policy after the Conservative victory in May 1979. Moreover, the rise in real interest rates and the stagnation of demand for their products that followed the second oil crisis pushed many of the developing and threshold nations and Eastern bloc countries to the brink of insolvency. This further impaired world trade and caused international interest levels to rise even higher. Consequently, other countries that had responded to the first crisis with an expansionary program were forced to practice at least monetary restraint this time around. In short, the preponderant response to the second oil crisis, both in the Western industrial nations and in the Third World, was deflationary. Everywhere policy makers sought to restrain aggregate demand in order to fight inflation and to manage their trade deficits.

The third and most significant distinction between the two crises was that the Federal Republic was not among the deflationary leaders this time. In keeping with the obligations it had undertaken at the Bonn summit, German monetary and fiscal policy was not restrictive on the eve of the second crisis. The federal government continued to stimulate aggregate demand even after the new crisis broke out. The unions were satisfied with a mere 4.9 percent increase in nominal hourly wages in 1979, despite the rise in prices triggered by the oil crisis. The increase in unit labor costs was well below the inflation rate. Hence, in contrast to 1974, the Bundesbank had no reason to restrain the money supply in order to quash a rapidly escalating domestic wage-price spiral. At the beginning of the second oil crisis, the Germans had apparently assembled the optimal combination of macroeconomic instruments which, if it had been in place in 1974, could have avoided the deep recession of 1975. Nevertheless, just as it had done in 1974, the central bank ultimately caused an even deeper recession in 1981 and 1982—but this is not to say that the bank could easily have avoided this result.

The change in economic conditions abroad limited the options for German monetary policy in comparison to 1974. Earlier the Bundesbank had decided on a high interest policy for Germany more or less on its own, which put some pressure on the other members of the European "snake," whose currencies were linked to the mark. Now the German bank found itself, together with other countries that had liberalized their capital markets, under pressure from the rising interest rates on the dollar—the currency in which most international financial transactions were and are carried out. Leaving aside the possibility of exchange controls (which would have been impracticable for the German mark, a secondary reserve currency compared to the dollar but still an important one), a "flight from the mark" could have been forestalled only if the interest advantage of the U.S. dollar had been offset by expectations of a continuous revaluation. But after 1979 this was not the case. On the other hand, because of its obsession with price stability the Bundesbank wanted to avoid devaluation of the German mark. It therefore had to match the American increase in nominal interest rates. Because of lower inflation in West Germany, this caused a very substantial increase in German real interest rates (Table 7.7).

Doubly burdened by an overvalued mark and increased energy prices, West Germany had a current accounts deficit in the second quarter of 1979, its first in nearly thirty years (see Table 7.6). Thanks to the success of the locomotive strategy, domestic demand was stronger on average than in other industrial nations. Thus imports continued to increase faster than exports, and the current accounts deficit rose from 6 billion marks in 1979 to a record high of 16 billion in 1980. In itself, even a deficit of this magnitude was not an economic catastrophe. After 1973 many countries had to live with trade deficits for long periods. But the deficit did limit the options for monetary and currency policy. In principle there were three possible responses, all of which entailed negative consequences.

Table 7.7 Long-term nominal and real interest rates: Federal Republic and United States, 1975–1982 (%)

	1975	1976	1977	1978	1979	1980	1981	1982
Long-term nominal interest rates								
Federal Republic	8.5	7.8	6.2	5.7	7.4	8.5	10.4	8.9
USA	7.0	6.8	7.1	7.9	8.7	10.8	12.9	12.2
Long-term real interest rates								
Federal Republic	2.3	4.3	2.4	1.4	3.3	3.9	5.9	4.1
USA	−2.0	0.9	1.2	0.4	0.2	1.1	3.7	4.9

Source: OECD *Historical Statistics,* 1960–1983.

1. The Bundesbank could have passively accepted the currency drain caused by the trade deficit, and the concomitant fall in the mark's exchange rate. This strategy, practiced by Japan, would have reduced German imports and led to an increase in German exports, and thus would have helped to balance current accounts. In the meantime, however, climbing import prices would have increased price levels and perhaps restarted the inflationary spiral.

2. The bank could have tried to finance the trade deficit by selling currency reserves, which would temporarily stabilize the mark. But this entailed the risk of speculation against the mark and the consequent waste of reserves in defense of an untenable rate of exchange.

3. Finally, the bank could finance the trade deficit by capital imports, which would also stabilize the rate of exchange. This was the path Austria had chosen to follow with its hard currency policy, despite chronic trade deficits. But after the worldwide increase in dollar interest rates, capital could be imported only at competitive rates of interest. Thus this third response demanded a policy of domestic monetary restraint that was contrary to fiscal expansion and the goal of full employment.

The Bundesbank ultimately chose the third response: an extreme strategy of domestic deflation. But one must give the bank its due; it chose this path reluctantly and without the monetarist cheer it had shown in 1973–74. Initially, monetary restraint was applied with caution. The discount rate was not raised until spring 1979, and then only by a percentage point, from its previous low of 3 percent. However, it then rose from quarter to quarter to a high of 7.5 percent in summer 1980, where it remained until summer 1982. Other interest rates also increased over the course of the year. This sufficed at first to guarantee that capital imports would offset the trade deficit in 1979 and stabilize the exchange rate.

But when American monetary and fiscal policy tightened still further between late 1979 and early 1980, this response was no longer adequate. The Bundesbank now turned to the second of the above strategies, supporting the mark by intervening in the currency market, with initial success. But as an earlier central bank president had said, reserves that have to be used soon stop being reserves. Between October 1979 and April 1980 the central bank lost nearly a quarter of its currency reserves, and when it finally had to reduce interventions in summer 1980, the German mark began to fall rapidly not only against the dollar but against other currencies as well (Bundesbank, 2/1981:7, 36ff., Appendix, Tables IX, 10, 11).

The Bundesbank now had to choose between accepting the mark's fall or countering it with even higher monetary restraint. It chose the second option. The volume of money (M1) was reduced and interest rates escalated in the first months of 1981, reaching the exotic highs of over 11 percent for loans and over 15 percent for consumer credit (SVR, 1982–83:143–46)—with an inflation rate that was under 6 percent, one of the world's lowest in 1981. It was not plausible this time, as it had been in 1974, to speak of a division of labor between fiscal policy and monetary policy after the Bonn summit set public finances on an expansionary course for the budget years 1979 and 1980, and the extremely cumbersome fiscal provisions of the German constitution did not allow short-term revisions of fiscal plans. Moreover, 1980 was an election year. Thus the Tax Relief Act of 1981, for instance, would have reduced tax revenues by 17.5 billion marks in 1981 and 1982 in the form in which it was presented by the government on February 20. By the time the bill was passed out of committee on July 3, it had been changed to provide tax relief measures and family and housing allowances of more than 27 billion marks for 1981–82. Moreover, the economic decline that had begun in 1980 naturally brought with it decreased income and government revenues and increased outlays. In short, the total public sector deficit, which had been reduced from 63.8 billion marks in 1975 to 31.2 billion in 1977, rose in 1981 to 75.7 billion marks and remained almost at that level in 1982 (BMF *Finanzbericht* 1986:66).

Fiscal policy was thus in an even more exposed position in 1980–81 than it had been in 1975–76. Starting in early 1975, the government's fiscal policies had been accommodated by a moderately expansionary monetary policy; now the situation was reversed. The increasingly restrictive policy of the central bank neutralized the expansionary impulses of fiscal policy, and the steep rise in interest rates caused debt service on the (higher) public debt to increase from 25 billion marks in 1979 to 45 billion in 1982 (SVR, 1982–83: Table 25). At 8 percent of total government outlays, debt service constituted a serious political concern, even though the warnings of an impending government bankruptcy during the election campaign of 1980 were not serious. The extremely tight money policy of 1980 and 1981 ran exactly counter not only to the economic and employment policy goals of the federal government but also to its interest in political survival. Nevertheless, in my interviews I gained the impression that during its last two years the social-liberal government accepted the central bank's policy either as an inevitable necessity or as an unavoidable misfortune.

One could, however, question the compelling necessity for such a restrictive policy. In a minority opinion in the 1982–83 annual report of the Council of Economic Advisers (SVR, 1982–83:150), Hans-Jürgen Krupp correctly pointed out that the Bundesbank could also have chosen the "Japanese option." It could have accelerated the devaluation of the mark instead of trying to prevent it with all the means at its disposal. Then, from the position of an undervalued currency (which observers expected would be revalued), West Germany could have managed to stay below the American interest rates for the duration. Domestic expansion could have continued and the undervalued currency would have improved the international competitive position of the German economy and soon eliminated the trade deficit, as in Japan. From a social democratic and union point of view, this was a much more attractive scenario than what actually happened, and this was also the path chosen by the Swedish Social Democrats in autumn 1982.

But in West Germany in 1975 responsibility for currency had passed from the federal government to the federal bank, and the devaluation strategy never had a chance in the central bank council. It would have allowed import prices to climb and thus would have raised the inflation rate at least temporarily. Moreover, from the bank's perspective there was no guarantee that things would stop with the imported inflation. The rise of standard hourly wages had increased throughout 1980, and unit labor costs had taken a jump upward; they were now above the inflation rate again. At the same time profits had receded sharply, especially because of the world economic downswing, so that the relative distributive position of the workers had improved although real wages were stagnant (Table 7.8).

As in 1973–74, the oil price inflation resulted in domestic wage and price increases, and once again the Bundesbank was unwilling to accommodate these increases. In its explanation of the projected money supply target for 1981 it warned that even the very modest increase of 4 to 7 percent could be tolerated only "if 'homemade' price and cost push diminished, the mark stabilized, and the trade deficit diminished," and at the same time it cautioned that these conditions had not been met at

Table 7.8 GDP growth, consumer prices, standard hourly
wages, real wages, and unit labor costs in industry
(changes from previous year in %); adjusted wage share
and unemployment (%): Federal Republic, 1979–1982

	1979	1980	1981	1982
GDP growth	4.2	1.8	0.0	−1.0
Consumer prices	4.1	5.5	6.3	5.3
Industrial wages	5.2	6.0	5.5	4.5
Real wages	1.1	0.5	−0.8	−0.8
Unit labor costs	2.4	7.3	5.2	4.1
Adjusted wage share	63.4	64.7	65.4	64.9
Unemployment	4.3	3.7	3.7	5.3

Sources: OECD Historical Statistics, 1960–1983; SVR, 1984–85.

the beginning of 1981 (Bundesbank, 2/1981:9). And even before its
warnings could have been heard or acted upon, credit was drastically
tightened. In February 1981, the Bundesbank increased the Lombard
rate at which it accepted commercial paper to an astronomical 12 percent. The increase triggered a general escalation of interest rates in 1981
(Bundesbank, 1/1983:14–26).

Unlike in 1973–74, the unions immediately responded to the restrictive policy of the central bank, although they criticized it. In both 1981
and 1982 not only increases in unit labor costs but also hourly wages
remained below the inflation rate. Nevertheless, the bank lending rate
was kept at record levels through autumn 1981. Not until the following
summer, when the current account had once again moved back into
balance, did the Bundesbank appreciably lower bank lending rates and
the discount rate. As a result all government attempts to use fiscal policy
to combat unemployment, which increased rapidly after 1981, were
doomed to failure. Consequently, after some delay, the second recession
of the decade hit the Federal Republic as well.

For political reasons, the federal government would have been unable
to continue its expansionary fiscal policy in any case, although on the
whole it had been successful in maintaining employment. Though the
social-liberal coalition had been returned to office by the legislative elections of autumn 1980, the opposition warnings about an impending
government bankruptcy and the currency reform necessary to combat it
had their effect. Election year polemics predictably focused on the
federal budget, which had to bear the burden of increased payments to
the European Community and of most of the new tax reforms. The
federal debt thus increased 252 percent between 1973 and 1979, more
than the states' debt, at 197 percent, and much more than the municipal

governments', at 40 percent (Simmert and Wagner, 1981:451). Even the SPD's budget analysts considered this development to be unhealthy and saw the need to trim back some excesses of the locomotive strategy. To reduce outlays, the chancellor also proposed the elimination of a variety of programs that were jointly financed by the federal government and the states (H. Schmidt, 1980a).

The FDP, however, did not only want to reduce the deficit, which it could have achieved by means of higher taxes and social security contributions. The party wanted to reduce the size of the public sector, and especially the taxes on business and property incomes. The FDP emerged stronger from the legislative election in 1980, and after Franz-Josef Strauß lost the race for leadership of the CDU/CSU, it once again had the option of changing coalition partners. Thus the FDP held the balance of power in the legislature and was able to impose its fiscal policies on the SPD. But even more important than the marginal shifts in the legislative balance of power was the change in the constellation of economic and political interests supporting the coalition, a change that was hardly recognized at first but that nevertheless had an effect.

The FDP had joined the social-liberal coalition in 1969 on the basis of shared foreign policy goals. In addition, its program had emphasized "idealistic" reform goals in the fields of criminal law, educational and university reform, and environmental policy. Although the party had lost much of the support of its traditional middle-class constituency when it switched coalition partners, in the coalition it consistently played the role of brakeman with respect to the expansion of social welfare and codetermination programs (Baring, 1982:183ff). While this role was not much emphasized initially, the FDP became ever more clearly the representative of business interests within the coalition after it took over the ministry of economics in the fall of 1972, and especially after the onset of the economic crisis. Even in this more realistic allocation of roles, however, the interest profile of the FDP was compatible with the primary orientation of the SPD toward worker interests—at least as long as both could be satisfied only by an economic policy aiming at higher rates of growth. This underlying harmony of interests became strained when interest rates began to rise worldwide after 1979.

At that point, economic growth had become much more difficult to achieve. Worse yet, the income interests of capital owners could not be directly satisfied on the national and international financial markets, whereas previously, despite all conflicts over distribution, capital interests and worker interests could only be satisfied jointly. As a consequence, policies promoting economic growth had become less important to the FDP clientele than distributive and tax policies. In the last analysis,

153

after all, it was tax policy that would determine how much one could retain of capital incomes achieved in the market. It was this change in the payoffs of the capital side that transformed the political economy of the social-liberal coalition from a mixed-motive game to a zero-sum game.

The new conflict of interests within the social-liberal coalition found its ideological expression in the debate between Keynesian demand management and supply-side economics, which rose to prominence in the 1970s among academic economists, in the Council of Economic Advisers, and finally in the economic policy of the FDP (Buttler, Kühl, and Rahmann, 1985; Giersch, 1983; Flassbeck, 1982; Meißner, 1980). Supply siders started with the correct premise that internationally high interest rates meant that the investment necessary to combat unemployment had to come from higher profits. They then drew the one-sided conclusion that expected profits had to be increased by lowering wages, taxes, and social security contributions, and not by raising macroeconomic demand, as advocated by Keynesian economists, the unions, and the Social Democrats. The Social Democrats probably would have accepted the distributive consequences of the supply-side policy demanded by the FDP if they had been sure that higher capital income would lead to investment and finally to increased employment. But since German tax law did not systematically favor reinvested over distributed profits and had not done so since the 1960s, there was every reason to believe that the tax relief and business subsidies demanded by the supply siders would merely accelerate capital transfers from firms into the internal money markets and high-interest government loans (Hankel, 1984:121–32; Hickel, 1985:342–52).

Following the 1980 elections, the FDP's new concerns were reflected in what now seems to have been an incompetent and economically counterproductive government austerity program. The budget draft for 1981 passed by the cabinet in December was highly deflationary, with expenditures growing only 4.1 percent, which was well below the inflation rate, and net borrowing limited to 27.4 billion marks. But owing to the worldwide recession, whose effects were accentuated at home by the central bank's tight money policy, tax revenues continued to fall while expenditures for unemployment benefits increased rapidly. Hence, the federal budget passed in June provided for net borrowing of 33.76 billion marks, and fiscal year 1981 closed with expenditures increased by 8 percent and a deficit of 37.4 billion marks. The same discrepancy occurred in the following year. The budget law passed in January for 1982 had limited net borrowing to 26.8 billion marks, but the actual deficit ran to 37.7 billion (BMF *Finanzbericht* 1986: Table 1).

For the government of Helmut Schmidt, who depended heavily on a reputation for professional competence, this was an extremely painful process. Unrealistic budgets had to be corrected over and over again under the unforgiving scrutiny of the media. At the same time, economists, including the Council of Economic Advisers (SVR, 1982–83:167), criticized the self-defeating attempt to reduce deficits resulting from the economic downswing by reducing expenditures, according to the motto "Save, whatever it may cost." But, while the government's austerity program drove the economic policy makers of the SPD to despair (and caused Labor Minister Herbert Ehrenberg to resign), the FDP remained implacable. With the threat to switch coalition partners, which remained unmentioned but was on everyone's mind, it was able to put almost unlimited pressure on the SPD. And for the FDP and its constituents, the austerity program was not nonsensical at all but extraordinarily attractive.

The austerity program was pushed through in a simple tactic against which the SPD never found an effective defense. The outlay reductions and tax increases needed to reduce the budget deficit had to come at the expense of social consumption and mass incomes if they were to make a quantitative difference. When the SPD, over the FDP's resistance, asked for new initiatives to combat increasing unemployment, then the compromise solution was inevitably a reduction of business taxes and increased capital subsidies. And since the opposition was able to block unpopular tax increases in the state chamber of the Bundesrat, the self-imposed obligation to reduce the deficit made additional budget cuts necessary. Of course, these cuts were again directed against the interests represented by the SPD. No wonder that even the DGB unions, which were loyal almost to the point of self-abnegation, finally organized massive protests against the governing Social Democrats.

It is hardly worthwhile to detail the process of decline. The 1981 budget included cuts in areas that were particularly dear to the SPD, such as federal contributions to pension insurance. Moreover, the oil and gasoline tax and some other consumption taxes were raised. When it became clear that the previous consolidation efforts would be overwhelmed by rising unemployment (and also by extremely high military procurement overruns), the government adopted "Operation 82" in the summer of 1981. This operation followed the model of the Budget Structure Act of 1975 by plugging holes where they existed. Its most important goal was again to close the gap in the unemployment insurance fund by raising contributions, cutting unemployment benefits, and eliminating job creation programs. Cuts in the family allowance (which had just been raised) and workers' savings allowances followed suit. Since something still had to be done about unemployment, the government also shortened depreciation schedules for plant and equipment and increased subsidies for the steel industry.

When the number of unemployed reached almost two million at the beginning of 1982, the government could no longer resist the pressure for new employment initiatives. In February, the cabinet proposed a "joint initiative for jobs, growth, and stability" whose main element was a temporary investment subsidy—which, after the experiences of 1975, no one expected would have much effect. In return for this "concession" by the FDP, the Social Democrats had to accept a deregulation of rental housing that was supposed to stimulate private investment in apartment construction. An increase in the value-added tax that was proposed at the same time failed to pass the Bundesrat in May. Therefore, and because unemployment continued to rise and tax estimates had to be corrected downward once more, the government was again forced to cut expenditures and raise more revenue. The cabinet decided to further increase contributions to the unemployment insurance fund, to cut the contributions of the unemployment fund to the pension insurance for unemployed workers, to require pensioners to contribute to their own health insurance, and to charge a certain share of health costs directly to health insurance patients. However, all of these cabinet decisions went into effect only after the social-liberal coalition fell and was replaced by the new conservative-liberal government in October of 1982.

With this "Operation 83," the Social Democrats and the unions finally reached the end of their patience. When, in late summer of 1982, FDP Minister of Economics Count Otto Lambsdorff presented the chancellor with a position paper making even more extreme demands, even the most loyal Social Democrats had to realize that this was a game they could not win. Given the Bundesbank's monetary constraint, the FDP's distributive goals, and the CDU/CSU's veto in the Bundesrat, there simply was no way to achieve social democratic goals. But before it reached that conclusion, the SPD had agreed to extreme cuts in the "social safety net" and had taken responsibility for increasing unemployment to the two million mark.

Unlike the Swedish Social Democrats in 1976, the German SPD did not leave to its successors in office the legacy of a policy of "full employment at any price," which may have been too expensive but was nevertheless successful. On the contrary, they were politically responsible for the rise of mass unemployment, so that the new conservative-liberal government was able to concentrate on fighting inflation and balancing the budget without political risk. For the great majority of employed workers it meant a great deal that the situation on the labor market at least did not worsen after 1983. Thus the new government had little to fear from social democratic criticism of their neglect of persistent mass unemployment as long as the memory of the obvious ineffectiveness of employment initiatives in the last years of the social-liberal regime remained alive.

PART III

COMPARATIVE ANALYSIS

CHAPTER EIGHT

Economic Problems and Strategic Options, 1973–1979

The foregoing sketches of economic developments and policy actions and reactions of the four nations describe how each tried to defend full employment and stable prices during the decade of crisis and how, despite identical social democratic–Keynesian goals and analyses, the policies of the four produced quite different results. Of course, these accounts are historically incomplete. My aims were not detailed description but "narrative explanations" of how distinct policy mechanisms worked. Thus even in these case studies I relied on comparisons among the four countries to clarify developments by distinguishing the economic or institutional conditions that made one country different from the others. In the following chapters I review the material presented from an explicitly comparative and theoretical perspective in order to explain similarities and differences. My aim is not greater historical precision, but theoretical simplification. In other words, I am trying to derive satisfactory explanations for the policy results observed using the smallest number of variables possible.

For this purpose, in the second chapter I introduced the analytical distinction between (1) a given economic situation, (2) strategies appropriate to that situation (given certain goals), and (3) institutional arrangements constraining the choice of strategies. To be successful, an economic strategy must satisfy two requirements. It must be appropriate to the (constantly changing) economic conditions that actually obtain, and it must also be feasible under existing (but equally changeable) institutional arrangements. Abstract analysis could and should go no further than this. Now, on the basis of the historical experiences of the four countries, it is possible to outline a set of concrete propositions about the effects of various configurations of economic and institutional conditions. My intention is not to propose universal, quasi-scientific laws of social, economic, and political development, but to formulate explanatory "theories of limited application" that are not necessarily valid everywhere but that should hold where situations of the specified type exist. One cannot ask more of the social sciences (Scharpf, 1983:11; 1986).

CRISIS SITUATIONS AND STRATEGIC OPTIONS, 1973–1979

Delimiting the situation to be interpreted is of course crucial for the development of "theories of limited application." If the boundaries are drawn incorrectly, one ends up with comparisons that are not subject to precisely the same conditions, and one may not discover behavioral relationships that are in fact present. That is why I limited my investigation to Western European social democratic industrial nations during the period of global crisis after 1973. In this way, I hoped to assure a similarity of economic conditions and of political priorities that would facilitate comparisons according to the "most similar systems" method (Przeworski and Teune, 1970). For present purposes, it is further necessary to make the periodization of global economic conditions more precise. I touched on that periodization in some of the case studies, but there it was in competition with other ways of grouping the data.

There are several ways to define the historical divide—by the turn to monetarism of the American Federal Reserve Bank, by the second oil price shock, or by the culmination of the international debt crisis. In any event, the world economic problems during the first half of the 1980s were so different from those of the 1970s that the (accurate) reference to a global economic crisis that has persisted since the early 1970s is more likely to confound than to help analysis. For that reason, I will distinguish the situation between 1973 and 1979 from the situation between 1980 and 1984. The first period includes roughly the time from the first to the second oil price increase; the second runs up to the beginning of the decline in oil prices and dollar exchange rates. A crucial difference between both periods is defined by the extreme rise of dollar interest rates and the dollar exchange rate after 1980, and by the worldwide rise of real interest rates that was linked to both these factors.

My present concern is with the period between 1973 and 1979. For all the differences in detail, the four nations faced essentially identical problems that arose from fundamental changes in international economic conditions (McCracken et al., 1977). All four had benefited from being integrated in the postwar years into an international economy in which the political and economic hegemony of the United States guaranteed the reduction of trade barriers, stable rates of exchange, and a sufficient, but not inflationary, supply of American dollars, which functioned as a "world currency" (Keohane, 1982; 1984). All four suffered under the erosion of the world economic order after the United States exploited its position as the "world's banker" in the second half of the 1960s to finance the Vietnam War by creating money rather than by raising taxes. Up to the end of the Bretton Woods regime of fixed exchange rates in spring 1973, all European nations were thus exposed to worldwide dollar inflation, repeated waves of currency speculation, and the turbulence of frequent changes in rates of exchange. As a consequence, even relatively stable wage-price relations at home became unstuck, and this "homemade" variety intensified the inflation on the world market.

Just when the transition to flexible rates of exchange seemed to offer new opportunities for domestic stabilization, the industrial nations were caught by the first oil price shock. It generated two problems at once. The jump in crude oil prices raised the production costs for firms and energy costs for private households, and the rapidly increasing payments to the OPEC nations reduced private demand in the industrial nations. Thus most industrial countries entered an acute crisis during 1974 with very high inflation rates, drops in production, rising unemployment, and high trade deficits. The crisis peaked in 1975.

Soon, however, the hoarded "petrodollars" flowed back into international financial markets (especially the Eurodollar markets), where they made possible an unparalleled expansion of the volume of international credit with initially very low interest rates (Gerhardt, 1984; Hankel, 1984; Pecchioli, 1983). It also made it easier for the Western industrial nations to bridge the first crisis years through a credit-financed expansionary policy. In the following years, up to the second oil price shock, the trade deficits of the West European nations receded again, because of reduced use of oil, because of rapidly increasing imports by the OPEC nations, and because of drops in the dollar's value (in which oil prices were to be paid). For the rest, the negative real interest rates on the international capital markets and the devaluation of the dollar promoted increased indebtedness on the part of the developing nations and the Eastern bloc nations, and their demand promoted a further expansion of world trade that was favorable to the industrial nations. Toward the end of the 1970s the inflation rates in the industrial nations were still quite high but were receding gradually; growth rates were markedly lower than before the crisis, but at least they were again positive; and even if unemployment persisted, employment was increasing almost ev-

Table 8.1 OECD nations as a whole: Current account balance (% of GDP), GDP growth, consumer prices, and employment (changes from previous year in %)

	1973	1974	1975	1976	1977	1978	1979	1980
Current account balance	0.3	−0.7	0.1	−0.4	−0.4	0.2	−0.5	−0.9
GDP growth	6.1	0.5	−0.2	4.8	3.9	4.0	3.2	1.0
Consumer prices	7.8	13.4	11.3	8.6	8.8	7.9	9.8	12.9
Employment	2.2	1.0	−0.7	1.2	1.6	1.7	1.6	0.6

Sources: OECD *Economic Outlook* 38; OECD *Historical Statistics,* 1960–1983.

erywhere (Table 8.1). Still, the development of the European Monetary System and the agreements at the "economic summit meetings" inspired the hope that the Western industrial nations might achieve a form of economic policy coordination that was capable of assuming the role that American hegemonic power had once played (Keohane, 1984; Putnam and Bayne, 1984).

The above will suffice to characterize the international economic conditions and the average development of the Western industrial nations during the first crisis period. But I am less concerned with similarities among the nations than with their differences, and less with the efforts to restore a functioning international economic order, however important they were, than with domestic opportunities to cope with the crisis. I therefore focus on the factors that allowed Austria and Sweden to avoid unemployment and even to increase employment during the 1970s, contrary to the general trend, and in Austria even with an inflation rate well under the international average.

These two countries used very different strategies to pursue the social democratic priority of full employment after the crisis began. Austria successfully used a Keynesian policy of growth and stability to fight unemployment and inflation at the same time, whereas Swedish economic policy failed in this undertaking. Nevertheless, Sweden did not abandon its commitment to full employment but successfully pursued it with the "second-best" means of an active labor market policy and an expansion of public sector employment; it was, however, less successful in combating inflation. The Federal Republic, on the other hand, did best in the battle against inflation and worst in maintaining employment, whereas the Labour government in Great Britain failed at both goals.

Precisely because of the differences in the strategies they adopted, Austria and Sweden demonstrate that widespread unemployment in Western Europe was not an unavoidable fate during the crisis. The social democratic governments were equally committed to full employment. If some were nevertheless unable to avoid unemployment, then the reasons must lie less in economic conditions than in the varying institutional arrangements of the individual countries. The analyses that follow concentrate on these conditions. First, however, let us recapitulate briefly the economic factors that assured the success of the "Austrian strategy."

THE ECONOMIC LOGIC OF KEYNESIAN COORDINATION

The success of the Austrian strategy, as we have seen, resulted from the reasonably effective combination of an expansionary government monetary and fiscal policy with a relatively restrained wage policy on the part of the unions, at least after 1975. This success was not unique. Whenever one of the four countries succeeded in achieving a similar combination of monetary, fiscal, and wage impulses in the period between the first and the second oil crises, it was able to stabilize employment or at least to raise it significantly while lowering or even stabilizing the inflation rate. Such conditions were met not only in Austria after 1975 but also in Great Britain during the time of the Social Contract, in the Federal Republic during the "locomotive" period, and in Sweden in 1974–75. The reverse is also true. Where this particular combination of government expansion and union restraint was not achieved, the results were unsatisfactory; restrictive monetary and fiscal policy typically produced rising unemployment, and aggressive union wage policy typically produced increased inflation.

Nor was there anything original in the theoretical foundation of Austria's strategy, which for the most part reflected the enlightened Keynesianism that was widely, if not universally, accepted by economists and policy makers during the 1960s and early 1970s. I call this position "enlightened" because it reflects Kalecki's (1943) insight that a Keynesian full-employment policy driven wholly by government fiscal and monetary policy would run into fundamental difficulties as a country approached full employment. The unions would then be tempted to launch a wage offensive aimed at changing the distribution of income and wealth between capital and labor. When this happened, one of two consequences would follow. If prices remained stable, firm profits would fall and unemployment would rise again. If full employment was to be maintained, the government would have to continue its expansive monetary policy in order to permit higher wage costs to be passed through into continuously rising prices (Cassel and Thieme, 1977:37–48; Weintraub, 1978).

But if neither high unemployment nor high rates of inflation is acceptable, government demand management is condemned to a stop-and-go policy, braking recoveries too soon in order to prevent rising inflation and switching to stimulation too soon in order to avoid rising unemployment. Under such conditions, economic policy can neither exploit the full growth potential of the economy nor keep prices stable in the long run. The British experience during the crisis-free postwar decades illustrates this fundamental weakness of a purely statist Keynesianism. In contrast, the Austrian strategy was based on the concept of a "corporatist Keynesianism," that is, on the explicit recognition of the need to coordinate government monetary and fiscal policy and union wage policy. That strategy presupposed that the unions, even under conditions of full employment, would refrain from exploiting their bargaining power to the utmost, and that instead of attempting to achieve redistribution through an aggressive wage offensive (a strategy that is always threatened by inflation or unemployment), they would pursue a "growth-oriented wage policy." Such a policy would respect the need for sufficient profits even in periods of full employment and leave room for government demand expansion during periods of recession (Lang, 1978:79–83).

In the 1973 crisis, however, smoothing the business cycle and avoiding inefficient stop-and-go policies was no longer sufficient. The crisis was characterized by the twin threats of galloping inflation and mass unemployment, a combination which, according to Keynesian dogma, should not have occurred at all. One threat was triggered (or accelerated) by the increase in crude oil and other raw materials prices, the other by the sudden transfer of purchasing power from the industrial countries to OPEC. This coincidence of cost-push inflation and demand-deficient unemployment confronted governments not merely with the usual trade-off on the Phillips curve but with a veritable dilemma. Left to their own devices, governments could either combat unemployment through expansionary fiscal and monetary measures or fight inflation with a restrictive fiscal and monetary policy—but they could not do both at once. If a government chose full employment, however, it was not merely compelled to let energy prices run their course but it also had to accept an acceleration of the domestic wage-price spiral if the unions, protected against the threat of unemployment, tried to make up for the higher oil bill through higher wage increases. In this way, the inflationary expectations of all parties to the economic process could become so hardened that it would be difficult for a later anti-inflation policy to break them again.

If the government instead gave priority to the fight against inflation, it would have to prevent firms from passing through their increased costs of production into prices. To this end it was necessary to reduce already insufficient macroeconomic demand still further. The unavoidable consequence was that more jobs would be lost. And if wages did not yield quickly, one could expect secondary effects through which profits and investment, and hence production and employment, would be still further reduced, possibly resulting in a structural jobs deficit that could not easily be corrected, even by subsequent increases in aggregate demand. In both cases, therefore, the exclusive reliance on demand management would not merely have required policy makers to accept politically unpleasant tradeoffs between inflation and unemployment, which could be corrected in the next round of stop-and-go policy making. Worse yet, the decision to pursue one goal would produce a deepening and hardening of the neglected problem that could later be corrected only at very high economic and social cost. Under such conditions, the claim that social democratic Keynesianism was capable of managing the economy and avoiding both inflation and mass unemployment necessarily loses all credibility.

Prospects were fundamentally improved, however, when union wage policy was able to act in partnership with a Keynesian government. Even if the unions merely refrained from demanding compensation for the higher oil bill, the freedom of action of government policy was increased. Governments could then have chosen to let the oil price inflation run its course and use their own policy instruments for the short-term stabilization of aggregate demand to avoid rising unemployment. In hindsight, this was probably the least painful way to cope with the crisis.

In 1974, Sweden had started down this path and was thus able initially to avoid a deep recession. In the other three countries, however, wage increases in 1974–75 were later judged to have been much too high. Even when Keynesian coordination was missed at the outset of the crisis, however, countries did have a second chance, although its implementation was somewhat more difficult. To achieve overall price stability despite the oil price push while avoiding mass unemployment, businesses had to be relieved of other costs to compensate for the higher oil bill. This called for a reduction of business taxes and for noticeably lower real unit labor costs. In order to assure full employment, however, government demand expansion would have to be more vigorous than would have been necessary in the first case.

This was the strategy Austria and Great Britain were forced to adopt in 1975, after excessive wage settlements in 1974 and 1975 had pushed inflation rates to politically unacceptable levels (although these levels were quite different in the two countries). Austria was successful in maintaining this strategy until the end of the 1970s, whereas Great Britain achieved impressive initial successes and then failed dramatically. In the Federal Republic, and also in Sweden before 1982, governments and unions acted like their counterparts in Austria from time to time, but since neither country had explicitly defined the coordination of monetary, fiscal, and wage policy as a common strategy during the 1970s, neither pursued it with the same persistence.

In the second part of this study I described the full range of country-specific reasons for the failure to achieve the promise of social democratic–Keynesian concertation. The following chapters focus more narrowly on the institutional arrangements that facilitated or prevented strategic concertation between the government's monetary and fiscal policy and the unions' wage policy. Institutional conditions on the government and the union side are obviously important here, and so is the system of collective bargaining between employers' associations and unions. Beyond that, however, institutions on the side of capital and business are not part of our investigation, for reasons that need to be explained.

Obviously, the allocation of financial assets by banks and other financial institutions and by large firms is at least as important from an economic policy point of view as is the unions' wage policy, and the same is true of the aggregate investment, pricing, and employment decisions of the individual firms. It is doubtful, however, whether the concept of "policy" can be used in the same sense in all spheres. Economic theory, at any rate, would interpret all business decisions about capital allocation, investment, production, employment, and price formation as parametric adjustments of microeconomic subjects to given conditions of the economic environment rather than as "policy" choices guided by a collective rationality. Anything else would be suspect from the point of view of normative economic theory, and perhaps illegal as a violation of antitrust and competition law. In this view, capital investors and firms are, or at least should be, incapable as a matter of principle of collectively pursuing rational strategies. Unlike the unions (and the employers' associations in the context of collective bargaining), they are objects, not subjects, of economic policy.

CHAPTER NINE

Voluntary Wage Restraint

To appreciate the achievement of the Austrian strategy and the difficulty of imitating it, we must specify the interests of its participants more carefully than we have done so far. Let us start with the perspectives of social democratic governments when confronted with a combination of cost-push inflation and demand-deficient unemployment (Figure 9.1).

If the government's first priority is full employment but it will be in political trouble if inflation rates climb steeply, the optimal outcome is clearly the "cooperative" solution of cell 1—expansionary fiscal and monetary policy and voluntary wage restraint on the part of the unions. If the unions fail to cooperate and the government nevertheless pursues expansionary fiscal and monetary policies, full employment can be maintained, but rising wage costs and increasing demand will accelerate inflation (cell 2). If the government then moves to a restrictive policy, the inflation rate will fall but unemployment will increase. The worst case from a social democratic point of view is the "noncooperative" solution shown in cell 4, where the unions persist in their aggressive demand for higher wages while the government reduces aggregate demand via budget cuts and tight money. In that case the collision between demand constraint and continued cost push would necessarily result in very high levels of unemployment. Hence, from the standpoint of a social democratic government, the "cooperative" solution in cell 1 is clearly optimal and the "noncooperative" solution in cell 4 is to be avoided if at all possible, while the two remaining outcomes are intermediate—each associated with both positive and politically unattractive negative effects.

The failure to coordinate macroeconomic policies can be attributed to the fact that there are important differences between the perspectives of the unions and those of the government. In the first place the unions use

Monetary and fiscal policy	Wage policy	
	Restrained	Aggressive
Expansionary Unemployment Inflation	(1) Low Low	(2) Low Very high
Restrictive Unemployment Inflation	(3) High Low	(4) Very high Very high

Figure 9.1. Coordination from the perspective of the social democratic government

a different set of criteria when evaluating outcomes (Figure 9.2). Insofar as the government wished to remain in office, it could not ignore inflation entirely, even if full employment remained its most important goal. For the unions, however, given the interests of their members, only unemployment (or at least the threat of job losses) was a problem of high salience. Inflation, however, need not directly concern union leaders. What mattered instead was the increase in workers' real incomes. Of course, since wage negotiations determine nominal rather than real wages, unanticipated inflation may impair workers' real incomes. But the most plausible union reaction to unanticipated inflation is not wage restraint, which would be best for reestablishing price stability, but more aggressive wage demands that would compensate workers for inflationary losses and anticipate future price increases.

That makes unions uncertain partners in the game of social democratic–Keynesian policy concertation. As long as the government's monetary and fiscal policies are in fact able to avoid unemployment, the unions are always tempted to defect from their "cooperative" strategy of voluntary wage restraint (cell 1) and to improve the distributive position

Monetary and fiscal policy	Wage policy	
	Restrained	Aggressive
Expansionary Unemployment Real wages	(1) Low Stagnant	(2) Low Increasing
Restrictive Unemployment Real wages	(3) High Stagnant	(4) Very high Increasing

Figure 9.2. Coordination from the perspective of the unions

of workers by fully exploiting their bargaining power, which is quite high under full employment (cell 2).

If, however, the government could switch to monetary and fiscal restraint despite the effect of such a policy on employment, self-interest would lead the unions to behave differently, since job security is even more important to workers than higher real incomes. In the face of rising unemployment, rational self-interested unions would try to avoid the loss of additional jobs (cell 4); self-interest would persuade them to practice wage restraint in order to stabilize firm profits and (in the best case) employment as well (cell 3). Consequently the government could once more pursue full employment by stimulating aggregate demand, and as soon as it succeeded, the cycle could begin anew.

The model sketched here, a cycle of full employment, inflation, unemployment, stabilization, and full employment, is politically improbable, however, although it was approximated by developments in the Federal Republic. Its implausibility is obvious from a common payoff matrix representing the rank orders of preferences of the unions and of a social democratic government (Figure 9.3). "Cooperative" strategies are defined for the government to stimulate aggregate demand and for the unions to practice voluntary wage restraint.

This figure shows that a social democratic government committed to the pursuit of full employment is fundamentally defenseless against uncooperative unions. As long as the government is unwilling to increase unemployment intentionally, it cannot respond to aggressive wage claims (cell 2) with deflation, because the result (cell 4) would be as unacceptable to a social democratic government as it would be to the unions. But if a social democratic government is forced by its own priorities to maintain a cooperative strategy, the unions are free to defect to a noncooperative strategy serving their own short-term interests. The result is high rates of inflation (Brittan and Lilley, 1977; Calmfors, 1982).

Voters usually hold the government in power responsible for economic performance. If, however, inflation forces a social democratic govern-

	Unions	
Social democratic government	Cooperative	Uncooperative
Cooperative	(1) 2, 1	(2) 1, 2
Uncooperative	(3) 0, 0	(4) −1, −1

Figure 9.3. Joint payoff matrix for unions and social democratic governments

ment to reorder its priorities to stay in power or the Social Democrats are replaced by a government with conservative-monetarist preferences, the nature of the game with the unions changes (Figure 9.4). A government that is willing to accept high unemployment and to concentrate instead on price stability (and other political issues) cannot be "exploited" by the unions. Instead, under pressure of high unemployment the unions will be forced by their own priorities to cooperate with government policy. By voluntarily restraining wages, the unions can at least reach their second-worst payoff (cell 3), whereas noncooperation would lead to their worst-case outcome (cell 4). Since a conservative-monetarist government would have no incentive to move from cell 3, which would be its optimum, the full employment-inflation-unemployment-stabilization cycle would thus end here.

The unions' vulnerability to conservative-monetarist policies, which the payoff matrix makes apparent, is often overlooked in the literature on corporatism. For instance, Lange and Garrett (1985), in analyzing the strategic interaction between unions and government, assert that unions can be expected to practice wage restraint only where a "leftist" government will reward them for their cooperation with full employment policies. In truth the situation is the exact reverse. Only a social democratic–Keynesian full employment policy can tempt unions to pursue aggressive wage demands, whereas a restrictive policy executed by a government that is relatively indifferent to rising unemployment will force even ideologically militant unions to moderate their wage demands.

The difficulty of realizing social democratic–Keynesian concertation thus results from a paradoxical asymmetry of interests between the unions and the government. As long as the government undertakes to ensure the unions' primary interest in job security through its expansionary policy, voluntary wage restraint seems an unattractive and hence precarious concession by the unions to the government. But as soon as the government switches to conservative-monetarist policies, wage restraint ceases to be a concession and becomes a self-interested union response—albeit under much less attractive conditions.

	Unions	
	Cooperative	Uncooperative
Conservative-monetarist government		
Cooperative	(1) 1,1	(2) −1,2
Uncooperative	(3) 2,0	(4) 0,−1

Figure 9.4. Joint payoff matrix for unions and conservative-monetarist governments

Moreover, as long as the government can live with the high unemployment resulting from its tight money policies, the unions cannot escape from cell 3 on their own. Aggressive wage demands will be punished by higher unemployment (cell 4), and, as long as the government restricts aggregate demand, further wage restraint will not produce full employment. In contrast to the voluntary but unstable union cooperation under expansionary monetary and fiscal policies, the union response to monetarism is involuntary but lasting and reliable. In other words, a social democratic–Keynesian full employment policy is the prisoner of the unions' wage policy, but the unions are prisoners of a conservative-monetarist stabilization policy.

Thus if the unions had a motive to cooperate with social democratic economic policy in the 1970s, that motive was not economic in the narrow sense, but political. As long as the government guaranteed full employment, the unions had no direct interest in playing their assigned role as inflation fighters, but they had every reason to avoid the trap of a conservative-monetarist regime that would drastically reduce their own range of options.

In the absence of this political risk, however, an egoistically rational union will pursue aggressive wage demands—even in a recession. Thus in 1976–82 the centrist coalition governments in Sweden never had a chance of coming to terms with the unions over an incomes policy. The fall of that coalition would have implied not a switch to monetarism but a more effective full employment policy. But since the election victory of the Social Democrats in autumn 1982, the centrist opposition has increasingly turned to a conservative-monetarist position in economic policy. This has strengthened the bargaining position of the politically weak Social Democrats vis-à-vis the unions so much that, despite all the difficulties within the unions, the government was able to persuade them to moderate their wage demands in the election year 1985.

CONDITIONS FAVORING THE STRATEGIC
CAPABILITY OF UNIONS

The search for explanations of economic policy success or failure in the four countries can thus be narrowed to the following question: under which institutional conditions were unions able to pursue their long-term and common interest in preserving a politically precarious full employment policy at the expense of their short-term interest in higher real-wage gains?

Analytically, this issue has two aspects. In the temporal dimension, wage restraint involves sacrificing short-term advantage for the sake of longer-term gains. In the interorganizational dimension, it involves orienting the individual unions and their subdivisions toward the common interest of the union movement as a whole. Both aspects of strategic competence are difficult to attain (i.e., they are not simply a matter of acting upon intellectual insight) because the interests in play may have different meanings from the point of view of different organizational units. Institutional structure is thus a very important element of the difficulties unions have to overcome in pursuing their long-term and common interest in a social democratic–Keynesian coordination between wage policy and government monetary and fiscal policy.

The neocorporatist literature has with good reason emphasized the problem of interorganizational strategic competence. Oriented toward the paradigm of collective goods, external effects, and the prisoners' dilemma, the neocorporatist literature stresses the fundamental discrepancy between a pluralistically fragmented organizational and decision-making structure and the pursuit of joint or macroeconomic goals. According to this thinking, small unions that compete with one another and decentralized negotiation systems would be incapable of collectively mounting rational strategies, whereas a corporatist structure with large, monopolistic, or "encompassing" (Olson, 1982:47–53) union organizations and centralized collective bargaining would be able to adopt a wage strategy that effectively promoted the common welfare of all workers and hence of the economy as a whole (Blaas, 1984; Cameron, 1984; Tarantelli and Willke, 1981; Streeck, 1978). In theory, this argument is correct.

Its practical significance is sometimes exaggerated, however. Not all union goals are collective goods and not all interactions between individual unions are governed by the destructive logic of the prisoners' dilemma. Moreover, monolithic, centralized organizations are not the only means to overcome these problems. To be sure, wage competition among individual unions has a dynamic of its own that drives wages up and contributes to inflation. And organizational boundaries certainly play an important role in this dynamic. Industrial unions that negotiate on an industry-wide basis generate less competitive pressure than do craft unions that negotiate independently of each other within the same plant.

So far, so good. But the prisoners' dilemma is not an unavoidable fate, as Axelrod demonstrated (1984), if the participants are engaged in a long-term relationship with one another or if they otherwise have the chance to come to terms about common and enforceable norms of distributive justice. The regulation of wage differentials is a prime example of such possibilities, and the Swedish and British unions have frequently developed rules for comparability and compensation designed to regulate and contain wage competition. Under relatively stable economic conditions they usually succeeded in doing so. Thus even with a fragmented union structure, the Hobbesian war of all against all is not an inevitable state of affairs.

The second limitation of the corporatist hypothesis seems even more important to me. Not all forms of "cooperative" union strategies (as seen from the state's point of view) have the nature of a collective good for the unions. Discussion seems to have focused too exclusively on the fight against inflation, in which it is indeed not worthwhile for small, competing unions to exercise restraint in wage demands unless others go along. And if many others go along, then it becomes worthwhile to defect from the alliance and push aggressively for higher wages. But is this also true when the aim is to avoid unemployment—which is different from re-establishing full employment? Full employment may be a public good, but unemployment also has the character of a "private bad" that affects individual regions, branches, plants, or job groups to varying degrees and which, to the extent that job loss can be traced back to inadequate profits, also can be combated within the individual plant by particularized wage restraint.

In any case many workers during a recession see the threat to their jobs in that way and behave accordingly. This is one of the most important reasons for the unions' vulnerability to a conservative-monetarist economic policy. The low wage demands that are desirable from the government's point of view coincide with the voluntary behavior of the rank and file when job losses are perceived as a real threat. Such responses are almost independent of the differing structures of union organization. Indeed, it is reasonable to presume that small unions would be even quicker to make concessions in negotiations at the firm level, hoping thereby to save their jobs at someone else's expense, while large and centralized unions might be able to avoid such a competitive race to cut wages, which would be ruinous from both a distributive and a macroeconomic point of view. Consequently, a conservative-monetarist policy does not depend on the organizational power, solidarity, and discipline of the large unions and can even afford to undermine them through legislative action (Streeck, 1984a).

The social democratic–Keynesian program is different. Because it guarantees full employment, it socializes the otherwise private or individual risk of unemployment. Thus it foregoes the possibility of exposing workers to the pressure of threatened job loss to force them to moderate their wage demands. Social democratic policy is thus completely dependent on voluntary union restraint in wage demands, and in this case restraint is indeed a collective good from the perspective of individual workers and small, egoistically rational unions, realized at the expense of their own immediate self-interest. Thus if social democratic–Keynesian coordination is to have a chance of success, it must rely on institutional mechanisms that replace the particularized calculus of interests with an orientation toward interests that are common to all unions.

But that is still not enough. Even a completely unified union movement would have an objective short-term interest in exploiting government-assured full employment in their wage negotiations. The social democratic–Keynesian coordination can thus succeed only if the unions orient themselves not only toward common as opposed to individual interests but also toward future as opposed to present interests. This requirement increases the difficulties of strategy as well as of theoretical analysis. An orientation toward the future and the sacrifice of present advantages for the sake of deferred gratification are highly precarious capabilities even at the level of individual action, although they can be supported by measures that discipline the freedom of spontaneous action (Elster, 1979). Institutions have precisely that function, and they are in principle able to achieve a degree of future orientation that extends beyond the individual horizons of their members. On the other hand, institutions can act only through representatives, and so they lack the freedom of the sovereign individual to toss egoistic interests to the winds. If institutions are to act in a future-oriented way, then their actions must be based on their institutional self-interest rather than on altruistic motives.

Under what conditions then could it be worthwhile for an egoistically rational union to subordinate its present wage demands to concern for the future stability of a social democratic–Keynesian full employment policy? We can approximate a provisional answer with the help of a thoughtful but highly abstract essay on "political exchange" by Alessandro Pizzorno (1978). Pizzorno emphasizes that unions' intertemporal strategic competence depends on their ability to see themselves as actors exercising a critical influence on future economic development. Indeed, actors who see themselves as impotent are not only relieved of moral responsibility, as expressed by the ethical maxim "duty implies capability," but would also have every egoistically rational motive to exploit all short-term advantages and to respond to the future only when it has become the present.

On what does mastery of the future then depend? It is not the same as the always-possible ex post attribution of economic effects to wage policy impulses. What is crucial is rather the ex ante estimate of those effects that can be brought about by one's own purposeful action. One's own intentions can be crossed by two kinds of events: by the strategic actions of other actors on the national economic policy scene and by unexpected changes in the international economic environment. The boundary between the two kinds of events is of course variable. Otherwise uncontrollable framing conditions can be influenced by shifts in the power relations between the actors, and shifts in the economic environment may change the power relations between the actors. Nevertheless, the distinction is analytically useful.

In the relatively stable economic environment of the 1950s and 1960s, even actors with little power, while unable to realize all desired goals, were able to anticipate the effects of their own actions with fair accuracy and orient their choices accordingly. That enabled actors to achieve a kind of "ecological coordination" or "spontaneous field control" (Dahl and Lindblom, 1953:99–105), made possible by mutual anticipation and adjustment, which largely prevented the uncontrolled escalation of negative developments. Even under the unfavorable conditions in Great Britain, with its fragmented industrial relations, wage-cost inflation in the 1950s and 1960s remained within narrow limits, despite near full employment.

As the world economic environment became more turbulent in the late 1960s, it became more difficult to anticipate not only economic conditions but also the reactions of other actors. Thus as the future became more uncertain, the temporal horizon of union wage policy had to become shorter, everything else being equal, unless a higher degree of explicit coordination with other actors could compensate for the increased uncertainty. Several authors consider this compensation for uncertainty to be the real secret of the "Austro-Keynesian" success (Ostleitner, 1982; Tichy, 1982). The theoretical foundation for this connection is obvious. For each individual the possibilities of controlling the environment are limited by the possible actions of others. However, to the extent that several actors cooperate within the framework of a common strategy, their potential for action increases over against their economic environment, and so does the chance that environmental turbulence may either be stabilized or neutralized in its effect.

Under crisis conditions, however such coordination could not have been achieved by means of the implicit "ecological" adaptation or the "partisan mutual adjustment" (Lindblom, 1965) that is characteristic of pluralistic democracies. It required the explicit orientation of economic policy measures to the demands of a common strategy, and a readiness to modify these measures on short notice if need be. Such coordination depends on power or consensus and hence on institutional conditions that favor either "hierarchical" or "hegemonic" or "cooperative" coordination of the most significant economic policy actors. Since compulsory coordination of union wage policy would have been neither economically sensible nor politically feasible in the four countries during the 1970s, the social democratic–Keynesian policy necessarily depended on informal hegemonic or cooperative solutions. These had to be solutions that guaranteed a "social memory" for all necessary contributions and sacrifices, so that participants would be relieved of the need to seek immediate compensation, a need that would otherwise undermine their cooperation (Ouchi, 1984:28–31).

INSTITUTIONAL PRECONDITIONS IN THE FOUR NATIONS

The institutional conditions for the coordination of wage policy were best met in Austria during the 1970s. In the following I compare these conditions from three angles: the unions' relation to the employers' side, the unions' relation to government policy, and finally the relation of the individual unions to one another and to the central union federation.

The Unions' Relation to the Employers' Side

In the unions' relation to employers, Austria has two institutional peculiarities whose importance for the success of the Austrian strategy is sometimes overestimated but certainly cannot be ignored. They are the large share of nationalized firms and the Commission for Prices and Wages. Both have their roots in the political compulsion to consensus that shaped Austria in the early postwar period, and both contributed to maintaining the postwar consensus even after the disappearance of the generation that experienced the leveling of political differences between the Catholic and Socialist factions in the Nazi concentration camps.

As noted in chapter 4, under political influence the nationalized firms and firms belonging to nationalized banks contributed considerably to stabilizing overall employment in Austria at the beginning of the crisis. However, for a number of years afterward they had to contend with the consequences of structural adjustment that was irresponsibly delayed in reliance on government support. In hindsight, the evaluation of their direct contribution to overcoming the crisis is thus rather ambivalent (Bauer, 1986). Because the nationalized firms did not belong to the business associations of the private sector, one also cannot assume a direct influence on their strategies. Nevertheless, their influence on the situational analysis and options for Austrian economic policy is extraordinarily important.

178

The following connection seems crucial to me. The Social Democrats and the Catholics have shared the leading positions in the nationalized industries since the Austrian Grand Coalition of the immediate postwar era. Thus the possibility of a management career is always one of the professional options for an ambitious unionist or socialist. In contrast to patterns of upward social mobility in other countries, their further career continues to depend on their continued good standing in their own camp. In the management and supervisory councils of nationalized firms and banks there is thus always a group of "practicing" socialists and union members who in cases of conflict will opt in favor of the goals of their original organizations (Dittrich, 1985:221–32). At the same time, however, they will take the management view of problems and will represent the firm's interests aggressively in discussions within the leftist camp. Moreover, there will be close "collegial" relations across political "camps" that generally promote the chances of consensus between the parties.

Relations between the unions and the Socialist party and the private sector of the economy have also benefited from the existence of the nationalized sector, since the private sector's problems are not fundamentally different from those of market-oriented public firms. Moreover, the private sector often benefits from measures that are taken primarily to assist nationalized industry. Thus the Austrian Left is not fundamentally estranged from the entrepreneurial function, as is often the case elsewhere. Despite all conflicts, in its practical politics since World War II the Left has emphasized the common interests of labor and capital rather than their competing interests. It has stressed the growth of investment, production, employment, and income, and the necessity for Austria to catch up with the richer nations of Western Europe, rather than conflicts over the distribution of income.

Cooperation in the Commission for Prices and Wages, which was formally instituted in 1957, also contributes to the convergence of perspectives. The commission has representatives from the federal government, the employers' side (Chambers of Commerce and Agricultural Chambers), and the workers (ÖGB [the Union Federation] and Labor Chambers), and it is viewed as the very embodiment of the Austrian social partnership (Matzner, 1975; Pelinka, 1981; Lang, 1981; Marin, 1982; Talos, 1985). The commission might best be understood as a continuation of the postwar practice of relying on agreements among the social partners rather than formal laws, which had to be approved by the Allies and thus were subject to Soviet veto. Even after the treaty of state of 1955 obviated the external necessity of "substitute lawmaking," the government of the Austrian Grand Coalition (and even more so the single-party governments after 1966) stressed the importance of maintaining and cultivating the consensus with the social partners. For this purpose the commission was eminently suitable. It seemed to accommodate the unions' demand for macroeconomic codetermination without fulfilling it expressly, and for that very reason it was marginally acceptable to private firms as well. Accordingly, participants even today stress not its positive functions but the complete voluntariness of the commission's proceedings and the absolutely nonbinding nature of its resolutions.

The explicit functions of the commission—approval of price increases (for part of the domestic supply) and permission to initiate wage negotiations—nevertheless have a direct and practical importance for economic policy (Ostleitner, 1982; Tichy, 1984). The time spent on the commission's proceedings delays the spontaneous reactions of prices to exogenous cost increases, and discussion about planned wage demands within the circle of peak organizations clarifies the macroeconomic implications and at the same time avoids overly emotional confrontations between unions and employers in the individual branches. Wage increases found acceptable by the commission are usually put through without strikes. The third subcommittee of the commission, founded in 1963, the Advisory Board for Economic and Social Issues, is another important influence in bringing about consensus with respect to politically controversial topics. In 1984, the year of the German strikes, for instance, the board suggested solutions for shortening the work week that were then adopted without much public attention in the bargaining agreements of the individual branches.

The institutional conditions for intertwining the interests of employers with the perspectives of the Social Democrats and the unions are much less well developed in the other countries than in Austria. Great Britain, of course, also has an above-average share of public firms, but the management careers for socialists and union members, which are guaranteed by proportional representation in Austria, are not available in Great Britain. British nationalized industries are thus a source of conflict rather than an institutional basis for social partnership. In Sweden and the Federal Republic, on the other hand, the number of government-owned firms is too small to have an influence on economic policy perspectives, although the semipublic status of Volkswagen was of considerable importance in shaping the strategies of the German metalworkers' union (Streeck, 1984b).

The relationships in the German coal and steel codetermination arrangement are the closest approximation to the Austrian model. But apart from the special legal position of the labor directors, the unions did not have the opportunity (or interest) to use their mandates on the supervisory boards in order to place their own people in the management of the codetermined firms. At the same time, however, the reform of 1972 strengthened the collaborative rights of works councils and established central works councils for all the plants of large firms (Streeck, 1984). As a consequence, codetermination provides the works councils, and the unions as well, with access to information and a considerable measure of influence, especially on personnel decisions, strengthening the social partnership in plants and firms. In individual areas, as in the nuclear industry, works councils and management have sometimes taken joint action, dictated by an "egoism of the firm." Nevertheless, in the Federal Republic there is nothing like the general convergence (or diffuseness) of interests and political perspectives of unions and management that one finds in Austria.

In Sweden there was significant nationalization only under the centrist coalition governments in the second half of the 1970s, and Social Democrats and the unions did not consider the nationalized firms a desirable increase of their influence but rather a limitation on their freedom to act in terms of economic policy. The Social Democrats thus worked even harder to liquidate or reprivatize the nationalized firms after 1982 then the centrist opposition parties demanded. On the other hand, since the end of the 1950s the public sector had supplied a substantial part of the private sector's investment capital from the reserves of the pension fund. And after the public sector became the debtor of the private sector as a result of the budget deficiencies of the late 1970s, the union movement attempted to gain influence on the investment decisions of the firms through the workers' fund. However, it is neither likely nor intended that the perspectives of unions and firms will come to converge as they do in Austria. The unions' strategic emphasis on distributive goals speaks against this possibility, as does their hegemonic self-image. Since the late 1930s the Swedish unions have seen themselves in control of the economy rather than as cooperative "social partners" of employers.

The British unions had no chance to become social partners for exactly the opposite reasons. They were and are too fragmented in their organization and too weak politically to entertain seriously any vision of hegemonic control of a capitalist economy. They also lack the ability to cooperate as partners in plants and firms. Without guaranteed rights of codetermination, they must rely exclusively on the fighting power and willingness of their rank and file and on the shop stewards mobilizing them (Degen, 1976; Taylor, 1978:125–46). The shop stewards, however, have neither the motive nor the competence to form any kind of partnership with management. They are exclusively the representatives of the immediate self-interest of the rank and file. Their willingness to engage in conflict may be influenced by moral appeals to the solidarity of the union movement, but otherwise it is determined only by prevailing conditions on the labor market and the mood of their members.

The institutions of macroeconomic partnership between capital and labor also have no direct counterparts outside Austria. In the Federal Republic, Concerted Action did not have the opportunity to develop into a functional equivalent of the Commission for Prices and Wages. And not even the Social Democrats seriously supported the establishment of economic and social councils that the unions constantly demanded. Codetermination in the Federal Republic is oriented toward plants or, at most, toward firms and thus cannot fulfill the functions of macroeconomic social partnership along Austrian lines (Dittrich, 1985). With the beginning of the employment crisis it has become apparent that there are very narrow limits to defending workers' interests in individual firms (Esser, 1982; Esser, Fach, and Väth, 1983; Hohn, 1984). Up to now, however, the German unions have not found a lever to exert stronger influence on macroeconomic development, and in any case they have been on the defensive since the beginning of the crisis.

In Sweden the peace agreement of Saltsjöbaden of 1938 has kept the level of conflict in industrial relations low in the postwar period. Moreover, the centralization of wage negotiations pushed through by the employers in the 1950s and accepted by the Swedish union federation (LO) had created the institutional conditions for a common orientation toward macroeconomic demands. At the end of the 1960s this common orientation was expressed in the wage-setting formula of the EFO model. However, after the model was invalidated by the crisis, strong rivalries emerged among the individual unions, and union goals were radicalized. The early 1980s saw a spread and intensification of strikes on a level unknown since before World War II. The employers reacted with an attempt to do away with centralized wage negotiations altogether. That would have undermined the institutional bases not only for solidaristic wage policy but also for macroeconomic social partnership, but in the increasing ideological polarization of the 1980s employers were willing to accept those consequences. The social democratic government and the leadership of the LO, on the other hand, used all means at their disposal to maintain or reestablish the conditions for the macroeconomic orientation of wage policy.

In Great Britain, finally, the organizational weakness of the central union federation, the TUC, is exceeded, if that is possible, by the weakness of the Confederation of British Industry on the employers' side (Grant and March, 1977). Thus an incomes policy worked out by the peak associations was out of the question. Even the Social Contract of the

1970s, which was in part successful, was limited to an understanding between the Labour government and the unions and did not include the employers. As a consequence, the employers' associations also failed to support the government's attempt to keep businesses from making excessive wage concessions in autumn 1978.

Conditions were more favorable in the field of economic development, where, in contrast to incomes policy, distributive conflicts between capital and labor may be subordinated to a common interest in growth (and subsidies). The Conservatives created the National Economic Development Council in the 1960s, and subsequent Labour governments gave it their full support. The council initiated discussion between employers and unions in individual branches and with the government over economic development policy; in several areas it achieved visible gains in modernization (Grant, 1982; Wilks, 1984; Middlemas, 1983). In the crisis period this policy dialogue broke down, however, because of the growing discrepancy between the ambitious aspirations of leftist Industry Minister Tony Benn's comprehensive economic development planning and the practical necessity to save endangered large firms without reference to any preconceived plans. The Thatcher government finally extended its hostility to any form of government planning or government-organized social partnership, even to the National Economic Development Council, although it has not been formally abolished.

The Relationship between the Unions and the Government

The unions' relationship with the government is also closer in Austria than in other nations. One reason is the pattern of proportional representation in leadership positions in public and quasi-public sector entities (for instance the central bank), and in the numerous committees that advise the government, an arrangement that was initiated by the coalition government of the immediate postwar era (Lehmbruch, 1967; Katzenstein, 1984). As a consequence, the unions, which have members in both camps, have every reason to see themselves as equal participants in the republic. An even more important relationship runs in the opposite direction, through the political parties that form factions within the unions (as well as within other sectors of the corporatist structure of associations and chambers) and draw up their own slate of candidates in union elections.

An important consequence of this legal and overt politicization is the relatively low importance of the principle that the unions should be "neutral" or "independent" as to party politics; that principle has merely rhetorical presence. A member of the socialist faction within the union federation (ÖGB), for instance, is naturally and legitimately a Socialist party politician, and it is just as natural that as a Socialist politician he is also a union official. Because there are no formal or informal norms against holding multiple offices, it is apparently not a problem in Austria that a federal minister or president of the legislature might concurrently hold office as president of an individual union or even of the ÖGB. At least under a social democratic government, the personal and cognitive distance between union and government policy in Austria is smaller than in any of the other three countries.

None of the other countries has a practice corresponding to the Austrian system of proportional representation. Nevertheless, Swedish unions have an even greater substantive influence than Austrian unions in the investigative commissions and other consensus-building procedures that usually precede political decisions (Anton, 1980; Elder and Thomas, 1982). Their position in the networks of institutionalized participation in government decision-making processes was so strong that even under centrist governments important decisions could not be put through over their opposition (Korpi, 1978; 1983; Esping-Andersen and Korpi, 1984). And if the Social Democrats were running the government, then the unions were not concerned with proportional representation at all; they had the initiative in all areas of economic and labor market policy that mattered to them. To be sure, that is in principle always an initiative from without. The complete interpenetration of union policy and party politics that characterizes Austria does not exist in Sweden. Swedish white-collar unions are neutral as to party politics to begin with, and while LO locals may become collective members in the local organizations of the Social Democratic party, at the central level both sides scrupulously observe the independence of the party from the union. Cabinet ministers cannot be active union officials at the same time.

In the Federal Republic, there are also certain parallels to Austrian proportional representation. The government in office is not completely free in its selection of political appointees. There is first the need to balance the claims of the coalition parties (and within each party, there is a need for a balanced presentation of regional subdivisions or of religious denominations). In addition, the requirements of federalism, and in some cases constitutional or statutory rules of selection, work to assure a certain balance in the representation of social groups on many decision-making or advisory bodies. However, the balance among the social partners is only one of numerous party-political, denominational, regional, or professional criteria of representation. As a consequence, the unions in the Federal Republic have no reason to see themselves as partners in a bilateral monopoly governing an Austrian-style "corporatist" republic.

Moreover, the relationship between the unions and the Social Democratic party in the Federal Republic is less intimate than in Austria or Sweden. Even without the threat of a serious schism, German unions, in which there are no official party-political factions, must respect the principle of political neutrality. Conversely, the SPD cannot hope to win the support of a majority of the voters simply by identifying itself with the interests of the unions, which represent only about 30 percent of the employed workers, as opposed to about 60 percent for the counterpart organization in Austria (see Table 9.1). Thus union officials frequently hold party office, and union membership is practically obligatory for SPD politicians (and even in the CDU it is not infrequent). But active union officials are not permitted to hold government office, and the unions do not dominate the policy of the Social Democrats even when the party is in opposition, let alone when it is in power as part of a coalition. On the other hand, social democratic chancellors and ministers are not immune from the criticism and public protest of the unions. At its best the relationship between the Social Democrats and the unions constitutes an effective

Table 9.1 Union membership, membership share of the large union federations, and number of member unions

	Austria	FRG	GB	Sweden
Percentage of employed workers organized in unions				
1973	59.8	32.7	50.6	72.2
1979	59.3	35.9	57.7	79.1
1983	60.5*	35.5	52.3	82.6
	ÖGB	DGB	TUC	LO
Percentage of organized workers belonging to the largest union federations				
1982–83	100	85	90	60
Percentage of workers belonging to the largest union federations				
1982–83	60.5	30.2	47.1	49.6
Number of member unions in the largest union federations				
1960	16	16	183	43
1970	16	16	142	27
1978–82	15	17	109	24

Sources: Visser, 1985; author's own calculations.
*1982.

partnership in Germany, but without the sense of an inviolable identity of interests and perspectives that one finds in Austria.

The relationship between the Labour party and the unions in Great Britain is even more troubled than in the Federal Republic. A first-past-the-post election system and the dominance of one-party governments have produced an adversarial winner-take-all political culture that could not conceivably coexist with the practice of proportional patronage. At the same time, however, the influence of political parties is less pervasive in Britain than in the other countries. The policy influence of the civil service and of politically neutral royal commissions ensures broader consensus and greater political continuity than one might expect given the brutal rules of prime ministerial government (Crossman, 1979; Ashford, 1981). However, the unions benefit less from the prepolitical balancing of interests in Britain than they do in Austria or Sweden. In the 1970s, for instance, there were radical leftist Keynesians among academic experts and even among the otherwise predominantly conservative higher officials of the Treasury. But the distance between the classes was and is so great in Britain that the unions could not see that their interests were represented by members of the Establishment, however ideologically close they may have been.

The relationship of the British unions to government policy is thus shaped by the lower classes' basic distrust of "those up there," which is mitigated but not eliminated when the Labour party comes to power (Panitch, 1976). But when that happens the extremely close organizational involvement (due to collective union membership in the party and the party's financial dependence on compulsory contributions by union members) is a constant cause of frustration and disappointment (Crouch, 1982a). It creates muddy political relations because the unions, which hardly participate in the day-to-day work in the party organization, cast the votes of their collective members at the yearly party congresses and can push through almost any of their demands in a spirit of paying the piper and calling the tune. As a consequence, the parliamentary party and the opposition leader or the elected head of government are practically compelled to insist on their formal independence and on the sovereignty of Parliament as a matter of principle, and to ignore party congress resolutions almost routinely. Anything else would amount to an abdication of political responsibility.

It is clear that this tension does the relationship between the party and its members in Parliament no good. It was one of the structural reasons for the growing distance between the party's rank and file and its political leadership that finally led to the secession of the SDP in 1979. From the unions' point of view, the lesson to be learned from such experiences was that the party and its resolutions could not be trusted, especially once a Labour government was in power. Thus in 1972 the unions began to make their political support in parliamentary elections dependent on formal, quasi-contractual commitments by Labour leadership on what the unions considered the most important issues of government policy. They also established a standing committee, the TUC–Labour Party Liaison Committee, to ensure continuing coordination at the highest levels of union and party leadership. After the election, however, it turned out that although the government kept its part of the bargain at first, the unions found it extremely difficult to produce the voluntary wage restraint that they had promised. The reasons for that difficulty lay exactly where theorists of neocorporatism would look for them: in the internal structure of the union organization and in the interrelations among the individual unions.

The Internal Structure of the Union Organization

In comparison with Great Britain, the internal structure of the union organization is much more unified in the other three nations. Whereas the Trades Union Congress contains more than one hundred individual unions (with a still larger number of small and very small unions outside of the TUC), the three other countries have only 15 to 25 separate unions, which are predominantly organized according to industry. Nevertheless, even here the differences are important. We can differentiate in three dimensions.

1. The level of unionization (and hence its potential political influence and its potential effectiveness in case of strikes) is highest in Sweden, with more than 80 percent of the employed work force organized in unions. It is lowest in the Federal Republic, with a mere 36 percent (Table 9.1). In Sweden, however, the largest union federation represents only 60 percent of the total number of organized workers, whereas in the Federal Republic it represents 85 percent, in Great Britain 90 percent, and in Austria 100 percent.

2. However, the organization of unions into one large federation is not a sufficient condition for avoiding inflationary wage competition between individual unions. What matters is rather the demarcation of union jurisdictions and the power relations among them. In the Federal Republic the unions are organized on industry lines, and the German labor union federation (DGB) unions represent both blue-collar and white-collar workers (and sometimes civil servants as well). These unions do not compete for members nor do they compete for wages within the same branch or the same plant, as is true in Great Britain and Sweden.

187

The German white-collar union (DAG), which is not part of the DGB federation, has steadily lost influence. In 1983 it represented only 24 percent of the white-collar workers in the private sector who belonged to unions. As a rule, DAG collective bargaining agreements follow those of the DGB unions. In the public sector, the German Federation of Civil Servants (DBB) represents only 25 percent of organized public employees (Visser, 1985: Table 5). If we consider only federal civil servants, the DBB share is higher; however, the salaries of civil servants, who cannot strike under German law, are not determined by negotiation but are set by law. To be sure, they closely follow the results achieved by the ÖTV, the large DGB union for employees and laborers in the public sector. Thus the negotiation monopoly of the industrial unions federated in the DGB is not seriously challenged by competing unions.

In Austria, as in Sweden, only the blue-collar unions are organized on an industry basis. But the white-collar union belongs to the ÖGB federation and orients its wage demands to those of the blue-collar unions. Similar conditions prevailed in Sweden during the 1950s and 1960s. However, the greater number of white-collar and civil servant unions and their organizational and political independence from the blue-collar LO federation made hegemonic coordination more difficult as their membership and organizational strength increased. Negotiation cartels organized by the white-collar unions contained the rivalry between professional groups, but the basic conflict between the interests of civil servants and higher-level white-collar employees and the LO's goal of maximal equalization of wage incomes intensified. Since the 1970s this conflict has been the basic structural problem of the Swedish union movement.

In Great Britain, finally, with its fragmented union structure and its coexistence of different organizational principles, industrial unions compete with a multitude of professional and craft unions and also with the large "general unions" that transcend individual branches. The rivalry between the individual unions is mitigated by the prohibition, sanctioned by the TUC, on recruiting members from other unions, and it is sometimes constrained by common wage negotiations. Nevertheless, union rivalry still shapes industrial relations in Britain. The Donovan Report of 1968 saw it as the main cause of the inflationary wage-cost push that limited the options for government economic policy more severely in Great Britain than in comparable nations. Neither the Thatcher government's antiunion laws nor the deep crisis of the British economy have basically changed these structural conditions.

3. The third dimension describes the degree of vertical centralization within the unions. Austria has the highest degree of centralization in its

formal organization. There are no unions outside the ÖGB federation, and internally the ÖGB has a legal and financial monopoly. It collects membership contributions and passes shares on to the individual unions, it hires the secretaries for the individual unions, and the wage agreements bargained out by the individual unions are formally concluded in the name of the federation. None of the other countries has comparable conditions. As far as actual wage policy decisions are concerned, however, Sweden seems to have the greatest degree of centralization; it is the only country in which wage negotiations for all industry branches are conducted between the central union federation and the central employers' association. In the three other countries there are at best branchwide wage agreements by individual unions. If we look more closely, however, these seemingly clear distinctions begin to disappear.

The clearest and simplest situation is that in the Federal Republic, with its one-step system of collective wage negotiations. The DGB federation is excluded from any direct participation in wage setting, and it has even given up its statutory responsibility for wage coordination. The individual unions are legally independent and solely responsible for wage settlements for their branches, with agreements concluded nationally or regionally (and in a few exceptional cases, by firm). These settlements have direct legal effect on the individual employment contracts. Collective negotiations beneath the level of standard wage agreements are not a union matter but are carried out by legally institutionalized elected works councils that have neither the competence to negotiate wage issues nor the right to lead strikes, although they are authorized to negotiate for other benefits that may have a monetary value, for instance, in exchange for the approval of overtime (Streeck, 1984). Wage drift, which exists in the Federal Republic as well, is thus always the result of "voluntary" payments by employers that exceed their legal obligation. Such payments occur under the pressure of labor scarcity in regional or craft-specific labor markets (or under the compulsion of wildcat strikes with which unions and works committees may have nothing to do). But wage drift never results from union wage negotiations on the lower levels.

In the three other countries, in contrast, the system of collective wage negotiations has at least two levels. In Austria the wage agreements concluded by the individual unions for the whole branch dominate. But before these negotiations can be opened, the Commission for Prices and Wages must give its approval based on a presentation by the ÖGB federation of the negotiation goals of the individual unions. Thus well before negotiations begin there is an informal clarification, which does not amount to an explicit wage guideline by the federation but does nevertheless contribute to a common understanding about wage levels that are macroeconomically sound. This informal understanding is reinforced in the unions by intensive communication within the "Socialist party faction" of the ÖGB, which brings top union officials together with government economic policy makers every two weeks. Within the Commission for Prices and Wages, the connection between the subcommittee on wages and the subcommittee on prices also plays an important role, facilitating discussions of the probable effects of wage increases on prices and vice versa. The attempt to push through above-average wage increases in a branch of industry with high earnings, which would entail the approval of above-average price increases, thus meets resistance not only from the employers but also from the other unions.

Unlike works councils in the Federal Republic, Austrian works councils, which are formally independent of the unions, can exploit the higher ability to pay of prosperous firms to reach local agreements on over-scale wage increases. In the next round of bargaining the increased effective wage rate is locked in and is thus removed from the employer's discretion while increases in the general standard wages will gradually catch up. In this way there is little room for wage drift that is not controlled by the unions, even if this practice runs counter to the goal of lessening wage differentials among different branches (Elliott and Fallick, 1981). Nevertheless, negotiations at the level of individual plants remain a possible source of problems from the macroeconomic perspective of ÖGB headquarters, and they receive constant attention. The individual unions therefore take pains to include as many representatives of works councils as possible in their collective bargaining delegations, in order to ensure a better understanding of economic conditions at the plant level.

But ÖGB headquarters dare not rely solely on this mechanism. According to its firm conviction, the lower negotiation levels must not only understand macroeconomic necessities but also feel the pressure of international competition if they are to maintain a stability-oriented wage policy. Thus the ÖGB took a position opposite to that of unions in the other nations. Even during the crisis it was a consistent opponent of all attempts to loosen the Austrian hard currency policy, believing that the wage restraint that had been accepted since 1975 would be jeopardized by such a change. In the ÖGB's view, the best proof was the development in Sweden, where after autumn 1976, when the Swedish krona was uncoupled from the German mark, the hoped-for competitive advantages of repeated devaluations were always consumed by an accelerated wage-price spiral. But of course, institutional conditions in Sweden were less favorable than those in Austria, and not only because of competition among the unions.

From the mid–1950s until the early 1980s there were three formal negotiation levels between employers and unions in Sweden: the central negotiations between the LO federation and the National Employers' Association, SAF, the branch negotiations, and the local wage negotiations between the union representatives in individual plants (who can lead legal strikes, unlike the German and Austrian works councils) and the individual firms. With the increasing precision of regulations for the central wage structure and the progressive reduction of permissible wage differentials, however, the branch level lost its importance. The real tension (apart from growing conflicts with the white-collar unions) was thus between the central and the local negotiation levels. The local level had never submitted to a strict discipline from LO headquarters, and the democratization movement of the 1970s had further increased the combativeness of union representatives in profitable or nationalized firms.

It is true that the effects of increasing wage drift on the goals of a solidaristic wage policy are reduced by the proliferation of compensation clauses, but only at the price of a structural wage-cost inflation that cannot be contained by union headquarters. The attempt of employers to abolish centralized wage negotiations only intensified these problems, because the strong branch unions were now able to achieve maximum settlements for themselves and still supported the demands of the weaker LO unions by solidarity strikes. When the three-step negotiation system was reintroduced, however, the intensity of central regulations was reduced to allow more scope for branch negotiations.

In Great Britain, finally, there have never been central wage negotiations for the whole economy in any formal sense. In the 1960s and 1970s the branchwide agreements that had dominated in the early postwar years became less important for the private sector, although they continued to dominate in the public sector. At the same time the practical importance of wage negotiations by shop stewards at the plant level, which are informal and may be enforced by walkouts, has also decreased. Instead, the larger firms have shifted to firmwide or at least plantwide formal wage agreements with the unions and they have also tried to limit wage negotiations with shop stewards as much as possible. The significance of branchwide agreements was thereby restricted to ensuring minimum wage conditions (Flanagan et al., 1983:363ff.). But even if these efforts to tame the militancy of the shop stewards could be maintained under more favorable labor market conditions (which is uncertain), the British system of collective wage negotiations would still be the most decentralized among the four countries. If we also consider the extreme horizontal fragmentation of the union structure, the institution-

	Austria	FRG	GB	Sweden
Macroeconomic level	x		x	xxx
Branch level	xxxx	xxxxxx	x	x
Plant level	x		xxxx	xx

Figure 9.5. Significance of wage negotiations on the macroeconomic, branch, and plant levels

al conditions for a wage policy oriented toward macroeconomic requirements are indeed extraordinarily unfavorable.

The success of the voluntary incomes policy in the three years from 1975 to 1978 thus becomes all the more impressive. As noted, it arose primarily from an extreme exertion of the leadership authority in the TUC and in several large unions, and from the political and moral pressure for solidarity that was generated. Solidarity received some institutional help from the rule in the TUC constitution according to which majority decisions at the annual congress were binding on all member unions under punishment of exclusion (in which case other unions were allowed to raid the excluded union's members). However, such crude means could be used to push through only extremely simple, "moral" guidelines that could easily be checked on the plant level, such as the limitation of wage increases to a fixed sum that was the same for everyone. By the same token, this type of incomes policy changed the income differentials among professional groups in ways that were not previously legitimated and that could not long be accepted by the craft and technicians' unions. Thus under the institutional conditions of British union organization, voluntary wage restraint was feasible only in a morally exceptional situation and could succeed only for a short time.

The distribution of responsibilities for wage negotiations among the three levels differs significantly from nation to nation (Figure 9.5). In Austria and especially in the Federal Republic the emphasis is on branch-level negotiations; in Sweden in the 1970s it was on central negotiations, and in Great Britain it is on plant negotiations.

COMPARATIVE INTERPRETATION

We can draw the following conclusions from this comparative survey of the institutional conditions that facilitate longer-term perspectives and a macroeconomic orientation of union wage policy.

Austria

Austria had the optimal set of institutional arrangements for cooperative coordination in its relationship between the unions and the employers as well as in its relationship between the unions and government
policy. The unions emphasized growth instead of distribution; there was
widespread appreciation of the management point of view within the
"Socialist camp"; and there was a tradition of cooperation in social partnership going back to the early postwar years. These factors permitted
the peak associations to develop a common view of economic problems
and an understanding of the goals, options, and constraints on each side
that was not reached in any of the other countries (Matzner, 1975). The
proportional representation rule extended social partnership far into
the reaches of government, where it was again intensified by the near
identity between union policy and Socialist party policy (and a somewhat
lesser coincidence of views between the People's party, ÖVP, and the
employers).

Nevertheless, Austria is not a "union state." Even under a socialist
government, and even under the charismatic leadership of Bruno
Kreisky, the Left never achieved the hegemonic position that the Swedish Social Democrats occupied together with the LO in the first three
postwar decades (Esping-Andersen and Korpi, 1984). One reason is that
in Sweden the centrist camp was politically divided, while in Austria it
was represented by a large party capable of winning a majority. A second, probably more important reason is the institutional system itself,
based as it is on the principles of parity representation, political balance,
and unanimity. Given these rules, both sides accept that they must try to
find consensual solutions.

But why are the rules still accepted when clear parliamentary major-
ities would permit unilateral decisions? The institutions of social partnership in Austria are not based on the constitution and are by and large
not even written into law but are completely voluntary, in contrast to
German "cooperative federalism" that had imposed a need for political
compromise in the 1970s (Scharpf, 1985). Unlike the situation in the
Federal Republic, in Austria an emphatic "socialist" policy of confrontation would not have jammed the political works but would have destroyed the institutions based on consensus, as employers' complaints
about codetermination completely ruined Concerted Action in West
Germany or as the unilateral adoption of the workers' fund may have
disabled the previous rules of consensus democracy in Sweden.

But the vulnerability of Austrian institutions is also the source of their
power to shape behavior. For the top officials of the unions, employers'

associations, and political parties in Austria, the trauma of 1934 still seems fresh: the short civil war between the Catholics and the Socialists, followed by Austrofascism, the Anschluß, the war, and total defeat. There is in Austria, as I learned through my interviews, a primordial fear of the possible disastrous consequences of open political confrontation. This fear provides even the succeeding generation of Austrian leaders with a plausible motive for their unrelenting commitment to achieving understanding among the social partners and their political camps. As a consequence, Austria is governed by an elite cartel or a "pluralistic alliance for advancement" (the phrase is Egon Matzner's) among careerists in both camps.

The actual problem for Austrian unions is thus not so much the search for possible compromises with employers, which has been "objectified" as much as possible, but rather the acceptance of the elite consensus by the membership of their own organizations. The strict centralization of internal personnel and career decisions within the union helps in this undertaking. For all their good fellowship in social contact and all the demonstrative respect for the autonomy of individuals and subordinate organizations, the rules of the game in the socialist camp seem to be much more brutal than in the conservative camp, where one can still retreat into the private sector. Anyone who wants to get ahead must be accepted (by the other side as well); anyone who wants to maintain a position must toe the party line; and anyone who no longer belongs can get nowhere further in his or her own camp or in the career fields it controls, neither in politics nor in the civil service, neither in the associations nor in state-owned industry, neither in academia nor in journalism. Thus the Austrian consensus extracts a price from those who produce and maintain it, but coordination between union wage policy and government economic policy is indeed easier to achieve there than elsewhere.

Great Britain

In comparison, we can now identify those institutional problems in each of the other countries that make cooperative coordination between union wage policy and government economic policy more difficult. They are especially apparent in Great Britain, where the unions do not have with either the employers or the government apparatus long-term cooperative relations that might reduce uncertainty and encourage a longer-term orientation. At the same time the fragmented and decentralized union organization is an obstacle to concerted efforts within and among individual unions. The only element on the positive side in the past was the very close but also difficult and stressful link with the Labour party.

Under the pressure of an acute crisis, that connection was sufficient to mobilize political and emotional loyalties in the union movement that temporarily disabled otherwise effective institutional constraints. But the success of voluntary incomes policy could not be maintained over the long run under given institutional conditions, and it could not have been achieved at all under a different government.

Thus it is not surprising that the Thatcher government gave up any attempt to revive statutory or voluntary incomes policies. As long as it was willing and politically able to use high unemployment to ensure noninflationary wage settlements (Flanagan et al., 1983:436–46), its program did not depend on the voluntary cooperation of the unions. For the opposition, however, which cannot simply strike massive unemployment from its catalog of horrors, the uncontrollable dynamics of wage competition are a problem whose importance intensifies with any increase in employment. The Labour party is once again pinning its hopes of controlling inflation on its special political relationship to the unions, while the "alliance" of the SDP and the Liberals would have embraced a tax-based incomes policy, an idea developed in the United States by Wallich and Weintraub (1971; see also Layard, 1982; Layard and Jackman, 1982). In the United States, with weak or no unions, this proposal might work. But in Great Britain, the structure of industrial relations is so deranged that the proposal would probably encounter nearly as many institutional problems as the central incomes policy of the Labour party it is supposed to replace.

The suggestion of permanently institutionalized machinery for the mediation of strikes to ensure an employment-oriented wage policy seems hardly more promising to me (Meade, 1982:108–18). It underestimates the institutional causes of the British inclination to strike (Cameron, 1984) and postulates an economic rationality for the unions' wage policy that cannot be maintained in the fragmented, decentralized, and competitive structure of British labor relations. Anyone who spends time thinking about the possible modalities of Keynesian coordination between incomes policy and full employment policy in Great Britain ought to conclude that reform of the unions' organizational structure is the first order of business (Streeck, 1978). I do not, however, see any sign that the British Left has resumed serious discussion about structural reforms, which it dropped after the Donovan Report (1968) and the failure of the Industrial Relations Act of 1971.

Sweden

The institutional conditions in Sweden are different from those in Great Britain in almost every respect. Swedish unions had maintained

hegemonic-cooperative relations with their counterparts on the employer side for decades, and they not only had every opportunity for equal
participation in the preparation of government decisions but have usually initiated such decisions in areas of importance to them. At the same
time, their own structure was and is much more strongly concentrated
and centralized than that of the British unions. Nevertheless, in the last
decade the coordination between government economic policy and the
unions' wage policy encountered problems resembling those in Great
Britain. Coordination was obviously possible only if political loyalty to a
social democratic government could be mobilized. And as in Britain
after 1975, voluntary wage restraint was maintained in Sweden after
1982 only with much sound and fury and by dramatic appeals to the
national responsibility of the unions, and still it was threatened by rivalries among individual unions.

One might thus conclude that the decisive factor for wage policy is the
coexistence of competing unions in the same branch of industry and in
the same plants—which is the only significant feature that Swedish industrial relations share with those in Great Britain. This is also the only
significant weakness in comparison with Austria. Such an interpretation
would indeed have a certain microsociological plausibility. As "voluntary
organizations" (Streeck, 1981), unions must be highly sensitive to the
danger of losing their members, regardless of their formal constitution.
Let us further assume that if wages in one job are below those in neighboring jobs in the same firm, workers will regard that "relative depriva-
tion" as a serious injury to their interests. When that is so, any situation
in which wages for neighboring jobs are bargained out by separate
unions independently is potentially unstable. If one of the unions
achieves above-average wage increases, the others in the next round
must break even or gain an advantage in order to keep the loyalty of
their own members. This condition was met in Sweden when the white-
collar unions united to form the bargaining cartel PTK in the 1970s and
from then on were no longer willing to follow the leadership of the blue-
collar unions in matters of pay.

But that is not the whole explanation. The coordination of separate
bargaining cycles for blue-collar workers and for white-collar employees
in the same branch should not have posed insoluble problems for organizations with the strategic, tactical, and communicative competence of
the Swedish unions. The EFO model at the end of the 1960s, which
permitted wages in sectors oriented toward the domestic market to be
coordinated with wages in the export sector, demonstrated this. Thus
the Swedish unions' inability to coordinate blue- and white-collar wages
in the 1970s and 1980s cannot simply be attributed to organizational

factors. Rather, I believe that two kinds of distributive conflict were crucial, conflicts that did not exist to the same degree in other countries.

Both conflicts, although they may have had different vectors, resulted from the increasingly uncompromising drive to equalize primary incomes that the blue-collar LO federation launched beginning in the mid–1960s. There is reason to think that the LO could not have been quite as relentless if it had also represented the interests of white-collar employees. On the one hand, this radicalization of solidaristic wage policy has helped greatly to increase the general awareness of "unjustifiable" wage differentials in comparison to other firms, even in distant branches or regions. No other country has developed such a perfect system of compensation clauses assuring the transmission of local wage drift throughout the economy. At the same time, however, the internal democratization of Swedish unions and the accountability of negotiators in local wage rounds create conditions under which all opportunities for generating local wage drift will in fact be exploited.

At the same time, however, qualified workers and technicians, professionals, civil servants, and doctors seem to have become less willing to sacrifice their own interests to the imperatives of solidaristic wage policy or to refrain from exploiting their bargaining power in the key sectors of public and private services and in the export industries (De Geer et al., 1986). Even Sweden apparently has its "me generation" and its yuppies. Consequently, even the metalworkers' union was recently forced by its members to accept a management offer of greater wage differentials, so it is no wonder that the nonsocialist white-collar and civil service unions have begun to oppose the LO's moral imperialism and to demand higher raises for their members.

The growing difficulties of wage policy coordination in Sweden are thus not entirely organizational in nature. They express a deep conflict between the LO's extremely demanding aspirations to equality and the new ideological self-confidence not only of Swedish entrepreneurs but also of highly qualified workers and professionals. Both sides contribute to the inflationary wage dynamic. It results equally from the privileged groups' more ruthless exploitation of their labor market power and from the LO's stubborn refusal to recognize the interests of professionals or to accept the unequal distribution of primary incomes that results from unequal market power. The first of these causes may be unavoidable under present conditions of rapid technological and structural change, but the second depends on the LO's strategic orientation, which could be changed. I thus believe that the recent wage conflicts in Sweden were never an unavoidable tragedy, as they were in Great Britain in 1978–79. For all the obvious parallels, the Swedish struggle was strategically calculated, waged by an "encompassing" union organization, intact and self-confident. Since the end of the 1960s that union has lost its uncontested dominance of the labor movement but not its capacity for strategic action.

Federal Republic

Where does the Federal Republic stand in this comparison of the unions' capacity for strategic action? Labor-management relations at the level of the firm are far more cooperative in the Federal Republic than they are in Great Britain. But on the branch level the institutions and modes of behavior characteristic of Austria's social partnership have evolved in only a few areas, for instance in mining, construction, and the textile and chemical industries. In other sectors relations between employers' associations and unions tend to be more distant and adversarial (Streeck, 1981; 1982). On the central level, before Concerted Action and again after its demise, there were and are occasional summit discussions between the DGB's board and the boards of the peak employers' and business organizations. But neither Concerted Action nor these contacts can be compared with the Austrian social partnership or with Swedish peak negotiations.

Before the Grand Coalition of the 1960s, union participation in the formulation of government economic policy was at arm's length, as in Great Britain, although the unions played a more important role in the formulation of labor and social security policy through their participation in the public insurance corporations. During the Grand Coalition the perspectives of unions and employers began to converge under Keynesian auspices, but that ended with the decline of Concerted Action and the passing of the Ministry of Economics to the Free Democrats. Afterward the relationship of the German unions to government policy depended on their relationship with the Social Democrats and on that party's influence on economic policy, as it did in Great Britain and Sweden. In the last years of the social-liberal coalition the relationship became more distant and conflictual, and after the political turn in autumn 1982 the relationship between unions and government even became hostile on both sides.

Finally, internal conditions in the German unions were not especially favorable for a macroeconomically coordinated wage policy. In the DGB federation there is neither a level of central wage negotiations, as in Sweden, nor an equivalent to the common discussion and approval of individual union wage demands, as in the Austrian Commission for Prices and Wages. Unlike even the TUC, the DGB cannot bind the wage

Table 9.2 Increase in real hourly wages in industry, 1973–1979 (%)

	1973	1974	1975	1976	1977	1978	1979
Austria	4.7	5.1	8.6	1.4	3.0	2.0	2.3
FRG	3.5	3.3	2.1	1.9	3.7	2.3	1.3
GB	3.4	1.0	4.7	2.8	−9.6	9.2	1.4
Sweden	1.4	1.0	4.6	6.9	−4.3	−1.1	0.5
OECD Europe	5.2	3.8	7.1	3.2	0.9	4.7	2.1

Source: OECD *Historical Statistics*, 1960–1983.

policy of its member unions even in a national emergency by a majority decision of its board of directors or even of the assembly of the whole. Nevertheless, the actual wage development in the Federal Republic after 1974 was more moderate than in almost any other OECD country, and of the four countries in this study it corresponded most closely to the requirements of a Keynesian coordination at the beginning of the crisis period (Table 9.2). Is this a contradiction, and if so, how can it be resolved?

Some economists have pointed out that unemployment in the Federal Republic rose especially quickly and forced the unions to keep their wage demands down (Calmfors, 1985). This interpretation cannot be rejected out of hand, especially if we refer not to registered unemployment (which was much higher in many countries) but to the job losses experienced in the plants. However, it does not explain the relatively moderate wage increases before the crisis began or during the years after 1977 when employment was increasing. If there is a mechanism in the structure of German labor relations that systematically favors wage restraint, then it must be located in the internal organization of the individual unions and in their relation to one another, since it is obviously not located in the union relationship to employers, the government, or the central labor federation.

Jurisdictions of the seventeen DGB unions are unambiguously demarcated by industry, and they often include several industrial branches at the same time. Within their own areas, individual unions exercise an even clearer monopoly on negotiations than is true in Austria. Moreover, union wage agreements have a greater binding force, because they usually apply to all firms within an industrial branch and cannot be supplemented or changed by plant-level negotiations. Thus workers in the Federal Republic have less cause than elsewhere to make unfavorable comparisons with wages in neighboring jobs at the same plant or within the same industry.

Of course, comparison between branches is still important. In the

199

annual wage rounds one of the large individual unions, usually the Metalworkers' Union but sometimes the Chemical Union or the Public Service, Transportation, and Traffic Union, will assume the leadership in wage negotiations, and other wage agreements will be oriented toward those results. In fact, for some of the smaller unions "negotiations" are limited to ratifying those results with the necessary modifications. Just as in Austria, a small union would also expect difficulties with the other unions (say, if it wanted to borrow from the union-owned bank in order finance a long strike) if it set its wage demands far above the limit defined by the wage leaders. Still, the German unions have so far not treated income equalization between industries as a high priority, as the Swedish unions have done.

Wage differentials among industries and regions thus do not necessarily entail economy-wide adjustments in the Federal Republic. Moreover, unified agreements on wage structure at the industry level suppress the inflationary dynamic caused by the struggle to reduce or defend wage differentials between different jobs and professional groups that is characteristic of British (and to a lesser extent of Swedish) conditions. The German unions are thus less compelled than are the Swedish and British unions to respond to wage developments that are not controlled by their own wage policy. At the same time they are much better informed about economic conditions in the firms of their industry than are their counterparts in Great Britain, Sweden, or even Austria, because of the supervisory council mandates they exercise under the codetermination laws. They are thus capable of judging, on the basis of their own expertise, the probable consequences of their wage demands for earnings of firms within their industries and for employment.

Unlike Swedish unions up to the middle of the last decade, German unions are not part of an "encompassing" organization in Mancur Olson's sense. But the "wage leaders" are still able to anticipate the macroeconomic consequences of their wage policy. Moreover, the absence of competition, the binding nature of industry wage agreements, and the unions' direct access to information favors a German wage policy sensitive to differences and changes in the earnings of individual industries in a way that would be impossible in Great Britain and even in Sweden. That does not preclude the possibility of miscalculations or the necessity to respond to changes in the mood of the rank and file or to spontaneous strikes and rising wage drift. But on the whole, institutional conditions are as favorable to a macroeconomic orientation to wage policy in the Federal Republic as they are in Austria.

This, I believe, explains the fact that wages in the Federal Republic responded more quickly and reliably to the worldwide economic crisis after 1974 than did wages in the other three nations. If Keynesian coordination between wage policy and monetary and fiscal policy, as measured by employment, was less successful in the Federal Republic than even in Great Britain, the immediate cause for the failure was not the same as in Great Britain and Sweden. The wage policy of the German unions did not confront government policy with the hard choice between galloping inflation and widespread unemployment during the crisis period. More than even in Austria, actual wage developments in the Federal Republic would have permitted an expansionary government policy to defend full employment without escalating wage-price inflation. If Keynesian coordination failed in the Federal Republic, the explanation must lie on the government side rather than the union side.

CHAPTER TEN

The Limits of Government Action

In the previous analysis I simply assumed that governments had the institutional capability to adopt economically plausible full-employment strategies. For both Austria and Great Britain, a closer examination supports this assumption, despite the differences between the countries. The Austrian government successfully executed its strategy, and if the British government failed to do so, its failure was due to external factors, capital markets, the IMF, or the unions, but not to any internal inability of the government to implement its plans. The politically heterogeneous centrist coalition governments in Sweden had greater difficulties implementing their economic program, but even they finally found a strategy that avoided mass unemployment.

This was not true of the Federal Republic of Germany. In the 1970s, West Germany lost far more jobs than did the other three nations. But unlike the Thatcher government in Great Britain, the German government had not intended this result, nor did external economic pressure or excessive union demands compel the government to accept it. Instead, the rise of mass unemployment in the Federal Republic was caused by difficulties of coordination within the state itself. The primary reason for policy failure was, at the beginning of the crisis and then again after 1980, the undeclared conflict between the extremely ambitious stabilization goals of the Bundesbank and the proclaimed full-employment policy of the federal government. Institutional factors inhibiting fiscal coordination among the levels of government and another set of factors that prevented the aggressive use of Swedish-style active labor market measures played a secondary role. Since I am now dealing with problems peculiar to the Federal Republic, the following analysis concentrates mainly on conditions in that country.

THE CENTRAL BANK

I noted the extreme importance of monetary and currency policies for the success of a social democratic–Keynesian full employment policy in the second chapter. This importance results from the fact that the instruments of fiscal policy, which are controlled by the government, and the instruments of monetary policy, which are controlled by the central bank, affect the same parameters of macroeconomic demand. From a macroeconomic perspective, fiscal and monetary policy are not two different instruments, each aimed at a different target. Instead, their effects combine to produce a net impulse that is either expansionary or restrictive, according to the weight of its components (Neumann, 1973; 1978). Very high deficit spending, like that practiced in the United States after 1982, can stimulate the economy despite high interest rates, while the economic effect of a moderately expansionary fiscal policy can be completely overwhelmed by determined reduction of the money supply. The central bank and the government thus have their hands on the same lever. The second, independent lever is controlled by the unions.

But even if they must side with the unions in the coordination game, the bank and the government will not necessarily have the same priorities. I presented the perspectives and preferences of a social democratic–Keynesian government that is committed to full employment but must also respond to inflation in Figure 9.1. The preferences of a central bank that is committed to the priority of stable prices would look rather different and much less ambivalent in the same game-theoretic form (Figure 10.1). Regardless of how unions behave, the goal of price stability will be realized to a greater degree if the net impulse of social and monetary policy is restrictive than if it is expansionary. But it is unrealistic to assume that even a politically independent central bank would be completely unconcerned with the state of employment. At least in the 1960s and 1970s, the Bundesbank would probably have been

Monetary and fiscal policy	Wage policy	
	Restrained	Aggressive
Expansionary Unemployment Inflation	(1) — Low	(2) — Increasing
Restrictive Unemployment Inflation	(3) — Very low	(4) — Low

Figure 10.1. Coordination from the perspective of the independent central bank

willing to accept the government's preferred "cooperative" solution in cell 1, even though it was only second-best in terms of price stability. But in order to accept the cooperative solution, the bank would have had to be very certain that the unions were permanently committed to a wage policy that respected the requirements of price stability.

That certainty, however, cannot be inferred from the objective interests of the unions. A glance at the game-theoretical pay-off matrix (Figure 10.2) shows why. The unions are always tempted to defect from the cooperative strategy in cell 1 to cell 2, which is optimal for them. For the bank, however, that outcome is the worst possible, and it is duty bound to avoid it at any cost. The only certain way to avoid this worst-case outcome is through restrictive policies pursued by the state as a whole. Speaking in purely economic terms, the central bank could also achieve this result on its own if it was willing to deploy the instruments of monetary and currency policy, which are under its own control, so restrictively that any expansionary effects of government fiscal policy would be neutralized.

In a coordination game with an independent central bank (and one that follows its own preferences exclusively), the unions are in an even less favorable situation than in the interaction with a conservative-monetarist government (Figure 9.4), for which rising unemployment also represents a certain political risk. If the bank succeeds in putting through a restrictive policy, unemployment increases and the unions are forced to practice wage restraint (cell 3) in order to avoid their worst outcome (cell 4). For the bank, however, cell 3 is the best outcome by far and the bank has less reason to leave that cell than would a conservative-monetarist government.

In game-theoretic terms, the interaction between the bank and the unions is thus not a prisoners' dilemma, as is sometimes assumed, where longer-term interaction can produce a cooperative solution that is advantageous for both sides (Axelrod, 1984). Instead, it is an asymmetrical game of "deadlock" in which a noncooperative solution is in the interest of one of the parties and thus cannot be overcome by the interaction of

| Independent central bank | Unions | |
	Cooperative	Uncooperative
Cooperative	(1) 0,1	(2) −1,2
Uncooperative	(3) 2,0	(4) 0,−1

Figure 10.2. Joint payoff matrix for unions and an independent central bank

purely self-interested players (Jervis, 1978; Axelrod and Keohane, 1986). For the bank, this outcome is optimal; the unions have no strategy that could free them from this trap.

From the perspective of a social democratic government, however, the stable solution arising from the interaction between the bank and the unions is a political catastrophe. Continuing high unemployment hurts its constituents, and the groups that are helped by price stability are unlikely to renounce their allegiance to the centrist parties. The government would thus greatly prefer the "cooperative" solution of cell 1. To achieve this outcome, the preferences of the bank must be changed. In theory this could be done by subordinating the bank to the government's policy or by removing or significantly reducing the risk of a cooperative strategy from the bank's viewpoint.

The first solution was adopted by Great Britain and Sweden. The management of the Swedish Imperial Bank is elected by the legislature each legislative period, so that the government in office always has a voting majority at the bank. The minister of finance supervises the bank, and it is up to him how much the political priorities of the government actually shape the central bank's policy. Thus in the centrist coalition the conservative minister of finance was initially able to permit a very restrictive monetary policy, but in the course of the crisis the bank was forced to accommodate the government's highly inflationary credit requirements. The same was true in Great Britain, where the Bank of England operates under the directives of the Treasury (Caesar, 1981:353–402). Thus the switch from easy money to a policy that reflected greater concern with price stability was not instigated by the central bank on its own but instead was compelled by capital flight and the conditions imposed by the IMF.

In Austria, too, the power relations are clear. The National Bank is legally obligated to support the government's policy. The bank is formally organized as a private legal corporation whose shares are held by the state and the social partners. These shareholders see to it that the bank's top management is appointed according to the principles of proportional representation. The Austrian National Bank could not possibly defect from a consensus between the government and the social partners. Nor could it have responded to the much-too-high wage agreements that resulted from the common misperception of the economic situation in summer 1974 by imposing a punitively restrictive monetary policy, as happened in Germany. To be sure, the Austrian model also includes a common sensitivity to the problems of price stability and international competitiveness that the bank can rely on. The hard currency policy is supported by a broad consensus and especially by the unions. By tying the schilling to the German mark, Austrian monetary policy changed to a kind of "imported monetarism" in the second half of the 1970s that reduced or even eliminated its fitness for a full-employment policy. But even if this outcome corresponded to the "natural" preferences of the bank (Marin et al., 1984), what lay behind it was not a unilateral imposition but a mutually accepted strategy, which the government and the social partners could also have changed.

In West Germany the central bank and the federal government also placed great value on presenting a united front (which, however, did not include the unions). But this public presentation reflected power relations fundamentally different from those in the other countries (Wooley, 1985; Kloten et al., 1985; Caesar, 1981:167–214). According to the Federal Bank Act of 1957 the bank's mission is to "guarantee the currency," and it is "independent of instructions from the federal government in carrying out the duties assigned to it by law." At the same time, however, it is to "support the general economic policy of the federal government while carrying out its mandate" (Sections 3, 12, Federal Bank Act). Representatives of the federal government can take part in the meetings of the central bank council without voting, make motions, and request that a decision be deferred to the next meeting. Conversely, the bank has a general duty to advise and inform the federal government, and its president is to participate in cabinet deliberations about "matters of importance to currency policy."

The influence of the government on bank personnel is also limited, at least in the short run. The president, vice-president, and eight other members of the central bank council are nominated by the federal government, but the eleven presidents of the state central banks (who also have seats on the central bank council) are formally named by the state chambers of the legislature (which amounts to selection by the state where each bank is located). Each of the members serves an eight-year term. Political influence on appointments to leadership positions is further attenuated by the requirement that the members have "technical expertise" and that the central bank council must be heard before a new member is nominated. In practice, the governments led by the SPD had observed a kind of proportional representation in filling the positions of president and vice-president and have tried to achieve a consensus with the central bank council and the big private banks in filling other positions. Moreover, since even the states led by the SPD have sometimes applied political criteria, but hardly ever economic policy criteria, in selecting their state central bank presidents, Keynesians were always in the minority in the German central bank, which was dominated by monetarists and traditional bankers for the entire duration of the social-liberal coalition.

Thus unlike the governments in Sweden and Great Britain, the West German government could not impose its preferences on the bank, and unlike the management of the Austrian National Bank, the committee running the Bundesbank does not reflect the consensus of social partners. If the federal government had wanted to gain the support of the bank's monetary and currency policy to cope with the crisis of 1974–75 or 1980–81 in Keynesian fashion, it would have had to convince the bank that despite high and rising inflation rates, the bank could loosen its restrictive policy without putting price stability seriously at risk. That would have been asking a great deal because what the government could have promised the bank was only the second-best result from the bank's point of view. But it was not a hopeless situation. After all, during the high time of Concerted Action, even the Bundesbank was willing to cooperate in a Keynesian coordination of wage policy, fiscal policy, and monetary policy.

Since that time, however, there were years of increasing estrangement between the bank and the unions. In 1970 and again after 1972, the unions threw all appeals to price stability to the winds, and the bank had had so little success with its own measures up to 1973 that its extremely restrictive policy in 1973 and 1974 was not considered credible by the unions. Under such conditions only explicit communication between the parties might have brought success. It might have made clear to the unions how serious the new situation was, because the tight monetary policy would be much more effective after the move to floating exchange rates, and it might also have convinced the bank that the unions would no longer jeopardize price stability by exploiting a full-employment policy supported by monetary policy.

I suspect that if the unions had offered an explicit "stability pact" in late 1973 or early 1974, the bank would have cooperated. After all, unlike in the situation of 1980–81, the bank had not yet tested the effectiveness of its new instruments and survived the threatening political conflict unharmed. Thus it should still have been interested in over-riding the confrontation. The further course of events was therefore decided by the fact that no one on the union side was willing and able to offer the bank such a pact. We can further clarify the question implicit in this statement. After 1974 the German unions did in fact pursue a wage policy that was extremely restrained from a comparative point of view. It did correspond to all reasonable demands of a cooperative, "Austrian" solution. Why then should the unions not also have been able to commit themselves at the beginning of the crisis (winter 1973–74) to the wage policy line that they actually followed in the coming years? The reasons lie in the characteristic tension between the German unions' rhetorical self-presentation and the policy they actually practice.

The unions, then as now, present themselves as being primarily concerned with distributive issues. Despite their positional gains in codetermination and despite their practical concern with the competitiveness and investment position of German firms, they have never explicitly given economic growth the priority that the Austrian Union Federation has. Even though the actual practice of German and Austrian unions is quite similar, this distinction is important. As the tacit and unofficial cooperation "without theory" reaches its limits when new strategies would be needed to deal with technical progress at the plant level (Streeck, 1986), the tacitly practiced macroeconomic orientation of wage policy reached its limits in a situation where only an explicit commitment could have helped.

Even at the time of Concerted Action, however, the unions had no choice but to avoid such commitment because on the level of the federation there was no possibility that a formal DGB commitment to wage restraint could bind the individual unions. The issue was not free collective bargaining along British lines but rather that the large, wage-leader unions, especially the metalworkers' union, refused to allow the DGB board to interfere with their own prerogatives. That, and the coincidence that in 1974 wage leadership was exercised by the "crisis-free" public service unions, rather than by the metal workers, who were shaken by the crisis in the automobile sector, doomed what was probably the last chance of a cooperative solution of the crisis in the winter of 1973–74.

The Federal Republic has paid a high price for letting the unions' most important contribution to economic policy remain latent despite the chancellor's indications that social peace is an important factor of production.[1] If parties cannot talk about an issue, they cannot bargain about it. As it was, there was no explicit coordination mechanism, and the wage leadership of the large industrial unions could not have been made the object of agreements without injuring the smaller unions' sense of dignity and autonomy. As a consequence, the German unions were unable to respond to the Bundesbank's increasingly urgent appeals and warnings with the offer of an explicit "stability pact." Worse yet, while most

1. The functions of latency seem to have received more attention in the literature of the social sciences (see Elster, 1983) than its dysfunctions. In game-theoretical terms, latency limits interactions to noncooperative equilibria that are often Pareto-inferior to the outcomes that could be achieved with explicit communication.

union leaders privately considered the course of the 1974 wage round unfortunate, the Bundesbank's interpretation of these events from a distance was much more sinister. The bank leadership, with no personal links to the social partners, could not empathize with their internal deliberations and implicit motives. The leadership thus saw the 1974 wage round as an expression of the unions' determination to exploit all possible opportunities for wage increases. If that were the case, an easy money policy defending full employment would indeed necessarily have entailed galloping inflation.

No central bank could want that, and the Bundesbank was institutionally independent and tactically skilled enough to pursue a restrictive policy to regain price stability. Winning this battle consolidated its institutional position and confirmed its analysis of the situation: it was not necessary to try to reach an accord with the unions. The unions obviously understood only one language, the threat of unemployment. But unlike their British counterparts (Wegner, 1986), they understood that language very well. Moreover, experience had shown that a social democratic federal government was not willing to oppose a monetarist central bank policy that entailed widespread unemployment. The bank had no reason to depart from this successful course.

From that point on, the power relations were changed in such a way that the Bundesbank no longer needed to purchase coordination among monetary policy, fiscal policy, and wage policy—which it continued to regard as desirable—with concessions regarding its goal of price stability. Instead, it could define the conditions under which the two other partners had any chance to approach their goal of full employment. Between 1975 and the onset of the second oil crisis, moreover, these conditions were no longer extremely restrictive and even permitted considerable growth in employment during the locomotive period. Thus the Bundesbank's almost unimaginable "monetarist" freedom of action explains the unusually deep crisis of 1975, but it does not explain the relative impotence of the government's fiscal impulses or the Federal Republic's failure to pursue full employment through active labor market programs along Swedish lines.

FISCAL POLICY

In examining monetary policy, we did not need to discuss the institutional conditions that make for strategic competence. If it is allowed to do so, a central bank can always influence interest rates, the money supply, and exchange rates according to its priorities. That distinguishes it from government fiscal policy, where the capability for strategic action is as problematic as it is in the case of an incomes policy. One important difference is that macroeconomic goals are the principal focus of monetary policy. In contrast, unions are primarily concerned with increasing real wages and employers with containing production costs. The macroeconomic effects that result are by-products of their negotiations, and it is obvious to neither side that the parameters of their distributive battle can also be powerful instruments of economic policy. It is therefore difficult to translate this idea into action.

But it is equally difficult to instrumentalize public budgets for the purposes of macroeconomic control. Taxes, social security contributions, borrowing on the revenue side, and especially expenditures for personnel and supplies, social services, subsidies, and public investment are the result of political conflicts about the purpose of government and the distribution of burdens and benefits. They have their own objectives and a distributive logic that cannot simply be placed at the service of the frequently changing demands of macroeconomic management. To these general problems of countercyclical fiscal policies, West Germany adds the difficulties of a federal fiscal constitution. These difficulties can be likened to the those associated with implementing voluntary wage restraint. In both instances control must be exercised in large part by organizations for which macroeconomic success would have the character of a collective good: individual unions or states and municipalities.

For the policy of price stability, the foregoing is true in a strict sense. In an integrated economy with uniform currency, individual communities and states cannot choose their own inflation rates, and their influence on nationwide inflation is hard to identify. The situation is somewhat different with regard to unemployment, which represents a local evil for communities and states (as well as for small unions) and which states and communities might combat through local employment initiatives. Their degree of effectiveness would be relatively small from the perspective of local policy, however, because the demand that was increased through local or regional expenditures could not be contained and would spill over into the economy at large by the next round at the latest. An egoistically rational cost-benefit analysis would thus encourage communities and states to ignore the macroeconomic consequences of their actions in a way similar to the justification given above for small individual unions ignoring macroeconomic effects (Kock, 1975).

The expenditure behavior of communities and states during recession is thus oriented less toward the criteria of macroeconomic demand management than toward their internal goals and constraints. One can thus expect a "delayed procyclical" budgetary adjustment during recessions.

For political, administrative, and legal reasons, subnational governments will try to continue their middle-term spending plans at the beginning of the recession. When revenue decreases and indebtedness increases, however, these plans have to be modified for fiscal and political reasons. In municipalities, the reaction is accelerated by the state's budget oversight that makes borrowing contingent on the development of municipal revenue. States are able to use debt financing to a greater degree. After a certain delay, however, egoistically rational calculation will also cause their budgets to generate procyclical rather than countercyclical impulses.

It is fitting that primary political responsibility for fighting inflation and unemployment is assigned to the central government. It is only at this level, within a national frame of reference, that the causal connection between budget policy and macroeconomic control can be made politically plausible. However, as economic cycles have increasingly become internationally interdependent, national fiscal policy is also confronted with externalities. In countries with a high share of imports in the GDP, much of the newly created demand will go abroad, and in countries with a high export share, constraints on domestic demand may be offset by foreign markets. Large countries such as the United States or Japan with a relatively small share of international trade in their GDP are at a fundamental advantage over small countries with a large external contribution. Even among the four countries of our study there are significant differences in this respect, although all of them would be listed among the group of "small open economies" in international comparisons (Table 10.1).

Other things being equal, domestic fiscal expansion has been somewhat less effective in Austria than in the other three countries, which are not quite so dependent on imports. During the course of the decade, Sweden and Great Britain kept their import share constant or reduced it, whereas in Austria and the Federal Republic (especially during the locomotive period), imports increased markedly. Both countries thus "exported" part of their expansionary fiscal impulses. However, much of their additional demand went to other European countries, which in turn had a propensity to import from the Federal Republic.

The international interdependence of national economies was thus not yet an insurmountable constraint on European fiscal expansion in the 1970s. On the other hand, differences between the fiscal constitutions of the four countries were all the more important for their capacity to carry out an anticyclical fiscal policy. The relationship may be derived from three premises of macroeconomic management: (1) the economic effect of a fiscal stimulus depends on the volume of the stimulus relative

Table 10.1 Imports as a percentage of gross domestic product, 1974–1984

	1974	1975	1976	1977	1978	1979	1980	1981	1982	1983	1984
Austria	33	31	34	35	33	36	39	40	36	36	38
FRG	22	22	24	23	23	25	27	28	28	27	29
GB	33	27	29	24	30	28	25	24	25	26	29
Sweden	33	28	29	29	27	31	32	30	33	33	32
USA	9	8	9	9	10	10	11	10	10	9	10

Sources: OECD *National Accounts*, 1960–1984; author's own calculations.

to the volume of aggregate demand in the economy at large; (2) the political and administrative difficulties of achieving a certain fiscal stimulus depend on the magnitude of budgetary changes required relative to the total volume of the budget in question; and (3) in vertically differentiated fiscal constitutions, the main burden of fiscal demand management must be borne by the budget of the central government.

The second of these premises is crucial. It assumes that because of the importance of the "normal" allocational and distributive functions of the budget, changes are always difficult, and that great changes in a small budget are harder to deal with politically and administratively than small changes in a large budget, even if the absolute volume of the changes and hence the economic stimulus is the same in both cases. If that is true, the institutional response to seemingly identical requirements of Keynesian demand management must create very different difficulties for government policy in different countries. Countries within which public expenditures already account for a large part of the gross national produce are in a favorable position. Small changes in their public budgets will suffice to achieve relatively large effects on macroeconomic demand.[2]

The relation between the possible economic uses of fiscal control and their economic and political costs is thus especially favorable in nations with a large public sector and a strongly centralized fiscal constitution. The conditions for Keynesian control are especially unfavorable in nations where public expenditures have a low share of the gross national product and the central government has a small share of the total public budget; Switzerland could serve as an extreme example (Table 10.2).

Table 10.2 shows that the conditions for fiscal demand management by the central government were relatively favorable in Great Britain and even more so in Sweden. In West Germany (and even more so in Switzerland), they were much less favorable. In order to generate a fiscal impulse of 1 percent of the GNP in 1979, the central budget in Sweden would have had to raise expenditures or reduce revenues by 2.8 percent of its volume. In West Germany, the budgetary changes necessary to

2. To be more accurate, one would have to relate the variation in public expenditures not to the gross national product but to the volume of the private sector (that is to be influenced by Keynesian controls). The differences among countries would then be even more pronounced. But since the burden of countercyclical demand control is to be borne primarily by the central government, the degree of fiscal centralization is also important. Thus nations whose central budget accounts for a relatively high share of the total public budget are also favored. If both effects are considered together, the difficulty of fiscal demand management may be measured by the percentage by which the central government's budget must be changed to bring about a 1 percent change in aggregate demand.

Table 10.2 Difficulty of fiscal policy control, 1979

	Austria	Switz.	FRG	GB	Sweden
Public sector*	42.8	27.2	33.3	37.5	57.3
Degree of centralization[†]	57.5	37.3	43.6	88.4	62.7
Degree of difficulty[‡]	4.1	9.9	6.9	3.0	2.8

Sources: BMF *Finanzbericht*, 1982; author's own calculations.
*Total public expenditures as % of GNP.
[†]Central government share of total expenditures (%).
[‡]Budgetary changes by the central government that correspond to 1% of the GNP.

bring about the same result were two and a half times greater, and in Switzerland they were three and a half times greater. Austria, where the central government clearly predominates despite a federal constitution, falls in the middle of this comparison. Switzerland apparently concluded from the unfavorable conditions of its federal constitution that it should not even try to use fiscal policy for purposes of a Keynesian full-employment policy, whereas the Federal Republic nevertheless has made the effort (Table 10.3).

The comparison of total government borrowing shows that the total budget in the Federal Republic at the first peak of the crisis in 1975 actually produced expansionary impulses in a magnitude comparable with those produced in Austria and Sweden. Only in Great Britain were the deficits higher at first; they were reduced after the intervention of the IMF in 1977. Switzerland, on the other hand, which is again introduced for purposes of comparison, refused to engage in deficit spending and had to accept high losses in employment while reducing registered unemployment by repatriating guest workers (M. Schmidt, 1985). It is worth noting that in West Germany the total government deficit was reduced much more quickly than in Austria after 1975, although unemployment was high in the Federal Republic and low in Austria. In terms of economic and employment policy this was a counterproductive response, whose institutional explanation becomes clear when we distinguish between the levels of government in both countries (Table 10.4).

The comparison reveals that the deficit as a share of federal expenditures in the two nations was at about the same level until the change of government coalitions in Bonn. Thus one cannot assert that Austria owed its more favorable development to a more aggressive federal fiscal policy. But although the federal government in both nations held to approximately the same fiscal policy line, the economic effects were different because of the varying sizes of the federal budget. In Austria (and to a lesser extent in Sweden and Great Britain as well) borrowing by subnational governments had no practical significance for mac-

Table 10.3 Deficit (surplus) of the total government (% of GNP), 1974–1984

	1974	1975	1976	1977	1978	1979	1980	1981	1982	1983	1984
Austria	+0.3*	4.3	4.5	3.8	4.1	3.5	2.9	2.6	4.1	5.3	4.9
Switz.	1.6	1.6	1.8	1.0	0.3	0.8	0.6	0.2	0.7	0.9	0.9
FRG	2.9	6.4	4.3	2.6	3.1	3.2	3.8	4.9	4.4	3.3	2.6
GB	6.7	7.8	8.1	5.4	5.3	4.9	7.0	3.1	3.9	4.8	3.2
Sweden	4.5	5.2	2.7	5.9	7.3	9.1	10.5	11.5	11.9	10.2	8.1

Sources: BMF Finanzberichte, 1977, 1979, 1982, 1986; author's own calculations.
* + = surplus.

Table 10.4 Deficit (surplus) as share of federal and subordinate jurisdiction expenditures: Austria and the Federal Republic, 1974–1984 (%)

	1974	1975	1976	1977	1978	1979	1980	1981	1982	1983	1984
Austria											
Federal government	+0.6*	18.9	19.3	16.0	16.8	14.4	12.2	10.5	16.0	19.5	18.2
Subordinate jurisdictions	+0.9	+1.2	+1.2	+0.1	+0.5	+0.2	+0.4	n.v.	n.v.	n.v.	n.v.
FRG											
Federal government	7.3	21.3	16.1	12.9	14.0	12.7	12.8	16.3	15.4	12.9	11.4
Subordinate jurisdictions	9.2	14.0	8.5	4.0	4.7	6.0	9.0	11.0	9.5	6.5	4.8

Sources: BMF Finanzberichte, 1977, 1979, 1982, 1985, 1986 (n.v.: available numbers are not comparable); author's own calculations.
*+ = surplus.

Table 10.5 Deficit (surplus) of subordinate governments as percentage of the central government deficit, 1975–1979

	1975	1976	1977	1978	1979
Austria	+5.7*	+5.5	+0.7	+2.6	+0.9
FRG	89.0	67.8	42.8	52.1	74.1
GB	27.0	22.0	12.7	6.1	17.5
Sweden	29.0	40.0	2.7	+12.5	+5.3

Sources: BFM *Finanzberichte*, 1977, 1979, 1982; author's own calculations.

*+ = surplus.

roeconomic fiscal policy (Table 10.5). Their net borrowing does not have any clear tendency, but there is no indication of a restrictive fiscal policy on the part of states and communities that is directed against the policy of the federal government.[3]

This is not true of the Federal Republic. The relatively small size of the federal budget meant that the macroeconomic effect of a basically similar national borrowing strategies was necessarily much less in the Federal Republic than in Austria, Sweden, or Great Britain. A countercyclical fiscal policy was possible in the Federal Republic only if subnational governments would participate as well. In fact, as Table 10.4 shows, states and communities made a substantial contribution to the expansionary impulses of fiscal policy by increasing their deficits in both 1975–76 and 1981–82. But these data do not allow us to conclude that their contributions resulted from successful fiscal coordination. If we look more closely, we see considerable instability and a much more rapid deficit reduction after the height of the crisis. Between 1975 and 1977 the federal government decreased its deficit by 36 percent, while subnational governments reduced their deficit by almost twice as much (69 percent). The statistical picture thus supports the hypothesis developed above, that states and communities pursued a delayed procyclical fiscal policy.

The high deficits at the beginning of the crisis were due less to a desire to maintain growth and employment than to the cumbersome nature of budgetary decision making. Budget cuts always meet with strong political and bureaucratic resistance, and it is usually necessary to meet legally binding obligations and to carry out projects that cannot be stopped for

3. Subnational governments in Austria regularly show budget surpluses. These are apparently the bookkeeping reflex of loans to private and nonprofit building societies financed from federal funds but paid out by the states and communities. In any case, in Austria, as in Sweden and Great Britain, only the central government sets and is engaged in fiscal policy for macroeconomic purposes.

technical reasons. Thus it takes time to implement even an intentionally procyclical fiscal policy, and in the interval the deficit increases. The differences between a procyclical fiscal policy and a serious countercyclical policy will not appear at the height of the crisis but only in the following years, when adjustments have had their effect. And in the Federal Republic these differences are clear.

It is true that even the German federal government reduced its budget deficit faster than Austria did after 1975, and faster than would have been desirable from a Keynesian point of view (Teschner and Vesper, 1983). But compared to the dramatic reduction of state and local deficits in 1976–77, the policy of the federal government was considerably less precipitous. At that time, unlike the situation in 1974–75, both the German central bank's monetary policy and the unions' wage policy were more or less aligned according to Keynesian prescriptions. Hence, the renewed recession of 1977, which halted the steep upswing of the previous year, must be ascribed primarily to state and local governments' delayed but clearly procyclical fiscal reaction to the crisis.

The Stability and Growth Act of 1967 and the 1969 reform of the federal fiscal constitution had been passed in order to overcome precisely such procyclical reactions; both were meant to improve the institutional conditions for coordinating the fiscal policies of the federal government and of subnational governments. The reasons why this fiscal coordination was largely ineffective have been analyzed a number of times (Kock, 1975; Knott, 1981; Reissert, 1984). If we relate these reasons to the potentially available instruments of lowering taxes, expenditures to increase private demand, increase of public investment, and expansion of public employment, we reach the conclusions presented below.

Lowering Taxes

While the Stability and Growth Act of 1967 expressly grants the German federal government the authority to raise and lower tax rates temporarily, this economic policy instrument is still not as readily available as it is in Great Britain. The main obstacle is the fact that the federal government, the states, and the municipalities share income tax revenues and that the federal government and the states also share corporate tax and value-added tax revenues. In the upswing of the business cycle, it was generally easy to obtain the states' approval in the Bundesrat for temporary tax surcharges. Difficulties were more likely to originate in the lower house of the legislature, where SPD members opposed proportional tax increases in the early 1970s and the FDP tried to protect its clientele from progressive tax increases.

During a recession, on the other hand, tax reductions would so upset the precarious balance between the functions assigned to each level of government and the fiscal means of carrying them out that an immediate renegotiation of intergovernmental fiscal transfers would become unavoidable. The necessary result could be predicted from the experience in the 1970s, when tax schedules had to be adjusted to offset the bracket creep caused by inflation. The federal government, operating under high political pressure to make those adjustments, was forced repeatedly to purchase the agreement of the Bundesrat (where states governed by the CDU/CSU had a majority) with concessions about the apportionment of the value-added tax. As a result, the federal share of public sector revenues fell from 53 percent to 48 percent between 1970 and 1983 (BMF, 1985). Hence, it is not surprising that the federal government did not try to use general tax cuts on the British or American model as an instrument of macroeconomic demand management. The sharing of federal and state revenues also discouraged the use of tax incentives to promote investment in the private sector on the Austrian model, since here too the tax shortfall would have had to be borne partly by state and local governments.

Promotion of Private Investment and Consumer Demand

On the expenditure side, fiscal policy options were also limited by the federal fiscal constitution. Direct subsidies for private investment (as opposed to tax reductions) were used widely after 1975 to promote aggregate demand, especially in Austria. In West Germany, however, investment subsidies took the form of tax abatements that also decreased the revenues of state and local governments. For this reason, instead of a long-term subsidy program that could have influenced the investment plans of firms, the investment subsidies of 1975 and 1982 were so short-lived that they caused a flurry of activity but failed to stabilize the propensity to invest over the medium term.

On the private consumption side, the federal government did have the option of raising or reducing payments to the unemployed, pensioners, families, and trainees. Thus the family allowance reform of 1975, although it was passed before the crisis began, did in fact contribute to stabilizing private demand. But that does not mean that social welfare spending was available as a major instrument of demand management. During the recession the social welfare insurance budgets were unbalanced in any case, and the financial burden caused by their deficits was borne almost exclusively by the federal government. At the same time, once social welfare expenditures had been increased, it would be extremely difficult from a political point of view to reduce benefits again. Thus it is understandable that even Keynesian fiscal policy makers in the federal government emphasized the need to consolidate the social welfare budget rather than its function in stabilizing demand.

Public Investments

Fiscal policy discussion in West Germany concentrated almost exclusively on public works and investment. Public works spending has two advantages: (1) its immediate effect on demand is local and concentrated, and (2) increased public works spending is less likely to become irreversible through long-term legal obligations. Its disadvantage is that the stimulus is concentrated on construction, so that the attempt to stabilize the economy as a whole destabilizes the construction industry, subjecting it to extreme fluctuations that are detrimental to steady employment (Nerb et al., 1977). But an even greater disadvantage of public works spending is that public works are the responsibility of the governmental bodies least capable of mounting a countercyclical fiscal policy. The federal government, which is responsible for economic stabilization, spent only 15 percent of the total public investment expenditures in 1978, while municipalities spent more than 62 percent (BMF *Finanzbericht,* 1982:252). Hence the capacity to influence investment behavior in the municipalities and states is a necessary condition for the success of the federal government's fiscal policy.

The only sure way for the federal government to influence state and local public investment is through fiscal incentives. The constitutional authority to provide such incentives had been granted by the 1969 reform, which added to the federal fiscal constitution provisions permitting the federal government to participate in the financing of joint undertakings with the states (Article 91a and 91b, Basic Law) and permitting it to provide financial aid for such "investments by state and local governments . . . as are necessary to prevent macroeconomic disequilibrium" (Article 104a, Paragraph 4, Basic Law). These amendments legalized existing practices and increased the capacity of the federal government to use direct subsidies to influence state and local investment expenditures. From 1974 on, the federal government took advantage of this option with several short-term investment support programs and the medium-term ZIP program (Investment in the Future) of 1977.

In practice, however, the effectiveness of joint financing as an instrument of economic policy was impaired by delays caused by the need for intergovernmental consensus and by the cumbersome multiple bureaucratic clearances (Scharpf, Reissert, and Schnabel, 1976; H. Schmidt, 1980; Scharpf, 1985). Even more damaging were the ubiquitous income and substitution effects at the local level. Municipalities did not simply reduce their own expenditures by the amount of the federal grant, nor did they increase their own investment spending. Instead, matching grants tied to a specific purpose mainly influenced the selection of investment projects but generally not the level of local expenditures (Reissert, 1984). Therefore, while the levels of public investment under federal investment programs increased over what they otherwise would have been, the increase probably did not exceed the amount of the federal grants. Far from correcting the procyclical fiscal propensities of state and local governments, these antirecession programs merely served to increase the federal debt much more rapidly than the debt of state and local governments.

Public Employment

The state of affairs with respect to public sector employment was even worse than with respect to public investment. Even if the federal government had been politically able to tolerate much higher debt levels, it would not have been able to use the additional funds, as the Swedish government did, to expand public and social services. Federal employment was only 11.8 percent of public employment in 1979, even less than the federal share of public investment, and during the years of crisis it decreased still further. As in Sweden, the clear preponderance of public employment lay with the state and local governments, which are responsible for schools and universities, hospitals, and social services. In Sweden the expansion of public services was supported by the combination of central government subsidies and autonomous local decisions that raise the level of municipal and county income taxes. Under the German fiscal constitution, on the other hand, both of these options were blocked. The reforms of 1969 authorize the federal government to use its funds to subsidize capital investments but not the operating expenditures of state and local governments, and the discretion of subordinate governments to set their own revenue levels is much more limited in federal West Germany than in unitary Sweden.

Tax revenues flowing to the states, even where tax sharing is not involved (Article 105, Basic Law), are generally determined by federal legislation. Whereas that requires the agreement of a majority of state votes in the Bundesrat, tax rates for the individual states are set by law and cannot be changed by political decisions at the state level. The same is true in principle for local governments that received a share of the unitary federal income tax but do not have the right to set surcharges on their share of the tax (Reissert, 1986). Unlike the Swedish regions and localities, social democratic German states and local governments were thus unable to increase employment in hospitals, schools, kindergartens, old-age homes, or counseling and to finance these positions by raising their own taxes. They remained dependent on federal legislation for their revenue and hence also on political consensus with the conservative majority in the Bundesrat. Their own political choices were hence limited on the expenditure side of the budget as well.

During the crisis period, therefore, the German fiscal constitution, with its unique division and interpenetration of political decisions over public revenue, public responsibilities, and public expenditures, prevented an expansion of public services inspired by social democratic principles. Public sector employment did grow in Germany in the 1970s, but as chapter 3 details, the growth was slower than in the other three countries and remained well below the level reached there. According to an OECD report, between 1970 and 1982 public employment rose from 11.2 percent of total employment to 15.6 percent in the Federal Republic. In Austria, it increased from 13.7 percent to 19.2 percent, in Great Britain from 18 percent to 22.4 percent, and in Sweden from 20.6 percent to 31.8 percent (OECD, 1985:63). These figures conceal even more basic structural differences that are not entirely due to West Germany's fiscal constitution.

A simple comparison of public employment ignores the fact that health care services in Sweden and Great Britain are almost exclusively publicly provided, whereas in West Germany ambulatory care is publicly financed but provided by private doctors. In contrast, in some other countries private schools and universities play a much greater role than in the Federal Republic. The American sociologist Martin Rein (1985) has therefore tried to determine employment figures in the "social welfare industry" (health care, social services, education) regardless of whether the services are publicly or privately financed or provided. His study does not include Austria. Nevertheless, even by this more inclusive measure the Federal Republic still lags behind the other countries (Table 10.6).

The Federal Republic's lag is evident in all three branches of the social welfare industry. This lag becomes even more significant when one considers that labor force participation was higher in the other countries than in West Germany. The differences cannot be explained by the assumption that the other countries were simply prepared to spend

Table 10.6 Social welfare industry employment as
percentage of total employment, 1970–1973 and
1981–1983

	FRG	GB	Sweden	USA
Social welfare industry				
1970–73	7.4	10.9	17.8	15.6
1981–83	10.7	15.0	25.5	17.8
Health care services				
1970–73	3.1	4.2	7.5	6.2
1981–83	4.9	5.8	10.1	7.3
Social services				
1970–73	1.2	0.9	4.6	1.3
1981–83	1.3	2.2	7.8	2.2
Education				
1970–73	3.0	5.8	5.7	8.1
1981–83	4.6	7.0	7.7	7.8

Source: Rein, 1985.

more for the services of the modern welfare state on the basis of different political and private preferences. Great Britain and the United States spent less of their GNP for health, social services, and education and still employed a greater percentage of the population of employable age in the social welfare industry. The public and private funds expended in West Germany thus have a weaker employment effect than in the other countries (Table 10.7).

Partial explanations for these differences are the smaller amount of part-time work in the Federal Republic and its traditionally higher level of transfer payments (Scharpf, 1986). The centralized social security system developed early in Germany, and it had originally favored transfer payments over social services. This historical priority is eroding, but it is still visible in the structure of public expenditures (Table 10.8). In the Federal Republic the percentage of the total budget dedicated to social

Table 10.7 Employment intensity of social welfare expenditures, 1981

	FRG	GB	Sweden	USA
(1) Social welfare expenditures (% of GNP)*	31.3	22.8	38.0	27.0
(2) Social welfare employment (% of 15-to-64-year-olds)	6.8	8.9	20.0	11.8
(3) Employment intensity (2:1)	0.22	0.39	0.53	0.44

Source: Rein, 1985.
*Expenditures for social transfers and for services of the social welfare industry.

Table 10.8 Transfer intensity of public social welfare expenditures, 1970 and 1981

	FRG	GB	Sweden	USA
(1) Total social welfare expenditures (% of government expenditures)				
1970	63.6	51.2	62.9	44.9
1981	66.4	52.6	60.9	51.8
(2) Expenditures for social welfare transfers (% of government expenditures)				
1970	39.0	26.2	29.6	25.7
1981	38.8	27.2	30.6	33.3
(3) Share of transfers in total social welfare expenditures (2:1)				
1970	0.61	0.51	0.47	0.57
1981	0.58	0.52	0.50	0.64

Sources: Rein, 1985; author's own calculations.

welfare expenditures is even higher than in Sweden, but the expenditures largely serve to finance transfer payments which, even if they flow into private consumption, have a smaller employment effect than direct financing of public services.

This is still not the whole explanation, however. The role of transfer payments is chiefly relevant to social welfare policy in the narrow sense, in which the dominant transfer orientation may indeed impede the development of counseling services, educational and rehabilitational measures, and personal care (Gross, 1983). But the discrepancy between financial expenditure and employment shows up in the health care industry as well, where personal services cannot simply be supplanted by money payments (Table 10.9).

Here too, the relative employment effect of expenditures in the United States and Great Britain was about one and a half times that in West Germany, and in Sweden it was nearly two and a half times as high. Perhaps the German form of financing privately provided health care services with public or collectively raised funds tends to favor a form of expensive, high-tech medical treatment, whereas public health services in Sweden and Great Britain may provide incentives for expanding labor-intensive personal care. But it could also be the case that in West Germany a higher portion of expenditures goes to highly paid professionals, whereas in the health sector and in the social welfare industry generally either the incomes in the other countries are generally lower or a higher percentage of employment goes to professional groups with low incomes. In any event, an OECD study showed that in the Federal Republic in 1975, per capita incomes in the public sector exceeded incomes

Table 10.9 Employment intensity of health care expenditures, 1981

	FRG	GB	Sweden	USA
(1) Health care industry: Expenditures (% of GNP)	7.9	5.6	8.6	9.2
(2) Health care industry: Employees (% of 15-to-64-year-olds)	3.1	3.5	8.0	5.2
(3) Employment intensity (2:1)	0.39	0.62	0.93	0.57

Source: Rein, 1985.

in the private sector by a factor of 1.3. In the United States incomes in both sectors were about the same, whereas public sector incomes in Sweden (0.94 percent) and Great Britain (0.96 percent) were even lower than private sector incomes (OECD, 1982).

We cannot continue our discussion of the West German public sector employment system and the social welfare industry (see Krupp, 1986). What we have said is sufficient, however, to highlight the difficulties facing an expansion of publicly financed services in the Federal Republic. The federal fiscal constitution makes it harder to spend public funds on services. And even if the financing problem could have been solved, this form of full-employment policy would have been much more costly in West Germany than in Sweden. The German social security and health care systems are comparatively less labor intensive and the expansion of the labor-intensive educational system is made more expensive by the relatively high salaries in public services. To combat unemployment by the rapid expansion of publicly financed services, West Germany would have needed basic reforms not only of the fiscal constitution but also of the existing systems of social welfare provision and public service, which are defended by powerful interests. Obviously, this variant of the successful Swedish employment policy could not have been pursued in West Germany under the conditions required to maintain a political majority in the 1970s.

WHY NOT ACTIVE LABOR MARKET POLICY?

In view of the extraordinary difficulties confronting Keynesian full-employment policy on the Austrian model, the question arises as to why the Federal Republic did not choose to fight unemployment using a version of the Swedish active labor market policy. The question is pertinent because by 1969, when the Grand Coalition passed the Labor Promotion Act, all the active labor measures that were used in Sweden were available to West Germany. Moreover these measures were not subject to political veto by the Bundesrat or the Free Democrats. Of course the question, like all questions about nonoccurrences, can be answered only with plausible arguments, not with absolute certainty (see also Webber, 1982; 1984).

In the first place, there were important temporal, conceptual, and organizational differences between Sweden's active labor market program and West Germany's. Sweden had worked from the late 1950s on to develop its labor market policy into an effective countercyclical instrument, and from recession to recession it increased its financial support for the program and the number of its participants. When the global crisis finally reached Sweden, the institutional infrastructure and the methods for continuing education, retraining, and job creation were fully developed and completely adapted to the anticyclical fight against unemployment.

In the Federal Republic, on the other hand, full employment since the late 1950s had allowed the quantitative and qualitative competence of active labor programs to wither. Consequently, the labor market administration responded to the short recession of 1966–67 almost exclusively with the "passive" measures of unemployment and short-time compensation. Macroeconomic policy measures worked so quickly to overcome the recession that it did not seem necessary to consider a new role for labor market programs. The discussion about reforming labor market policy at that time was thus not directed at cyclical unemployment but exclusively at the newly discovered problem of structural unemployment.

This problem became visible during the crisis in coal mining in the Ruhr and Saar regions, where in the midst of a fully employed economy miners were out of work or being forced into early retirement despite labor shortages in other regions and other skilled occupations. Unemployment also persisted on the East German border, and it was expected that the transition to a Common European Agrarian Policy would also produce structural unemployment in other regions. At the same time, educationists emphasized the importance of a highly trained labor force to a competitive economy and the necessity for lifelong learning in view of accelerating technological and structural change. In short, reform of German labor market policy in the late 1960s centered on anticipating structural change by promoting mobility and training (Blankenburg, Schmid, and Treiber, 1975).

That was not an easy task for the German labor administration, whose personnel had dropped in number, capacity, and competence after the late 1950s, when it had been reduced to administering a small number of unemployed workers and the growing number of foreign workers. Even so, no institutional changes were contemplated. In the Federal Republic, as opposed to Sweden, Great Britain, France, and other countries, reform efforts entailed neither an organizational nor a financial separation between passive and active labor market programs (Bruche and Reissert, 1985; Schmidt, Reissert, and Bruche, 1986). Both aspects were and are financed by contributions to the unemployment insurance fund, and both are administered by the self-governing Federal Institution for Labor with its local and regional labor bureaus under the tripartite control of the social partners and state and federal governments. In contrast to Sweden, the German labor administration also lacked a comprehensive network of government training centers. Instead, to carry out its new assignment it had to contract with private and nonprofit trade schools and other educational institutions to provide the continuing education and retraining needed.

Despite these unfavorable starting conditions, the labor administration was able to develop technical and vocational continuing education into a functioning labor market policy instrument within an extremely short time. The number of annual new entrants into educational programs rose to 288,000 in 1971 and stabilized at that high level (Garlichs and Maier, 1982:96). Given the labor market situation at the time, of course, hardly any of the participants were unemployed, and the technical and vocational schools responded to student demand by developing courses for skilled laborers interested in upgrading their qualifications and for housewives preparing for reentry into the paid labor force. Thus when unemployment rose again in 1974 the available courses were hardly adapted to the needs of the unemployed. Even though the unemployed constituted one-third of the participants by 1975, training programs did not reach the group of unskilled workers hit hardest by the crisis.

Thus the new training measures of the labor program were vulnerable to criticism as an unjustified luxury after the crisis began. Since unemployment compensation payments (which were still politically sacrosanct at the time) increased exponentially, so that the unemployment insurance fund went deeply into deficit, it seemed politically most expedient to reduce the outlays for continuing technical and vocational education. In the Budget Structure Act of 1975, support payments for participants in continuing education and retraining programs (which had provided 90 percent of the participant's previous net wage) were reduced to 80 percent for the unemployed and for participants without any technical and vocational training and to 58 percent for all others. Financially the act was highly successful. The total number of new entrants into educational programs dropped by half between 1975 and 1977, from 271,000 to 136,000, and expenditures fell from DM 1.99 billion in 1975 to DM 771 million in 1977 (Schmid, 1982:50).

In terms of labor market policy goals, however, the act was a failure. Instead of redirecting technical and vocational training to help unemployed workers acquire marketable skills, the effect was to lower the rate at which unemployed workers participated in training programs. Their number fell from 84,000 new entrants in 1975 to 50,000 in 1976 and began to increase again only after 1978. The reason for this decline was less the small reduction in support payments for unemployed participants than the drastic effect the cuts had on the course offerings of the private technical and vocational training institutions. Existing courses could no longer be filled and teaching staff had to be let go in many cases, while the development of new courses that might have "sold" under the new conditions took so long that the number of unemployed participants, now the favored target group, did not reach the 1975 level again until 1979.

Then, when unemployment climbed again after 1980 and the budget of the unemployment insurance fund again went into deficit, this lesson was forgotten. The Labor Program Consolidation Act of 1981 again changed and worsened the conditions for participating in training programs, forcing the educational institutions to restructure their course offerings once again. Job creation measures were even harder hit by the Consolidation Act's cuts. These measures had played a very small role in 1975. Their volume had gradually been increased by the labor bureaus, from 16,000 participants in 1975 to 51,000 in 1978 and 1979. The emphasis was on community work on parks and green belts and in public offices. Special federal programs also supported work in the social services area (Maier, 1982). The public service unions, however, regarded these job creation measures with suspicion from the outset. They feared that it would supplant regular job opportunities in the public sector and in the long run would create second-class employment conditions unprotected by collective bargaining agreements. When it became known that some communities had placed job creation program participants in jobs they had previously filled with regular employees, the Federal Institution for Labor unilaterally reduced the scale of the program even before the Consolidation Act substantially restricted it and imposed still more restrictive conditions. All told, in the last years of the social-liberal coalition the number of job creation participants fell from 51,000 in 1979 to 29,000 in 1982 and increased significantly only after the new coalition took over (IAB, 1983; 1984).

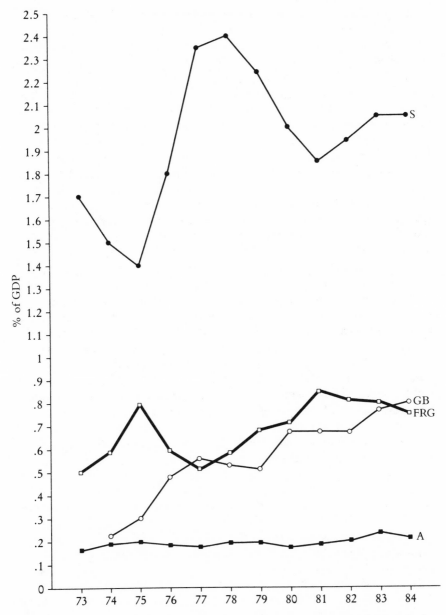

Figure 10.3. Expenditures for the active labor market programs. Sources: Wösendorfer, 1980; Schmid, 1982; Reissert, 1985; Schmid, Reissert, and Bruche, 1986.

Comparatively speaking, German expenditures for active labor market measures lie between the Swedish and Austrian extremes (Figure 10.3). The same is true of net employment effects (Table 10.10). But whereas in the 1970s Austria, with its generally successful economic policy, had no cause to use active labor market programs to fight widespread unemployment (Wösendorfer, 1980:108–26), the Federal Republic and Great Britain had every reason to deploy the active labor market instruments as aggressively as in Sweden. In fact, however, their expenditures and the effects they achieved were closer to the Austrian than the Swedish position. Nevertheless, over the course of time there were also important differences between these two countries.

In Great Britain the organizational separation between job placement and unemployment insurance at the beginning of the 1970s led to the foundation of a self-governing central labor market authority, the Manpower Services Commission, in 1974. At first the commission was responsible for placement, continuing education, and retraining; later it was also charged with job creation programs. During the reorganization and in the years immediately following, the main bottleneck of British labor market policy was implementation capacity (Reissert, 1985:99–101). In 1975 total expenditures for active measures were far below the German level, but they climbed steeply and surpassed German spending in 1977 and 1984. On the whole, this expansion (which increased again under the Conservative government after 1979) reflected the continuing increase of measures directed at youth unemployment, wage subsidies, and a temporary rise in job creation programs (Reissert, 1985:65, Table 13). All told, the relative contribution of British labor market policy to coping with the employment crisis, while far below Swedish levels, nevertheless increased with the rise of unemployment (Figure 10.4).

In the Federal Republic, on the other hand, the comparatively high level of expenditures during the crisis years 1975 and 1981–82 was due more to the "automatic" increases in short-time compensation than to

Table 10.10 Active labor market programs: Expenditures and job creation effects, 1978

	Austria	FRG	GB	Sweden
Expenditures (% of GDP)	0.18	0.56	0.53	2.40
Job creation effects (% of wage earners)	0.3	1.3	1.1	3.9
Registered unemployment (% of wage earners)	2.1	3.5	6.0	2.2
Potential unemployment without active labor market programs (% of wage earners)	2.4	4.8	7.1	6.1

Sources: Wösendorfer, 1980; Schmid, 1982; Schmid, Reissert, and Bruche, 1986; Reissert, 1985.

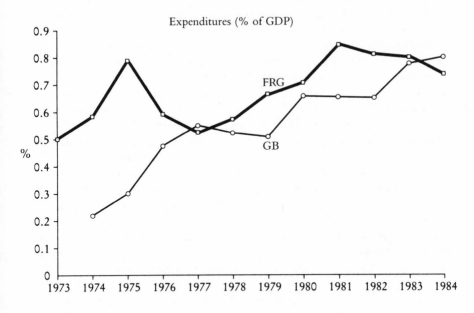

Expenditures (% of GDP)

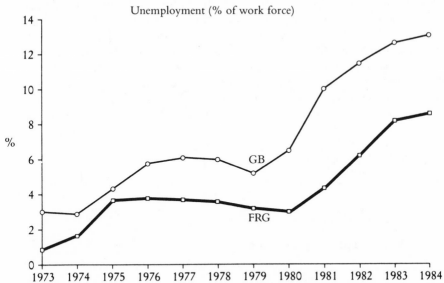

Unemployment (% of work force)

Figure 10.4. Unemployment and expenditures for active labor market programs: Federal Republic and Great Britain, 1973–1984. Sources: Schmid, Reissert, and Bruche, 1986; OECD *Economic Outlook* 39; author's own calculations.

training and job creation programs (IAB, 1983: Table 6). The Federal Republic is thus the only country in which initially rising expenditures for the active labor market measures were procyclically decreased after 1976 and 1982, even before unemployment had peaked (Table 10.11).

The institutional reasons for this perverse expenditure behavior and for the the failure to use labor market measures for the active fight against rising unemployment have been attributed to the way labor market programs are financed (Bruche and Reissert, 1985; Schmid, Reissert, and Bruche, 1986). In Sweden and Great Britain active labor market measures are financed exclusively from tax revenues by the central government. Only unemployment compensation payments are wholly or partially met by contributions to unemployment insurance. In Austria and the Federal Republic, on the other hand, the unemployment insurance fund pays for both branches of the labor market programs. This difference plausibly accounts for the different behavior of the labor administrations.

When active and passive measures are jointly financed from the budget of the insurance fund, both branches of the labor market policy compete for the same resources. As long as unemployment was low, there was financial room even for less pressing measures (later criticized as "luxuries"). When the crisis began, however, contributions dropped and unemployment increased. According to the legal and political logic of the insurance principle, unemployment compensation now had a clear priority. Therefore, when reserves were exhausted and resources became scarce, the insurance fund was practically compelled to economize by saving money on discretionary services (for instance, job creation measures, continuing education, and retraining programs). Even though the obligation to guarantee unemployment compensation and to carry out active measures technically had the same legal status (Section 3,

Table 10.11 Gross expenditures per annum per capita for job creation programs and public investment: Federal Republic, 1977 and 1981–1983 (German marks)

	Job creation not comparable	Public investment
1977	n.v.	42,000 *
Federal and Federal Institute share	15,285 †	21,000 ‡
1981–83	41,000 ‡§	119,000 ‡‖
Federal and Federal Institute share	25,600 ‡§	58,520 ‡‖

Sources: * J. Schmidt, 1977. † Schmid, 1982. ‡ Bruche and Reissert, 1985. § Spitznagel, 1982. ‖ Seidler and Zwiener, 1982.
Note: n.v. = given value is not comparable.

Paragraph 2; Section 5, Labor Promotion Act), active measures would have been disadvantaged by a simple budgetary calculus. Job creation or continuing education and retraining were much more expensive per capita and per year than unemployment compensation.[4]

Thus we seem to have an internally consistent explanation that fits actual developments in the Federal Republic. In contrast to the Federal Republic and Austria, countries that financed active labor market measures out of general revenue like Sweden, Great Britain, and France were less tempted to cut their most effective programs in an employment crisis. This simple institutional explanation does not seem fully satisfactory, however, because it exaggerates the separateness of the insurance fund budget. Both as a matter of law and as a matter of fact, the fiscal autonomy of unemployment insurance is quite restricted, and its budget is connected through several channels not only to the federal budget but to the budget of the old-age insurance fund as well.

The first of these links results from the federal government's legal obligation to finance supplementary unemployment assistance, which is paid to unemployed workers without other income after their unemployment compensation benefits are exhausted. By changing eligibility standards for unemployment compensation, financial burdens can be shifted back and forth between the federal budget and the insurance fund. Similar mechanisms connect the budgets for unemployment insurance and old-age insurance. Thus in order to balance the pension fund in 1978 the unemployment fund was required to pay pension insurance contributions for unemployed workers based on their previous wages. In 1983, in order to relieve the burden on unemployment insurance, contributions were based on unemployment compensation payments and thereby substantially reduced. The most important connection, however, is the federal government's legal obligation to cover the operating deficits (Section 187, Labor Promotion Act) and the concomitant authority to supervise the formulation and execution of the annual budget of this formally independent insurance corporation (Section 216, Paragraph 2, Section 217, Paragraph 2, Sections 218, 224, Labor Promotion Act;

---

4. This fiscally based tendency was reinforced by administrative pressures. If, as in West Germany and Austria, the same authorities are responsible for both kinds of labor programs, rising unemployment leads to personnel shortages in the labor bureaus. Because their staff must be used primarily for the quick processing of unemployment compensation claims, there is less time for job training and job creation just when these tasks become harder and more important (Scharpf, Garlichs, Maier, and Maier, 1982; Bruche and Reissert, 1985:153–54). The organizational separation between the administration of unemployment insurance and the implementation of active labor market programs in Sweden, Great Britain, and other nations was thus introduced with good reason (Bruche, 1983; Reissert, 1985).

Bruche and Reissert, 1985:63–80). Furthermore, the federal government always had the authority to finance additional labor market programs and to have them carried out by the labor administration.

Thus an institutional analysis that considers only the budget of the unemployment insurance fund and its constraints falls short of the mark. In fact, decisions about the size, scope, and timing of labor market programs and their financing were the responsibility of the central government in West Germany as well: up to the Lower House of the legislature (since the Bundesrat inclined to a generosity that would cost the states nothing) and to the federal government, especially the federal minister of labor. Since the deficits for pension insurance and for unemployment insurance were to be covered by his budget, in the 1970s as today he was and is the actual switchman at the "Bonn switching yard." If the government and its parliamentary majority had wanted, the very restricted fiscal autonomy of the unemployment fund would never have been able to prevent them from mounting a Swedish-style offensive against unemployment using active labor market measures.

Institutional impediments could not have been so effective if labor market programs had had more political support in the Federal Republic. The lack of support was doubtless due to the fact that political discussion was fixated on the macroeconomic and fiscal instruments of full-employment policy. Even according to the understanding of labor market policy specialists, combating widespread unemployment was the job of the Stability and Growth Act of 1967 and not the Labor Promotion Act of 1969 (Kühl, 1982). Especially Social Democrats and union leaders, who assigned high priority to full employment, were convinced that active labor market measures, while perhaps mitigating the effects of unemployment, were incapable of combating mass unemployment. In short, the Federal Republic locked itself into the "Austrian way" to such an extent that the second-best Swedish option was not considered even when the preferred strategy obviously failed to maintain full employment. A series of special problems that impaired the reputation and effectiveness of labor market programs also contributed to this outcome.

In the first place, the same ministry was responsible for oversight of both the active labor market and unemployment compensation programs and all social welfare and pension programs. Thus political outsiders tended to associate active labor market policy with the impenetrable and threatening dynamics of social welfare expenditures, whose containment was the avowed goal of even social democratic budget policy makers after 1974. Their intent was to stop government handouts, and time and again they saw this intent frustrated by social democratic bleeding hearts in the legislature and the tricky bargaining tactics of the labor minister. At the same time, comprehensive oversight gave the labor minister an opportunity to end the pension finance crisis that had received much attention in the 1976 election by requiring the unemployment fund to contribute to social security for the unemployed. This elegant solution had a price, however: the recently consolidated budget of the unemployment fund ran into deficit again in 1979, when unemployment was falling, and thus earned the critical attention of budget policy makers.

As a consequence, the proponents of fiscal responsibility in the government took as dim a view of labor market programs in general as they did of social welfare policy. Moreover, a few of the additional labor market measures designed and financed by the federal government had received bad press, and the public service unions continued to oppose the expansion of job creation programs. Even calculations showing that job creation was hardly more expensive for the general government than the costs of unemployment had no effect in this generally skeptical atmosphere (Spitznagel, 1982; 1985; Reissert, 1983).

There was little political resistance to the worldview of the fiscalists, according to which labor market policy had to make do with the means available through unemployment insurance contributions. The federal government was obligated to cover deficits, but if this emergency recourse was necessary, things were seriously disordered. They had to be reordered as quickly as possible by means of higher contributions and lower expenditures on the part of the insurance fund. Confronted with this choice, even the unions finally decided to accept the unavoidable cuts primarily in the realm of the active labor market programs.

The unions' clear preference for defending unemployment compensation payments was decisive in this choice. If it proved impossible to achieve a significant increase in compensation benefits, as seemed likely, then successful support for active labor market programs would have cost either higher contributions or a decrease in unemployment insurance benefits. The first was unpopular with the membership and met political resistance from the employers and the FDP; the second would have harmed the vital interests of the organized "core groups" of the labor market, which at that time had reason to anticipate the possibility of layoffs but not of long-term unemployment (Freiburghaus, 1978). For them job creation or retraining programs were distant, hypothetical possibilities, but cuts in their unemployment compensation benefits would have diminished the value of entitlements earned during long years of contribution and hence violated the "social contract" of the insurance system in the most blatant way. In short, if cuts were unavoidable, the unions had to defend unemployment compensation payments in the

Table 10.12 Effect of the offensive and defensive labor
market policy in 1978: Sweden and the Federal Republic
(in relation to employment figures for 1974 and in % of
members of the paid work force)

	Sweden	FRG
Unemployment rate, 1978	2.2	3.5
Relief of the labor market by:		
Active labor market programs	3.9	1.3
Reduction in number of workers over age 55 (78/74)	0.2	1.5
Reduction in the number of foreign workers (78/74)	−1.2	1.7
Potential unemployment rate, 1978	5.1	8.0

Sources: BMA, Arbeits- und Sozialstatistik, Hauptergebnisse, 1975;
1979; SCB, aku, 1974; 1978; F. Schmidt, 1978; author's own
calculations.

interest of their members. In their search for the path of least resistance
budget policy makers had reason to concentrate the cuts they considered
necessary on those programs that might have been able to combat unemployment directly. Hence the German labor administration was never
asked to offset the failure of macroeconomic policy by launching an
active labor market offensive against mass unemployment.

That does not mean that the Federal Republic failed to use labor
market programs to combat registered unemployment, only that its efforts were aimed at reducing the labor supply rather than promoting employment. We showed in chapter 3 that in none of the other countries in
this study did work force participation of 60–to–65–year–olds decline
as much as in West Germany during the 1970s, and in no other country
did the participation of women increase so little. If we add in the reduction in the number of foreign workers (which also occurred in Austria),
we can establish a comparison with the Swedish model (Table 10.12).

German labor market policy in the 1970s did keep the consequences
of poor economic performance from becoming fully visible in the unemployment statistics. But West Germany achieved that effect by ceasing
recruitment of foreign workers and using the flexible age limit, disability
pensions, and other means of retiring older workers instead of expanding job creation and retraining programs. Employers then had a welcome chance to part with older workers who would otherwise have had
job security, and the unions and works committees did not oppose shifting the employment risk to their older colleagues; some actively supported it. One could conceivably read this as a reflection of low German

pleasure in work, at least as compared to Sweden and some other nations (Noelle-Neumann and Strümpel, 1984:62).

In contrast to Austria, the options for a social democratic–Keynesian coordination of economic policy instruments were limited in West Germany by the autonomy of the central bank and the constraints of the federal fiscal constitution. But unlike their counterparts in Sweden, Social Democrats and the unions in West Germany were still not prepared to respond to the failure of a Keynesian full-employment strategy with massive expansion of active labor market policy, although there were no insurmountable institutional obstacles to such a strategy.

CHAPTER ELEVEN

1979–1985: The End of the Keynesian Interlude

In the 1970s, as our analysis has shown, there was a plausible macroeconomic strategy that permitted even small countries to defend full employment during the crisis and to keep inflation within bounds. It required a social democratic–Keynesian coordination of expansionary fiscal policy and an accommodating monetary policy as well as voluntary union wage restraint to keep unit labor costs below the rate of inflation. In Austria the institutional conditions were favorable to such coordination and the strategy was predictably successful. In Great Britain the unions were ultimately unable to restrain wages for institutional reasons, and in Sweden in the second half of the 1970s neither the centrist coalition governments nor the unions were capable of policy coordination. Instead, there was a substantial, somewhat unplanned expansion of public employment and an extraordinary intensification of efforts to promote employment through active labor market policy.

In the Federal Republic, finally, Keynesian coordination failed first because of the institutional autonomy of the German central bank and later because of procyclical deficit reductions, especially at the state and local levels, while the unions did their full share in the successful battle against inflation. The attempt to secure full employment on the Swedish model, by expanding public employment and through active labor market measures, failed because of the difficulties peculiar to Germany's unique brand of fiscal federalism and because of institutional conditions governing the financing of the labor market programs, which disadvantaged programs designed to promote employment just as unemployment was rising.

In short, during the crisis of the 1970s it was possible to defend full employment either through an economic policy strategy pursued jointly by the government and the unions or through a labor market strategy pursued by the government alone. Where social democratic governments succeeded with neither strategy, we can find special institutional constraints that explain their failure.

Conditions in the first half of the 1980s were no longer so favorable to the success of a full-employment policy. Austria and Sweden, which were still or again governed by Social Democrats, continued to do well in international comparisons of unemployment and employment levels, but they no longer unambiguously belonged in the top group as they had in the 1970s (Table 11.1). With unemployment, moreover, the comparatively positive figures can be explained partly as the delayed effect of early success. If instead of absolute values we compare the relative change in unemployment from 1973 to 1979 and 1979 to 1985 (Figures 11.1 and 11.2), then the Austrian and Swedish figures are closer to the German and British in the second period, although Great Britain stopped pursuing a social democratic full-employment strategy in 1979 and the Federal Republic stopped in 1982 at the latest.

The Austrian and Swedish strategies have thus lost a great deal of their effectiveness since the late 1970s. Our case studies of Austrian and Swedish developments after 1979, and the history of the last years of the social-liberal coalition in the Federal Republic, offer one explanation. Between 1979 and 1985 there was no economically plausible strategy for

Table 11.1 Unemployment and employment in selected OECD nations, 1973–1979 and 1979–1983/85

	Average annual unemployment rate		Total change in number employed	
	1973–79	1979–85	1973–79	1979–84
Austria	1.7	3.0*	2.4	−2.0
FRG	2.9	6.0	−3.4	−2.7
GB	4.7	10.3	1.5	−5.6
Sweden	2.0	2.7	7.8	1.8
Belgium	5.8	11.6	0.2	−4.4
Switzerland	0.4[†]	0.6	−7.5	1.4
France	4.3	8.0	2.2	−1.8
Italy	6.5	9.0	6.3	1.8
Japan	1.8	2.4	4.2	5.2
Norway	1.8	2.4	13.2	5.2
Netherlands	4.5[‡]	10.3	3.1	3.0
USA	6.4	7.7	16.2	6.3

Sources: OECD *Economic Outlook* 39; OECD *Labour Force Statistics Yearbook*, 1963–1983; 1964–1984.
* Until 1984. [†] From 1975 on. [‡] From 1974 on.

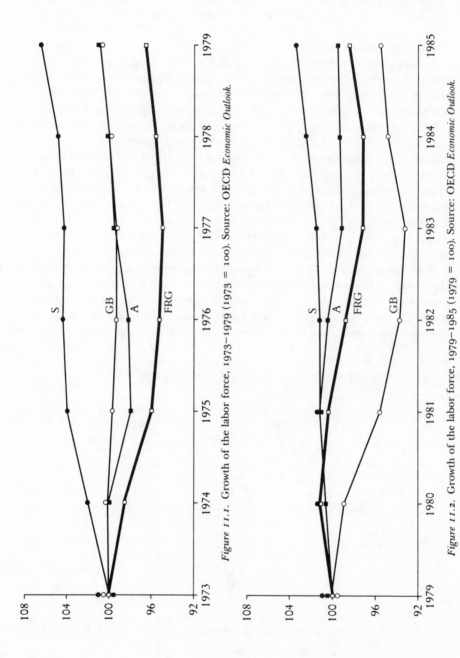

Figure 11.1. Growth of the labor force, 1973–1979 (1973 = 100). Source: OECD *Economic Outlook.*

Figure 11.2. Growth of the labor force, 1979–1985 (1979 = 100). Source: OECD *Economic Outlook.*

240

dealing with the crisis that was also in tune with social democratic criteria, as there had been earlier. There were only attempts to maintain the old goals and employ the old instruments under increasingly unfavorable conditions while trying to meet a number of increasingly incompatible demands at once. What had changed?

The crisis of the early 1980s was characterized by the coincidence of three developments whose importance (if not their relative weights) is now generally acknowledged. A short recapitulation will suffice to describe them.

As in 1973–74, the trigger was an oil price shock. Since 1975 the OPEC nations had increasingly been spending their oil income on imported consumer goods, industrial plants, and armaments, and had in part managed once more to run up negative current account balances. At the same time they saw the real price of oil sales fall as the American dollar dropped in value. When the Iranian revolution and the Teheran hostage crisis once again destabilized oil markets, the OPEC countries took the opportunity to escalate the dollar oil price by a factor of three relative to the level of 1978. The result was a repetition of the primary effects of the first oil price shock. OPEC surpluses shot up again, from $79 billion in 1979 to $120 billion in 1980; predictably, the industrial countries found themselves again with current account deficits. The reduction in aggregate demand again resulted in a worldwide increase in unemployment, and price increases in petroleum and petroleum-based products pushed inflation rates up once more.

This was accompanied by a second development in the international money and capital markets (Mayer, 1982; Gerhardt, 1984; Hankel, 1984). As early as the 1950s and 1960s, international credit markets, the "Euro" or "offshore" dollar markets, had grown up outside of the control of the national central banks. Offshore transactions were conducted in places like Luxembourg, the Bahamas, and Singapore, tax oases with liberal bank regulations, by "extraterritorial" branches of major American and European banks. At first, they primarily benefited the Soviet Union, the multinational companies, and large American banks, all of which were interested in financial transactions in the global currency of U.S. dollars that were not subject to the control of the U.S. government. Their turnover increased with the rise in importance of forward markets in currencies after the end of the 1960s.

After 1973 this development accelerated again. The number of German bank branches in offshore locations rose from 23 to 88 between 1973 and 1981, and their volume of business increased by a factor of eight during the same time, from 15 to 125 billion marks (Huber, 1982:350). The same development occurred in the other OECD countries as well. On average, the foreign business share of all bank transactions doubled between 1970 and 1981 (Pecchioli, 1982:19). Several developments coincided to produce this result. On the one hand the Eurobanks were ideal partners for the OPEC nations in managing and investing their current account surpluses. On the other, in the industrial nations the transition to flexible rates of exchange increased the interest of monetary institutions, firms, and private investors in forward transactions to protect themselves against changes in rates of exchange and in speculating on exchange rates. At the same time the demand for credit also increased in those countries that had to finance their trade deficits with capital imports.

But the Eurodollar business went far beyond the mere recycling of petrodollars. Eastern bloc and Latin American exports were especially hard hit by the stagnation of world trade, which jeopardized their development and investment plans. For them, the practically unlimited credit offered by the Eurobanks—unlimited because it was not subject to central bank or IMF control—was an irresistible temptation to continue their investment programs in the hopes that the world economy would soon improve. But when the the second oil price shock brought recovery to an abrupt halt in 1979, these countries were unable to service their loans. To avert a global bank crisis, the loans had to be rolled over, interest payments had to be postponed, and additional credit had to be extended to pay interest when it came due. Debts were piled upon debts in order to avoid the default of practically bankrupt debtor countries and the collapse of the creditor banks. In Latin America alone the sum of public foreign debts rose from $59 billion in 1975 to $257 billion in 1983 (Table 11.2).

This debt crisis had two repercussions for the Western industrial countries that intensified their own problems. Because the debtor nations had to commit not only their export earnings but also new loans exclusively to debt service, their demand for imported goods, especially capital goods, decreased. This primarily affected countries such as the Federal Republic that exported capital goods and specialized in building indus-

Table 11.2 Public foreign indebtedness in the Third World (billions of U.S. dollars)

	1975	1977	1979	1981	1983
Total Third World	180	276	407	515	634
Latin America	59	96	145	184	257

Source: World Bank, Annual Reports, 1983 and 1985.

trial facilities abroad. Second, in refinancing Third World debts the creditor banks imposed substantial risk premiums on interest rates, and the oligopolistic structure of credit markets allowed them to obtain the higher yields they needed to cover foreign risks in their domestic business as well (Schulmeister, 1986:40–41).

The major impetus for the worldwide increase in interest rates, however, came from the United States. The Federal Reserve Bank abandoned its previous liberal policy in autumn 1978, in the face of climbing inflation rates, trade deficits, and a constantly falling dollar. It had decided to pursue a monetarist tight money policy, just as the German Bundesbank had done earlier. The Fed intensified this policy in the second half of 1979 to prevent the second oil price shock from being translated into general price increases. The immediate results of monetary restraint for the American economy echoed the German experience of 1974 and 1975. The sharp contraction between 1980 and 1982 and the rise of unemployment were, however, accepted politically during the changeover from the Carter to the Reagan administration. The inflation rate, on the other hand, fell rapidly from more than 13 percent in 1980 to 6.1 percent in 1982 and 3.2 percent in 1983. The monetarist cure took.

As the Federal Reserve pursued its monetarist course, American interest rates rose sharply. The annual average interest rate on long-term government securities increased from 9 percent in 1979 to more than 14 percent in autumn 1981 (SVR, 1984–85:11–20). As the inflation rate dropped, real interest rates climbed dramatically. In the United States, unlike the Federal Republic, they had been strongly negative until 1980; by 1982 they had risen to 6 percent and by 1983–84 to more than 8 percent (Funke, 1986: Table A8).

The Federal Reserve Bank relaxed its grip on the money supply in summer 1982. Nevertheless, interest rates remained very high. They were held up by the large federal deficits that were produced by a combination of supply-side tax cuts and greatly increased defense spending. From an international perspective, the American deficits were less remarkable for their size than for their breathtaking rate of increase (from $64 billion or 0.9 percent of GNP in 1981 to $179 billion or 4.1 percent in 1983; BMF *Finanzbericht*, 1986: Übersicht 17). Despite efforts to reduce the deficit, the increase continued and in 1985 reached the record high of $212 billion. In its economic effect, this was a "Keynesian" fiscal impulse whose intensity far exceeded the efforts of social democratic European countries in the mid–1970s (Teschner and Vesper, 1983). This impulse can explain the steep economic upswing of the

American economy, with growth rates of 3.7 percent in 1983 and 6.8 percent in the election year of 1984, if we also take into account the supply-side effects of the tax cut (SVR, 1984–85:6–10).

The economic impulse of the budget deficit was intensified by the fact that it was covered to a great extent by capital imports, because the American savings rate was too small to meet capital requirements in any case. Thus the federal deficit acted domestically as pure supplemental demand without a corresponding crowding-out effect. Capital imports were attracted by the high American real interest rates and by the fact that the dollar's exchange rate had stopped its downslide with the turn to monetarism in autumn 1978 and had been climbing steadily since early 1981. At the same time, the capital imports raised international demand for American currency and drove the dollar's value up still further. For a few years there was a dynamic movement feeding on itself, a virtuous circle or a vicious one, depending on perspective, in which capital imports were stimulated by the expectation of further revaluation and the actual revaluation was intensified by capital imports, while the deficit in the American current account balance continued to increase (precisely because of the revaluation).

KEYNESIAN COORDINATION IS BLOCKED

Our subject is not the United States, however, but the Western European industrial nations and their opportunity to pursue a successful full-employment policy in the 1980s. For them the restrictive phase of American monetary policy between 1979 and 1982 was a catastrophe, and the fiscal expansion after 1982 a mixed blessing. Along with the American economic upswing and the further revaluation of the dollar, it brought improved opportunities for export sales to the United States, but the high dollar interest rates constrained the policy options available to the European countries. These constraints can be summarized as follows.

1. In the 1970s the internationalization of the money and capital markets was institutionally completed in all but a few countries (among them Japan). Government exchange controls were dismantled or they lost their effectiveness for the portfolio decisions of monetary institutions that were ever more closely linked internationally, as well as for "nonbanks" looking for investment opportunities abroad. As the dollar's exchange rate stabilized and began to rise again, the large American capital market, with its guaranteed government loans and very high real interest rates, became more attractive. Countries that were dependent on capital imports to offset their current account deficits were thus forced

to offer conditions to international capital that were at least as attractive as those that obtained in the United States.

In practice, real interest rates in European countries had to rise in step with the dollar rates. If this condition was not met, massive capital out-flows resulted. If a country then tried to defend its exchange rate, these outflows first exhausted the currency reserves of the national bank and then forced a massive devaluation of the nation's own currency. At least this was the experience of the new socialist government in France, whose Keynesian expansionary strategy was able to reduce long-term real inter-est rates in autumn 1981 but which was forced by the realities of the international capital market to capitulate by the summer of 1982. As long as American real interest rates were negative in the 1970s, the "smaller" currencies were able to choose their own positive or negative real interest level (as long as they were not members of the D-mark bloc with their currencies tied to the German mark). But by winter 1980–81, when real interest rates became positive in the United States, real inter-est rates had become positive in all the other Western industrial nations (except Switzerland) as well (Table 11.3).

In other words, as the capital markets became international, national monetary policy lost the freedom to undercut the rate of return offered for financial investments in the dollar market—and with the rise in real interest rates for long-term dollar investment, what had been a latent condition became a manifest constraint. National monetary policy had lost its sovereignty over interest rates.

2. Therefore national monetary policy was disabled as an element of Keynesian control as long as the dollar interest rate was high. Con-sumers, builders, and firms faced a tight and expensive credit market, which reduced domestic consumer and investment demand, although underutilized production capacities and high unemployment would have called for an expansion of demand. If a country nevertheless wanted to pursue a Keynesian full-employment policy, the burden of expanding demand would have to be borne by fiscal policy alone. To achieve a given economic impulse, however, the budget deficit would have to be larger than would have been necessary with monetary policy support.

At the same time higher interest rates increased the cost of an expan-sionary fiscal policy. If real interest rates do not fall in a period of weak growth but continue to climb, the increase in the public debt (desirable from an economic point of view) becomes a serious financial policy prob-lem. According to "Domar's Law," when real interest rates rise above the real growth rate (and thus above the growth of tax income), the escala-tion of debt service must progressively limit fiscal maneuverability (Domar, 1944). Thus interest payments increased from 8 percent of

Table 11.3 Long-term real interest rates, 1979–1984

Quarter	USA	FRG	France	GB	Sweden
1979					
Q1	−1.38	4.03	−0.43	3.78	3.94
1980					
Q1	−3.10	3.03	0.38	−4.66	−1.69
1981					
Q1	0.81	4.17	2.24	1.14	0.71
Q2	2.85	4.99	3.69	2.47	0.38
Q3	2.74	4.63	3.44	4.02	0.75
Q4	3.65	3.16	2.57	3.78	3.35
1982					
Q1	5.81	3.89	2.37	3.55	3.71
Q2	6.14	3.74	2.41	4.38	4.17
Q3	6.40	4.07	4.87	4.29	4.91
Q4	5.83	3.47	6.23	4.66	3.83
1983					
Q1	6.82	3.57	5.58	6.41	3.67
Q2	7.01	4.41	5.58	6.75	3.35
Q3	8.63	5.19	4.26	6.25	2.77
Q4	8.02	5.57	4.24	5.37	4.13
1984					
Q1	7.06	5.18	5.04	5.15	3.49
Q2	8.36	5.16	6.08	5.68	3.69
Q3	8.15	6.06	6.19	6.43	6.23
Q4	7.31	5.12	5.53	5.65	4.81

Source: Funke, 1986.
Note: Interest rates for long-term government securities, deflated using the consumer price-inflation rate of the preceding period.

central government expenditures to 15 percent between 1977 and 1985 in the United States, from 5 percent to 11 percent in the Federal Republic, and from 5 percent to 23 percent in Sweden (Table 11.4). To be sure, the nations varied greatly in their political tolerance for such developments, but for budgetary reasons it is certain that they could not have continued indefinitely (Simmert and Wagner, 1981).

3. With high dollar interest rates, the possibility of Keynesian demand expansion was seriously constrained in Western European countries. Still more serious, however, were the supply-side effects. Countries that had not been able to avoid mass unemployment in the 1970s depended on additional investment to create new jobs. In the face of the rapid technological and structural changes, however, even countries that had been more successful in their employment policies faced a similar necessity to invest. With the increase in global interest rates, investment credit became more expensive, and the opportunity cost of savings increased at the same rate. As a result, the yield thresholds that investment projects

Table 11.4 Debt of the total state (% of GNP) and debt service (% of expenditures)

	Public sector debt			Debt service		
	1977	1980	1984	1977	1980	1985
Austria	27	37	48	4.5	7.5	10.6
FRG	27	31	41	5.0	6.5	11.3
GB	63	58	50	8.5	10.7	14.5
Sweden	39	52	77	4.6	8.6	23.0
USA	52	47	54	8.3	10.9	15.0

Source: BMF *Finanzberichte,* 1979; 1982; 1987.

had to meet were raised. When real interest rates were negative in the 1970s, any project that promised positive cash flows could find financing; now projects could be financed only if their expected rate of return was significantly higher than the real interest rate of 6 to 8 percent on American government securities.

Other things being equal (costs, returns, risks), investment had to decrease because of the higher interest rates. And even if profits increased, perhaps because government economic policy succeeded in increasing aggregate demand and in persuading the unions to pursue a "cooperative" wage policy, the effects were less than in the 1970s. As long as medium-term profit expectations did not surpass the minimum rate of return of the international capital markets, the higher profits of firms would flow into financial investments rather than into real investments that would create jobs (Faxén and Normann, 1984).

Thus when supply-side analyses in the early 1980s attributed the rise in unemployment to weak investment and this in turn to insufficient expectations of profit, they were only technically correct. Certainly in some countries firm profits decreased during the recession, but the dramatic rise in the rate of return of competing financial investments was no less significant. Social Democrats and union leaders were right to protest against supply-side theorists, who blamed weak investment and employment in the European economies on excessive wage costs, nonwage labor costs, and taxes. It was not these burdens on firms that had risen dramatically as the 1970s became the 1980s; instead, profits had diminished with the worldwide stagnation of demand, and at the same time the international interest level had drastically raised the standard for a "sufficient" expectation of profit from the perspective of capital investors.

But this theoretical battle had little practical significance. The gap had opened between firm profits and the yields of financial investment, and investment and employment decreased. As long as the domestic economic policies of European countries could neither determine the international level of interest nor effectively limit the mobility of capital, the only policy options in the early 1980s were to accept further loss of jobs in the private sector or to increase the rate of return of productive investment so much that it could again compete with nonproductive financial investments. In that sense, capitalist logic supported the supply-side formulas. If it is impossible to resist a redistribution in favor of capital, then other claims on firms' product must be reduced, and one does not have to be particularly critical of government or hostile to unions to conclude that most of those reductions have to come at the expense of government and workers.

In summary, as capital markets became internationalized and the international level of interest rates was raised, the terms of trade between capital, labor, and government shifted in favor of the capital side. For that reason any attempt to maintain or restore full employment in the private sector in the early 1980s had to be paid for by a massive redistribution in favor of capital incomes. The only question was, who would pay this price and how.

THE NEED FOR SUPPLY-SIDE ORIENTED REDISTRIBUTION

None of the four countries in our study tried to shield its own capital markets from the international interest level by introducing or increasing controls on capital transfers. Austria and Sweden were no longer able to do so because they depended on capital imports to equalize their balance of payments. Great Britain and the Federal Republic, on the other hand, again had current account surpluses after 1981, but their capital markets were so integrated into the international markets and their currencies were held to such a great extent by foreigners that even the announcement of restrictions would have caused uncontrollable capital movement with incalculable effects on the exchange rates. The French experience of 1981–82, at any rate, seemed to justify such fears precisely because the franc was much less of an international reserve currency than either the British pound or the German mark.

If it was impossible to avoid the pressure for redistribution by uncoupling from the international capital markets, then how should nations give in to them, and with what consequences for what groups and what economic and social goals? In my view, this should have been the focus of the strategic discussion of the early 1980s, but in fact it was conducted in such a one-sided way that the available options were insufficiently explored. At fault was the fact that a conservative, monetarist version of supply-side economics dominated the discussion, taking its solutions from the American model. In the United States a massive tax cut combined with the increasing erosion of union influence on wage setting, cuts in social services, and an active policy of deregulation (and, of course, with the demand stimulus of a huge budget deficit) to raise firm profits to such high levels that both private investment and employment increased markedly despite the high interest rates. The message, propagated with missionary zeal by neoclassical theorists of all nations, was that the same result must be possible with the same or similar means in Europe as well (Giersch, 1983; Lindbeck, 1980; 1986; Minford, 1983).

The weakness of social democratic and union counterarguments in this debate was that they refused to recognize the necessity for redistribution. As long as these camps refused to accept defeat in the battle over redistribution, it was impossible to develop reasonable concepts for containing the damage and morally convincing solutions for distributing the resulting burdens. Instead, the European Left concentrated on criticizing the integration of the world market (Fröbel et al., 1986) and the distributive implications of supply-side policy (Meißner, 1980) and demanded the return to a Keynesian demand policy (Hickel, 1985) or the transition to a policy of "qualitative growth" that would also be based on deficit financing (Meißner and Zinn, 1984). Those who recognized and understood the significance of international constraints on domestic Keynesianism concentrated their hopes on the chance of regaining Keynesian options on the international level, either on the high road of macroeconomic coordination between the United States, Japan, and Western Europe (H. Schmidt, 1986) or on the low road of economic policy integration in the European Community (Glotz, 1985). I shall return to this point.

Thus there is as yet no explicit social democratic strategy that acknowledges the necessity to adapt national economies to the constraints of the international capital market, at least temporarily. Accordingly, the surviving social democratic governments responded to the problems of the early 1980s without a clear view of what they were doing. Austria persisted in its Austro-Keynesian combination of investment subsidy and wage restraint, whose supply-side accent became even more important under the new conditions. Although this combination was less effective in terms of economic and employment policy in the 1980s than before (Leibfritz and Meurer, 1984:126ff., 154ff.), Austria still had an above-average profit level and an above-average investment rate (Table 11.5). Nevertheless, unemployment increased and employment declined between 1979 and 1984, and despite all subsidies (or perhaps because of

Table 11.5 Gross capital formation (% of GDP), 1979–1984

	1979	1980	1981	1982	1983	1984
Austria	25.1	25.5	25.2	23.0	22.2	21.8
FRG	21.8	22.7	21.8	20.5	20.6	20.3
GB	18.8	18.1	16.4	16.4	16.4	17.4
Sweden	19.8	20.2	19.2	18.8	18.7	18.4
OECD Europe	21.0	21.3	20.5	19.8	19.3	19.2

Source: OECD Economic Outlook 39.

them), the nationalized industries were caught in a structural crisis that has caused massive layoffs and that precludes their further use as an employment buffer. But even though Austrian self-satisfaction has long since given way to a deep unease, expressed in a plethora of self-critical analysis (Seidel et al., 1982; Arndt, 1982; Gerlich et al., 1985; Nowotny and Tieber, 1985), the discussion has not yet produced plausible alternative strategies or a willingness to call into question the institutions of neocorporatist social partnership and the consensus politics on which it is based.

One might say that the Austrian economic policy makers know that they haven't got a clue, but they seem to prefer their joint bewilderment to battling over patent solutions that would advantage one side at the expense of the others and could therefore not meet with consensus. This battle over solutions that defy consensus has dominated academic and political discussion not only in Great Britain and the Federal Republic but also in Sweden since the late 1970s. In Sweden, the LO unions and the Social Democrats started the fight with their campaign for the wage earners' fund as the "first step to socialism" or at least to economic democracy (Eidem and Öhman, 1978). Conservatives and employers responded with a political mobilization and ideological radicalization that had a clear agenda of redistribution from below to above (Faxén and Normann, 1984). They also attempted to destroy the system of centralized wage negotiations.

The practical program of the Social Democrats since 1982, however, has been almost unaffected by this ideological polarization. Like their predecessor centrist governments, they tried to improve the international competitiveness of Swedish industry by devaluating the krona. However, they were more decisive in doing so and set the rate of devaluation so high when they entered office that the previously overvalued Swedish krona traded below its value for a while. Because the government and the leadership of the LO unions also succeeded, despite all difficulties, in dampening wage increases, the devaluation effects were not immediately neutralized by increased inflation. Thus the devaluation actually helped Swedish exports, or at least Swedish export industries. Exporters did not pass along devaluation to their foreign customers, but (in keeping with the assumptions of the EFO model) continued to act as price takers in foreign markets. The quantitative export boom that the government had hoped for therefore did not materialize (and the Swedish balance of trade benefited more from the American import boom than from devaluation), but at least there was a steep rise in profits in the export sector.

The Social Democrats were thus able to create conditions under which the gap between the rate of return of real investments and the interest paid on financial investments could be closed (Faxén and Normann, 1984:23, 48). Nevertheless, it took until 1984 for rapidly climbing profits finally to pull even with slightly declining interest rates, so that investment in Swedish industry, which had declined until 1983, also increased again. As a result the Swedish Social Democrats did in fact meet the conditions specified by the supply-side economists, but they did so with a strategy that was designed to raise firm revenues rather than to reduce the costs of production. This camouflaged the need for redistribution but did not obviate it. The devaluation could not have increased profits substantially if the unions had obtained a wage compensation for the higher import prices and had then exploited the improved capacity of firms to pay, as had happened in the 1970s. An increase in profits was to be had only through redistribution to the disadvantage of the workers. According to calculations of the German Council of Economic Advisers (SVR), the "real wage position" (which takes into account the inflation rate, productivity, and terms-of-trade effects) has been reduced in Sweden more than in the other countries since the Social Democrats' return to office (Table 11.6).

Table 11.6 Annual change in real wages, 1977–1984

	1977	1978	1979	1980	1981	1982	1983	1984
Austria	+0.1	+2.2	−4.2	−0.6	+1.3	−9.0	−1.4	−2.4
FRG	−0.3	−0.7	−0.3	+1.9	−0.2	−2.2	−2.9	−1.3
GB	−5.3	−0.1	−0.0	+3.8	−1.1	−3.5	−1.3	+0.9
Sweden	+4.4	−1.0	−1.5	−1.2	−0.6	−3.5	−4.4	−4.0
Switzerland	−0.1	+1.6	−0.0	+0.6	+0.5	+1.4	−0.8	−1.7
Japan	−1.2	−2.8	+0.4	−1.5	−1.7	−0.3	+0.1	−2.8
USA	+0.1	+0.5	+0.8	+0.7	−2.2	+1.6	−1.2	−1.6

Source: SVR, 1984–85.
Note: The change in employee income was deflated using the consumer price index minus the change in real gross domestic product per employee, after adjusting for the income effect of the change in real terms of trade.

Workers in Sweden and Austria, the two countries with Social Democratic governments and strong, centralized unions, were not particularly well protected against redistribution to the capital side in the 1980s. On the contrary, they gave in to that pressure even more than did their colleagues in countries with conservative governments and with weak or organizationally fragmented unions such as Great Britain, Japan, Switzerland, and the United States.

That outcome seems paradoxical only if one considers positional gains in the distributive battle with the capital side as the highest goal of the labor movement. But if one assumes instead that full employment is the highest goal, and if one further assumes that under given economic conditions that goal could not be defended without a drastic increase in business profits, then reductions of labor income may be interpreted not only as a sign of economic weakness but also as a demonstration of the organizational strength of solidaristic labor unions. In economic effect, after all, the conservative-monetarist constellation, which I described as a danger in chapter 9, had now come about in all countries. As governments practiced monetary and fiscal restraint willy-nilly, the unions were forced to choose between two unattractive options. While a more aggressive wage policy could have maintained or increased the real incomes of employed workers, it would also have entailed even higher job losses. Real wage cuts, on the other hand, could at least slow down, and perhaps stop, job losses.

It is less easy to decide which institutional conditions would favor execution of this "second-worst" solution than it was to determine the institutional conditions favoring the social democratic–Keynesian coordination discussed above. In the 1970s that coordination could work in the long run only given a strongly centralized and concentrated union organization. In contrast, as I have tried to show, conservative-monetarist policy does not depend on the strategic capabilities of strong and unified unions. But that conclusion presupposed a conservative government primarily interested in price stability rather than a government that was trying to promote investment in order to increase employment.

The neoclassical proponents of supply-side economics consider strong unions to be evil in principle. In the best of all possible worlds they believe equilibrium would be secured in the labor market by flexible employment contracts and individually negotiated wages. Therefore, the existence of unions and collectively determined (monopolistic) wages and employment conditions can only hinder the otherwise certain tendency toward full employment in a free-market economy, and the stronger the unions are the more they hinder (Brittan and Lilley, 1977; Calmfors, 1982; 1985; Risch, 1983). But at least this last conclusion contains a logical error. Apart from the issue of whether labor markets tend to a stable equilibrium (Spahn and Vobruba, 1986), neoclassically inspired investigations have shown that the one-sided dominance of employers both in the labor market and within enterprises would be economically inefficient (Addison, 1985; Freeman and Medoff, 1984; Mueller, 1980). But some countervailing power of unions is economically desirable, and if collective bargaining over wages and working conditions takes place at all, then the union-busting campaign conducted by employers and conservative parties in many countries makes no economic sense.

The market model guarantees full employment in theory only because it assumes that the unemployed will compete with the employed for wages. This competition would then keep wages at the market-clearing level. But if wages are collectively determined at all, the wage competition postulated by neoclassical theory disappears and the market mechanism will not automatically adjust wages so as to avoid involuntary unemployment. Wages are set through a process of collective decision making in which the unemployed do not participate. Whether wages will correspond to supply-side requirements does thus not depend on the degree to which various bargaining structures mimic the market. What matters are the criteria of collective rationality of the participating organizations, and they speak against rather than for the neoclassical prejudice in favor of small and weak unions.

It is true, as I mentioned above, that the threat of unemployment is an individual rather than a collective bad. It will force small unions or shop committees to make wage concessions in the interest of the firm. But their willingness to make concessions ends, according to the same egoistically rational logic, when their own jobs are no longer in immediate jeopardy. Moreover, unions that represent workers in bottleneck professions or in plants that are employed to capacity would have no self-interested reason at all to forego any wage increase the traffic will bear. And unions in less profitable sectors are often still strong enough to push through compensation for higher wage agreements reached next door, despite their higher risk of job losses. This combination of scarcity wages and demands for comparability explains why real wages were rising in Great Britain despite very high unemployment.

The situation is different for an industrial union that is responsible for large branches. It is here that such unions are able, by their sheer power, to force the employers in individual firms, branches, or regions to their knees, and this explains the zeal of their critics. But the principle of solidarity to which they owe their strength compels them to an economic rationality that is foreign to smaller organizations. Even if they orient themselves exclusively toward the interests of their employed members in an egoistically rational way, the heterogeneous conditions of firms within their jurisdiction would force them to take into account the weakest members of their constituency as soon as these are seriously threatened with unemployment. The result of uniform wage contracts negotiated by large industrial unions is thus unexploited surplus earnings in profitable firms. These surpluses work to the advantage of industrial policy in that they give a supply-side push to the more competitive firms and branches, which can and should expand at an above-average rate. Thus it is difficult to see the Swedish and German demands for decentralized wage negotiations as an expression of particular strategic wisdom by employers and their conservative political partners. But that is not our topic.

The institutional structures that favored a social democratic–Keynesian coordination in the 1970s have facilitated the supply-side-oriented wage policy demanded in the 1980s. In other words, under the economic conditions of the 1980s the weak American unions or the small and decentralized British or Japanese unions were able to offer little resistance to the increased exploitative capacity of the capital side. Therefore they were comfortable partners for employers. But their narrow plant egoism precluded their becoming partners in a supply-side strategy of government employment policy. That would have depended on the capacity to intentionally refrain from wage increases that could have been obtained by full exertion of their bargaining power. This capacity for actively promoting the macroeconomically necessary redistribution in favor of capital income was always much greater in the large and centralized monopoly unions of Sweden and Austria (and in the industrial unions of the Federal Republic). That explains why the "American employment miracle" was due more to expansionary government policy than to wage restraint by American workers.

"Encompassing" and solidaristic unions were thus more capable of self-exploitation under the economic conditions of the 1980s than pluralistic, fragmented systems of interest representation, which were less able to resist exploitation by employers. Hence reports about the demise of corporatist institutions may have been premature after all. But all this does not change the fact that this "second-worst solution" is deeply unsatisfactory. Social Democrats and union leaders who must derive masochistic pride from the fact that they are able to organize an economically necessary redistribution in favor of capital more effectively than the capitalists themselves could have done may still be able to thrive on their own professionalism. But they are clearly incapable of turning their practice into a plausible, integrative vision of the future. Therefore I close this interpretive stocktaking of the experiences of the 1970s and early 1980s with a cautious, speculative look at the chances for renewing a social democratic–Keynesian policy of full employment through international cooperation.

CHAPTER TWELVE

Hopes at the End of the Eighties

In summer 1986, it almost seemed that the economic problems of Western industrial nations might solve themselves. At least it seemed that we again had conditions under which the techniques of Keynesian demand management that had been successful in the 1960s and early 1970s might work again. The dramatic fall of oil prices since 1985 (the effect of which was intensified in the Federal Republic by the simultaneous devaluation of the dollar) generated economic impulses that were a mirror image of the impulses of the oil price shocks that triggered the crisis of 1973–74 and 1979–80. Thus there was a widespread feeling that the crisis had passed.

Oil prices were now not driving inflation but rather helping to stabilize prices. West Germany, for instance, had negative inflation for the first time in decades. According to the logic that called for voluntary wage restraint to fight inflation when oil prices were increasing, it should have been possible to increase real wages without triggering inflationary pressures. The German wage agreements of 1986 were accordingly higher.

At the same time consumer savings from lower oil prices were available to increase domestic demand in the industrial countries. In the Federal Republic, for example, the oil bill in 1986 was half what it was in 1985, which had the effect of giving Germans an additional 20 billion marks with which they could buy domestic goods and services or other imports. Twenty billion marks represents a far greater demand stimulus than any of the programs of the 1970s provided (Beyfuss and Kroper, 1986). To the same degree, of course, the income of the oil-producing countries was falling, and with it their potential demand for imports. How soon the positive and negative demand effects would work themselves out or to what extent they would be mitigated or delayed by higher savings or higher borrowing remained to be seen, just as in summer 1974 no one could have predicted the actual course of the first oil price crisis.

Moreover, real dollar interest rates were somewhat lower, and the dollar had fallen 40 percent against the German mark since its high in February 1985. These changes decreased the price advantages of European and Japanese exporters in the American market, but at the same time they reduced external pressures on the central banks, which now no longer had to defend exchange rates with a tight money policy that was choking off all impulses toward domestic economic expansion.

On the contrary. In summer 1986 the U.S. government, which brought about the devaluation as a means of correcting the enormous current account deficit but remained dependent on capital imports to cover its budget deficit, pressured its trading partner nations to reduce interest rates still further in order to boost domestic demand in Europe and Japan, which would benefit both American exports and American capital imports. Even the U.S. threat to drive the dollar exchange rate down still further if its partners should fail to cooperate made economic sense. After a certain point undervaluation of the dollar would reduce not only profits from exports to the United States but also their quantity, and thus would have to improve the American balance of trade. If a flight from the dollar should ensue, it might be possible to pay off old debts at favorable exchange rates, and afterward a greatly undervalued dollar would give rise to expectations of revaluation and would again favor capital imports.

Just as was true at the Bonn summit in 1978, European self-interest now spoke in favor of yielding to American pressure. If the interest rate differential, which was necessary from an American point of view, could be stabilized at a lower level of real interest rates, the result for Europe would be a greater use of productive capacity and additional investment. Moreover, the public debt would not have to be increased as it was in 1978. Quite the reverse; further reductions in the interest rates would make it easier to consolidate the budget. Unfortunately, however, the American demands this time were not addressed to the German federal government, which then as now could hardly withstand serious American pressure. They were addressed to the German central bank, which is autonomous, combative, and obviously insatiable in its desire to stabilize prices. Thus in late July 1986 (when the inflation rate was −0.5 percent) the Bundesbank's vice-president justified the vigorous rejection of any further reductions in the interest rate with reference to the threat of renewed inflationary pressure (Schlesinger, 1986). The institutional chances for remounting the locomotive strategy were thus less favorable in the Federal Republic than they had been in summer 1978, and if the

257

German central bank remained firm, the hands of all the countries in the European "Deutschmark bloc" were tied as well.

Therefore, the European countries might be unable to seize the opportunity to boost growth and reduce unemployment presented by unexpectedly favorable oil prices, dollar interest rates, and the dollar exchange rate. But even if the Bundesbank were to abandon its monomaniacal pursuit of price stability and accord the same significance to increasing employment, it would be a mistake to infer that the fall in oil prices has recreated the stable conditions in the world economy that facilitated Keynesian full-employment and stabilization policy on the domestic level in the 1960s.

Such a belief is belied not only by the persistence of very high real interest rates, the danger of a global debt crisis, and the risk of a new increase in oil prices. More important, it is belied by the fact that world market integration, which was economically and institutionally completed in the 1970s, has constrained the scope of a national macroeconomic policy permanently and fundamentally (Pecchioli, 1983). The institutional changes that have made the world market the sole relevant frame of reference for capital investors seem to be irreversible. Why else, in the absence of an international catastrophe, should banks, savings associations, and insurance companies close their foreign branches and break up their lucrative international business connections, and why should firms decide to fire their foreign financial investment specialists?

The internationalization of money and capital markets not only limits the effectiveness of domestic Keynesian demand management; it also creates a fundamental uncertainty of expectations for all participants in the economic process. How should long-term investment plans be calculated in view of the fact that the real dollar interest rate went from −4.44 percent to 2.85 percent between spring 1980 and spring 1981 and in the next year jumped to 6.40 percent? Or how can export strategies be planned when the dollar lost a third of its value between fall 1985 and spring 1986? This uncertainty reduces the willingness of capital owners to make long-term real investments and increases their preference for liquid forms of investment. This in turn increases the volume of mobile capital for international speculation. The same process of internationalization that reduces domestic economic policy options generates and intensifies the economic turbulences that could be controlled only by an authority outside the marketplace.

For neoclassical economics, these problems prove the error of domestic government intervention in the free play of the international capital and money markets, whereas Marxists like Fidel Castro see the problems as the harbingers of the imminent collapse of the capitalist world economy (Altvater, 1985). Keynesians, who do not share the neoclassical belief in the inscrutable wisdom of the market and nevertheless cannot hope for its removal, must hold fast to their optimism about the possibility of control even under the much less favorable conditions of the late 1980s. If economic crisis mechanisms have become internationalized, then strategies to avoid and master economic crises must also be internationalized. Keynesians must try to reestablish on the international level the institutional capability to control economic processes that they have lost on the national level.

From a European perspective there are basically two strategies by which to accomplish this, globalization or Europeanization of Keynesian controls. The two strategies are not mutually exclusive; indeed, they could reinforce each other in their effects. Both are unimpeachable in their economic logic—but their realization confronts such fundamental institutional and political difficulties that it seems highly risky to place the strategic hopes of the European Left in one of these variants of international Keynesianism.

WORLDWIDE COORDINATION OF KEYNESIAN CONTROL?

The goal of the first strategy is to reestablish the worldwide and stable economic order that existed in the postwar decades. At that time the United States had such a clear economic and political predominance that it was possible for it (or for its "internationalistic" leadership at the time) to define its own interests comprehensively and in the long term and to forego the use of its power for short-term, self-interested gains. The Marshall Plan and the GATT negotiation rounds on liberalizing world trade were examples for this responsible exercise of U.S. hegemony. But the most significant example was the American assumption of the role of a world banker that was willing and able to provide the world economy with a sufficient but not inflationary supply of American dollars, which had been elevated to the status of world reserve currency under the Bretton Woods regime.

The double role of the dollar as domestic currency and as the universal means of payment and liquidity basis for world trade was never without tensions (Hankel, 1984:47–95; Schulmeister, 1986). But it also became threatening with the relative decline of American economic power (Table 12.1). As American interests began to diverge from those of the world economy, the temptation for the United States to take advantage of its unique position at the expense of rest of the world increased.

259

Table 12.1 Erosion of the economic hegemony of the United States,
1950–1980

	1950	1960	1970	1980
GDP (U.S.) as % of GDP of (U.S. + Japan + European Community)	69.1	61.6	54.3	40.5
Foreign trade (U.S.) as % of foreign trade of (U.S. + Japan + European Community)	33.3	27.0	23.5	22.1
Money supply M1 (U.S.) as % of M1 of (U.S. + Japan + FRG + GB + Switz.)		76.1	65.0	42.3

Sources: Keohane, 1984; IMF *International Financial Statistics*, 1977; 1985.

The United States gave in to this temptation when President Lyndon Johnson decided to finance the Vietnam War through central bank credits. As long as the greater volume of dollars in circulation had to be accepted by the rest of the world at fixed rates of exchange, a part of the U.S. war burden could be shifted to its trading partners in real terms, while the inflationary consequences were also exported into the world economy. The ultimate destruction of the Bretton Woods system of fixed exchange rates in spring 1973 put an end to this unique possibility of burden shifting, but it did not replace the U.S. dollar as a universal currency. On the contrary, the simultaneous expansion of offshore markets expanded the dollar supply available worldwide relative to the American domestic money supply and provided the United States with access to external credit markets in its own currency that were roughly of the same magnitude as the domestic market.

The continuing role of the dollar as a world reserve currency permits the United States to pay for its trade deficit with borrowed dollars (rather than with debt denominated in the currencies of its trading partners) and to repay and service its debts in dollars. This largely frees the United States from the discipline of having to balance payments that all other countries face, a discipline that forced Jim Callaghan and François Mitterrand but not Jimmy Carter and Ronald Reagan to give up their fiscal expansion. Moreover the existence of the huge dollar supply in the currency reserves of other nations and in the money circulation of the offshore markets also results in a diffusion of the negative repercussions of monetary decisions. Much of the inflationary and crowding-out effects of American fiscal policy can be unloaded abroad, while the United States is not exposed to similar effects from the opposite direction. Because of the unequal volumes of the currencies involved, the United States is still largely immune to the monetary and fiscal policy decisions of other countries (Mayer, 1982).

The world economy and especially the other Western industrial nations benefited from this fundamental asymmetry in the postwar decades. It established the United States as a power capable of creating order, which could, if necessary, act without the agreement of selfish partners to provide the monetary conditions for twenty years of worldwide economic growth and relative prosperity (Keohane, 1984; 1984a). But the asymmetry became a problem when the United States lost its sense of invincibility in the era of Vietnam and Watergate. Then the hegemonic self-image of American policy, which was if not selfless at least comprehensive and oriented to the long term, was displaced by interpretations that were much more oriented toward America's particular interests and its acute problems than toward the requirements of the world economic order or of the Western alliance. But as soon as the United States, as the world's banker, began to act in a short-sighted, self-interested way, its policy ceased to be a stabilizing factor in the world economy and contributed more than anything else to destabilizing it.

This is the point of departure for a plethora of reform proposals, all of them aimed at either replacing the dollar as the world currency with an international liquidity reserve and replacing the United States as world banker with an international organization (Davidson, 1982; Hankel, 1984) or at least achieving a lasting rule-governed coordination of the fiscal and currency policies of the important industrial nations, which would also bind the United States (H. Schmidt, 1986). I have no fundamental objections to the economic logic of these proposals. Transferring currency and monetary policy responsibilities to a supranational world central bank would subject all nations to the same monetary discipline and still avoid the deflationary risks posed by a return to the gold standard, which performed the same function before World War I. But one would not have to go so far. Even a simple but binding agreement between the central banks in Washington, Tokyo, and Frankfurt to reflate the currency that was under the greatest pressure to revalue would suffice to reduce currency speculation and to permit a more stable monetary expansion in all countries (McKinnon, 1984).

But one should be skeptical about the political and institutional chances of realizing these reform proposals. They depend on the hope that it is possible to replace the postwar order of the world economy that had been unilaterally maintained by the United States with a new international order voluntarily agreed to by the larger Western industrial nations. The theoretical foundations for such a hope were explicated by Robert Keohane (1984; 1986). It must rest on the assumption that all countries share a fundamental common interest in establishing an international regime that would impose monetary discipline on all of them.

261

In theory, of course, such a regime would be threatened by the temptation of individual countries to free-ride on the monetary system upheld by others (Olson, 1965; Hardin, 1971).

But fortunately, so the argument goes, there is a solution for this free-rider problem if participants are few in number and engaged in continuous interaction rather than in a one-shot encounter. Under such conditions, rational actors will be able to punish free riders by following a tit-for-tat strategy that facilitates the evolution of long-term cooperative solutions even in the absence of hierarchical coercion or hegemonic leadership (Axelrod, 1984). Yet however valid this explanation of the evolution of international regimes may be in other areas, I doubt that its logic does in fact apply to the specific circumstances of international monetary coordination.

The more optimistic theoretical analyses assume that somehow the world economic situation has changed from hegemonic coordination to a constellation resembling the symmetrical prisoners' dilemma game. But in reality, this change has not taken place. Even though its economic power has declined, the United States is not merely one country among many. The dollar continues to be immune from the monetary decisions of countries with smaller currencies, and with its limited dependence on international trade, the United States could survive a protectionist trade war far more easily than could smaller industrial countries that depend much more on exports. The significance of this fact becomes clearer in a game-theoretical presentation contrasting the asymmetrical constellation of interests under posthegemonic conditions with the (also asymmetrical) hegemonic constellation and with the symmetrical prisoners' dilemma game (Figure 12.1).

Both sides, as usual, must choose between cooperation (C) and non-cooperation (NC). The payoff for the weaker players (columns) corresponds in all variants to the prisoners' dilemma, whereas the payoff for the dominant player (rows) varies from game to game. (The numbers in the payoff matrix refer only to the rank order of preferences and not to the order of magnitude of the given advantage.)

In the hegemonic constellation after 1945, American strength, European weakness, and the Soviet threat combined to define a situation in which it was in the interest of the United States to pursue a cooperative strategy toward Western Europe regardless of the strategies chosen by its weaker partners. The Western European countries therefore faced a constant temptation to free-ride on the alliance (Olson and Zeckhauser, 1966), unless they were restrained by the fear of American sanctions.

In the symmetrical prisoners' dilemma that is presupposed by theorists of international regimes created by voluntary self-coordination, on

	Hegemony		Posthegemony		Prisoners' dilemma	
	C	NC	C	NC	C	NC
C	2,1	1,2	0,1	−1,2	1,1	−1,2
NC	0,−1	−1,0	1,−1	0,−1	2,−1	0,0

Figure 12.1. Constellations of interests under hegemonic and posthegemonic conditions

the other hand, both partners have equal weight and have the same temptation to behave noncooperatively. The uncooperative result is equally unfavorable for both, and thus both have a common interest in finding a reliable way to cooperate. In long-term relationships, the temptation to exploit the cooperative behavior of the other side can be checked by punishing noncooperation.

But the prisoners' dilemma does not describe contemporary posthegemonic conditions. The dominance of the United States is no longer so great that it can carry the burden of cooperation alone, as it could in the postwar era. From its perspective, the partner countries are no longer clients but competitors whose noncooperation, as Jimmy Carter learned, can cause great difficulties for a cooperative economic policy in the United States. And as the Western European countries have become economically stronger, their potential vulnerability has also come to be of much less concern to the American national interest. Thus unilateral noncooperation by the United States would now be the best outcome from an American point of view (as was demonstrated during the Vietnam War), whereas mutual cooperation would be only second-best. More important, however, is the fact that the United States has less to fear from mutual noncooperation than its partner countries. Since its noncooperation cannot be punished effectively, the United States is tempted to pursue its own interests without regard for the interests of others. American willingness to participate in a permanent international monetary regime would thus depend on altruistic motives whose trustworthiness is regarded with great skepticism by all theories of rational action.

EUROPEAN KEYNESIANISM AS A WAY OUT?

This weakness of all proposals aimed at coordinating economic and currency policy worldwide is the point of departure for proposals for Eurocentric coordination. It also has economic logic on its side. The full integration of the European domestic market, which the European

Community plans to accomplish by the end of 1992, would create an economy comparable to that of the United States in size, whose internal dynamism would probably be greater and whose vulnerability to the world economy would be substantially less than the vulnerability of its component national economies (Table 12.2). Even more important, the planned development of the European currency system into a European Currency Union with a common European capital market controlled by a European central bank, which the German Social Democrats support (H. Schmidt, 1984; Glotz, 1985:86–87), would achieve about equal weight to the dollar capital market. The greater relative size of the European currency union would mean that its exchange rate would be less vulnerable to speculative flight than that of any of the European national currencies. At the same time a common European currency policy would increase Europe's bargaining power against the American Federal Reserve. The game about interest rates, capital imports, and relative rates of exchange could be played by both sides with roughly the same stakes and the same risks. This would improve the chances for lasting currency policy cooperation between the United States and Europe (and probably Japan as well) that would be based on their common interests.

How likely is it that such an extensive institutional reform would be realized, or that European institutions could function as expected with such expanded responsibilities? Several problems collide here; each is capable of calling the success of the Europeanization strategy into question. The first problem arises from the high need for consensus in European politics; this makes institutional reforms that require national gov-

Table *12.2* Relative size and openness, 1984

	GDP (billions of U.S. $)	Exports as percentage of GDP	
		Total	Goods
Austria	64.45	37.4	24.4
FRG	613.37	31.1	28.0
GB	423.39	29.1	22.1
Sweden	94.78	36.0	31.0
Japan	1,255.01	15.2	13.5
USA	3,634.58	7.5	6.0
European Community	2,182.59	n.v.	12.9

Sources: OECD *National Accounts*, 1960–1984; IMF *Direction of Trade Statistics*, 1978–1984.
Note: n.v. = given value is not comparable.

ernments to sacrifice some of their autonomy very difficult. And even if, under the pressure of a crisis, they agreed to expand the authority of European institutions in spite of the unanimity principle, national governments would have every reason and every opportunity to ensure their continuing ability to influence European decisions (Scharpf, 1985). A European authority that in every instance had to purchase its ability to act with concessions to the most reluctant national governments, on the model of the Common Agricultural Policy, would not be a particularly competent partner or opponent of the American Federal Reserve in the field of international currency policy, which demands quick, flexible decision making.

In contrast, the current European Monetary System, in which exchange rates are coupled in a more flexible regime (IFO Institute, 1985), may not be suited to realize a common European monetary policy for Keynesian purposes, but its strategic capability to act vis-à-vis the dollar is probably greater than a European currency union's would be. Practically speaking, the "foreign policy" of the European currencies that are now tied to the German mark is conducted by the German Bundesbank alone, whose ability to act is uncontested although one can criticize the criteria that govern its actions. The interests of the other members of the German mark bloc, which might deviate from the Frankfurt line, can and must assert themselves by varying exchange rates against the mark, but they have no veto over the policy of the leading currency. The German central bank's fierce resistance to any institutionalization of responsibility for currency and monetary policy on the European level is thus not only grounded in its fear of inflation and its interest in maintaining its own position of power, but it is also a defense of the existing capability for strategic action against the dollar in Europe.

However, two special problems of Keynesian demand control on the European level are even more important than the general inflexibility of European institutions. First, Keynesian macroeconomic control on a continental scale would depend on the coordination of fiscal policy, monetary policy, and wage policy, just as it does on the national level. At present, however, discussion is restricted to the Europeanization of monetary policy, whose coordination even with fiscal policy is being ignored. The European Community itself, whose budget is about one percent of the gross domestic product of the Community countries, is obviously incapable of implementing a countercyclical fiscal policy on its own. Thus the prospects for the success of macroeconomic control would depend on the likelihood of coordinating European monetary policy with the fiscal policies of the individual member countries. Mechanisms for such coordination are nowhere in sight. The task would, at any rate,

265

be even more difficult than coordinating the fiscal policy of the federal government, states, and communities, which failed in the Federal Republic. The national legislatures would certainly defend their sovereign right to decide on taxes, expenditures, and deficits against a European authority even more vigorously than against national coordinating efforts.

If coordination between monetary policy and fiscal policy should come about at all, then it would have to follow the "monetarist" model practiced in the Federal Republic since 1974, which does not formally encroach on national sovereignty. Like the German Bundesbank, a European central bank could announce its money supply goals in advance and then leave it to the national budget makers and social partners to fit their own decisions to the existing monetary framework. Any attempt at a disproportionate fiscal expansion would be punished by money becoming tight. At the end of this road, one would not have arrived at the European Keynesianism that Social Democrats hope for, but instead at an institutionally based (and thus politically irreversible) European monetarism. It is hard to imagine why that outcome should be preferred to domestic monetarism from a social democratic perspective—unless one should hope that a European central bank would pursue a less restrictive money supply policy than the German Bundesbank practices.

Even greater difficulties will confront attempts to coordinate monetary with wage policy, which remains necessary in the context of Keynesian demand control. A European monetary policy would be able to force a uniform rate of inflation upon the Community countries, but it could do nothing to ensure uniform increases of production costs in the various European countries. They are determined primarily by the wage policy of the unions, and coordinated wage settlements throughout Europe are even more unlikely than the coordination of national fiscal policies. For that reason there is good cause to assume that instead of Keynesianism, a monetarist form of coordination would occur, resulting in a high level of persistent unemployment.

The most serious problem, however, arises from the fact that not all European countries are subject to the same cost pressure. Domestic systems of industrial relations vary greatly, as we have seen, in their capacity to react with economic rationality to given macroeconomic conditions. The fragmented negotiating system in Great Britain produces above-average wage increases despite very high unemployment, and the same is true, under different structural conditions, in France and Italy. In the Federal Republic or in the Netherlands, wages adapt fairly quickly to changes in the profitability of individual industries and hence to changing macroeconomic conditions. The structure of the negotiation system in these two countries does not produce the endogenous wage cost inflation that is unexplained by external economic conditions, which is a common problem in other countries.

As a consequence, there have been varying rates of increase in unit labor costs and periodic alterations in exchange rates to balance the relative competitiveness of the European countries (Table 12.3). If all else were equal and the exchange rates between European countries had not changed after 1970 or even after 1982, the Federal Republic and the Netherlands would have swept the other countries from the marketplace.

Of course, such a thought experiment does not amount to a prognosis. It does show, however, where the main problem of the proposed European Currency Union would lie. The Common Market has functioned fairly well because, despite the "snake" and the European Monetary System, it has been possible to offset differences in the development of production costs by adjusting exchange rates. If, after 1992, the European Internal Market, which will permit the free movement of goods, services, and capital, were complemented by a currency union, this adjustment mechanism would be lost. If costs then continued to develop unevenly, less competitive regions would lose sales, production, and employment, whereas the more competitive regions could expand production and employment at their expense.

Economists, if they recognize this problem at all, usually assume that a common monetary policy would "discipline" national costs, but this hope is not worth much. The European Monetary System has already accomplished what could be accomplished by this mechanism without being able to eliminate the need for periodic exchange rate adjustments (IFO Institut, 1985). Wage costs depend on the institutions of collective wage determination, and different institutions will produce different wages under similar economic conditions. If these institutions are not more or less uniform throughout the unified currency area, the results will be structural disequilibria and shifts between the regions.

Since it is impossible at present to create uniform union organizations throughout Europe, a necessary condition for a common European economic and currency policy is lacking and cannot be brought into existence by government action. As long as industrial relations generate so much less inflationary pressure in the Federal Republic than in the other European Community countries, a fully integrated European Internal Market, with a unified monetary and currency policy, would become the perfect instrument of German economic imperialism. Hence, it would be irrational for the Federal Republic's trading partners to submit to a unified European monetary policy or to give up their freedom to adjust

Table 12.3 Unit labor costs and effective exchange rates in the European Community

	Belgium	FRG	Denmark	France	GB	Italy	Ireland	Netherlands
Unit labor costs in domestic currency, 1986 (1982 = 100)*	106	99	115	113	114	141	n.v.	93
Effective exchange rate, 1986† (1982 = 100)	102	115	102	96	87	92	98	108
Effective exchange rate, 1985† (1970 = 100)	101	171	86	78	65	38	62	133

Source: OECD Economic Outlook 39.
* In industry. † Trade-weighted exchange rates.

their exchange rates. Consequently, there is very little hope that the Keynesian control of macroeconomic demand, which has become increasingly less effective on the national level, could soon be replaced by a Keynesian full employment policy on the European level. What may be possible is better coordination among European countries, but the key to such coordination is more likely to be held in Frankfurt by the Bundesbank than in Brussels by the European Commission.

BEYOND KEYNESIANISM: SOCIAL DEMOCRATIC SUPPLY-
SIDE POLICY AND "SOCIALISM IN ONE CLASS"?

There is much to be said for the assumption that the Western European industrial countries will have to continue to fend for themselves. There is also much to be said for the assumption that the world economic conditions that evolved in the 1980s will continue. The only thing that can safely be predicted about them is their instability. Neither international interest rates nor exchange rates between the American dollar and other currencies are subject to international control, and they do not tend to a stable market equilibrium. Instead they seem to move in cycles that are driven by American policy decisions and speculative, self-reinforcing capital movements. These disequilibria are driven to (never quite predictable) extremes, at which point the dynamic reverses itself to move toward opposite extremes (Schulmeister, 1986).

The smaller industrial countries cannot isolate themselves from these large cycles of international capital markets. At best, they can try to exploit the limited tradeoff between the movements of exchange rates and interest rates. Strong currencies may be able to afford to have relatively low interest rates, whereas a weak currency can avoid capital flight only by above-average interest rates. It is true that Sweden tricked the international capital markets by an unexpectedly large devaluation in fall 1982, but this option was available only to a small country whose currency played no significant role in international portfolio investments. Moreover, the trick could neither be repeated at will nor could all countries improve their export opportunities by simultaneous devaluation. In general, therefore, the larger Western European countries cannot at present hope to shield their economies from global interest rate fluctuations or unilaterally improve their competitiveness by manipulating exchange rates.

This means that the limits to Keynesian demand control that became apparent in the early 1980s remain in place. To be sure, there can be phases of relative relaxation, in which dollar interest and exchange rates

269

fall and active governments can expand domestic demand and hence employment without being punished by capital flight or the devaluation-inflation spiral. But nothing supports the conclusion that such periods will be of long duration, and as long as the international real interest level remains high, the demand-driven investment boom that would make possible a lasting expansion of employment in the private sector is unlikely to occur in any case. Moreover, any expansion of private-sector employment continues to be subject to the supply-side imperative of high profits.

For Social Democrats and the unions, the distributive implications of neoclassical supply-side formulas were so provocative that they would deal with them only in polemical fashion. As a consequence, the responses of social democratic governments to the conditions of the early 1980s, when private-sector employment could be maintained only if business profits increased substantially, lacked a theoretical foundation. In practice, of course, Sweden and Austria had yielded to the necessity for redistribution, but none of the protagonists apparently found these responses plausible enough to raise them to the level of an explicit strategic concept. As was so often the case in the history of the labor movement, the strategies legitimated by socialist ideology were not practicable, while the pragmatic course of action that was in fact pursued could not be legitimated in socialist discourse. But what if the conditions that obtained between 1979 and 1984 should recur more frequently, and what if not only growth and full employment but also existing levels of government services and social welfare should continue to depend on high profits?

The Left has no intellectually honest answer to this question. Unions cannot see it as their role to increase the incomes of capital owners at the expense of the workers, and Social Democrats cannot make it their program to dismantle the welfare state in order to lighten the tax burden on business. If they nevertheless did both things, they did so with a bad conscience and more under the cover of darkness than in the full daylight of their programmatic debates. Ideologically, and in public debate, at any rate, the hour of supply-side policies has always been the hour of employers and conservative parties.

This did not have to be the case. If Social Democrats and unions had fought as hard to change the distribution of ownership and wealth as they did to increase workers' wages and the size of government, then we would be able today to use the descriptors "capital" and "labor" as neutral categories describing types of functional income rather than as descriptions of social classes. In an economy in which everyone would be in principle both a worker and a capitalist, in which everyone had a stock portfolio and a wage check in the mail, the shift from a demand-side to a supply-side policy would merely mean a marginal shift between two sources of household incomes, not strategic wins and losses in the class struggle.

But these are armchair fantasies. According to the latest available numbers, from 1973 (which also says something about the political priority of the topic), in the Federal Republic 1 percent of households owned 53.8 percent of the total productive assets, while the bottom 52 percent of households owned only 2.4 percent of those assets (Glastetter, Paulert, and Spörel, 1983:392). The distribution of monetary assets has become even more unequal since 1973, and I suspect that this is also true for productive assets (Euler, 1985). In the other countries things are not much better (Meidner, 1978; Robinson, 1973). During the period when distributive gains were still possible, even reformist unions preferred higher wages to people's capitalism (DGB, 1983). And Social Democrats were not self-confident or strong enough to pursue an active course of redistribution of wealth without the solid support of the unions. Only the Swedish campaign for the workers' fund made distribution of assets topical again for leftist politics, but unfortunately in a form that precluded compromises with the centrist camp and that therefore was hardly encouraging for the nonhegemonic labor movements in the rest of Western Europe.

With the distribution of assets that exists today, an accent on supply-side policy always benefits the class of capital owners at the expense of the class of workers and the recipients of public transfer payments. This explains the deep aversion of Social Democrats and unions to supply-side economics, but it does not solve their strategic problem.

Despite many demands for a version of supply-side economics that would meet social democratic criteria, and some attempts to meet those demands (Kromphardt, 1986; Milner, 1986; DeGeer et al., 1986; Williams, 1985; Piore and Sabel, 1985; Magaziner and Reich, 1982), an internally consistent strategic conception is not yet in sight. However, it is clear in what direction we must look for answers. Social Democrats and unions, concerned about workers' interests and about the obligations of the social welfare state, must counter the neoclassical obsession with lower real wages and lower taxes with concepts that are more microeconomic in character. A social democratic supply-side policy for the private sector must concentrate on increasing the returns on business investment, and to do so it must aim at improving the product strategies and production processes of firms. High wages and social services must be earned. If we are to meet the competition of the Japanese, Taiwanese, South Koreans, and other nations with lower wages and lower levels of government social welfare services, then our products must be more attractive and our labor productivity must be that much higher.

There is no shortage of attractive formulas for such a strategy, and many of them have already been put into practice in the Federal Republic. "Flexible specialization" in high value-added products (Piore and Sabel, 1985) and increased product differentiation have permitted the German automobile industry to expand despite the global crisis (Streeck and Hoff, 1983; Streeck, 1986). The high productivity achieved by combining microprocessor-controlled machine tools with a highly trained work force (Sorge et al., 1982; Sorge, 1985; Kern and Schumann, 1984) has guaranteed international competitiveness for German industry as a whole (Sabel et al., 1986). To be sure, government can do less to facilitate these trends than can the works councils and the unions; and what the government can do to help small and midsized firms grow (Hjern and Hull, 1983; Hull, 1986; Maier, 1986) seems to be easier for the conservative state governments in Baden-Württemberg, Bavaria, or Berlin than for the Social Democrats, who have traditionally tended to focus their attention on large firms.

Microeconomic strategies allow competitive advantages to be won or defended, and this is necessary. But there is no reason to think that microeconomic success will eliminate the macroeconomic constraints on the growth of industrial economies as a whole. Thus it seems unlikely that either the promotion of high-tech industries (Tomaskovic-Devey and Miller, 1983) or the productivity gains made possible by microelectronics and flexible manufacturing will suffice to regain full employment over the next decade in those countries where massive unemployment prevails today. If we seriously want full employment, we can no longer depend exclusively on traditional macroeconomic or new microeconomic growth strategies. Full employment has become a distributive problem.

Contrary to the conventional rhetoric of unions and leftist parties, however, this is not a distributive conflict between the production factors of capital and labor. The front lines of that battle are defined by the international capital markets and cannot be changed much at the national level. To be sure, these lines define only the minimum rate of return that productive and job-creating investment must receive. They do not affect the distribution of those incomes that are not inverted, whether derived from wages, profits, or rents. For political rhetoric this last distinction is important enough, but we should not fool ourselves. If achieving full employment is a distributive problem, the main burden must be borne by the workers. The other types of income do not count enough in quantitative terms. That is not to deny that social justice requires those who receive higher incomes to be more heavily burdened.

In a practical sense, the distributive solution to the unemployment problem has only two options: raising taxes to create additional employment opportunities that must be publicly financed or shortening the working week in order to redistribute existing employment opportunities. Neither of these options is easy to realize.

If additional employment is to be financed through higher taxes (assuming that large-scale deficit spending continues to be impractical), one must take withdrawal effects into account. Hence expenditures must be concentrated on projects that are clearly more labor-intensive than the private demand they displace. That means increasing social services rather than the large-scale public works favored by unions and Social Democrats in the past. But any expansion of social services, regardless of its desirability, will encounter the obstacles discussed in chapter 10 arising from the peculiarities of intergovernmental relations and fiscal federalism in West Germany. In the short and medium term, therefore, a significant expansion of active labor market measures based on the Swedish model might be the more promising course of action (Hellmich, 1982; Scharpf et al., 1982).

The attempt to pursue full employment by shortening the working week also has its characteristic difficulties. If unions and employers in the private sector are left to deal with this problem on their own, they must operate under the same constraints that ordinarily apply to wage negotiations. Whether used for wage increases at constant hours or for reductions of working time at constant wages, that margin is usually defined by the expected gains in labor productivity. Thus even if the unions were willing and able to forego higher incomes, the working week could be reduced only by such small increments that the impact on employment would hardly be noticed. In fact, this is exactly what happened in West Germany after 1984, when the working week was on average reduced by about half an hour each year. In order to have a significant impact on unemployment, the reduction of the working week would have to proceed by much larger steps, dropping from 40 to 35 hours per week within two or three years, for instance. Such large steps, however, would exceed the margin of expected productivity gains and hence would be counterproductive if undertaken by unions and employers acting on their own. If worker incomes should remain constant, unit labor costs of firms would drastically increase and overall employment might in fact be reduced. If, on the other hand, unit labor costs were held constant, worker incomes would have to fall, which would reduce aggregate demand and hence employment. Thus in order to be useful as an instrument of full employment policy, work-time reduction would have to be accompanied by government subsidies either to the production costs of firms or to worker incomes. It has been shown that such subsidies could be financed from the reduced fiscal costs of unemployment (Reissert et al., 1986).

However, my goal is not to propose patent solutions. What is important is the strategic insight that, for the time being, full employment cannot be recovered through strategies that are painless for the clientele of the labor movement. Neither deficit-financed growth nor redistribution at the expense of capital incomes are available to solve the employment problem. If it can be solved at all, it is through a redistribution of existing work opportunities and working incomes at the expense of the great majority of those who are presently employed.

This concludes my survey of the options for social democratic full employment policy under the foreseeable conditions of the world economy. The vision is bleak. Unlike the situation in the first three postwar decades, there is now no economically plausible Keynesian strategy that would permit the full realization of social democratic goals within a national context without violating the functional imperatives of the capitalist economy. Full employment, rising real wages, larger welfare transfers, and more and better public services can no longer all be had simultaneously—because growth rates are inadequate and because the distributive claims that capital is able to realize have increased.

But that need not be the end of social democratic strategies. On the contrary: when not all goals can be realized at the same time, the ability to set strategic priorities increases in importance. A prerequisite, however, is to acknowledge the change in the terms of trade among capital, labor, and government. If the labor movement's defeat in the distributive battle is not accepted as being irreversible for now, the attempt to pursue all goals at once will not lead to "system-transforming" reforms or to the realization of other postulates of an anticapitalist rhetoric, but only to a war of all against all within the Left. The most likely outcome in that case would be a deepening division between the majority of relatively privileged jobholders in the private and public sectors and a growing minority of persons in long-term unemployment, early retirement, or occasional employment, and of young people who never gain access to regular employment at all. This process is under way now, but it can be halted. In order to stop it, Social Democrats and unions must be able to demand that all workers pay higher taxes and contribute part of their work time and work incomes to facilitate the employment of all who are willing to work.

274

This, I believe, is the crucial question for the political future of social democracy. If Social Democrats are unwilling to face it, they will cease to shape the future, leaving the field to the social Darwinism of the market liberals and conservatives. Their hour might return only if, after a long period of prosperity, politics were once again to focus on the distribution of unclaimed gains from capitalist growth. For the foreseeable future, however, social democracy has a chance to shape economic policy only if it explicitly accepts the full harshness of worldwide economic conditions and hence the constraints on domestic policy options. But Social Democrats deserve this chance only if they hold firm to the solidaristic ideals of democratic socialism—even when these ideals can be realized only through solidarity within the working classes or through "socialism within one class."

References

Abele, Hanns, Ewald Nowotny, Stefan Schleicher, and Georg Winckler, eds. 1982. *Handbuch der österreichischen Wirtschaftspolitik*. Vienna: Manz.

Adam, Hermann. 1972. *Die Konzertierte Aktion in der Bundesrepublik*. Cologne: Bund-Verlag.

Addison, John T. 1985. "What Do Unions Really Do? A Review Article." *Journal of Labour Research* VI:127–146.

Agartz, Viktor. 1953. "Beiträge zur wirtschaftlichen Entwicklung 1953. Expansive Lohnpolitik." *WWI-Mitteilungen* 6:245ff.

Alemann, Ulrich von, ed. 1981. *Neokorporatismus*. Frankfurt: Campus.

Altvater, Elmar. 1985. "Das Jahr 2000, der Weltmarkt und Fidel Castro." In Elmar Altvater, Martin Baethge, et al., *Arbeit 2000: Über die Zukunft der Arbeitsgesellschaft*. Hamburg: VSA-Verlag, pp. 21–31.

Anton, Thomas J. 1980. *Administered Politics: Elite Political Culture in Sweden*. Boston: Martinus Nijhoff.

Arndt, Sven W., ed. 1982. *The Political Economy of Austria*. Washington, D.C.: American Enterprise Institute.

Ashford, Douglas E. 1981. *Policy and Politics in Britain: The Limits of Consensus*. Philadelphia: Temple University Press.

Aukrust, Odd. 1977. "Inflation in the Open Economy: A Norwegian Model." In Lawrence B. Krause and Walter S. Salant, eds., *Worldwide Inflation: Theory and Recent Experience*. Washington, D.C.: Brookings, pp. 135–38.

Axelrod, Robert. 1970. *Conflict of Interest: A Theory of Divergent Goals with Applications to Politics*. Chicago: Markham.

———. 1984. *The Evolution of Cooperation*. New York: Basic Books.

Axelrod, Robert, and Robert O. Keohane. 1986. "Achieving Cooperation under Anarchy: Strategies and Institutions." *World Politics* 38:226–254.

Bacon, Robert, and Walter Eltis. 1978. *Britain's Economic Problem: Too Few Producers*. London: Macmillan.

Bain, George Sayers, ed. 1983. *Industrial Relations in Britain*. Oxford: Basil Blackwell.

Ball, Terence. 1972. "On 'Historical' Explanation." *Philosophy of the Social Sciences* 2:181–92.

277

REFERENCES

Balogh, Thomas. 1982. *The Irrelevance of Conventional Economics*. London: Weidenfeld and Nicolson.

Baring, Arnulf. 1982. *Machtwechsel: Die Ära Brandt-Scheel*, Stuttgart: Deutsche Verlags-Anstalt.

Barnes, Denis, and Eileen Reid. 1980. *Governments and Trade Unions: The British Experience, 1964–1979*. London: Heinemann.

Barnett, Joel. 1982. *Inside the Treasury*. London: André Deutsch.

Bauer, Johannes M. 1986. "Grenzverschiebungen zwischen öffentlicher und privater Wirtschaft in Österreich 1970–1985." *Journal für Sozialforschung* 26:283–318.

Baum, Thomas M. 1983. "Empirische Analyse der Bundesbankautonomie." *Konjunkturpolitik* 29:163–86.

Berrington, Hugh. 1982. "The Labour Left in Parliament: Maintenance, Erosion, and Renewal." In Kavanagh, ed. (1982):69–94.

Besters, Hans, Burghard Freudenfeld, Gernot Gutmann, Rolf Henschel, Werner Meißner, Rainer Thoss, and Otto Vogel. 1975. *Investitionslenkung—Bedrohung der Marktwirtschaft?* Cologne: Deutscher Instituts-Verlag.

Beyfuss, Jörg, and Rolf Kroker. 1986. "Konjunktureffekte sinkender Ölpreise." *Iwtrends* 1/86:1–10.

Beyme, Klaus von. 1977. *Gewerkschaften und Arbeitsbeziehungen in kapitalistischen Ländern*. Munich: Piper.

———. 1982. *Parteien in westlichen Demokratien*. Munich: Piper.

Bieshar, Hans, and Alfred Kleinknecht. 1984. "Kondratieff Long Waves in Aggregate Output? An Econometric Test." *Konjunktürpolitik* 17:279–303.

Blaas, Wolfgang. 1984. "Stabilisierungspolitik: Zur politischen Ökonomie marktwirtschaftlicher Instabilität." *Der öffentliche Sektor* 10, 1/2-1984.

Blaas, Wolfgang, and Alois Guger. 1985. "Arbeitsbeziehungen und makroökonomische Stabilität im internationalen Vergleich." In Gerlich, Grande, and Müller, eds. (1985):255–78.

Black, Stanley W. 1977. *Floating Exchange Rates and National Economic Policy*. New Haven: Yale University Press.

Blankenburg, Erhard, Günther Schmid, and Hubert Treiber. 1975. "Legitimitäts- und Implementierungsprobleme 'aktiver Arbeitsmarktpolitik.'" In Rolf Ebbinghausen, ed., *Bürgerlicher Staat und politische Legitimation*. Frankfurt: Suhrkamp, pp. 247–80.

BMF. *Finanzberichte, 1977–1987*. Bonn: Bundesministerium der Finanzen.

———. 1985. *Die finanzwirtschaftliche Entwicklung von Bund, Ländern und Gemeinden*. Dokumentation 2/85. Bonn: Bundesministerium der Finanzen.

Boltho, Andrea, ed. (1982). *The European Economy: Growth and Crisis*. Oxford: Oxford University Press.

Bonß, Wolfgang. 1980. "Gewerkschaftliches Handeln zwischen Korporatismus und Selbstverwaltung: Die Konzertierte Aktion und ihre Folgen." In Volker Ronge, ed., *Am Staat vorbei: Politik der Selbstregulierung von Kapital und Arbeit*. Frankfurt: Campus, pp. 125–69.

Borchart, Knut. 1982. *Wachstum, Krisen, Handlungsspielräume der Wirtschaftspolitik: Studien zur Wirtschaftsgeschichte des 19. und 20. Jahrhunderts*. Göttingen: Vandenhoeck and Ruprecht.

———. 1984. "Wege aus der Arbeitslosigkeit: Die Diskussion in Deutschland in den frühen dreißiger Jahren." *Vierteljahreshefte zur Wirtschaftsforschung* 1/84:6–16.

Bornstein, Stephen, and Peter Gourevitch. 1984. "Unions in a Declining Economy: The Case of the British TUC." In Gourevitch et al., (1984):13–88.

278

Braun, Rachel Eisenberg. 1984. "Equal Opportunity and the Law in the United States." In Schmid and Weitzel, eds. (1984):92–106.

Brittan, Samuel, and Peter Lilley. 1977. *The Delusion of Incomes Policy.* London: Temple Smith.

Brown, William, ed. 1981. *The Changing Contours of British Industrial Relations: A Survey of Manufacturing Industry.* Oxford: Basil Blackwell.

Bruche, Gert. 1983. "Die Administration arbeitsmarktpolitischer Programme. Ein internationaler Vergleich (Frankreich, Niederlande, Österreich, Schweden, USA)." Discussion Paper IIM/LMP 83-10, Wissenschaftszentrum Berlin.

Bruche, Gert, and Bernard Casey. 1982. *Arbeit oder Rente? Beschäftigungs- und sozialpolitische Maßnahmen für ältere Arbeitnehmer in Frankreich, Großbritannien, den Niederlanden, Schweden und den USA.* Frankfurt: Campus.

Bruche, Gert, and Bernd Reissert. 1985. *Die Finanzierung der Arbeitsmarktpolitik: System, Effektivität, Reformansätze.* Frankfurt: Campus.

Bundesbank. *Monatsberichte der Deutschen Bundesbank, 1973–1983.*

——. 1974. *Auszüge aus Presseartikeln Nr. 17, 1974.*

——. 1974. *Geschäftsbericht der Deutschen Bundesbank für das Jahr 1974.*

Butschek, Felix. 1981. *Vollbeschäftigung in der Krise: Die österreichische Erfahrung 1974 bis 1979.* Vienna: Orac.

Buttler, Friedrich, Jürgen Kühl, and Bernd Rahmann, eds. 1985. *Staat und Beschäftigung. Angebots- und Nachfragepolitik in Theorie und Praxis. Beiträge zur Arbeitsmarkt- und Berufsforschung 88.* Nürnberg: Institut für Arbeitsmarkt- und Berufsforschung der Bundesanstalt für Arbeit.

Caesar, Rolf. 1981. *Der Handlungsspielraum der Notenbanken: Theoretische Analyse und internationaler Vergleich.* Baden-Baden: Nomos.

Calmfors, Lars. 1982. "Employment Policies, Wage Formation, and Trade Union Behavior in a Small Open Economy." *Scandinavian Journal of Economics,* no. 2:345–73.

——. 1985. "The Roles of Stabilization Policy and Wage Setting for Macroeconomic Stability—The Experiences of Economies with Centralized Bargaining." *Kyklos* 38:329–47.

Calmfors, Lars, and Henrik Horn. 1984. "Classical Unemployment, Accommodation Policies, and the Adjustment of Real Wages." University of Stockholm, Institute for International Economic Studies, Seminar Paper No. 270.

Cameron, David R. 1978. "The Expansion of the Public Economy: A Comparative Analysis." *American Political Science Review* 72:1243–61.

——. 1984. "Social Democracy, Corporatism, Labour Quiescence, and the Representation of Economic Interest in Advanced Capitalist Society." In Goldthorpe, ed. (1984):143–78.

Carsten, F. L. 1986. *The First Austrian Republic 1918–1938: A Study Based on British and Austrian Documents.* Aldershot: Gower.

Cassel, Dieter, and H. Jörg Thieme. 1977. *Einkommenspolitik: Kritische Analyse eines umstrittenen stabilitätspolitischen Konzepts.* Cologne: Kiepenheuer and Witsch.

Chaloupek, Günther. 1985. "Sozialpartnerschaft in der Zeit des Übergangs." In Gerlich, Grande, and Müller, eds. (1985):331–48.

Coates, David. 1980. *Labour in Power? A Study of the Labour Government, 1974–1979.* London: Longman.

Coombes, David. 1982. *Representative Government and Economic Power.* London: Heinemann.

Cripps, Francis, and Wynne Godley. 1978. "Control of Imports as a Means to Full

Employment and the Expansion of World Trade: The UK Case." *Cambridge Journal of Economics,* vol. II, no. 3 (September 1978):327–34.

Crossman, Richard. 1979. *The Crossman Diaries: Selections from the Diaries of a Cabinet Minister, 1964–1970.* Condensed Version. London: Methuen Paperbacks.

Crouch, Colin. 1982. *The Politics of Industrial Relations.* 2d ed. London: Fontana Paperbacks.

———. 1982a. "The Peculiar Relationship: The Party and the Unions." In Kavanagh, ed. (1982):171–90.

Crouch, Colin, and Alessandro Pizzorno, eds. 1978. *The Resurgence of Class Conflict in Western Europe since 1968.* Vol. 2, *Comparative Analyses.* London: Macmillan.

Dahl, Robert A., and Charles E. Lindblom. 1953. *Politics, Economics, and Welfare: Planning and Politico-Economic Systems Resolved into Basic Social Processes.* New York: Harper and Row.

Dahrendorf, Ralf. 1979. *Lebenschancen: Anläufe zur sozialen und politischen Theorie,* Frankfurt: Suhrkamp.

Davidson, Paul. 1982. *International Money and the Real World.* London: Macmillan.

De Geer, Hans, Eskil Ekstedt, Nils Elvander, Roger Henning, Lorentz Lyttkens, Lennart Norgren, Maivor Sjölund, and Solveig Wikström. 1986. *In the Wake of the Future.* Stockholm: FA-Radet.

Degen, Günther R. 1976. *Shop Stewards: Ihre zentrale Bedeutung für die Gewerkschaftsbewegung in Großbritannien.* Frankfurt: Europäische Verlagsanstalt.

Derek, Morris, ed. 1979. *The Economic System of the United Kingdom.* 6th ed. Oxford: Oxford University Press.

DGB. 1983. "Dokumentation: Stellungnahmen des DGB zur Vermögenspolitik." *WSI-Mitteilungen* 7/1983:453–57.

Dittrich, Walter. 1985. *Mitbestimmung-eine korporatistische Strategie? Eine international vergleichende Untersuchung zur Mitbestimmungspolitik in zehn europäischen Ländern.* Konstanz: Wisslit-Verlag.

Dohnanyi, Klaus von. 1986. "Der Markt schafft nicht genügend Jobs: Die Bundesregierung vernachlässigt die Beschäftigungspolitik." *Die Zeit* Nr.35 (22 August 1986): 20.

Domar, Eversey D. 1944. "The 'Burden of the Debt' and the National Income." *American Economic Review* 34:798–827.

Donovan Report. 1968. Royal Commission on Trade Unions and Employers' Associations, 1965–1968, Cmnd 3623. London: HMSO.

Edgren, Gösta, Karl-Olof Faxén, and Clas-Erik Odhner. 1973. *Wage Formation and the Economy.* London: Allen and Unwin (Translated from the 1970 Swedish edition).

Ehrlicher, Werner, and Diethart B. Simmert, eds. 1982. *Geld- und Währungspolitik in der Bundesrepublik Deutschland.* Berlin: Duncker and Humblot.

Eidem, Rolf, and Bernt Öhman. 1978. *Economic Democracy through Wage-earner Funds.* Stockholm: Arbetslivscentrum.

Eidlin, Fred. 1983. "Area Studies and/or Social Science: Contextually-Limited Generalizations versus General Laws." In Eidlin, ed., *Constitutional Democracy: Essays in Comparative Politics.* Boulder, Colo.: Westview Press.

Eklund, Klas. 1980. "Long Waves in the Development of Capitalism." *Kyklos* 33:383–419.

Elder, Neil, and Alastair H. Thomas. 1982. *The Consensual Democracies? The Government and Politics of the Scandinavian States.* Oxford: Martin Robertson.

Elliott, R. F., and J. L. Fallick. 1981. "Incomes Policies, Inflation Policies, and Relative

Pay: An Overview." In Elliott and Fallick, *Incomes Policies, Inflation, and Relative Pay.* London: Allen and Unwin, 246–63.

Elster, Jon. 1979. *Ulysses and the Sirens: Studies in Rationality and Irrationality.* Cambridge: Cambridge University Press.

———. 1983. *Sour Grapes: Studies in the Subversion of Rationality.* Cambridge: Cambridge University Press.

Elvander, Nils. 1983. Die Gewerkschaftsbewegung in Schweden: Geschichte, Programm, politische Beziehungen. In Rühle and Veen, eds. (1983):327–402.

Engels, Wolfram. 1984. *Arbeitslosigkeit: Woher sie kommt und wie man sie beheben kann.* Bad Homburg: Franfurter Institut für wirtschaftspolitische Forschung (Kronberger Kreis).

Esdar, Bernd. 1980. *Kooperation in der Einkommenspolitik: Eine empirische Untersuchung einkommenspolitischer Maßnahmen in ausgewählten Ländern Europas.* Tübingen: Mohr.

Esping-Andersen, Gösta. 1985. *Politics against Markets: The Social Democratic Road to Power.* Princeton: Princeton University Press.

Esping-Andersen, Gösta, and Walter Korpi. 1984. "Social Policy as Class Politics in Post-war Capitalism: Scandinavia, Austria, and Germany." In Goldthorpe, ed. (1984):179–208.

Eucken, Walter. 1959. *Die Grundlagen der Nationalökonomie.* 7th ed. Berlin: Springer.

Euler, Manfred. 1985. Geldvermögen privater Haushalte Ende 1983: Ergebnis der Einkommens- und Verbrauchsstichprobe." *Wirtschaft und Statistik* 5/1985:408–9.

Farr, James. 1982. "Historical Concepts in Political Science: The Case of 'Revolution.'" *American Journal of Political Science* 26:688–708.

Faxén, Karl-Olof. 1982. "Incomes Policy and Centralized Wage Formation." In Boltho, ed. (1982):365–89.

Faxén, Karl-Olof, and Göran Normann. 1984. *Profits for Employment.* Paris/Stockholm: OECD (BIAC)/NFD AB.

Fiedler, Jobst, and Rolf Schroedter. 1983. "Der 'Zweite Arbeitsmarkt' in Hamburg: Nützliche Beschäftigung statt Hinnahme und Finanzierung von Arbeitslosigkeit." In Michael Bolle and Peter Grottian, eds., *Arbeit schaffen—jetzt!* Reinbek: Rowohlt, pp. 165–85.

Flanagan, Robert J., David W. Soskice, and Lloyd Ulman. 1983. *Unionism, Economic Stabilization, and Incomes Policies: The European Experience.* Washington, D.C.: Brookings.

Flassbeck, Heiner. 1982. "Was ist Angebotspolitik?" *Konjunkturpolitik* 28:75–138.

Frantz, Peter. 1986. "Der 'Constrained Choice'-Ansatz als gemeinsamer Nenner individualistischer Ansätze in der Soziologie." *Kölner Zeitschrift für Soziologie und Sozialpsychologie* 38:32–54.

Freeman, Richard B., and James L. Medoff. 1984. *What Do Unions Do?* New York: Basic Books.

Freiburghaus, Dieter. 1978. *Dynamik der Arbeitslosigkeit: Umschlagsprozeß und Dauerverteilung der Arbeitslosigkeit in der Bundesrepublik, 1966–1977.* Meisenheim: Anton Hain.

———. 1980. "Internationaler Vergleich der Arbeitslosigkeit—ein mehrdimensionales Problem." In J. Hoffmann-Nowotny, ed., *Soziale Indikatoren im internationalen Vergleich.* Frankfurt: Campus, pp. 77–96.

Frey, Bruno S. 1981. *Theorie demokratischer Wirtschaftspolitik.* Munich: Vahlen.

Fröbel, Folker, Jürgen Heinrichs, and Otto Kreye. 1986. *Umbruch in der Weltwirtschaft. Die globale Strategie; Verbilligung der Arbeitskraft/Flexibilisierung der Arbeit/Neue Technologien.* Hamburg: Rowohlt.

Frye, Jon, and Robert J. Gordon. 1981. Government Intervention in the Inflation Process: The Econometrics of 'Self-Inflicted Wounds.'" *American Economic Review* 71:288–94.

Funke, Michael. 1986. "Nominalzinsen, Realzinsen, und Internationale Kapitalbewegungen." Discussion Paper IIM/LMP 86-11, Wissenschaftszentrum Berlin.

Fürst, Dietrich, Joachim Jens Hesse, and Hartmut Richter. 1984. *Stadt und Staat: Verdichtungsräume im Prozeß der föderalstaatlichen Problemverarbeitung.* Baden-Baden: Nomos.

Garlichs, Dietrich, and Friederike Maier. 1982. "Die arbeitsmarktpolitische Wirksamkeit der beruflichen Weiterbildung." In Scharpf, Brockmann, Groser, Hegner, and Schmid, eds. (1982):89–118.

George, Alexander L., and Richard Smoke. 1974. *Deterrence in American Foreign Policy.* New York: Columbia University Press.

Georgescu-Roegen, Nicholas. 1987. "Das Wechselspiel von Institution und Materie." In Egon Matzner, Jan Kregel, and Alessandro Roncaglia, eds., *Arbeit für alle ist möglich: Über ökonomische und institutionelle Bedingungen erfolgreicher Beschäftigungs- und Arbeitsmarktpolitik.* Berlin: Edition Sigma.

Gerhardt, Wolfgang. 1984. *Der Euro-DM-Markt: Marktteilnehmer, Zinsbildung, und geldpolitische Bedeutung. Eine Untersuchung aus der Sicht der Bundesrepublik Deutschland.* Hamburg: Verlag Weltarchiv.

Gerlich, Peter, Edgar Grande, and Wolfgang C. Müller, eds. 1985. *Sozialpartnerschaft in der Krise: Leistungen und Grenzen des Neokorporatismus in Österreich.* Vienna: Böhlau.

Gerstenberger, Wolfgang, and Volker Hölterhoff. 1983. *Wechselwirkungen von Geldpolitik, Inflation und Strukturwandel.* IFO Studien zur Strukturforschung 2, Ergänzungsband. Munich: IFO Institut.

Giersch, Herbert. 1976. "Episoden und Lehren der Globalsteuerung." In Heiko Körner et al., *Wirtschaftspolitik—Wissenschaft und politische Aufgaben.* Bern: pp. 277–96.

———. 1983. *Wie es zu schaffen ist: Agenda für die deutsche Wirtschaftspolitik.* Stuttgart: Deutsche Verlags-Anstalt.

Giersch, Herbert, and Harmen Lehment. 1984. "Löhne, Zinsen, und Beschäftigung im Wirtschaftswachstum." In Helmstädter, ed., *Die Bedingungen des Wirtschaftswachstums in Vergangenheit und Zukunft.* Tübingen: Mohr, pp. 79–95.

Glastetter, Werner, Rüdiger Paulert, and Ulrich Spörel. 1983. *Die Wirtschaftliche Entwicklung in der Bundesrepublik Deutschland, 1950–1980: Befunde, Aspekte, Hintergründe.* Frankfurt: Campus.

Glotz, Peter. 1985. *Manifest für eine neue Europäische Linke.* Berlin: Siedler.

Goldthorpe, John H., ed. 1984. *Order and Conflict in Contemporary Capitalism: Studies in the Political Economy of Western European Nations.* Oxford: Clarendon Press.

Gourevitch, Peter, Andrew Martin, George Ross, Christopher Allen, Stephen Bornstein, and Andrei Markovits. 1984. *Unions and Economic Crisis: Britain, West Germany, and Sweden.* London: Allen and Unwin.

Grant, Wyn. 1982. *The Political Economy of Industrial Policy.* London: Butterworths.

Grant, Wyn, and David Marsh. 1977. *The Confederation of British Industry.* London: Hodder and Stoughton.

Gross, Peter. 1983. *Die Verheißungen der Dienstleistungsgesellschaft: Soziale Befreiung oder Sozialherrschaft?* Opladen: Westdeutscher Verlag.

Guger, Alois. 1983. "Die Arbeitskosten der verarbeitenden Industrie im internationalen Vergleich." *WIFO Monatsberichte* 1/83:26–39.

Gustafson, Siv. 1984. "Equal Opportunity Policies in Sweden." In Schmid and Weitzel, eds. (1984):132–54.

Haines, Joe. 1977. *The Politics of Power.* London: Jonathan Cape.

Hankel, Wilhelm. 1979. *Prosperität in der Krise. Eine Analyse der Wirtschaftspolitik in der Energiekrise am Beispiel Österreichs: Aktive Binnenbilanz durch passive Außenbilanz.* Vienna: Molden.

——. 1984. *Gegenkurs: Von der Schuldenkrise zur Vollbeschäftigung.* Berlin: Siedler.

Hardes, Heinz-Dieter. 1974. *Einkommenspolitik in der BRD. Stabilität und Gruppeninteressen. Der Fall Konzertierte Aktion.* Frankfurt: Herder and Herder.

Hardin, Garrett. 1968. "The Tragedy of the Commons." *Science* 132:1243–48.

Hardin, Garrett, and John Baden, eds. 1977. *Managing the Commons.* San Francisco: Freeman.

Hardin, Russell. 1971. "Collective Action as an Agreeable n-Prisoners' Dilemma." *Behavioral Science* 16:472–81.

Hartwich, Hans-Herrmann, ed. 1985. *Policy-Forschung in der Bundesrepublik Deutschland: Ihr Selbstverständnis und ihr Verhältnis zu den Grundfragen der Politikwissenschaft.* Opladen: Westdeutscher Verlag.

Hayek, Friedrich A. von. 1944. *The Road to Serfdom.* Chicago: University of Chicago Press.

Hellmich, Andres. 1982. "Allgemeine Maßnahmen zur Arbeitsbeschaffung als Instrument aktiver Arbeitsmarktpolitik: Ein Beitrag zur Wirkungsanalyse des Arbeitsmarktpolitischen Programms der Bundesregierung für Regionen mit besonderen Beschäftigungsproblemen." *Mitteilungen aus der Arbeitsmarkt- und Berufsforschung* 15:345–61.

Hennings, Klaus Hinrich. 1982. "West Germany." In Boltho, ed. (1982):472–501.

Hibbs, Douglas A. 1977. "Political Parties and Macroeconomic Policy." *American Political Science Review* 71:1467–87.

Hickel, Rudolf. 1985. "Programmvorrat als Voraussetzung nachfrageorientierter Arbeitsmarkt- und Beschäftigungspolitik." In Buttler, Kühl, and Rahmann, eds. (1985):337–82.

Hjern, Benny, and Chris Hull. 1983. "Förderung kleiner Industriebetriebe als Mittel der Beschäftigungspolitik vor Ort." In Scharpf and Brockmann, eds. (1983):101–20.

Hohn, Hans-Willy. 1983. "Interne Arbeitsmärkte und betriebliche Mitbestimmung: Tendenzen der 'sozialen Schließung' im 'dualen' System der Interessenvertretung." Discussion paper IIM/LMP 83-2, Wissenschaftszentrum Berlin.

Huber, Ludwig. 1982. "Internationalisierung des Bankgeschäfts und Auslandstöchter deutscher Banken." In Ehrlicher and Simmert, eds. (1982):349–61.

Hull, Chris. 1986. "Delivering Resources for Small-Firm Development: Local Intermediation as a Policy Strategy." In European Centre for Work and Society. *Fostering and Financing Local Business and Employment Initiatives.* Maastricht.

Huntford, Roland. 1971. *The New Totalitarians.* London: Penguin.

IAB. 1983. "Der Arbeitsmarkt in der Bundesrepublik Deutschland im Jahre 1983—insgesamt und regional." *Mitteilungen aus der Arbeitsmarktund Berufsforschung* 16:5–16.

——. 1984. "Der Arbeitsmarkt in der Bundesrepublik Deutschland in den Jahren 1984 und 1985." *Mitteilungen aus der Arbeitsmarkt und Berufsforschung* 17:435–40.

Ifo-Institut für Wirtschaftsforschung. 1982. *Spiegel der Wirtschaft: Struktur und Konjunktur in Bild und Zahl.* Frankfurt: Campus.

——. 1985. "Das Europäishe Währungssystem." *Ifoschnelldienst* 17/18–85.

ILO. *Yearbook of Labour Statistics, 1981; 1983.*
IMF. *Direction of Trade Statistics, 1978–1984.* Washington, D.C.; International Monetary Fund.
——. *International Financial Statistics: May 1977; May 1980; May 1985.* Washington, D.C.: International Monetary Fund.
Internationale Chronik zur Arbeitsmarktpolitik 4 1981. "Focus: Ausländerbeschäftigung und Arbeitsmarktpolitik." Wissenschaftszentrum Berlin.
Jarvie, I. C. 1972. *Concepts and Society.* London: Routledge and Kegan Paul.
Jervis, Robert. 1978. "Cooperation under the Security Dilemma." *World Politics* 30:167–214.
Jonung, Christina. 1984. "Patterns of Occupational Segregation by Sex in the Labor Market." In Schmid and Weitzel, eds. (1984):44–68.
Kahn, Hermann, Ernest Schneider, and John Trammell. 1983. *Österreich, Europa, und die Welt in den achtziger Jahren.* Vienna: Zentralsparkasse.
——. 1984. *Österreich: Wirtschaftliche Herausforderungen der 80er Jahre.* Vienna: Zentralsparkasse.
Kalecki, Michael. 1943. "Political Aspects of Full Employment." In Kalecki, *Selected Essays on the Dynamics of the Capitalist Economy.* London: Cambridge University Press, 1971, pp. 138–45.
Kanter, Rosabeth Moss. 1972. *Commitment and Community: Communes and Utopias in Sociological Perspective.* Cambridge: Harvard University Press.
Katzenstein, Peter. 1984. *Corporatism and Change: Austria, Switzerland, and the Politics of Industry.* Ithaca: Cornell University Press.
——. 1985. "Policy and Politics in West Germany: A Semi-Sovereign State." Ms. Cornell University, November.
Kavanagh, Dennis, ed. 1982. *The Politics of the Labour Party.* London: Allen and Unwin.
Keohane, Robert O. 1980. "The Theory of Hegemonic Stabiity and Changes in International Economic Regimes, 1967–1977." In Ole Holsti et al., *Change in the International System.* Boulder, Colo.: Westview Press.
——. 1984. *After Hegemony: Cooperation and Discord in the World Political Economy.* Princeton: Princeton University Press.
——. 1984a. "The World Political Economy and the Crisis of Embedded Liberalism." In Goldthorpe, ed. (1984):15–38.
——. 1986. "Reciprocity in International Relations." *International Organization* 40:1–27.
Kern, Horst, and Michael Schumann. 1984. *Das Ende der Arbeitsteilung? Rationalisierung in der industriellen Produktion.* Munich: C. H. Beck.
Kirchheimer, Otto. 1957. "Vom Wandel der politischen Opposition." *Archiv für Rechts- und Sozialphilosophie* XLIII:58–86.
Kitzmantel, Edith. 1986. "Steuerliche Investitionsförderung in Österreich—Umfang und Wirkung." *Der Öffentliche Sektor* 11, 1-1986:1–29.
Klauder, Wolfgang. 1982. "Arbeitskräfte-Potentialrechnung." In Dieter Mertens, ed., "Konzepte der Arbeitsmarkt- und Berufsforschung. Eine Forschungsinventur des IAB." *Beiträge zur Arbeitsmarkt- und Berufsforschung. BeitrAB* 70:99–119.
Kleinknecht, Alfred. 1984. "Innovationsschübe und Lange Wellen: Was bringen 'neoschumpeterianische' Kriseninterpretationen?" *Prokla* 57:55–78.
——. 1986. *Innovation Patterns in Crisis and Prosperity: Schumpeter's Long Cycle Reconsidered.* London: Macmillan.
Kloten, Norbert, Karl-Heinz Ketterer, and Rainer Vollmer. 1985. "West Germany's Stabilization Performance." In Lindberg and Maier, eds. (1985):353–402.

Knott, Jack H. 1981. *Managing the German Economy: Budgetary Politics in a Federal State.* Lexington, Mass.: Lexington Books.

Kock, Heinz. 1975. *Stabilitätspolitik im föderalistischen System der Bundesrepublik Deutschland: Analyse und Reformvorschläge.* Cologne: Bund-Verlag.

Köhler, Claus, ed. 1973. *Geldpolitik—kontrovers.* Cologne: Bund-Verlag.

———. 1985. *Hat sich das Bundesbankgesetz bewährt?* Bonn: Friedrich-Ebert-Stiftung.

Kondratieff, Nikolai M. 1926. "Die langen Wellen der Konjunktur." *Archiv für Sozialwissenschaft und Sozialpolitik,* no. 3/56.

Koren, Stephan. 1982. "Austrian Monetary and Exchange Rate Policies." In Arndt, ed. (1982):26–41.

Korpi, Walter. 1978. *The Working Class in Welfare Capitalism: Work, Unions, and Politics in Sweden.* London: Routledge and Kegan Paul.

———. 1983. *The Democratic Class Struggle.* London: Routledge and Kegan Paul.

Korpi, Walter, and Michael Shalev. 1979. "Strikes, Industrial Relations, and Class Conflict in Capitalist Societies." *British Journal of Sociology* 30:164–87.

Kromphardt, Jürgen. 1985. "Reallohnniveau und Beschäftigung in der keynesianischen Theorie." *WiSt Wirtschaftswissenschaftliches Studium* 14:597–602.

———. 1986. "Die Zukunft der Globalsteuerung—Theoretishe Perspektiven." In Körner and Uhlig, eds. *Die Zukunft der Globalsteuerung.* Bern: Haupt.

Krupp, Hans-Jürgen. 1986. "Die Erschließung von Arbeitsplatzreserven im Tertiärsektor als Beitrag zur Lösung struktureller Probleme." In Krupp, Rohwer, and Rothschild, eds. (1986):235–52.

Kühl, Jürgen. 1982. "Das Arbeitsförderungsgesetz (AFG) von 1969: Grundzüge seiner arbeitsmarkt- und beschäftigungspolitischen Konzeption." *Mitteilungen aus der Arbeitsmarkt- und Berufsforschung* 15:251–60.

Kühlewind, Gerhard. 1986. "Beschäftigung und Ausgliederung älterer Arbeitnehmer: Empirische Befunde zu Erwerbsbeteiligung, Rentenübergang, Vorruhestandsregelung, und Arbeitslosigkeit." *Mitteilungen aus der Arbeitsmarkt- und Berufsforschung* 19:209–32.

Lang, Werner. 1978. *Kooperative Gewerkschaften und Einkommenspolitik: Das Beispiel Österreichs.* Frankfurt: Peter Lang.

———. 1981. "Krisenmanagement durch Neokorporatismus: Das Modell Österreich." *Politische Vierteljahresschrift* 22:6–25.

Lange, Peter, and Geoffrey Garrett. 1985. "The Politics of Growth: Strategic Interaction and Economic Performance in the Advanced Industrial Democracies, 1974–1980." *Journal of Politics* 47, no. 3 (August 1985):792–827.

Latsis, Spiro J. 1976. *Method and Appraisal in Economics.* Cambridge: Cambridge University Press.

Layard, Richard. 1981. "Unemployment in Britain: Causes and Cures." Discussion Paper No. 87, Centre for Labour Economics, London School of Economics.

———. 1982. "Is Incomes Policy the Answer to Unemployment?" Discussion Paper No. 99 (revised), Centre for Labour Economics, London School of Economics.

Layard, Richard, and R. Jackman. 1982. "An Inflation Tax." Discussion Paper No. 111, Centre for Labour Economics, London School of Economics.

Lehmbruch, Gerhard. 1967. *Proporzdemokratie: Politisches System und politische Kultur in der Schweiz und Österreich.* Tübingen: Mohr.

Lehmbruch, Gerhard, and Philippe C. Schmitter, eds. 1982. *Patterns of Corporatist Policy Making.* London: Sage.

Lehner, Gerhard. 1979. *Die steuerlichen Investitionsförderungssysteme und die Unternehmensbesteuerung in der BRD, in Schweden, in der Schweiz, und in Österreich.* Vienna: Österreichisches Institut für Wirtschaftsforschung.

285

——. 1982. "Deficit-Spending in Österreich." *Wirtschaftspolitische Blätter* 29:24–35.

Leibfritz, Willy, and Cornelia Meurer. 1984. *Steuerliche Investitionsförderung im internationalen Vergleich.* Berlin: Duncker and Humblot.

Lindbeck, Assar. 1980. "Overcoming the Obstacles to Successful Performance of the Western Economies." *Business Economics* 15:81–84.

——. 1986. "Limits to the Welfare State." *Challenge* 29, no. 1:31–36.

Lindberg, Leon N. 1983. "Wirtschaftswissenschaftler als Politikberater. Der Rückzug aus Keynesianismus und Staatsinterventionismus in den USA nach 1970." *Journal für Sozialforschung* 23, no. 1:3–25 and no. 2:85–204.

Lindberg, Leon N., and Charles S. Maier, eds. 1985. *The Politics of Inflation and Economic Stagnation: Theoretical Approaches and International Case Studies.* Washington, D.C.: Brookings.

Lindblom, Charles E. 1965. *The Intelligence of Democracy.* New York: Free Press.

Lindner, Clausjohann. 1986. "Max Weber als Handlungstheoretiker." *Zeitschrift für Soziologie* 15:151–66.

LO. 1951. *Trade Unions and Full Employment.* Stockholm: LO 1953 (Translated from the 1951 Swedish document).

Lundberg, Erik. 1985. "The Rise and Fall of the Swedish Model." *Journal of Economic Literature* 23:1–36.

Lutz, Burkart. 1984. *Der Kurze Traum immerwährender Prosperität. Eine Neuinterpretation der industriell-kapitalistischen Entwicklung im Europa des 20. Jahrhunderts.* Frankfurt: Campus.

McCracken, Paul, Guido Carli, Herbert Giersch, Attila Karaosmanoglu, Ryutaro Komya, Assar Lindbeck, Robert Marjolin, and Robin Matthews. 1977. *Towards Full Employment and Price Stability: A Report to the OECD by a Group of Independent Experts.* Paris: OECD.

McKinnon, Ronald I. 1983. "Why U.S. Monetary Policy Should be Internationalized." Ms. Stanford University, Department of Economics.

——. 1984. *An International Standard for Monetary Stabilization.* Washington, D.C.: Institute for International Economics.

Magaziner, Ira C., and Robert B. Reich. 1982. *Minding America's Business: The Decline and Rise of the American Economy.* New York: Harcourt Brace Jovanovich.

Maier, Hans. 1982. "Arbeitsbeschaffungsmaßnahmen als Instrument aktiver Arbeitsmarktpolitik." In Scharpf, Brockmann, Groser, Hegner, and Schmid, eds. (1982):119–40.

——. 1986. *Schafft Energieeinsparung Arbeitsplätze? Qualitatives Wachstum durch kleine Unternehmen.* Opladen: Westdeutscher Verlag.

Maier-Rigaud, Gerhard. 1982. "Die Fiktion vom Produktionspotential." *Wirtschaftsdienst* 1982/7:357–60.

——. 1983. "Der Zins, das Potential und der Aufschwung." *Wirtschaftsdienst* 1983/1:45–50.

Malinvaud, Edmond. 1977. *The Theory of Unemployment Reconsidered.* Oxford: Blackwell.

Marin, Bernd. 1982. *Die Paritätische Kommission: Aufgeklärter Technokorporatismus in Österreich.* Vienna: Internationale Publikationen.

Marin, Dalia, Johann Maurer, and Michael Wagner. 1984. "Budget- und lohnpolitische Reaktionen auf Wachstumskrisen: Österreich 1952 bis 1982." Ms. Institut für Höhere Studien, Vienna.

Markovits, Andrei S., and Christopher S. Allen. 1984. "Trade Unions and the Economic Crisis: The West German Case." In Gourevitch et al., (1984):89–188.

Martin, Andrew. 1984. "Trade Unions in Sweden: Strategic Responses to Change and Crisis." In Gourevitch et al. (1984):189–359.

Matthews, R. C. O., C. H. Feinstein, and J. C. Odling-Smee. 1982. *British Economic Growth, 1856–1974.* Oxford: Clarendon Press.

Matzner, Egon. 1975. "Funktionen der Sozialpartnerschaft." In Heinz Fischer, ed., *Das politische System Österreichs.* Vienna: Europaverlag, pp. 429–51.

———. 1982. *Der Wohlfahrtsstaat von Morgen: Entwurf eines zeitgemäßen Musters staatlicher Interventionen.* Frankfurt: Campus.

———. 1986. "Der moderne öffentliche Sektor und das Phänomen Korruption." In Christian Brünner, ed., *Korruption und Kontrolle.* Vienna: Böhlau, pp. 329–47.

Mayer, Helmut. 1982. "Die Bedeutung der Offshore-Finanzmärkte für die inländische Geldpolitik." In Ehrlicher and Simmert, eds. (1982):363–85.

Mayntz, Renate. 1985. "Über den begrenzten Nutzen methodologischer Regeln in der Sozialforschung." In Bonß and Hartmann, eds., *Entzauberte Wissenschaft—Zur Relativität und Geltung soziologischer Forschung.* Soziale Welt. Sonderband 3. Göttingen: Schwarz, pp. 65–76.

Meade, James E. 1982. *Stagflation.* Vol. 1, *Wage Fixing.* London: Allen and Unwin.

Meidner, Rudolf (with Anna Hedborg and Gunnar Fond). 1978. *Vermögenspolitik in Schweden.* Cologne: Bund-Verlag.

Meidner, Rudolf, and Anna Hedborg. 1984. *Modell Schweden: Erfahrungen einer Wohlstandsgesellschaft.* Frankfurt: Campus.

Meißner, Werner. 1974. *Investitionslenkung.* Frankfurt: Fischer Athenäum.

———. 1980. *Die Lehre der fünf Weisen: Eine Auseinandersetzung mit den Jahresgutachten des Sachverständigenrats zur Begutachtung der gesamtwirtschaftlichen Entwicklung.* Cologne: Bund-Verlag.

Meißner, Werner, and Karl Georg Zinn. 1984. *Der neue Wohlstand: Qualitatives Wachstum und Vollbeschäftigung.* Munich: Bertelsmann.

Mensch, Gerhard. 1975. *Das technologische Patt: Innovationen überwinden die Depression.* Frankfurt: Umschau Verlag.

Mertens, Dieter, and Wolfgang Klauder, eds. 1980. "Probleme der Messung und Vorausschätzung des Erwerbspersonenpotentials." *Beiträge zur Arbeitsmarkt- und Berufsforschung. BeitrAB* 44.

Mesch, Michael. 1984. "Einkommenspolitik in West-Europa, 1945–1980." *Wirtschaft und Gesellschaft* 10:237–70.

Micheletti, Michele. 1985. *Organized Interest and Organized Protest: Difficulties of Member Representation for the Swedish Central Organization of Salaried Employees (TCO).* Stockholm Studies in Politics 29. Stockholm: University of Stockholm Press.

Middlemas, Keith. 1979. *Politics and Industrial Society: The Experience of the British System since 1911.* London: André Deutsch.

———. 1983. *Industry, Unions, and Government: Twenty-one Years of the National Development Office.* London: Macmillan.

Milner, Henry. 1986. "The Economics of Social Democracy." University of Stockholm, Department of Political Science.

Minford, Patrick. 1983. *Unemployment: Cause and Cure.* Oxford: Martin Robertson.

Mintzberg, Henry, and Alexandra McHugh. 1985. "Strategy Formation in an Adhocracy." *Administrative Science Quarterly* 30:160–97.

Mintzberg, Henry, and James A. Waters. 1985. "Of Strategies, Deliberate and Emergent." *Strategic Management Journal* 6:257–72.

Mises, Ludwig von. 1944. *Bureaucracy.* New Haven: Yale University Press.

Mueller, Dennis C. 1980. "Power and Profit in Hierarchical Organisations." *Statsvetenskaplig Tidskrift* 83:293–302.

Narr-Lindner, Gudrun. 1984. *Grenzen monetärer Steuerung. Die Restriktionspolitik der Bundesbank, 1964–1974*. Frankfurt: Campus.

Nerb, Gernot, Lutz Reyher, and Eugen Spitznagel. 1977. "Struktur, Entwicklung, und Bestimmungsgrößen der Beschäftigung in Industrie und Bauwirtschaft auf mittlere Sicht: Ergebnisse einer Unternehmensbefragung." *Mitteilungen aus der Arbeitsmarkt- und Berufsforschung* 10:291–310.

Neumann, Manfred J. M. 1973. "Zur relativen Bedeutung fiskalpolitischer und monetärer Impulse: Evidenz vom Konjunkturzyklus, 1967–1981." *WSI-Mitteilungen* 1/1973:14–25.

———. 1978. "The Impulse-Theoretic Explanation of Changing Inflation and Output Growth: Evidence from Germany." In Brunner and Meltzer, eds., *The Problem of Inflation*. Amsterdam: North Holland, pp. 233–69.

———. 1981. "Der Beitrag der Geldpolitik zur konjunkturellen Entwicklung in der Bundesrepublik Deutschland, 1973–1980." *Kyklos* 34/1981:405–31.

Noelle-Neumann, Elisabeth, and Burkhard Strümpel. 1984. *Macht Arbeit krank? Macht Arbeit glücklich? Eine aktuelle Kontroverse*. Munich: Piper.

Nowotny, Ewald. 1979. "Verstaatlichte und private Industrie in der Rezession— Gemeinsamkeiten und Unterschiede." *WISO—Wirtschafts- und Sozialwissenschaftliche Zeitschrift* 2:71–95.

Nowotny, Ewald, and Herbert Tieber, eds. 1985. *Perspektiven 90. Sozialdemokratische Wirtschaftspolitik—Eine Diskussion*. Vienna: Europaverlag.

OECD. *Economic Outlook, 1980–1986*. Paris: OECD.

———. *Economic Surveys: Austria, 1977–1985*. Paris: OECD.

———. *Economic Surveys: Sweden, 1977–1985*, Paris: OECD.

———. *Historical Statistics, 1960–1983, 1960–1984*. Paris: OECD.

———. *Labour Force Statistics, 1970–1982, 1963–1983, 1964–1984*. Paris: OECD.

———. *National Accounts*. Vol. 1, *Main Aggregates, 1951–1980, 1960–1984*. Paris: OECD.

———. *The Role of the Public Sector: Causes and Consequences of the Growth of Government*. OECD Economic Studies No. 4/Spring 1985. Paris: OECD.

Öhman, Berndt. 1982. "Solidary Wage Policy and Wage Earners' Funds." English summary. In *Solidarisk Lönepolitik och Löntagarfonder*. Stockholm: Statens Offentliga Utredningar, 1982, p. 47.

Olson, Mancur. 1965. *The Logic of Collective Action: Public Goods and the Theory of Groups*. Cambridge: Harvard University Press.

———. 1982. *The Rise and Decline of Nations: Economic Growth, Stagflation, and Social Rigidities*. New Haven: Yale University Press.

———. 1986. "A Theory of the Incentives Facing Political Organizations: Neo-Corporatism and the Hegemonic State." *International Political Science Review*.

Olson, Mancur, and Richard Zeckhauser. 1966. "An Economic Theory of Alliances." *Review of Economics and Statistics* 48:266–79.

Ostleitner, Herbert. 1979. "Handlungssequenzen, Herrschaftsverhältnisse und unfreiwillige Arbeitslosigkeit." In Kazimiers Laski, Egon Matzner, and Ewald Nowotny, eds., *Beiträge zur Diskussion und Kritik der neoklassischen Ökonomie, Festschrift für Kurt W. Rothschild und Josef Steindl*. Berlin: Springer, pp. 45–59.

———. 1982. "Zu den Grundlagen der wirtschaftspolitischen Konzeption der Sozialistischen Partei Österreichs (SPÖ)." In Abele et al., eds. (1982):133–42.

Ouchi, William G. 1984. *The M-Form Society: How American Teamwork Can Recapture the Competitive Edge.* Reading, Mass.: Addison-Wesley.

Paloheimo, Heikki. 1984. "Distributive Struggle, Corporatist Power Structures and Economic Policy of the 1970s in Developed Capitalist Countries." In Paloheimo, ed., *Politics in the Era of Corporatism and Planning.* Tampere: Finnish Political Science Association.

Panitch, Leo. 1976. *Social Democracy and Industrial Militancy: The Labour Party, the Trade Unions, and Incomes Policy, 1945–1947.* Cambridge: Cambridge University Press.

———. 1979. "The Development of Corporatism in Liberal Democracies." In Schmitter and Lehmbruch, eds. (1979):119–46.

Pecchioli, R. M. 1983. *The Internationalization of Banking: The Policy Issues.* Paris: OECD.

Pelinka, Anton. 1981. *Modellfall Österreich? Möglichkeiten und Grenzen der Sozialpartnerschaft.* Vienna: Braumüller.

Pencaval, John H. 1981. "The American Experience with Incomes Policies." In Elliott and Fallick, eds., *Incomes Policies, Inflation, and Relative Pay.* London: Allen and Unwin, pp. 155–86.

Peters, Aribert B., and Günther Schmid. 1982. "Aggregierte Wirkungsanalyse des Arbeitsmarktpolitischen Programms der Bundesregierung für Regionen mit besonderen Beschäftigungsproblemen: Analyse der Beschäftigungswirkung." Discussion Paper IIM/LMP 82-32, Wissenschaftszentrum Berlin.

Piore, Michael J., ed. 1979. *Unemployment and Inflation: Institutionalist and Structuralist Views.* White Plains, N.Y.: M.E. Sharpe.

———. 1982. "American Labour and the Industrial Crisis." *Challenge* 25:5–11.

Piore, Michael J., and Charles F. Sabel. 1985. *Das Ende der Massenproduktion: Studie über die Requalifizierung der Arbeit und die Rückkehr der Ökonomie in die Gesellschaft.* Berlin: Wagenbach.

Pizzorno, Alassandro. 1978. "Political Exchange and Collective Identity in Industrial Conflict." In Crouch and Pizzorno, eds. (1978):277–98.

Placone, Dennis, Holley Ulbrich, and Myles Wallace. 1985. "The Crowding Out Debate: It's Over When It's Over and It Isn't Over Yet." *Journal of Post-Keynesian Economics* 8:91–96.

Pöhl, Karl-Otto. 1985. "Widersprüche und Gemeinsamkeiten in der Politik der Bundesregierung und der Deutschen Bundesbank in der Zeit von 1978–1982." In Schmidt and Hesselbach, eds. (1985):222–26.

Pohl, Reinhard. 1973. "Zur geldpolitischen Diskussion: Bestätigt die westdeutsche Konjunktur von 1965 bis 1971 den Monetarismus?" *WSI-Mitteilungen* 4/1973:153–64.

Pohl, Rüdiger. 1974. "Für mehr Liquidität bei den Banken—Geldstromanalyse für den Sommer und Herbst 1974." *WSI-Mitteilungen* 12/1974:462–72.

———. 1975. "In der stärksten Rezession der Nachkriegszeit—Geldstromanalyse für das zweite Quartal 1975." *WSI-Mitteilungen* 9/1975:454–63.

Przeworski, Adam, and Henry Teune. 1970. *The Logic of Comparative Social Inquiry.* New York: Wiley-Interscience.

Putnam, Robert D., and Nicholas Bayne. 1948. *Hanging Together: The Seven-Power Summits.* London: Heinemann.

Rau, Jes. 1986. "Keine Angst vor Defiziten: Ein ungewöhnlicher Vorschlag zur Lösung der Außenhandelsprobleme zwischen den Vereinigten Staaten, Japan und der Bundesrepublik." *Die Zeit* 33 (8 August 1986):19–20.

Rehn, Gösta. 1952. "The Problem of Stability: An Analysis and Some Policy Proposals." In Ralph Turvey, ed., *Wages Policy under Full Employment.* London: William Hodge.

Rein, Martin. 1985. "Women in the Social Welfare Labor Market." Discussion Paper IIM/LMP 85–18, Wissenschaftszentrum Berlin.

Reissert, Bernd. 1983. "Langfristarbeitslosigkeit und 'temporärer Ersatzarbeitsmarkt'—Modellrechnungen zu einem arbeitsmarktpolitischen Sofortprogramm." *Wirtschaftsdienst* 4/83:178–84.

——. 1984. "Staatliche Finanzzuweisungen und kommunale Investitionspolitik." Ph.D. diss., Freie Universität Berlin.

——. 1985. "Die Finanzierung der Arbeitsmarktpolitik: Großbritannien." Discussion Paper IIM/LMP 84-21c, Wissenschaftszentrum Berlin.

——. 1986. "Kommunales Hebesatzrecht zur Einkommensteuer." *Demokratische Gemeinde* (March 1986):40–45.

——. 1986a. "Finanzielle Spielräume für kommunale Beschäftigungspolitik?" In Hans Maier and Hellmut Wollmann, eds., *Lokale Beschäftigungspolitik.* Basel: Birkhäuser Verlag.

Reissert, Bernd, Fritz W. Scharpf, and Ronald Schettkat. 1986. "Eine Strategie zur Beseitigung der Massenarbeitslosigkeit." *Aus Politik und Zeitgeschichte* B 23/86:3–21.

Reitzner, Rudolf N. 1983. "Gewerbeförderung am Beispiel der Existenzgründungsaktion." *Wirtschaft und Gesellschaft* 9:391–410.

Risch, Bodo. 1983. *Alternativen der Einkommenspolitik.* Kieler Studien 180. Tübingen: Mohr.

Robinson, Derek. 1973. *Incomes Policy and Capital Sharing in Europe.* London: Croom Helm.

Roth, Wolfgang. 1985. *Der Weg aus der Krise: Umrisse einer sozial-ökologischen Marktwirtschaft.* Munich: Kindler.

Rothschild, Kurt W. 1981. *Einführung in die Ungleichgewichtstheorie.* Berlin: Springer.

——. 1985. "Felix Austria? Zur Evaluierung der Ökonomie und Politik in der Wirtschaftskrise." *Österreichische Zeitschrift für Politikwissenschaft* 85/3:261–74.

Rothstein, Bo. 1985. "The Success of the Swedish Labour Market Policy: The Organizational Connection to Policy." *European Journal for Political Research* 13:153–65.

——. 1985a. "Managing the Welfare State: Lessons from Gustav Möller," *Scandinavian Political Studies* 8:151–70.

Rühle, Hans, and Hans-Joachim Veen, eds. 1983. *Gewerkschaften in den Demokratien Westeuropas.* Vol. 2, *Großbritannien, Niederlande, Österreich, Schweden, Dänemark.* Paderborn: Schöningh.

Sabel, Charles F., Gary B. Herrigel, Richard Deeg, and Richard Kazis. 1986. "Regional Prosperities Compared: Massachusetts and Baden-Württemberg in the 1980's." Ms. Department of Political Science, Massachusetts Institute of Technology.

Sarrazin, Thilo. 1985. "Die Finanzpolitik des Bundes 1970–1982." In Schmidt and Hesselbach, eds. (1985):195–201.

Sawyer, Malcolm. 1982. "Income Distribution and the Welfare State." In Boltho, ed. (1982):188–224.

——. 1982a. *Macro-Economics in Question: The Keynesian-Monetarist Orthodoxies and the Kaleckian Alternative.* Brighton: Wheatsheaf Books.

SCB, aku. Statistika Centralbyrau, *Arbetskrafsundersökningen 1974; 1978.*

Schäfer, Claus, and Hartmut Tofaute, eds. 1980. *Beschäftigungssichernde Finanzpolitik: Eine Chance für Vollbeschäftigung.* Frankfurt: Campus.

Scharpf, Fritz W. 1978. *Autonome Gewerkschaften und staatliche Wirtschaftspolitik: Prob-*

leme einer Verbändegesetzgebung. Schriftenreihe der Otto Brenner Stiftung. Cologne: Europäische Verlagsanstalt.

——. 1979. "Die Rolle des Staates im westlichen Wirtschaftssystem: Zwischen Krise und Neuorientierung." In *Staat und Wirtschaft: Schriften des Vereins für Socialpolitik,* NF, vol. 102. Berlin: Duncker and Humblot, pp. 15–44.

——. 1981. "The Political Economy of Inflation and Unemployment in Western Europe: An Outline." Discussion Paper IIM/LMP 81-21, Wissenschaftszentrum Berlin.

——. 1983. "Interessenlage der Adressaten und Spielräume der Implementation bei Anreizprogrammen." In Renate Mayntz, ed., *Implementation politischer Programme II: Ansätze zur Theoriebildung.* Opladen: Westdeutscher Verlag, 99–116.

——. 1984. "Economic and Institutional Constraints of Full-Employment Strategies: Sweden, Austria, and West Germany (1973–1982)." In Goldthorpe, ed. (1984):257–90.

——. 1985. "Die Politikverflechtungs-Falle: Europäische Integration und deutscher Föderalismus im Vergleich." *Politische Vierteljahresschrift* 26:323–56.

——. 1986. "Strukturen der post-industriellen Gesellschaft, oder: Verschwindet die Massenarbeitslosigkeit in der Dienstleistungs- und Informationsökonomie?" *Soziale Welt* 37:4–24.

Scharpf, Fritz W., Dietrich Garlichs, Friederike Maier, and Hans Maier. 1982. *Implementationsprobleme offensiver Arbeitsmarktpolitik: Das Sonderprogramm der Bundesregierung für Regionen mit besonderen Beschäftigungsproblemen.* Frankfurt: Campus.

Scharpf, Fritz W., Bernd Reissert, and Fritz Schnabel. 1976. *Politikverflechtung: Theorie und Empirie des kooperativen Föderalismus in der Bundesrepublik.* Kronberg: Scriptor.

Scharpf, Fritz W., and Marlene Brockmann, eds. 1983. *Institutionelle Bedingungen der Arbeitsmarkt- und Beschäftigungspolitik.* Frankfurt: Campus.

Scharpf, Fritz W., Marlene Brockmann, Manfred Groser, Friedhart Hegner, and Günther Schmid, eds. 1982. *Aktive Arbeitsmarktpolitik: Erfahrungen und neue Wege.* Frankfurt: Campus.

Schiller, Karl. 1970. *Reden zur Wirtschaftspolitik.* Vols. 1–7. Bonn: Bundesministerium für Wirtschaft.

Schlesinger, Helmut. 1975. "Geldbremsen gelöst, doch Exportventil bleibt geschlossen: Politik der knappen D-Mark sollte Preise dämpfen." *Deutsche Bundesbank. Auszüge aus Presseartikeln* 67/1975:1–3.

——. 1986. "Schlesinger warnt vor Inflationspotential." *Süddeutsche Zeitung* (26/27 July 1986):33.

Schmid, Günther. 1980. *Strukturierte Arbeitslosigkeit und Arbeitsmarktpolitik.* Königstein, Czechoslovakia: Athenäum.

——. 1982. "Arbeitsmarktpolitik in Schweden und in der Bundesrepublik." In Scharpf, Brockmann, Groser, Hegner, and Schmid, eds. (1982):29–62.

——. 1984. "Die Finanzierung der Arbeitsmarktpolitik: Schweden." Discussion Paper IIM/LMP 84-21a, Wissenschaftszentrum Berlin.

——. 1984a. "Women in the Labour Market and Equal Opportunity Policy in Sweden, United Kingdom, United States, and West Germany." In Schmid and Weitzel, eds. (1984):1–19.

Schmid, Günther, Bernd Reissert, and Gert Bruche. 1986. *Arbeitslosenversicherung und aktive Arbeitsmarktpolitik—Finanzierungssysteme im internationalen Vergleich.* Berlin.

Schmid, Günther, and Klaus Semlinger. 1980. *Instrumente gezielter Arbeitsmarktpolitik: Kurzarbeit, Einarbeitungszuschüsse, Eingliederungsbeihilfen. Durchführung, Wirksamkeit und Reformvorschläge.* Frankfurt: Campus.

Schmid, Günther, and Renate Weitzel. 1984. *Sex Discrimination and Equal Opportunity: The Labour Market and Employment Policy.* Aldershot: Gower.

Schmidt, Erich. 1985. "Subvention und Wirtschaft—Subventionswirtschaft." *WISO* 1/1985:81–89.

Schmidt, Folke, ed. 1978. *Discrimination in Employment.* Uppsala: Almqvist and Wiksell.

Schmidt, Helmut. 1980. "Grundsatzfragen der Struktur des Gesamtstaates. Rede des Bundeskanzlers in der 494. Sitzung des Bundesrates am 19.Dezember 1980." *Bulletin* 134. Bonn: 23. 12. 1980: 1137–41.

——. 1984. "Some Proposals for Further Progress of the European Monetary System." Ms. Bonn.

——. 1985. "Glanz und Elend der Gipfeldiplomatie und ihre Notwendigkeit." In Schmidt and Hesselbach, eds. (1985):235–39.

——. 1986. *Eine Strategie für den Westen.* Berlin: Siedler.

Schmidt, Helmut, and Walter Hesselbach, eds. 1985. *Kämpfer ohne Pathos: Festschrift für Hans Matthöfer zum 60.Geburtstag am 25.September 1985.* Bonn: Neue Gesellschaft.

Schmidt, Jochen. 1977. *Zur Bedeutung der Staatsausgaben für die Beschäftigung.* Berlin: Deutsches Institut für Wirtschaftsforschung.

Schmidt, Manfred F. 1980. "Staat und Wirtschaft unter bürgerlichen und sozialdemokratischen Regierungen: Ein Beitrag zur vergleichenden Analyse des Steuerstaates, des Wohlfahrtsstaates und der Lage auf dem Arbeitsmarkt." In P. Grottian, ed., "Folgen reduzierten Wachstums für Politikfelder." *Politische Vierteljahresschrift,* Sonderheft 11/80: 7–37.

——. 1982. "Does Corporatism Matter? Economic Crisis, Politics, and Rates of Unemployment in Capitalist Democracies in the 1970s." In Lehmbruch and Schmitter, eds. (1982):237–58.

——. 1983. "The Welfare State and the Economy in Periods of Economic Crisis: A Comparative Study of Twenty-three OECD Nations." *European Journal of Political Research* 11:1–26.

——. 1985. *Der Schweizerische Weg zur Vollbeschäftigung: Eine Bilanz der Beschäftigung, der Arbeitslosigkeit, und der Arbeitsmarktpolitik.* Frankfurt: Campus.

Schmitter, Philippe C. 1974. "Still the Century of Corporatism?" *Review of Politics* 36:85–131. Reprinted in Schmitter and Lehmbruch, eds. (1979):7–52.

——. 1981. "Interest Intermediation and Regime Governability in Contemporary Western Europe and North America." In Suzanne Berger, ed., *Organizing Interests in Western Europe: Pluralism, Corporatism, and the Transformation of Politics.* Cambridge: Harvard University Press, pp. 287–327.

Schmitter, Philippe C., and Gerhard Lehmbruch, eds. 1979. *Trends towards Corporatist Intermediation.* London: Sage.

Schulmeister, Stephan. 1986. "Zur Krise der Weltwirtschaft in den siebziger und achtziger Jahren—ein Rekonstruktionsversuch." Ms. WIFO-Institut, Vienna.

Schumpeter, Joseph A. 1950. *Capitalism, Socialism, and Democracy.* 3rd ed. New York: Harper and Row.

Seidel, Hans. 1979. *Die österreichische Wirtschaft: Entwicklung, Erfolge, und Probleme.* Vienna: WIFO-Institut.

——. 1982. "Austro-Keynesianismus." In Seidel et al. (1982):11–15.

Seidel, Hans, and Peter Szopo. 1983. "Der österreichische Weg de Inflationsbekämpfung." *Wirtschaft und Gesellschaft:* 373–90.

Seidel, Hans, et al. 1982. "Der Austro-Keynesianismus: Schwerpunkt-Thema." *Wirtschaftspolitische Blätter* 29, no. 3.

Seidler, Horst, and Rudolf Zwiener. 1982. "Kürzung öffentlicher Investitionen führt nicht zur Konsolidierung." *DIW-Wochenbericht* 50/82:619–24.

Semlinger, Klaus. 1982. "Die Wiedereingliederung schwervermittelbarer Arbeitsloser." In Scharpf, Brockmann, Groser, Hegner, and Schmid, eds. (1982):63–88.

Shonfield, Andrew. 1965. *Modern Capitalism: The Changing Balance of Public and Private Power*. London: Oxford University Press.

Simmert, Diethard B. 1974. "Reform der Geldpolitik—Konsequenzen für die Tarifpartner." *WSI-Mitteilungen* 2/1974:47–56.

Simmert, Diethard B., and Kurt-Dieter Wagner, eds. 1981. *Staatsverschuldung kontrovers: Schriftenreihe der Bundeszentrale für politische Bildung*. Vol. 174. Bonn: Bundeszentrale für politische Bildung.

Simon, Herbert A. 1978. "Rationality as Process and as Product of Thought." *American Economic Review* 68:1–16.

Smith, Eric Owen. 1983. *The West German Economy*. New York: St. Martin's.

Socher, Karl. 1982. "Vom Austro-Keynesianismus zum Austro-Monetarismus." In Seidel et al. (1982):43–49.

Sorge, Arndt. 1985. *Informationstechnik und Arbeit im sozialen Prozeß: Arbeitsorganisation, Qualifikation, und Produktivkraftentwicklung*. Frankfurt: Campus.

Sorge, Arndt, Gert Hartmann, Malcolm Warner, and Ian Nicholas. 1982. *Mikroelektronik und Arbeit in der Industrie: Erfahrungen bei der Anwendung von CNC-Werkzeugmaschinen in Großbritannien und der Bundesrepublik Deutschland*. Frankfurt: Campus.

Spahn, Heinz-Peter. 1986. *Stagnation in der Geldwirtschaft: Dogmengeschichte, Theorie und Politik aus keynesianischer Sicht*. Frankfurt: Campus.

Spahn, Heinz-Peter, and Georg Vobruba. 1986. "Das Beschäftigungsproblem: Die ökonomische Sonderstellung des Arbeitsmarktes und die Grenzen der Wirtschaftspolitik." *Wirtschaft und Gesellschaft*, no. 4.

Spindler, Joachim von, Willy Becker, and O.-Ernst Starke. 1973. *Die Deutsche Bundesbank: Grundzüge des Notenbankwesens und Kommentar zum Gesetz über die Deutsche Bundesbank*. 4th ed. Stuttgart: Kohlhammer.

Spitznagel, Eugen. 1982. "Arbeitsbeschaffungsmaßnahmen (ABM): Beschäftigungswirkung, Zielgruppenorientierung, und gesamtfiskalischer Kostenvergleich." In Dieter Mertens, ed. "Konzepte der Arbeitsmarkt- und Berufsforschung." *Beiträge zur Arbeitsmarkt- und Berufsforschung* 70:278–98.

———. 1985. "Arbeitsmarktpolitische Maßnahmen: Entlastungswirkungen und Kostenvergleiche." *Mitteilungen aus der Arbeitsmarkt- und Berufsforschung* 18:20–23.

Steinkühler, Franz. 1984. "Einbahnstraße Technik? Das Verhältnis der Gewerkschaften zu den 'neuen Technologien.'" *Blätter für deutsche und internationale Politik*: 188–96.

Sterner, Mariann, and Gunilla Fürst Mellström. 1985. *Das schwedische Experiment: Beschäftigungsförderung für Frauen im öffentlichen Dienst*. Bonn: Verlag Neue Gesellschaft.

Strauss, Anselm. 1978. *Negotiations: Varieties, Contexts, Processes, and Social Order*. San Francisco: Jossey-Bass.

Streeck, Wolfgang. 1978. "Staatliche Ordnungspolitik und industrielle Beziehungen: Zum Verhältnis von Integration und Institutionalisierung gewerkschaftlicher Interessenverbände am Beispiel des britischen Industrial Relations Act von 1971." In Udo Bermbach, ed., *Politische Wissenschaft und politische Praxis. Politische Vieteljahresschrift* 19, Sonderheft 9/1978:106–39.

———. 1981. *Gewerkschaftliche Organisationsprobleme in der sozialstaatlichen Demokratie.* Königstein: Athenäum.

———. 1982. "Organizational Consequences of Neo-Corporatist Cooperation in West German Labour Unions." In Lehmbruch and Schmitter, eds. (1982):29–81.

———. 1983. "Interessenverbände als Hindernisse und Vollzugsträger öffentlicher Politik." In Scharpf and Brockmann, eds. (1983):179–98.

———. 1984. "Co-determination: The Fourth Decade."In Bernhard Wilpert and Arndt Sorge, eds., *International Perspectives on Organizational Democracy.* New York: John Wiley.

———. 1984a. "Neo-Corporatist Industrial Relations and the Economic Crisis in West Germany." In Goldthorpe, ed. (1948):291–314.

———. 1984b. *Industrial Relations in West Germany: A Case Study of the Car Industry.* London: Heinemann.

———. 1986. "Kollektive Arbeitsbeziehungen und industrieller Wandel: Das Beispiel der Automobilindustrie." Discussion Paper IIM/LMP 86-2, Wissenschafszentrum Berlin.

———. 1986a. "Zwischen Solidarität und Modernisierung: Die schwierige Gratwanderung der westdeutschen Gewerkschaften." Ms. Wissenschaftszentrum Berlin.

Streeck, Wolfgang, and Andreas Hoff. 1983. "Manpower Management and Industrial Relations in the Restructuring of the World Automobile Industry." Discussion Paper IIM/LMP 85-5, Wissenschaftszentrum Berlin.

Streeck, Wolfgang, and Philippe C. Schmitter. 1985. *Private Interest Government: Beyond Market and State.* London: Sage.

Surrey, Michael. 1982. "United Kingdom." In Boltho, ed. (1982):528–53.

SVR. *Sachverständigenrat zur Begutachtung der gesamtwirtschaftlichen Entwicklung: Jahresgutachten 1970/71–1985/86.* Stuttgart: Kohlhammer.

SWS. 1986. "SWS Meinungsprofile: Einschätzung der wirtschaftlichen Lage Österreichs 1975–1985." *Journal für Sozialforschung* 26:275–82.

Szanton, Peter, ed. 1981. *Federal Reorganization: What Have We Learned?* Chatham, N.J.: Chatham.

Talos, Emmerich. 1985. "Sozialpartnerschaft: Zur Entwicklung und Entwichlungsdynamik kooperativ-konzertierter Politik in Österreich." In Gerlich, Grande, and Müller, eds. (1985):41–83.

Tarantelli, Ezio, and Gerhard Willke, eds. 1981. *The Management of Industrial Conflict in the Recession of the 1970s: Britain, Germany, and Italy.* Florence: Le Monnier.

Taylor, Robert. 1978. *The Fifth Estate: Britain's Unions in the Seventies.* London: Routledge and Kegan Paul.

Teschner, Manfred, and Dieter Vesper. 1983. *Budgetpolitik Österreichs im internationalen Vergleich.* Deutsches Institut für Wirtschaftsforschung. Beiträge zur Strukturforschung, no. 75. Berlin: Duncker and Humblot.

Thoss, Rainer. 1975. "Ansatzpunkte einer systemkonformen Investitionslenkung." In Besters et al. (1975):125–48.

Tichy, Gunther. 1980. "Investitionsverhalten in Österreich: Ist die hohe Investitionsneigung eine Folge der weitgehenden staatlichen Förderung?" In Gottfried Bombach, Bernhard Gahlen, and Alfred E. Ott, eds., *Neuere Entwicklungen der Investitionstheorie und -politik.* Schriftenreihe des wirtschaftswissenschaftlichen Seminars Ottobeuren, vol. 9. Tübingen: Mohr, pp. 131–76.

———. 1982. "Austro-Keynesianismus—Gibt's den? Angewandte Psychologie als Konjunkturpolitik." In Seidel et al. (1982):50–64.

———. 1984. "Strategy and Implementation of Employment Policy in Austria: Successful Experiments with Unconventional Assignment of Instruments to Goals." *Kyklos* 37:363–68.

Tilley, Nicholas. 1982. "Popper, Historicism, and Emergence." *Philosophy of the Social Sciences* 12:59–67.

Tinbergen, Jan. 1967. *Economic Policy: Principles and Design.* 4th ed. Amsterdam: North Holland.

Tomaskovic-Devey, Donald, and S. M. Miller. 1983. "Can High-Tech Provide the Jobs?" *Challenge* 26, no. 2:57–63.

Trapp, Peter. 1976. *Geldmenge, Ausgaben, und Preisanstieg in der Bundesrepublik Deutschland.* Tübingen: Mohr.

Triffin, Robert. 1969. *Gold and the Dollar Crisis.* New Haven: Yale University Press.

Ullmann-Margalit, Edna. 1977. *The Emergence of Norms.* Oxford: Clarendon Press.

Verkstadsföreningen. 1984. *Verkstadsinidustrin inför avtalsrörelsen 1984.* Stockholm: Sveriges Verkstadsförening.

Vesper, Dieter, and Rudolf Zwiener. 1982. "Finanzpolitik und konjunkturelle Entwicklung—Einige Bemerkungen und Simulationsergebnisse zur Effizienz finanzpolitischer Konjunktursteuerung." *WSI-Mitteilungen* 10/1982:587–96.

Visser, Jelle. 1985. "European Trade Unions in Retreat." Ms. Sociologisch Institut, Universiteit van Amsterdam.

Wallich, Henry C., and Sidney Weintraub. 1971. "A Tax-Based Incomes Policy." *Journal of Economic Issues* 5:1–19.

Webber, Douglas. 1982. "Zwischen programmatischem Anspruch und politischer Praxis: Die Entwicklung der Arbeitsmarktpolitik in der Bundesrepublik Deutschland von 1974 bis 1982." *Mitteilungen aus der Arbeitsmarkt- und Berufsforschung* 15:261–75.

———. 1984. "German Social Democracy in the Economic Crisis: Unemployment and the Politics of Labour Market Policy in the Federal Republic of Germany from 1974 to 1982." Ph.D. diss., University of Essex, Department of Government.

Wegner, Manfred. 1986. "Das 'britische Experiment' nach sechs Jahren: Überblick über die Wirtschaftspolitik der Regierung Thatcher." *Ifo-Schnelldienst* 8/86:3–14.

Weintraub, Sidney. 1978. *Capitalism's Inflation and Unemployment Crisis.* Reading, Mass.: Addison-Wesley.

Weizsäcker, Carl Christian von. 1975. "Grenzen der traditionellen Globalsteuerung." *Jahrbücher für Nationalökonomie und Statistik* 189:1–41.

Welsch, Johann. 1980. *Globalsteuerung in der Bundesrepublik Deutschland.* Cologne: Bund-Verlag.

Weltbank. *Jahresberichte 1983 und 1985.* Washington, D.C.: Bank für Internationalen Wiederaufbau und Entwicklung/Weltbank.

Wiener, Martin J. 1981. *English Culture and the Decline of the Industrial Spirit, 1850–1980.* Cambridge: Cambridge University Press.

WIFO. 1974. "Österreichisches Institut für Wirtschaftsforschung: Die Österreichische Konjunktur Mitte 1974." *WIFO Monatsberichte* 6/1974:261–315.

———. 1982. *Arbeitszeitverkürzung als Instrument der Beschäftigungspolitik: Zwischenbericht zur Studie.* Vienna: Österreichisches Institut für Wirtschaftsforschung.

Wilensky, Harold. 1976. *The New Corporatism: Centralization and the Welfare State.* Beverly Hills: Sage.

———. 1981. "Democratic Corporatism, Consensus, and Social Policy: Reflections on

Changing Values and the 'Crisis' of the Welfare State." In OECD, *The Welfare State in Crisis: An Account of the Conference on Social Policies in the 1980s*. Paris: OECD.

Wilks, Stephen. 1984. *Industrial Policy and the Motor Industry.* Manchester: Manchester University Press.

Williams, Shirley. 1985. *A Job to Live: The Impact of Tomorrow's Technology on Work and Society.* Harmondsworth: Penguin.

Wilpert, Bernhard, and Jörg Rayley. 1983. *Anspruch und Wirklichkeit der Mitbestimmung.* Frankfurt: Campus.

Woolley, John T. 1985. "Central Banks and Inflation." In Lindberg and Maier, eds. (1985):318–51.

Wösendorfer, Johann. 1980. *Arbeitsmarktpolitik: Beurteilungskriterien für das Arbeitsmarktförderungsgesetz.* Linz: Österreichisches Institut für Arbeitsmarktpolitik.

WSI. 1974. "Die wirtschaftliche Lage in der Bundesrepublik Deutschland im Jahre 1974." *WSI Mitteilungen* 3/1974:73–88.

———. 1975. "Die wirtschaftliche Lage in der Bundesrepublik Deutschland im Jahre 1975." In: *WSI-Mitteilungen* 3/1975:105–20.

———. 1975a. "Diskriminierende Wirkungen der Geldpolitik." *WSI-Mitteilungen* 9/1975:446–47.

Index

INDEX

Great Britain (*cont.*)
sectoral employment patterns, 52–54
social partnership, institutions of, 194–95
structural consolidation, 81–82
unions, 73–74, 180–82, 186–88, 191–92
wage controls, 72–73
wage negotiations, 191–92
wage policy: Thatcher government and, 87; unions and, 74–75, 77, 79–80, 82–88
women in work force, 79
Great Depression of 1930s, 3

Hard currency policy, 61, 63
Healey, Dennis, 77, 82–84
Health insurance, federal, 106
Heath, Edward, 70, 74–75
Hegemonic and posthegemonic conditions, constellation of interests under, 262–63
Hicks, John, 21
High-tech industries, promotion of, 272

Incomes policy. *See* Wage policy
Industrial policy, 72
Industrial sectors, employment in, 52–54
Inflation
comparative indicators (1973–79), 42–45
inflation-unemployment combination, 169–70
Keynesian economics and, 27, 30–31
as macroeconomic problem, 25–27
oil prices and, 41–42
side effects of management policies, 31–33. *See also under* individual countries
wage policy and, 34–35
Institutions (political and social), 10–11
Interest rates
Austria, 66–67
economic crisis of 1980s and, 244–46
Federal Republic of Germany, 148–49, 152, 257
Internationalization of money and capital markets, 257–59
International monetary coordination, proposed, 261–63
International Monetary Fund (IMF), 81–82

Interorganizational strategic competence, problem of, 174–75
Inventory maintenance subsidies, 100, 102
Investment, 18–19, 246–48. *See also under* Austria; FRG
Iranian revolution, 241
Italy, 266

Japan, 144, 146, 149, 151, 211, 244
Job creation measures, 228, 233
Johnson, Lyndon B., 260
Jones, Jack, 77, 79–80, 86

Kaldor, Nicholas, 81
Keohane, Robert, 261
Keynes, John Maynard, 3, 20, 36
Keynesian economics, 3, 21–22, 165–68, 259–69
capitalism, perspective on, 17, 19–21
inflation and, 27, 30–31
macroeconomic policy instruments, 30–31
social democrats' alliance with, 23–25, 35–37
unemployment and, 25–26, 30
Kluncker, Heinz, 129, 130
Kondratieff, Nicolai, 5
Korean War, 117
Kreisky, Bruno, 63, 193
Krupp, Hans-Jürgen, 151

Labor force participation rates, 48, 50–51
Lambsdorff, Otto, 156
Latency in economic policy, 208n
Latin America, 242
Liquid assets, 18–19
Locomotive strategy for economic recovery, 144–46, 153
Lutz, Burkart, 5

McCracken Report (1977), 5
Market coordination, 17–22
Marshall Plan, 259
Marxist economics
capitalism, perspective on, 17, 19–20
internationalization and, 258–59
Maternity leave, 145
Matthöfer, Hans, 145
Matzner, Egon, 194
"Me generation" and yuppies, 197
Meidner, Rudolf, 90, 112
Memorandum Group, 20

300

Cornell Studies in Political Economy

EDITED BY PETER J. KATZENSTEIN

Library of Congress Cataloging-in-Publication Data

Scharpf, Fritz Wilhelm.
   [Sozialdemokratische Krisenpolitik in Europa. English]
   The political economy of social democratic Europe during a decade
of crisis / by Fritz W. Scharpf; translated by Ruth Crowley and
Fred Thompson.
     p.   cm.—(Cornell studies in political economy)
   Translation of: Sozialdemokratische Krienpolitik in Europa.
   Includes bibliographical references and index.
   ISBN 0-8014-2221-3 (alk. paper)
   ISBN 0-8014-9942-9 (pbk.: alk. paper)
   1. Europe—Economic conditions—1945– 2. Socialism—Europe.
3. Europe—Full employment policies. 4. Wage-price policy—Europe.
I. Title. II. Series.
HC240.S29513 1991
339.5′094—dc20   90-55139